D0975229

A Clinical Guide to the
Treatment of the
Human Stress Response

The Plenum Series on Stress and Coping

Series Editor:
Donald Meichenbaum, *University of Waterloo, Waterloo, Ontario, Canada*

Editorial Board: Bruce P. Dohrenwend, *Columbia University*
Marianne Frankenhaeuser, *University of Stockholm*
Norman Garmezy, *University of Minnesota*
Mardi J. Horowitz, *University of California Medical School,*
San Francisco
Richard S. Lazarus, *University of California, Berkeley*
Michael Rutter, *University of London*
Dennis C. Turk, *University of Pittsburgh*
Camille Wortman, *University of Michigan*

A CLINICAL GUIDE TO THE TREATMENT OF THE
HUMAN STRESS RESPONSE
George S. Everly, Jr.

COPING WITH LIFE CRISES
An Integrated Approach
Edited by Rudolf H. Moos

COPING WITH NEGATIVE LIFE EVENTS
Clinical and Social Psychological Perspectives
Edited by C. R. Snyder and Carol E. Ford

DYNAMICS OF STRESS
Physiological, Psychological, and Social Perspectives
Edited by Mortimer H. Appley and Richard Trumbull

HUMAN ADAPTATION TO EXTREME STRESS
From the Holocaust to Vietnam
Edited by John P. Wilson, Zev Harel, and Boaz Kahana

A Continuation Order Plan is available for this series. A continuation order will bring
delivery of each new volume immediately upon publication. Volumes are billed only upon
actual shipment. For further information please contact the publisher.

A Clinical Guide to the Treatment of the Human Stress Response

George S. Everly, Jr.
Harvard University
Cambridge, Massachusetts

Plenum Press • New York and London

Library of Congress Cataloging in Publication Data

Everly, George S., 1950–
    A clinical guide to the treatment of the human stress response.

    (The Plenum series on stress and coping)
    Includes bibliographies and index.
    1. Stress (Psychology) 2. Stress management. I. Title. II. Series. [DNLM: 1. Stress—
physiopathology. 2. Stress—therapy. QZ 160 E93c]
    RC455.4.S87E84   1989   616.98   88-35676
    ISBN 0-306-43068-1

10 9 8 7 6

Notations concerning doses of pharmacologic agents are based on published sources and
relevant experience. Although believed to be accurate at the time of printing, the information cannot be guaranteed.

Printed in the United States of America

To Marideth Rose Everly, with love;
now older and wiser, she has helped me, once again,
to see the world through the eyes of a child.

Preface

In 1981, Plenum Press published a text entitled *The Nature and Treatment of the Stress Response* by Robert Rosenfeld, M.D., and me. That text attempted to do what no other text from a major publisher had previously attempted, that is, to create a clinically practical guide for the treatment of excessive stress and its arousal-related syndromes—this to be captured between the same covers in combination with a detailed, clinically relevant pedagogy on the neurological and endocrinological foundations of the stress response itself. That volume has enjoyed considerable success having found markets among practicing professionals and clinical students as well.

The fields of psychosomatic medicine, health psychology, behavioral medicine, and applied stress research have appreciably expanded their boundaries since the publication of the aforementioned volume. Although remarkably little of the clinical utility of that volume has been eroded with time, it was felt that an updated and more integrative clinical textbook needed to be offered to practicing clinicians and students within clinical training programs. Therefore, rather than simply create a second edition of the original volume, the decision was made to create a significantly revised and expanded volume that would cover many of the same topics as the original volume but would provide a primary emphasis on the treatment of excessive stress and that would employ an integrative phenomenological model to facilitate that end. This present volume entitled *A Clinical Guide to the Treatment of the Human Stress Response* is the result.

The current text resists the temptation to adopt a medical model as its basic epistemological perspective. Such a model would assume a "one-germ, one-disease, one-treatment" model. Pedagogically, its natural corollary would be a discussion of specific stress-related disorders, with a subsequent discussion of specific treatment recommendations for each of the specific disorders. Rather than reflecting such an approach, the present text views excessive stress arousal as the pathogenic foundation and the pathognomonic core of stress-related disease. As such, the primary target for therapeutic intervention becomes the stress response itself—the pathogenic arousal phenomenon that leads to related disease and dysfunction.

Thus, this text will devote its pages to a discussion of what stress arousal is and how the phenomenon of excessive stress arousal can be treated. This perspective in no way denies the importance of treating specific target-organ signs and symptoms. Nor does it deny the possibility that target-organ signs and symptoms may even become self-sustaining in some instances. Nevertheless, the perspective adopted within this volume reflects the choice to view the pathogenic stress arousal phenomenon itself as the phenomenological key to understanding and treating stress-related disease and dysfunction; as such, it is the primary topic of discussion within the covers of this volume.

Finally, it should be noted that this text is designed to be a to-the-point volume of practical value; therefore, a conscious effort was made to keep most discussions, especially in Part II, brief, concise, and clinically targeted. This was done with the knowledge that other, more comprehensive literature reviews exist elsewhere, and that this volume cites a plethora of original research articles and scholarly reviews for those readers interested in more in-depth analyses of specific issues.

GEORGE S. EVERLY, JR.

Cambridge, Massachusetts

Acknowledgments

The author wishes to express his deepest gratitude to those individuals who, directly or indirectly, helped shape this volume: David C. Mc-Clelland, Ph.D., Harvard University; Joan Borysenko, Ph.D., Harvard Medical School; Theodore Millon, Ph.D., University of Miami; and Herbert Benson, M.D., Harvard Medical School, who provided the opportunity for me to reexamine the concept of arousal and its natural antithesis, the relaxation response. I would also like to thank Eileen Potocki, Joseph Mallet, Ph.D., Eileen Newman, Ph.D., and Robert Rosenfeld, M.D., for their scholarly contributions; Steve Beck for his superb contributions in the area of artwork; Frank Bond for his critique; and Richard Lanham for his technical assistance. My thanks also to Eliot Werner and Robert Jystad, editors at Plenum, and Donald Meichenbaum, Ph.D., all of whom contributed helpful suggestions at various stages in the development of the text.

Contents

Part II

The Treatment of the Human Stress Response 99

Chapter 6

Personologic Diathesis and Human Stress 103

Chapter 7

Control and the Human Stress Response 119

Chapter 8

Psychotherapy: A Cognitive Perspective 137

Chapter 9

A Neurophysiological Rationale for the Use of the Relaxation Response 149

Chapter 10

Meditation 171

Chapter 15

The Pharmacological Treatment of Excessive Stress **247**

Chapter 16

Physical Exercise and the Human Stress Response **261**

Part III

Special Topics in the Treatment of the Human Stress Response . . . **275**

The Nature of Human Stress

First study the science.
Then practice the art . . .
—Leonardo da Vinci

Part I is the first of three parts that constitutes this volume. It is dedicated to an in-depth analysis of the nature of human stress. The five chapters of Part I explore stress phenomenology.

Chapter 1, entitled "The Concept of Stress," provides the reader with a working definition of the stress response derived in the Selyean tradition. This chapter also reviews other related terms and concepts that provide a basic conceptual framework from which to study stress.

The purpose of Chapter 2, entitled "The Anatomy and Physiology of the Human Stress Response," is to examine the mechanisms that serve to "link" *stressor stimuli* with subsequent stress-related *target-organ arousal*. A systems model is constructed to assist the reader in understanding phenomenological processes. Also contained in this chapter is a comprehensive analysis of the physiological stress-response mechanisms originally studied by Walter Cannon and Hans Selye and most recently updated with the latest published and unpublished research findings. A unique diagrammatic summary of the "multiaxial" nature of the physiological stress response is provided as a pedagogical tool.

Chapter 3, entitled "The Link from Stress Arousal to Disease," examines several major models of target-organ pathogenesis. That is, Chapter 3 is designed to explore the mechanisms that link *stress arousal* to subsequent *target-organ disease* and dysfunction. Thus, as Chapter 2 explored the link from stimulus to stress arousal, Chapter 3 explores the link from stress arousal to disease.

Chapter 4, entitled "Stress-Related Disease: A Review," is the logical extension of Chapters 2 and 3, and as such Chapter 4 reviews common stress-related disorders that clinicians are likely to encounter during the course of clinical practice.

The final chapter in Part I is Chapter 5, entitled "The Measurement of the Human Stress Response." This chapter employs the same systems model constructed in Chapter 2, detailing stress phenomenology, and uses it to superimpose technologies that may be considered for the measurement of human stress. By graphically depicting assessment technologies in relation to the systems model of the stress response, it will facilitate greater phenomenological insight into the measurement process itself.

The fact that this volume, dedicated to the treatment of human stress, has as one-third of its contents a detailed discussion of phenomenology of the human stress response bears witness to the wisdom of da Vinci when he proclaimed, "First study the science. Then practice the art which is born of that science."

The Concept of Stress

'Tis in myself I meet my greatest foe.
—Moliere

BEHAVIOR AND HEALTH

Scientists investigating human health and disease are now reformulating the basic tenets upon which disease theory is based. For generations, the delivery of health care services was built upon the "one-germ, one-disease, one-treatment" formulations that arose from the work of Louis Pasteur. Although clearly one of the great advances in medicine, yielding massive gains against the infectious diseases that plagued humanity, the "germ theory" of disease also represents an intellectual quagmire that threatens to entrap us in a unidimensional quest to improve human health.

The germ theory of disease ignores the fact that by the year 1960, the primary causes of death in the United States were no longer microbial in nature. Rather, other pathogenic factors have emerged as well. Even a decade ago, it was noted, "New knowledge . . . has increased the recognition that the etiology of poor health is multifactorial. The virulence of infection interacts with the particular susceptibility of the host" (American Psychological Association, 1976, p. 264). Thus, in addition to mere exposure to a pathogen, one's overall risk of ill health seems also to be greatly influenced by other factors. Recent evidence points toward health-related behavior patterns and overall life style as important health determinants.

The significance of health-related behavior in the overall determination of health status is cogently discussed by Jonas Salk (1973) in his treatise *The Survival of the Wisest*. Salk argues that we are leaving the era where the greatest threat to human health was microbial disease only to enter an era where the greatest threat to human health resides in humanity itself. He emphasizes that we must actively confront health-eroding practices such as pollution, sedentary life styles, diets void of nutrients, and practices that disregard the fundamentals of personal and interpersonal hygiene at the same time that we endeavor to treat disease. As evidence of the validity of his assertions, we need only review Table 1.1 below as it presents the leading causes of premature death (i.e., death prior to the age of 75 years) and the factors that support them.

As Table 1.1 reveals, life-style is estimated to have the greatest single effect upon the eight leading causes of death in the United States. Furthermore, combining all 10 leading causes, we see that personal life style is estimated to account for 51% of the total effect of all 10 leading causes of premature death.

Just what is "life-style?" The term life-style refers to the overall manner in which one leads one's life. It subsumes factors such as occupation, hobbies, diet, exercise levels, and even the consistent manner in which one chooses to view the world, that is, one's "worldview." For example, does one see the world from a friendly, optimistic perspective or from a threatened, insecure, and pessimistic perspective? A major life-style factor is that of stress arousal. There is little disagreement with the notion that stress arousal plays a major role in the ultimate determination of human health. If we turn our focus toward the promotion of human health, then we must consider the factor of human stress. Let us take a closer look at the concept of human stress.

Table 1.1. Estimated Contribution of 4 Factors to the 10 Leading Causes of Death Before the Age of 75 (Expressed in Percentages)

	Factors			
Cause of death	Life-style	Environment	Biology	Other
Heart disease	54	9	25	12
Cancer	37	24	29	10
Motor vehicle accidents	69	18	1	12
Other accidents	51	31	4	14
Stroke	50	22	21	7
Homicide	63	35	2	0
Suicide	60	35	2	3
Cirrhosis	70	9	18	3
Influenza/pneumonia	23	20	39	18
Diabetes	34	0	60	6
All factors combined:	51	20	20	9

Source: U.S. Center for Disease Control, July 1980, June, 1984.

DEFINING STRESS

STRESS! A term heard so often that its meaning is frequently distorted and its implications taken for granted. Yet what this term represents touches virtually every aspect of American life. So pervasive are the effects of stress that one author (Manuso, 1978) has argued that:

1. As many as 25% of all Americans suffer the ill effects of excessive stress.
2. Approximately 50% of all general medical practice patients are suffering from stress-related problems.

In 1979, the office of the U.S. Surgeon General declared that when stress reaches excessive proportions, psychologic changes can be so dramatic as to have serious implications for both the mental and physical health of Americans (Public Health Service, 1979). Contained within the Surgeon General's Report, entitled *Healthy People*, this was the most significant indication that stress and its potentially pathologic effects were considered significant public health factors by the U.S. Government. If, indeed, the aforementioned appraisals appear credible, then what has emerged is a rationale for the study of the *nature and treatment* of the human stress response. To that end, this book has been developed.

This book is written for clinicians, and the focus is on the treatment of pathogenic stress. Yet it may be argued that effective treatment emerges from an understanding of the phenomenology of the pathogenic entity itself. In this first chapter, the reader will encounter some of the basic foundations and definitions upon which the treatment of pathogenic stress is inevitably based.

It seems appropriate to begin a text on stress with a basic definition of the stress response itself.

The term *stress* was first introduced into the allied health sciences in 1926 by Hans Selye. As a second-year medical student at the University of Prague, he noted that individuals suffering from a wide range of physical ailments all seemed to have a common constellation of symptoms. These included loss of appetite, decreased muscular strength, elevated blood pressure, and a loss of ambition (Selye, 1974). Wondering why these symptoms seemed to appear commonly, regardless of the nature of the somatic disorder, led Selye to label this condition as "the syndrome of just being sick" (Selye, 1956).

In his early writings, Selye used the term *stress* to describe the "sum of all nonspecific changes (within an organism) caused by function or damage" or, more simply, "the rate of wear and tear in the body." In a more recent definition, the Selyean concept of stress is "the nonspecific response of the body to any demand" (Selye, 1974, p. 14).

Paul Rosch (1986) provides an interesting anecdote. Recognizing that the term was originally borrowed from the science of physics, he relates how Selye's usage of the term did not conform to original intent:

> In 1676, Hooke's Law described the effect of external stresses, or loads, that produced various degrees of "strain," or distortion, on different materials . . .
> Selye once complained to me that had his knowledge of English been more precise, he might have labeled his hypothesis the "strain concept," and he did encounter all sorts of problems when his research had to be translated. . . . (Rosch, 1986, ix)

Indeed, confusion concerning whether stress was a "stimulus" as used in physics or a "response" as used by Selye has plagued the stress literature. As Rosch (1986) describes:

> The problem was that some used stress to refer to disturbing emotional or physical stimuli, others to describe the body's biochemical and physiologic response . . . , and still others to depict the pathologic consequences of such interactions. This led one confused British critic to complain, 35 years ago, that stress in addition to being itself was also the cause of itself and the result of itself. (p. ix)

To summarize so far, the term *stress* used in the Selyean tradition, refers to a response, whereas in its original usage within the science of physics it referred to a stimulus and the term *strain* referred to the response.

Using the term *stress* to denote a response left Selye without a term to describe the stimulus that engenders a stress response. Selye chose the term *stressor* to denote any stimulus that gives rise to a stress response.

In sum, drawing upon historical precedent and consistent with Selye's original notion, the term *stress* will be used within this volume to refer to a physiological reaction, or response, regardless of the source of the reaction. The term *stressor* will be used to refer to the stimulus that serves to engender the stress response.

With this fundamental introduction to the concept of stress, let us extend the conceptualization a bit further.

STRESS AND OTHER CONCEPTS

1. The stimulus that evokes a stress response is called a *stressor*. A stimulus becomes a stressor by virtue of the fact that it has, indeed, engendered a stress response. There are two generic types of stressors (Girdano & Everly, 1986), as will be discussed in Chapter 2: (1) psychosocial stressors and (2) biogenic stressors. *Psychosocial* stressors become stressors by virtue of the cognitive interpretation, or meaning, assigned to the stressor (Ellis, 1973; Lazarus, 1966; Lazarus & Folkman, 1984; Meichenbaum, 1977; Meichenbaum & Jaremko, 1983). *Biogenic* stressors become stressors by

virtue of the fact that the stressor possesses some electrical or biochemical property that is capable of initiating a stress response while bypassing higher interpretive mechanisms within the neocortex. For example, a traffic jam is a neutral event; it only becomes a stressor by virtue of the fact that the driver interprets the traffic jam as a threatening or otherwise undesirable situation. If the driver would interpret the traffic jam as having some positive or desirable aspect to it, no stress response is likely to evolve. On the other hand, certain biogenic stimuli, called *sympathomimetics*, act directly to cause a stress response by virtue of some direct physiological action. Coffee, tea, amphetamines, and even exercise, to mention only a few, all possess inherent stimulant qualities and will induce a stress response regardless of one's interpretation of them.

The inclusion of the biogenic sympathomimetic category of stressors in no way contradicts the work of Lazarus and others who have studied the critical role that interpretation plays in the formation of psychosocial stressors. Such an inclusion merely extends the stressor concept to recognize that stimuli that alter the normal anatomical or physiological integrity of the individual are also capable of activating many of the same psychoendocrinological mechanisms that we shall come to refer to as the *stress response*. Thus even if a patient convinces you that he or she really enjoys drinking 15 cups of caffeinated coffee per day, the clinician must be sensitive to the fact that those 15 "enjoyable" cups of coffee can serve as a powerful stressor activating an extraordinary systemic release of stress-response hormones such as epinephrine and norepinephrine and in doing so can be a contributing factor in cardiac conduction abnormalities, for example. Similarly, individuals who belong to "Polar Bear" clubs who voluntarily immerse themselves in frigid waters during the winter undergo an extraordinary stress response characterized by massive sympathetic nervous system arousal. Thus, even though the consumption of caffeine and the immersion of oneself into frigid bodies of water may truly be reinforcing to the individual, that person still experiences a form of physiological arousal that is accurately described as a stress response and that may pose some risk to the health of the individual depending upon the intensity and chronicity of the exposure to the stressors. These issues will be reiterated once again in Chapter 2.

In general, it is important for the clinician to understand that by far the greater part of the excessive stress in the patient's life is self-initiated and self-propagated. This is owing to the fact that it is the patient who interprets an otherwise neutral stimulus as possessing stress-evoking characteristics. Kirtz and Moos (1974) suggest that social stimuli do not directly affect the individual. Rather, the individual reacts to the environment in accordance with his or her interpretations of the environmental stimuli. These interpretations are affected by such variables as personality components or status and social-role behaviors. These cognitive–affective reactions are also

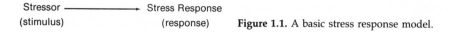

Stressor ──────────→ Stress Response

(stimulus)   (response)   Figure 1.1. A basic stress response model.

subject to exacerbation through usually self-initiated exposures to sympathomimetic stimuli, such as excessive caffeine consumption and the like. Having the patient realize and accept reasonable responsibility for the cause and reduction of excessive stress can be a major crossroads in the therapeutic intervention. Therefore, I shall discuss this issue in greater detail in a later chapter (Chapter 2).

2. Stress is a response, or reaction, to some stimulus. This notion is captured in Figure 1.1.

3. The stress response represents a physiological reaction, as defined in the Selyean tradition (Cannon, 1914; Selye, 1956); Everly (Everly, 1985a; Everly & Sobelman, 1987) has extended this concept somewhat and conceptualizes the stress response as a "physiologic mechanism of mediation," that is, a medium to bring about a result or effect. More specifically, the stress response may be viewed as the physiological link between any given stressor and its target-organ effect. This then will be the working definition of stress as used in this volume: "stress is a physiological response that serves as a mechanism of mediation linking any given stressor to its target-organ effect or arousal." This notion is captured in Figure 1.2.

When communicating with patients or simply conceptualizing the clinical import of the stress response, however, Selye's (1974, 1976) notion that stress is the "sum total of wear and tear" on the individual, seems useful.

4. The stress response, as a physiological mechanism of mediation, can be characterized by a wide and diverse constellation of physiological mechanisms (Cannon, 1914; Makara, Palkovits, & Szentagothal, 1980; Mason, 1972; Selye, 1976). These mechanisms may be categorized as (1) neurological response axes, (2) neuroendocrine response mechanisms, and (3) endocrine response axes. These potential response mechanisms will be reviewed, in detail, in Chapter 2.

Although the mechanisms of the stress response are processes of arousal, and the target-organ effects are usually indicative of arousal, the stress response has been noted as entailing such forms of arousal as to cause

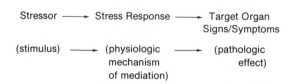

Figure 1.2 The stress response as a Mechanism of Mediation.

actual slowing, inhibition, or complete stoppage of target-organ systems (Engle, 1971; Gellhorn, 1968, 1969; Selye, 1971; Gray, 1985). These inhibiting or depressive effects are typically a result of the fact that upon occasion stress arousal constitutes the activation of inhibitory neurons, inhibitory hormones, or simply an acute hyperstimulation that results in a nonfunctional state (e.g., cardiac fibrillation). This seeming paradox is often a point of confusion for the clinician; hence its mention here.

5. Selye (1956, 1976) has argued for the "nonspecificity" of the stress response. Other authors (Everly, 1972; Humphrey & Everly, 1980; Mason, 1971; Mason, *et al.*, 1976) have argued that the psychophysiology of stress may be highly specific with various stressors and various individuals showing varying degrees of stimulus or response specificity, respectively. Current evidence strongly supports the existence of highly specific neuroendocrine and endocrine efferent mechanisms. Whether there exists another way of collectively categorizing stress response mechanisms may be as much a semantic issue as a physiological one (Everly, 1985a; Selye, 1980).

6. A vast literature argues that when stress arousal becomes excessively chronic or excessively intense in amplitude, target-organ (the organ affected by the stress response) disease and/or dysfunction will result (Everly, 1986; Selye, 1956). When stress results in *organic* biochemical and/or structural changes in the target organ, these results are referred to as a *psychophysioloical disease* (American Psychiatric Association, 1968) or a *psychosomatic disease* (Lipowski, 1984). Psychosomatic diseases were first cogently described by Felix Deutsch in 1927. However, it was Helen Dunbar (1935) who published the first major treatise on psychosomatic phenomena. In 1968, in the *Diagnostic and Statistical Manual of Mental Disorders*, 2nd edition (American Psychiatric Association, 1968), the term *psychophysiological disorder* was used to define a "group of disorders characterized by physical symptoms that are caused by emotional factors" (p. 46). Thus we see the terms *psychosomatic* and *psychophysiological* used interchangeably to refer to organically based physical conditions resulting from excessive stress.

Sometimes these terms are confused with the development of neurotic-like physical symptoms without any basis in organic pathology. The terms *conversion hysteria* or *somatoform disorders* are usually used to designate such nonorganic physical symptomatology.

The current *Diagnostic and Statistical Manual of Mental Disorders*, 3rd edition, revised (1987), uses the designation "Psychological Factors Affecting Physical Condition" to encompass stress-related physical disorders. By virtue of its multiaxial diagnostic schema, this nosological manual allows clinicians to assess levels of stress and environmental support as they may affect not only physical symptoms but psychiatric symptoms as well. Physical symptoms without a basis in or manifestation of organic pathology are subsumed under the somatoform category.

In the context of this volume, it is recognized that stress can be directed toward discrete anatomic or physiological target organs and therefore can lead to physical disorders characterized by organic pathology (i.e., psychophysiological or psychosomatic disorders); yet we must also recognize that the human mind can serve as a target organ. Thus, in addition to somatic stress-related disorders, it seems reasonable to include psychiatric-stress-related disorders as potential target-organ effects as well.

In sum, the terms *psychosomatic* and *psychophysiologic* disorders will be considered in this book as terms that refer to disorders characterized by physical alterations initiated or exacerbated by psychological processes. If tissue alterations are significant enough, and if the target organ is essential, then psychosomatic disorders could be life threatening. Neurotic-like somatoform disorders, on the other hand, involve only functional impairments of the sensory or motor systems and therefore cannot threaten life. Like the psychosomatic disorder, somatoform disorders are psychogenic; unlike psychosomatic processes, somatoform disorders entail no real tissue pathology. Confusion between the psychosomatic concept, one one hand, and the somatoform concept, on the other, is easily understandable. Yet, such confusion may lead to an underestimation of the potential severity of the disorder, thereby affecting treatment motivation and compliance.

7. Although recent reports emphasize the negative aspects of stress, there do exist positive aspects as well.

Previous writers have viewed the stress response as an innate preservation mechanism, which in earlier periods of evolutionary development allowed us to endure the challenges to survival. Numerous researchers (Cannon, 1953; Chavat, Dell, & Folkow, 1964; also see Henry & Stephens, 1977, for a brief review) have concluded, and we shall see in later chapters, that the nature of the psychophysiological stress response is that of apparent preparatory arousal–arousal in preparation for physical exertion. When used in such a way, it is easy to see the adaptive utility of the stress response. Yet stress arousal in modern times under circumstances of strictly psychosocial stimulation might be viewed as inappropriate arousal of primitive survival mechanisms, in that the organism is aroused for physical activity but seldom is such activity truly warranted and therefore seldom does it follow (see Benson, 1975).

Selye (1956, 1974) further distinguishes constructive from destructive stress, clearly pointing out that not all stress is deleterious. He argues that stress arousal can be a positive, motivating force that improves the quality of life. He calls such positive stress "eustress" (prefix *eu* from the Greek meaning "good") and debilitating, excessive stress "distress." Figure 1.3 depicts the relationship between stress and health/performance. As Figure 1.3 indicates, as stress increases so does health/performance and general well-being. However, as stress continues to increase, a point of maximal

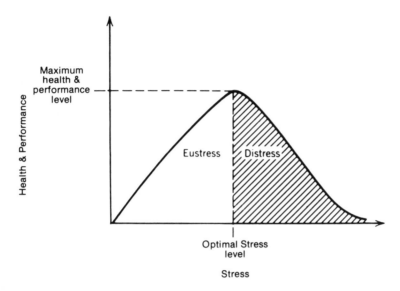

Figure 1.3. This figure graphically shows the relationship between stress arousal (horizontal axis) and performance (vertical axis). As stress increases, so does performance (eustress). At the optimal stress level, performance has reached its maximum level. If stress continues to increase into the "distress" region, performance quickly declines. Should stress levels remain excessive, health will begin to erode as well.

return is reached. This point may be called the *optimal stress level*, because as stress continues to increase, it becomes deleterious to the organism.

The point at which an individual's optimal stress level is reached, that is, the apex of one's tolerance for stress as a productive force, seems to be a function of genetic biological, acquired physiological, and behavioral factors.

8. Last in this series of assumptions about what stress is and what it is not, is the point that confusion exists regarding the role of the nonmedical clinician in the treatment of the stress response. This is so primarily because the target-organ effects or pathologies that result from excessive stress are mistakenly thought of as the psychophysiological stress response itself. It is important to remember the distinction that stress is a process of psychophysiological arousal (as detailed in Chapter 2), whereas the effects and pathologies (such as migraine headache, peptic ulcers, etc.) are the manifestations of chronically repeated and/or intense triggerings of the psychophysiological stress response (see Chapter 3). Treating the end-organ pathologies is clearly within the realm of the physician or non-medical specialist in behavioral medicine. However, the traditional psychologist, counselor, physical therapist, social worker, or health educator

can effectively intervene in the treatment of the stress arousal process itself. This includes treating the excessive stress/anxiety that accompanies, and often exacerbates, chronic infectious and degenerative diseases (see Basmajian & Hatch, 1979).

It is important to understand that this text addresses the clinical problem of excessive psychophysiological arousal—that is, the excessive stress-response process itself. It is not a detailed guide for psychotherapeutic intervention in the psychological trauma or conflict that may be at the root of the arousal (although such intervention can play a useful role). Nor is this a text that addresses the direct treatment of the pathologies' target organs that might arise as a result of excessive stress. We shall limit ourselves to a discussion of the clinical treatment of the psychophysiological stress-response process itself.

Based on a review of the literature, it may be concluded that treatment of the process of excessive psychophysiological stress arousal may take the form of three discrete interventions (see Girdano & Everly, 1986):

1. Helping the patient develop and implement strategies by which to avoid/minimize/modify exposure to stressors, thus reducing the patient's tendency to experience the stress response (Ellis, 1973; Lazarus, 1966; Meichenbaum, 1985; Meichenbaum & Novaco, 1978).
2. Helping the patient develop and implement skills that reduce excessive psychophysiological functioning and reactivity (Benson, 1975; Emmons, 1978; Gellhorn & Kiely, 1972; Girdano & Everly, 1986; Jacobson, 1938, 1970, 1978; Stoyva, 1976, 1977; Stoyva & Budzynski, 1974).
3. Helping the patient develop and implement techniques for the healthful expression, or utilization, of the stress response (see Chavat et al., 1964; Gevarter, 1978; Girdano & Everly, 1986; Kraus & Raab, 1961).

Finally, it has been suggested that the clinicians who are the most successful in treating the stress response are those who have training not only in the psychology of human behavior, but in medical physiology as well (Miller, 1978; Miller & Dworkin, 1977). Our own teaching and clinical observations support this conclusion. If indeed accurate, this conclusion may be owing to the fact that stress represents the epitome of mind–body interaction. As Miller (1979) suggests, mere knowledge of therapeutic techniques is not enough. The clinician must understand the nature of the clinical problem as well. Therefore, the reader will find the treatment section of this text preceded by a basic discussion of the functional anatomy and physiology of the stress response.

PLAN OF THE BOOK

The purpose of this text is to provide an up-to-date discourse on the phenomenology and treatment of pathogenic human stress arousal. As noted earlier, once target-organ signs and symptoms have been adequately stabilized, or ameliorated, the logical target for therapeutic intervention becomes the pathogenic process of stress arousal that engendered the target-organ signs and symptoms in the first place. To treat the target-organ effects of stress arousal while ignoring their pathogenic phenomenological origins is palliative at best, and often predicts a subsequent relapse.

The unique interaction of psychological and physiological phenomena that embodies the stress response requires a unique therapeutic understanding, as Miller has noted. Therefore, this volume is divided into three sections: Part I will address the anatomical and physiological nature of stress arousal. Also discussed will be measurement considerations. Part II will offer a practical clinical guide for the actual treatment of the human stress response. In this section a multitude of various technologies will be addressed. Finally, Part III will discuss several aspects of clinical practice that warrant special consideration. Also included in this volume is an appendix that provides a series of brief discussions on "special" topics relevant to the treatment of human stress arousal.

The Anatomy and Physiology of the Human Stress Response

It is highly dishonorable for a Reasonable Soul to live in so Divinely built a Mansion as the Body she resides in, altogether unacquainted with the exquisite structure of it.

—Robert Boyle

In the first chapter, the following working definition of the stress response was provided: "stress is a physiological response that serves as a mechanism of mediation linking any given stressor to its target-organ effect." By viewing the phenomenology of stress within the context of a "linking" mechanism, one can satisfy one of the most critical issues in psychosomatic medicine, that is, through what mechanisms can stressor stimuli, such as life events, lead to disease and dysfunction? The response to that query will be addressed within the next two chapters.

Chapter 2 will describe, within the boundaries of current findings and speculation, the anatomical and physiological foundations of the human stress response. This chapter will: (1) address basic neuroanatomical structures as well as (2) trace the psychophysiological effector mechanisms that actually represent the stress response, as currently defined. To assist in the pedagogical process, a basic model of the human stress response will be constructed to serve as a unifying thread for better understanding, not only of the phenomenology of human stress, but its measurement and treatment as well. Chapter 3 will pursue the logical extension by reviewing several models of pathogenesis, that is, the process by which stress arousal leads to disease.

NEUROLOGICAL FOUNDATIONS

In order to understand the stress response, we must first understand its foundations. These foundations reside in the structure and function of the human nervous systems.

The basic anatomical unit of the nervous systems is the *neuron* (see Figure 2.1). The neuron is indeed the smallest functional unit of the nervous system and serves to conduct sensory, motor, and regulatory signals throughout the body. The neuron consists of three basic units: (1) the *dendrites* and their outermost membranes—the postsynaptic dendritic membranes; (2) the *neural cell body,* which contains the nucleus of the cell; and (3) the *axon*, with its branching projections called the *telodendria* and their end points, the presynaptic membranes.

Neural Transmission

An incoming signal is first received by the postsynaptic membranes of the dendrites. Chemical (metabotropic) or electrical (ionotropic) processes are initiated upon stimulation of the postsynaptic dendritic membranes, which cause the neuron to conduct the incoming signal through the dendrites and the cell body. Finally, the neural impulse is relayed to the axon and travels down the axon until it reaches the telodendria and ultimately

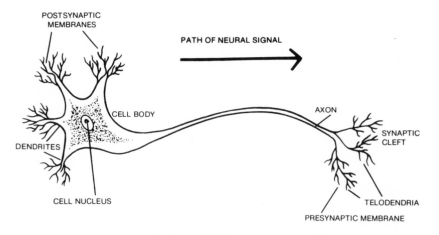

Figure 2.1. A typical neuron.

the presynaptic membranes. It is the task of the presynaptic membrane to relay the signal to the subsequent postsynaptic membrane of the next neuron. This is not easily achieved, however, because the neurons don't actually touch one another. Rather, there exists a space between neurons. This space is called the *synaptic cleft*.

In order for a signal to cross the synaptic cleft, chemical substances called *neurotransmitters* are called into play. Residing in storage vesicles in the telodendria, chemical neurotransmitters await the proper cues to migrate toward the presynaptic membrane. Once there, they are discharged into the synaptic cleft ultimately to stimulate (or inhibit) the postsynaptic membrane of the next neuron. Table 2.1 contains a list of major neurotransmitters and their anatomical loci.

Having completed a basic overview of the anatomy of neural transmission, it is necessary to return to a brief discussion of the dynamics of intraneuronal communication. For clinicians, this phenomenon is extremely important because it serves as the basis for electrophysiological events such as electromyography, electrocardiography, and electroencephalography.

Shortly after the incoming signal passes the postsynaptic dendritic

Table 2.1. Major Neurotransmitters and Their Loci

Neurotransmitter	Neuronal pathways
Norepinephrine (NE) (a major excitatory neurotransmitter)	Locus coeruleus Limbic system, especially Amygdala Hippocampus Septum and interconnecting pathways Postganglionic sympathetic nervous system Cerebellum
Serotonin (5-HT)	Brain stem Limbic system
Acetylcholine (Ach)	Neuromuscular junctions Preganglionic sympathetic nervous system Preganglionic parasympathetic nervous system Postganglionic parasympathetic nervous system Septal-hippocampal system
Gamma amino butyric acid (GABA) (a major inhibitory neurotransmitter)	Hippocampus Substantia nigra Limbic system—general
Dopamine (DA)	Mesolimbic system Nigrostriatal system

membrane and moves away from the cell body toward the axon, its nature becomes that of a measurable electrical event. It is this measurable electrical event that serves as the basis for electrophysiological techniques such as electrocardiography. The foundations of these electrical events are based upon the dynamics of ionic transport.

As a neuron sits at rest, it has ions within the boundaries of its membranes as well as outside around its membranes. Sodium (Na^+) is the positively charged ion that makes up the majority of the ionic constituency outside the neuron. The sodium concentration outside the neuron is about 0.142 M. Chloride (Cl^-) is a negatively charged ion that makes up the second largest ionic constituency outside the neuron (about 0.103 M). Whereas Na^+ and Cl^- predominate the extraneural space, negatively charged protein anions dominate the internal milieu of the neuron along with potassium (K^+). Thus relatively speaking, the outside of the neuron possesses a positive charge and the inside of the neuron possesses a negative charge. This resting status is called a polarized state *(polarization)*. The relative intensity of the negatively charged intraneuronal constituency is about −70 mV. This −70 mV is called the *resting electrical potential*.

When a neuron is in the act of transmitting a neural signal, the resting status of the neuron is altered. Ionically, Na^+ rushes across the membrane of the neuron and enters the intraneuronal space. This influx of Na^+ pushes the electrical gradient to about +50 mV (from the resting −70 mV). This process of sodium ion influx is called *depolarization* and represents the actual firing, or discharge, of the neuron. Depolarization lasts about 1.5 msec. Depolarization moves longitudinally along the axon as a wave of ionic influx. After 1.5 msec, however, the neuron begins to repolarize. *Repolarization* occurs as K^+ and Na^+ are pumped out of the neuron and any remaining Na^+ is assimilated into the neuron itself. The result of repolarization is the return of the +50 mV to a resting −70 mV, ready for subsequent discharge. This process is captured in Figure 2.2.

Basic Neuroanatomy

From the preceding discussion of basic neural transmission, the next step to be undertaken is an analysis of the fundamental anatomical structures involved in the human stress response.

The nervous systems are the functional structures within which millions upon millions of neurons reside. These nervous systems may be classified from either an anatomical perspective or a functional perspective. For the sake of parsimony, the nervous systems will be described from an anatomical perspective.

From an anatomical perspective, there exists two fundamental nervous systems: the *central nervous system* (CNS) and *the peripheral nervous system* (PNS) (see Figure 2.3).

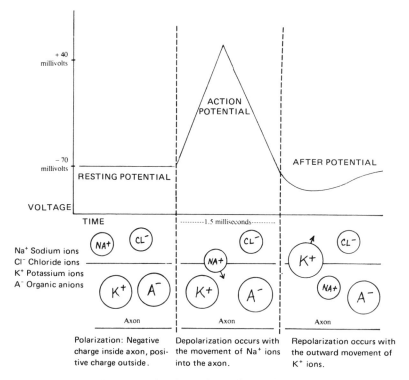

Figure 2.2. The electrochemical neural impulse.

The CNS

The CNS consists of the brain and the spinal cord (see Table 2.2). MacLean (1975) has called the human brain the "triune brain" because it can be classified as having three functional levels (see Figure 2.4). The *neocortex* represents the highest level of the triune brain and is the most sophisticated component of the human brain. Among other functions, such as the decoding and interpretation of sensory signals, communications, and gross control of motor (musculoskeletal) behaviors, the neocortex (primarily the *frontal lobe*) presides over imagination, logic, decision making, memory, problem solving, planning, and apprehension.

The *limbic system* represents the major component of the second level of the triune brain. The limbic brain is of interest in the discussion of stress because of its role as the emotional (affective) control center for the human brain. The limbic system is believed to be just that, that is, a *system*, consisting of numerous neural structures, for example, the *hypothalamus, hippo-*

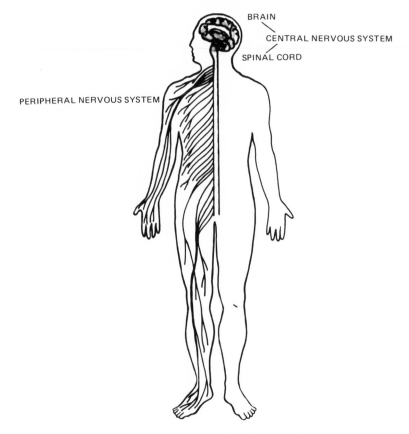

Figure 2.3. Nervous systems (adapted from Lachman, 1972).

Table 2.2. The Human Nervous Systems

I. The central nervous system (CNS)
   A. Brain
   B. Spinal cord
II. The peripheral nervous systems (PNS)
   A. The somatic branch
   B. The autonomic branches (ANS)
      1. Sympathetic (SNS)
      2. Parasympathetic (PSNS)

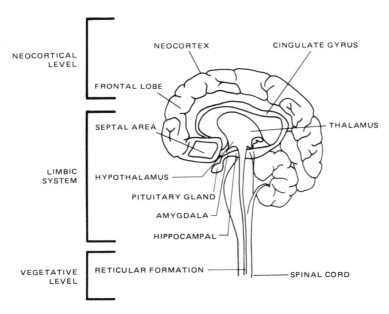

Figure 2.4. The human brain.

campus, septum, cingulate gyrus, and *amygdala.* The *pituitary gland* plays a major functional role in this system in that *it is a major effector* endocrine gland. The limbic system will be examined in greater detail in Chapter 9.

The *reticular formation* and the *brain stem* represent the lowest level of the triune brain. The major functions of this level are the maintenance of vegetative functions (heart beat, respiration, vasomotor activity) and the conduction of impulses through the reticular formation and relay centers of the *thalamus* en route to the higher levels of the triune brain.

As for the spinal cord, it represents the central pathway for neurons as they conduct signals to and from the brain. It is also involved in some autonomically regulated reflexes.

The PNS

The PNS consists of all neurons exclusive of the CNS. Anatomically, the PNS may be thought of as an extension of the CNS in that the functional control centers for the PNS lie in the CNS. The PNS may be divided into two networks: the *somatic* and the *autonomic* (ANS).

The somatic branch of the PNS carries sensory and motor signals to and from the CNS. Thus it innervates sensory organs as well as the striate musculature (skeletal musculature).

The autonomic branches carry impulses that are concerned with the regulation of the body's internal environment and the maintenance of the homeostasis (balance). The autonomic network therefore, innervates the heart, the smooth muscles, and the glands.

The autonomic nervous system can be further subdivided into two branches, the *sympathetic* and the *parasympathetic* (see Figure 2.5 for details of autonomic innervation). The sympathetic branch of the autonomic ner-

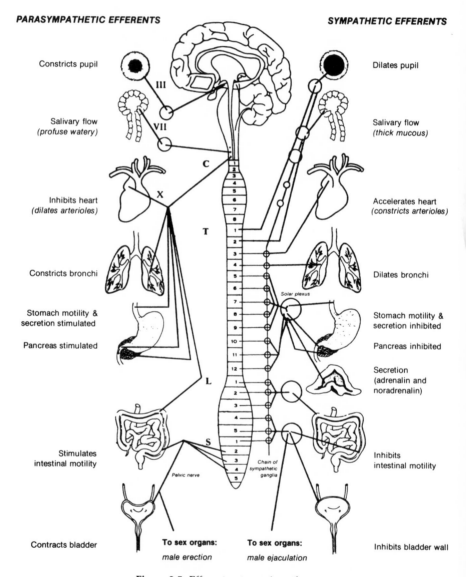

Figure 2.5. Efferent autonomic pathways.

vous system is concerned with preparing the body for action. Its effect on the organs it innervates is that of generalized arousal. The parasympathetic branch of the autonomic nervous system is concerned with restorative functions and the relaxation of the body. Its general effects are those of slowing and maintenance of basic bodily requirements. The specific effects of sympathetic and parasympathetic activation on end organs are summarized later in this chapter (see Table 2.3).

To this point I have briefly described the most basic of the anatomical and functional aspects of the human nervous system. We are now ready to see how these elements become interrelated as constituents of the human stress-response process.

A SYSTEMS MODEL OF THE HUMAN STRESS RESPONSE

The human stress response is perhaps best described within the context of the dynamic "process" it represents. This process may then be delineated from a "systems" perspective, that is, one of interrelated multidimensionality. Figure 2.6 details a systems perspective brought to bear upon the phenomenology of the human stress response. This model, which has evolved significantly in recent years, not only will serve as a unifying theme to assist in gaining a better understanding not only of the phenomenology of human stress but its measurement and treatment as well. These latter themes will be expanded upon later in the text.

An analysis of Figure 2.6 reveals the epiphenomenology of the human stress response to be that of a multidimensional interactive process possessing several key elements:

1. Stressor events (real or imagined)
2. Cognitive appraisal and affective integration
3. Neurologic triggering mechanisms (e.g., locus coeruleus, limbic nuclei, hypothalamic nuclei)
4. The stress response (a physiologic mechanism of mediation)
5. Target-organ activation
6. Coping behavior

A detailed analysis of each of these elements is appropriate at this point.

Stressor Events

Because Selye used the term *stress* to refer to a "response," it was necessary to employ a word that to delineate the stimulus for the stress response—that word is *stressor*. Stressor events, as noted earlier, fall in one

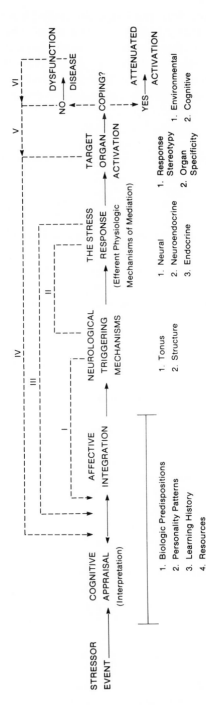

Figure 2.6. A systems model of the human stress response.

of the two categories: (1) psychosocial stressors and (2) biogenic stressors (Girdano & Everly, 1986).

Psychosocial stressors are either real or imagined environmental events that "set the stage" for the elicitation of the stress response. They cannot directly "cause" the stress response, but must work through cognitive appraisal mechanics. Most stressors are, indeed, psychosocial stressors. It is for this reason that one may argue that "stress, like beauty, resides in the eye of the beholder."

Biogenic stressors, however, are stressors that actually "cause" the elicitation of the stress response. Such stimuli bypass the higher cognitive appraisal mechanisms and work directly on affective and neurologic triggering nuclei. Thus, by virtue of their biochemical properties, they directly initiate the stress response without the usual requisite cognitive–affective processing. Examples of such stimuli include

- amphetamine
- phenylpropanolamine
- caffeine
- theobromine
- theophylline
- nicotine
- certain physical factors such as pain-evoking stimuli, extreme heat, and extreme cold

As just mentioned, however, most stressors are not biogenic stressors. Therefore, in clinical practice, therapists will most likely be treating patients who are plagued by environmental events, real, imagined, anticipated, or recalled, that are perceived in such a manner as to lead to activation of the stress response. To better understand this process we move now to the second step in the model: the cognitive–affective integration stage.

Cognitive–Affective Domain

Practically speaking, there is simply no such thing as "reality" without considering the human perspective that might be brought to bear upon it. The cognitive–affective domain is delineated within this model in order to capture that notion.

Cognitive appraisal refers to the process of cognitive interpretation, that is, the meanings that we assign to the world as it unfolds before us. *Affective integration* refers to the blending and coloring of felt emotion into the cognitive interpretation. The resultant cognitive–affective complex represents how the stressors are ultimately perceived. In effect, this critical integrated perception represents the determination of whether psychosocial *stimuli* become psychosocial *stressors* or not. Such a perceptual process, however, is uniquely individualized and vulnerable to biological predispositions (Millon & Everly, 1985; Strelau, Farley, & Gale, 1985), personality patterns (Millon, 1981), learning history (Lachman, 1972), and available resources for coping (Lazarus & Folkman, 1984; Ray, Lindop, & Gibson, 1982).

Although Figure 2.6 portrays a reciprocity between cognitive and affective mechanisms, it should be noted that there exists substantial evidence (see Chapter 8) supporting the cognitive primacy hypothesis. That is, cognition determines affect (felt emotion) and thus assumes a superordinate role in the process of restructuring human behavior patterns. Let us explore this important notion further.

Perhaps the earliest recognition that cognition is superordinate to affect has been credited by Albert Ellis to the fifth-century Greco-Roman philosopher Epictetus who reportedly said, "Men are disturbed not by things, but by the views which they take of them." The science of physiology follows in kind. Hans Selye, also known as the father of modern endocrinology, has summarized over 50 years of research into human stress with the conclusion, "It is not what happens to you that matters, but how you take it." Similarly, the noted neurophysiologist Ernest Gellhorn (Gellhorn & Loofbourrow, 1963) recognized the preeminent role of the prefrontal lobe cognitive processes in felt and expressed emotion in his research spanning the 1950s, 1960s and 1970s. Today, influential authors such as Arnold (1970, 1984), Cassel (1974), Ellis (1977), Lazarus (1982), Meichenbaum (Meichenbaum, 1985; Meichenbaum & Jaremko, 1983), and Selye (1976) strongly support the cognitive primacy position as it relates to human stress.

An extended physiological perspective may be of value at this point. If a given, nonsympathomimetic, stimulus is to engender a stress response, it must first be received by the receptors of the PNS. Once stimulated, these receptors send their impulses along the PNS toward the brain. According to Snyder (1974) and Penfield (1975), once in the CNS, collateral neurons diverge from the main ascending pathways to the neocortical targets and innervate the reticular formation. Snyder has noted that "via these collaterals, events perceived in the environment may be integrated with . . . emotional states encoded in the hypothalamus and limbic system" (p. 221). These collaterals diverge and pass through limbic constituents, but seldom are such afferent diversions sufficient to generate full-blown emotional reactions. Rather, such diversions may account for nonspecific arousal (startle or defense reflexes) or subtle affective coloration ("gut reactions"). Cognitive theorists do not regard these momentary acute ontogenetically primitive events as emotions (Lazarus, 1982).

These divergent pathways ultimately reunite with the main ascending pathways and innervate the primary sensory and appraisal loci. Arnold

(1984) has written that, "the sheer experience of things around us cannot lead to action unless they are appraised for their effect on us" (p. 125). She has hypothesized the anatomical locus of such appraisal to be the cingulate gyrus and the limbic–prefrontal neocortical interface.

Arnold (1984) notes that the granular cells of the limbic–prefrontal interface contain relay centers that connect all sensory, motor, and association areas. She states:

> These connections would enable the individual to appraise information from every modality: smells, via relays from the posterior orbital cortex; movement and movement impulses, via relays from frontal and prefrontal cortex; somatic sensations can provide data via relays from parietal association areas; and things seen could be appraised over relays from occipital association areas. Finally, something heard can be appraised as soon as relays from the auditory association area reach the hippocampal gyrus. (pp. 128–129)

As noted in Figure 2.6, appraisal is a function of any existing biological predispositions, personality patterns, learning history, and available coping resources. Once appraisal is made, efferent impulses project so as to potentiate the stimulation of two major effector systems:

1. Impulses project back to the highly sensitive emotional anatomy in the limbic system (Arnold, 1984; Gellhorn & Loufbourrow, 1963; Gevarter, 1978; Nauta, 1979); especially the hippocampus (Reiman *et al.*, 1986), for the experience of stimulus-specific felt emotion and the potential to trigger visceral effector mechanisms.
2. Impulses similarly project to the areas of the neocortex concerned with neuromuscular behavior where, through pyramidal and extrapyramidal systems, muscle tone (tension) is increased and the intention to act can be potentially translated to actual overt motor activity (Gellhorn, 1964).

Thus far, we have seen that psychosocial stimuli, once perceived, excite nonspecific arousal and cognitive appraisal mechanisms. If the appraisal of the stimulus is ultimately one of threat, challenge, or aversion, then emotional arousal will likely result.

In most individuals, activation of the limbic centers for emotional arousal leads to expression of the felt emotion in the form of visceral activation and neuromuscular activity. Such visceral and neuromuscular activation represents the multiaxial physiological mechanisms of mediation Selye called the "stress response." Thus in the final analysis, it can be seen that physiological reactions to psychosocial stimuli result from the cognitive interpretations and emotional reactions to those stimuli, *not* the stimuli themselves.

Before turning to a discussion of the multiaxial nature of the stress response, we must first discuss a mechanism that prefaces activation of the stress response axes. Research in the last several years has necessitated specific consideration of mechanisms that serve to "trigger" the elicitation of the multiaxial stress response. These mechanisms are referred to as *neurological triggering mechanisms*.

Neurological Triggering Mechanisms

The next step in the model depicted in Figure 2.6 is the neurological triggering mechanisms consisting of the locus ceruleus (LC), limbic system, hypothalamic efferent triggering complex. Linked through ventral and dorsal adrenergic as well as serotonergic projections (among others), this complex appears to consist of the locus ceruleus, the hippocampus, the septal-hippocampal-amygdaloid complexes, and the anterior and posterior hypothalamic nuclei (Everly, 1985b; Nauta & Domesick, 1982; Reiman *et al.*, 1986). These structures appear to be the anatomical epicenters for the visceral and somatic efferent discharges in response to emotional arousal (Gellhorn, 1964, 1965, 1967; MacLean, 1949; Nauta, 1979; Redmond, 1979). That is, these structures appear to give rise to the multiaxial stress response. Indeed, these centers even seem capable of establishing an endogenously determined neurological tone that is potentially self-perpetuating (Everly, 1985b; Gellhorn, 1967; Weil, 1974). This notion of a positive feedback loop is initially depicted in Figure 2.6 by the dotted line labeled I. Subsequent dotted lines appear in Figure 2.6 and are labeled with Roman numerals to show other feedback mechanisms that maintain what Gellhorn (1957) has called a state of "egotropic tuning" and what Everly (Everly & Benson, 1988) calls "limbic hypersensitivity" (discussed in Chapter 3), and what Weil (1974) has called a "charged arousal system." Each of these terms is indicative of a predisposition for physiological arousal.

More specifically, these terms describe a preferential pattern of sympathetic nervous system (and related arousal mechanism) responsiveness. Such a chronic tonic status may, over time, serve as the basis for a host of psychiatric and psychophysiological disorders (Gellhorn, 1967). The mechanisms by which such neurological tone can exert an effect upon a given target organ is the subject of the next phase of the system's model: the stress response—a physiological mechanism of mediation.

The Stress Response

One may recall that the question that has plagued psychosomatic research involves the issue of through what mechanisms of pathogenic mediation a stressor and its subsequent appraisal can ultimately affect a target organ to such a degree as to result in dysfunction and disease. Although a definitive answer on *all* levels has yet to be found, research in applied

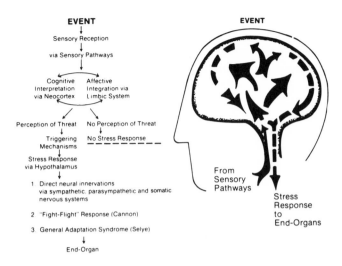

Figure 2.7. The stress response.

physiology has yielded considerable insight into the mechanisms of pathogenesis by which stressors cause disease. This section will detail three such physiological pathways known to demonstrate extraordinary responsiveness with respect to psychosocial stimuli: (1) the neural axes, (2) the neuroendocrine axis, and (3) the endocrine axes (see Figure 2.7).

The Neural Axes—Stress Response via Neural Innervation of Target Organs

There are three neural pathways that comprise the neural stress axes: (1) the sympathetic nervous system, (2) the parasympathetic nervous system, and, (3) the neuromuscular nervous system. The three neural pathways are the first of all stress response axes to become activated during stress arousal. This phenomenon is based upon the fact that the structure of these pathways, from origination to target-organ innervation, are completely neural, and therefore quickest.

It is clear that autonomic nervous system activation occurs during states of emotional arousal in human beings (Duffy, 1962; Johnson & Spaulding, 1974; Lindsley, 1951). These neural axes are the most direct of all stress pathways. Following the complex neocortical and limbic integrations that occur in the interpretation of a stimulus as "threatening," neural impulses descend to the posterior hypothalamus (in the case of a sympathetic activation) and the anterior hypothalamus (in the case of a parasympathetic activation). From here sympathetic neural pathways descend from the posterior hypothalamus through the thoracic and lumbar regions of the spinal cord. Having passed through the sympathetic chain of ganglia, the sympathetic nerves then innervate the end organs. Parasympathetic pathways descend from the anterior hypothalamus through the cranial and sacral spinal-cord regions. Parasympathetic nerves then innervate the end organs.

Generally speaking, the release of the neurotransmitter norepinephrine from the sympathetic telodendria is responsible for changes in most end-organ activity. Acetylcholine is the neurotransmitter in the remaining cases and for the parasympathetic postganglionic transmissions as well.

The effects of neural activation via the sympathetic system are those of generalized arousal within the end organs—what Hess (1957) referred to as an "ergotropic" response. The effects of activation via the parasympathetic system are inhibition, slowing, and "restorative" functions—what Hess called a "trophotropic" response. The specific end-organ effects of the sympathetic and the parasympathetic nervous systems are summarized in Table 2.3.

Although the most common form of neural autonomic stress responsiveness in human beings is in the form of the ergotropic response (Johnson & Spalding, 1974), simultaneous trophotropic responses have been observed in human beings as well (Gellhorn, 1969). The trophotropic stress response may be perceived by some clinicians as paradoxical, owing to the expectation of manifestations of somation "arousal." However, the important work of Gellhorn (1968, 1969) and Williams (1986), in addition to the clinical observations of Carruthers and Taggart (1973), Engle (1971), Everly (1985b), and Karasarsky (1969), have demonstrated that sympathetic stress arousal can be accompanied by parasympathetic trophotropic activation.

Finally, there is evidence (Gellhorn, 1967, 1958a, 1958b, 1964b; Malmo, 1975; Williams, 1986) that the skeletal muscular is also a prime target for immediate activation during stress and emotional arousal. Such activation, if excessive, may lead to a host of neuromuscular dysfunctions as well as increased limbic excitation (Gellhorn, 1958b; Malmo, 1975; Weil, 1974) and therefore heightened emotional arousal (Everly, 1985b).

Although neuromuscular activation may last virtually indefinitely, hence the proliferation of various neuromuscular dysfunction syndromes, the major effects of autonomic neural activation on target organs are immediate, but not potentially chronic. This is because of the limited ability of the sympathetic telodendria to continue to constantly release neurotransmitting substances under chronically high stimulation (LeBlanc, 1976). Therefore, in order to maintain high levels of stress arousal for prolonged periods, an additional physiological stress axis must be activated. This axis is the neuroendocrine "fight or flight" response axis.

Table 2.3. Responses of Effector Organs to Autonomic Nervous System Impulses

	SNS	PSNS
Function	Ergotropic; catabolism	Trophotropic; anabolism
Activity	Diffuse	Discrete
Anatomy		
Emerges from spinal cord	Thoracolumbar	Craniosacral
Location of ganglia	Close to spinal cord	Close to target organ
Postganglionic neurotransmitter	Noradrenalin[a] (adrenergic)	Acetylcholine (cholinergic)
Specific actions		
Pupil of eye	Dilates	Constricts
Lacrimal gland	—	Stimulates secretion
Salivary glands	Scanty, thick secretion	Profuse, water secretion
Heart	Increases heart rate	Decreases heart rate
	Increases contractility	Decreases metabolism
	Increases rate of idiopathic pacemakers in ventricles	
Blood vessels		
Skin and mucosa	Constricts	—
Skeletal muscles	Dilates	—
Cerebral	Constricts	Dilates
Renal	Constricts	—
Abdominal viscera	Mostly constricts	—
Lungs: Bronchial tubes	Dilates	Constricts
Sweat glands	Stimulates[a]	Constricts
Liver	Glycogenolysis for release of glucose	—
		Expels bile
Spleen	Contracts to release blood high in erythrocytes	—
Adrenal medulla	Secretes adrenaline (epinephrine) and noradrenaline (norepinephrine)[a]	—
Gastrointestinal tract	Inhibits digestion	Increases digestion
	Decreases peristalsis and tone	Increases peristalsis and tone
Kidney	Decreases output of urine	?
Hair follicles	Piloerection	—
Male sex organ	Ejaculation	Erection

[a]Postganglionic SNS neurotransmitter is acetylcholine for most sweat glands and some blood vessels in skeletal muscles. Adrenal medulla is innervated by cholinergic sympathetic neurons. Partially adapted from Hassett (1978).

The "Fight or Flight" Response—The Neuroendocrine Axis

In the same year, 1926, that Selye first described the "syndrome of just being sick," physiologist Walter Cannon first wrote about a phenomenon that he termed *homeostasis*. Homeostasis was described as the effort of the physiological systems within the body to actively maintain a level of functioning, within the limits of tolerance of the systems, in the face of ever-changing conditions. Homeostasis was the adaptational effort of the body to stay in balance. From his early efforts, it was clear that the work of Cannon was to parallel and augment that of Selye in terms of understanding the psychophysiological stress response.

Cannon wrote extensively on one particular aspect of the autonomic nervous system's role in the stress response—the neuroendocrine process. He researched what he termed the "fight or flight" response. The pivotal organ in this response is the adrenal medulla—thus giving this response both neural ANS characteristics and endocrine characteristics (Cannon, 1914, 1953; Cannon & Paz, 1911).

The "fight or flight" response is thought to be a mobilization of the body to prepare for muscular activity in response to a perceived threat. This mechanism allows the organism either to fight or to flee from the perceived threat (Cannon, 1953).

Research has demonstrated that the homeostatic, neuroendocrine "fight or flight" response can be activated in human beings by numerous and diverse psychological influences, including varied psychosocial stimuli (Ametz et al., 1986; Froberg, Karlsson, Levi, & Lidberg, 1971; Levi, 1972; Mason, 1968a, 1972; Roessler & Greenfield, 1962).

The dorsomedial-amygdalar complex appears to represent the highest point of origination for the "fight or flight" response as a functionally discrete psychophysiological axis (Lang, 1975; Roldan, Alvarez-Palaez de Molina, 1974). From that point, the downward flow of neural impulses passes to the lateral and posterior hypothalamic regions (Roldan et al., 1974). From here neural impulses continue to descend through the thoracic spinal cord, converging at the celiac ganglion, then innervating the adrenal gland, more specifically, the adrenal medulla.

The adrenal gland in mammals consists of two constituents that are functionally and histologically discrete: the adrenal medulla and the adrenal cortex. The adrenal medulla consists of chromaffin cells (pheochromoblasts) that lie at the core, or center, of the adrenal gland (medulla means stalk). Chromaffin cells are responsible for the creation and secretion of adrenal medullary catecholamines. This process is referred to as *catecholaminogenesis*.

The hormonal output of the neuroendocrine stress response axis is the secretion of the adrenal medullary catecholamines. There are two adrenal medullary catecholamines: norepinephrine (noradrenalin) and epinephrine (adrenalin). These two hormones are collectively referred to as adrenal medullary catecholamines because of their origin and the chemical nature. That is, these hormones are secreted by the two adrenal medullae that lie at the superior poles of the kidneys. Furthermore, the biochemical structure of these hormones is related to a group of organic compounds referred to as *catechols* (or pyrocatechols).

The adrenal medullary cells are divided into two types: A-cells, which secrete epinephrine, and N-cells, which secrete norepinephrine. About 80% of the medullary catecholamine activity in humans is accounted for by epinephrine (Harper, 1975). It is critical to note at this juncture that nor-epinephrine is secreted not only by the adrenal medulla, but also by the adrenergic neurons of the central nervous system and the SNS. The biosynthesis and actions are the same regardless of whether the norepinephrine originates in the medulla or in the adrenergic neurons of the CNS or SNS (see Appendix F).

Upon neural stimulation, the adrenal medulla releases the medullary catecholamines as just described. The effect of these medullary catecholamines is an increase in generalized adrenergic somatic activity in human beings (Folkow & Neil, 1971; Maranon, 1924; Wenger, Clemens, Coleman, Cullan & Engel, 1960). The effect, therefore, is functionally identical to that of direct sympathetic innervation (see Table 2.3), except that the medullary catecholamines require a 20- to 30- second delay of onset for measurable effects and display a tenfold increase in effect duration (Usdin, Kretnansky, & Kopin, 1976). Also, the catecholamines only prolong the adrenergic sympathetic response. Cholinergic responses, such as increased electrodermal activity and bronchiole effects, are unaffected by medullary catecholamine release (Usdin *et al.*, 1976).

The "fight or flight" response has been somewhat reformulated by writers, such as Schneiderman (McCabe & Schneiderman, 1984), who view this system as an "active coping" system. This active coping system has been referred to as the "sympatho-adrenomedullary system" (SAM).

Specific somatic effects that have been suggested or observed in humans as a result of activation of this axis in response to psychosocial stressor exposure are summarized in Table 2.4.

Williams (1986) has identified two distinctive patterns of ANS activation that may be relevant to the formation of coronary artery disease: (1) a "defense" pattern (Pattern 1), where the sympathetic nervous system seems so highly activated as to result in increased neuromuscular activation, increased heart rate and cardiac output, and vasodilitation of the skeletal muscles (thus somewhat offsetting, in terms of blood pressure, other SNS activity), and (2) A "vigilance" pattern (Pattern 2), where heart rate and cardiac output are vagally inhibited, and there is vasoconstriction in the skeletal muscles while other SNS activity seems elevated. The pri-

Table 2.4. Effects of Adrenal Medullary Axis
Stimulation[a]

Increased arterial blood pressure
Increased blood supply to brain (moderate)
Increased heart rate and cardiac output
Increased stimulation of skeletal muscles
Increased plasma free fatty acids, triglycerides, cholesterol
Increased release of endogenous opioids
Decreased blood flow to kidneys
Decreased blood flow to gastrointestinal system
Decreased blood flow to skin
Increased risk of hypertension
Increased risk of thrombosis formation
Increased risk of angina pectoris attacks in persons so prone
Increased risk of arrhythmias
Increased risk of sudden death from lethal arrhythmia, myocardial ischemia, myocardial fibrillation, myocardial infarction

---

[a]See Brod, 1959, 1971; Froberg, Karlsson, Levi, & Lidberg, 1971; Henry & Stephens, 1977; Ametz, Fjellner, Eneroth, & Kallner, 1986; Axelrod & Reisine, 1984; McCabe & Schneiderman, 1984, for reviews.

mary hormone active in the defense pattern appears to be epinephrine, whereas the primary hormone active in the vigilance pattern appears to be testosterone. Testosterone is the primary male androgenic hormone.

This brings us to a discussion of the third and final stress response mechanism—the endocrine axes.

Endocrine Axes

The most chronic and prolonged somatic responses to stress are the result of the endocrine axes (Mason, 1968b). Four well-established endocrine axes have been associated with the stress response:

1. The adrenal cortical axis
2. The somatotropic axis
3. The thyroid axis
4. The posterior pituitary axis

These axes not only represent the most chronic aspects of the stress response, but also require greater intensity stimulation to activate (Levi, 1972).

Reviews by Axelrod and Reisine (1984), Levi (1972), Makara, Palkovits, and Szentagothal (1980), Mason (1968c, 1972), McCabe and Schneiderman (1984), McKerns and Pantic (1985), and Selye (1976) demonstrate that these axes can be activated in humans by numerous and diverse psychological stimuli, including varied psychosocial stimuli.

The Adrenal Cortical Axis. The septal-hippocampal complex appears to represent the highest point of origination for the adrenal cortical axis as a physiologically discrete mechanism (Henry & Ely, 1976; Henry & Stephens, 1977). From these points, neural impulses descend to the median eminence of the hypothalamus. The neurosecretory cells in the median eminence release corticotropin releasing factor (CRF) into the hypothalamic-hypophyseal portal system (Rochefort *et al.*, 1959). The CRF descends the infundibular stalk to the cells of the anterior pituitary. The chemophobes of the anterior pituitary are sensitive to the presence of CRF and respond by releasing adrenocorticotropic hormone (ACTH) in the systemic circulation. At the same time, the precursor to the various endogenous analgesic opioids (endorphins) is released. This precursor substance is beta lipotropin and yields the proliferation of endogenous opioids during human stress (Rossier, Bloom, & Guillemin, 1980).

ACTH is carried through the systemic circulation until it reaches its primary target organ: an endocrine gland, the adrenal cortex. The two adrenal cortices are wrapped around the two adrenal medullae (neuroendocrine axis) and sit at the superior poles of the kidneys.

ACTH appears to act upon three discrete layers, or zona, of the adrenal cortex. ACTH stimulates the cells of the zona reticularis and zona fasciculata to release the glucocorticoids cortisol and corticosterone into the systemic circulation. The effects of the glucocorticoids in apparent response to stressful stimuli are summarized in Table 2.5.

Table 2.5. The Effects of the Glucocorticoid Hormones[a] and HPAC Activation

Increased glucose production (gluconeogenesis)
Exacerbation of gastric irritation
Increased urea production
Increased release of free fatty acids into systemic circulation
Increased susceptibility arteherosclerotic processes
Increased susceptibility to nonthrombotic myocardial necrosis
Thymicolymphatic atrophy (demonstrated in animals only)
Supression of immune mechanisms
Exacerbation of herpes simplex
Increased ketone body production
Appetite supression
Associated feelings of depression, hopelessness, helplessness, and a loss of control

[a]See Henry & Stephens (1977), Selye (1976), Yates & Maran (1972), Yuwiler (1976), MaCabe & Schneiderman (1984), Makara, Palkovitz, & Szentagothal (1980) for reviews.

Similarly, ACTH allows the zona glomerulosa to secrete the mineralocorticoids aldosterone and deoxycorticosterone into the systemic circulation. The primary effects of aldosterone release are an increase in the absorption of sodium and chloride by the renal tubules and a decrease in their excretion by the salivary glands, sweat glands, and gastrointestinal tract. Subsequent fluid retention will be noted as a corollary of this process. Although cortisol does exhibit some of these properties, aldosterone is about 1,000 times more potent as an electrolyte effector. As the prepotent mineralocorticoid, aldosterone may effect other physiologic outcomes, among them increasing glycogen deposits in the liver and decreasing circulating eosinophils.

Excessive activation of mineralocorticoid secretion in human beings has been implicated in the development of Cushing's syndrome (hyperadrenocorticism) by Gifford and Gunderson (1970) and in high blood pressure and myocardial necrosis by Selye (1976).

As a tropic hormone, the main function of ACTH is to stimulate the synthesis and secretion of the glucocorticoid hormones from the adrenal cortex, yet ACTH is known to cause the release of cortical adrenal androgenic hormones such as testosterone as well. Finally, there is evidence that ACTH affects the release of the catecholamines described earlier in this chapter. Its effect on the catecholamines epinephrine and norepinephrine appears to be through a modulation of tyrosine hydroxylase, which is the "rate-limiting" step in catecholamine synthesis. This effect is a minor one, however, compared with other influences on tyrosine hydroxylase. Thus adrenal medullary and cortical activities can be highly separate, even inversely related, at times (Kopin, 1976; Lundberg & Forsman, 1978). See Axelrod and Reisine (1984) for an excellent review of hormonal interaction and regulation.

The adrenal cortical response axis has been referred to by various authors (e.g., McCabe & Schneiderman, 1984), as the hypothalamic-pituitary-adrenal cortical system (HPAC). Activation of this system in the aggregate has been associated with the helplessness/hopelessness depression syndrome, passivity, the perception of no control, immunosuppression, and gastrointestinal symptomatology. Behaviorally, the HPAC system appears to be activated when active coping is not possible; thus it has been called the "passive coping" system. Considering the HPAC system with respect to the SAM, Frankenhauser (1980) has concluded that:

1. Effort without distress → activation of the SAM response system.
2. Distress without effort → activation of the HPAC response system.
3. Effort with distress → activation of both SAM and HPAC.

The Somatotropic Axis. The somatotropic axis appears to share the same basic physiological mechanisms from the septal-hippocampal complex through the hypothalamic-hypophyseal portal system as the previous axis, with the exception that somatotropin releasing factor (SRF) stimulates the anterior pituitary within this axis. The anterior pituitary responds to the SRF by releasing growth hormone (somatotropic hormone) into the systemic circulation (see Makara et al., 1980; Selye, 1976).

The role of growth hormone in stress is somewhat less clearly understood than that of the adrenal cortical axis. However, research has documented its release in response to psychological stimuli in human beings (Selye, 1976), and certain effects are suspected. Selye (1956) has stated that growth hormone stimulates the release of the mineralocorticoids. Yuwiler (1976) in his review of stress and endocrine function suggests that growth hormone produces a diabetic-like insulin-resistant effect, as well as mobilization of fats stored in the body. The effect is an increase in the concentration of free fatty acids and glucose in the blood.

The Thyroid Axis.   The thyroid axis is now a well-established stress response mechanism. From the median eminence of the hypothalamus is released thyrotropin releasing factor (TRF). The infundibular stalk carries the TRF to its target—the anterior pituitary. From here, the tropic hormone thyroid stimulating hormone (TSH) is released into the systemic circulation. TSH ultimately stimulates the thyroid gland to release two thyroid hormones: triiodothyronine (T3) and thyroxine (T4). Once secreted into the systemic circulation system, these hormones are bound to specific plasma protein carriers, primarily thyroxin binding globulin (TBG). A small amount of the thyroid hormones remains as "free" unbound hormones. About .04% of T4 remains unbound, and about .4% of T3 remains unbound. Proper evaluation of thyroid function is best based upon an assessment of free thyroid hormones. At the level of target-cell tissue, only free hormone is metabolically active.

The T3 and T4 hormones serve to participate in a negative feedback loop thus suppressing their own subsequent secretion.

In humans, psychosocial stimuli have generally led to an increase in thyroidal activity (Levi, 1972; Makara et al., 1980; Yuwiler, 1976). Levi (1972) has stated that the thyroid hormones have been shown to increase general metabolism, heart rate, heart contractility, peripheral vascular resistance (thereby increasing blood pressure), and the sensitivity of some tissues to catecholamines. Hypothyroidism has been linked to depressive episodes. Levi therefore concludes that the thyroid axis could play a significant role as a response axis in human stress.

The Posterior Pituitary Axis and Other Phenomena.   Since the early 1930s, there has been speculation on the role of the posterior pituitary in the stress response. The posterior pituitary (neurohypophysis) receives neural impulses from the supraoptico nuclei of the hypothalamus. Stimulation from these nuclei results in the release of the hormones vasopressin (antidiuretic hormone, sometimes shortened to ADH) and oxytocin into the systemic circulation.

ADH affects the human organism by increasing the permeability of the collecting ducts that lie subsequent to the distal ascending tubules within the glomerular structures of the kidneys. The end result is water retention.

Corson and Corson (1971) in their review of psychosocial influences on renal function note several studies that report significant amounts of water retention in apparent response to psychological influences in human beings.

Although there seems to be agreement that water retention can be psychogenically induced, there is little agreement on what the specific mechanism is. Corson and Corson (1971) report studies that point to the release of elevated amounts of ADH in response to stressful episodes. On the other hand, some studies conclude that the antidiuretic effect is due to decreased renal blood flow. Some human subjects even responded with a diuretic response to psychosocial stimuli.

Nevertheless, Makara *et al.* (1980) in their review of 25 years of research found ample evidence for the increased responsiveness of ADH during the stress response. ADH is now seen as one of the wide range of diverse stress-responsive hormones.

Oxytocin is the other major hormone found in the posterior pituitary axis. It is synthesized in the same nuclei as ADH, but in different cells. Its role in the human stress response is currently unclear but may be involved in psychogenic labor contractions (Omer & Everly, in press) and premature birth.

Most recent research into the Type A behavior pattern has uncovered the role that testosterone plays in the stress response (Williams, 1986). Along with cortisol, testosterone is seen as one of the key responsive hormones in the Type A coronary-prone behavior pattern in males. Testosterone lies at the end of the gonadotropin-releasing factor–anterior pituitary–interstitial cell-stimulating hormone–response axis. Various investigations have shown that both interstitial cell-stimulating hormone (Sowers *et al.*, 1977), also known as luteinizing hormone, and testosterone (Williams, 1986) have been shown to be responsive to the presentation of various stressors.

Finally, the hormone prolactin has clearly shown responsiveness to psychosocial stimulation as well (see Makara *et al.*, 1980). The role of prolactin in disease or dysfunction phenomena, however, has not been well-established. Attempts to link prolactin with premenstrual dysfunction have yet to yield a clear line of evidence. The specific role of prolactin in stress-related disease needs further elucidation.

The "General Adaptation Syndrome"

As a means of integrating his psychoendocrinological research, Hans Seyle (1956) proposed an integrative model for the stress response. This model was known as the "General Adaptation Syndrome" (GAS).

The GAS is a triphasic phenomenon. The first phase Selye refers to as the "alarm" phase. This phase represents a generalized somatic shock, or "call to arms" of the body's defense mechanisms. The second phase is called the "stage of resistance." In this phase, there is a dramatic reduction in most alarm stage processes and the body fights to reestablish and maintain homeostasis. Stages 1 and 2 can be repeated throughout one's life. Should the stressor persist, however, eventually the "adaptive energy," that is, the adaptive mechanisms in the second stage, may become depleted. At this point, the body enters the third and final stage, the "stage of exhaustion." This final stage, when applied to a target organ, is indicative of the exhaustion of that organ and the symptoms of disease and dysfunction become manifest. When the final stage is applied to the entire body, life itself may be in jeopardy. The three stages of the GAS are detailed in Table 2.6.

The Stress Response: A Summary

In this section, we presented a unifying perspective from which to view the complex psychophysiological processes that have come to be known as the stress response. The intention was to provide the clinician with an understandable interpretation of the complexities of the stress-response process that he or she will often find himself or herself treating. Because effective treatment of the stress phenomenon is related to com-

Table 2.6. The General Adaptation Syndrome

Alarm Stage
    Sympathetic nervous system arousal
    Adrenal medullary stimulation
    ACTH release
    Cortisol release
    Growth hormone release
    Prolactin release
    Increased thyroid activity
    Gonadotropin activity increased
    Anxiety
Resistance Stage
    Reduction in adrenal cortical activity
    Reduction in sympathetic nervous system activity
    Homeostatic mechanisms engaged
Exhaustion Stage
    Enlargement of lymphatic structures
    Target organ disease/dysfunction manifest
    Increased vulnerability to opportunistic disease
    Psychological exhaustion: depression
    Physiological exhaustion: disease → death?

prehension of the nature of the problem (Miller, 1978, 1979), it is hoped that this discussion will prove of some utility for the clinician.

The unifying thread throughout this discussion has been the temporal sequencing of the stress-response process. We have shown that the most immediate response to a stressful stimulus occurs via the direct neural innervations of end organs. The intermediate stress effects are due to the neuroendocrine "fight or flight" axis. The reaction time of this axis is reduced by its utilization of systemic circulation as a transport mechanism. However, its effects range from intermediate to chronic in duration and may overlap with the last stress-response system to respond to a stimulus—the endocrine axes. The endocrine axes are the final pathways to react to stressful stimuli. This is primarily owing to the almost total reliance on the circulatory system for transportation, as well as the fact that a higher intensity stimulus is needed to activate this axis. The GAS provides an additional schema to extend the endocrine response axis in the adaptation of the organism to the presence of a chronic stressor (see Selye, 1956, for a discussion of diseases of adaptation). Figure 2.8 summarizes the sequential activation of the stress-response axes.

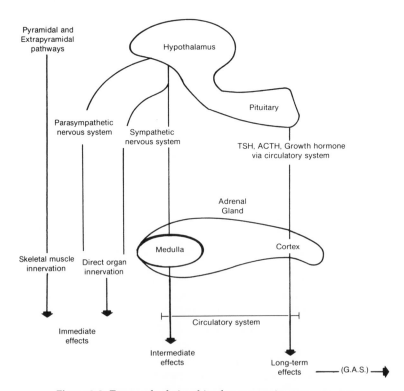

Figure 2.8. Temporal relationships between primary stress axes.

It is important to understand that there is a potential for the activation of each of these axes to overlap. The most common axes to be simultaneously active are the neuroendocrine and endocrine axes—both of which have potential for chronic responsivity (Mason, 1968a, c).

On the other hand, it is clear that all mechanisms and all axes detailed cannot possibly discharge each and every time a person is faced with a stressor. Perhaps clearest of all is the fact that each sympathetic and parasympathetic effect is not manifest to all stressors. Therefore, what determines which stress-response mechanisms will be activated by which stressors in which individuals? The answer to this question is currently unknown. However, there is some evidence to suggest the existence of a psychophysiological predisposition for some individuals to undergo stress-response pattern specificity (see Sternbach, 1966). We will expand on this topic in Chapter 3.

These then, are the stress-response axes and the various mechanisms that work within each. They represent the response patterns that can potentially result each time the human organism is exposed to a stressor. As to when each responds and why, we are unsure at this time. Current speculations will be reviewed in Chapter 3. Despite this uncertainty, the clinician should gain useful insight into the treatment of the stress response by understanding the psychophysiological processes involved once the stress response becomes activated. To assist the reader in putting the picture together, Figure 2.9 provides a unique "global" perspective into the multiaxial nature of psychophysiological stress.

As a final note, returning to Figure 2.6, feedback loops II and III simply indicate the ability of the physiological stress response described above to further stimulate the cognitive/affective domain as well as the neurologic triggering mechanisms so as to further promulgate the stress response. Such a feedback mechanism may provide the potential for a psychophysiologically self-sustaining response. This, then, is the physiology of human stress as currently understood.

Target-Organ Activation

The term *target-organ activation* as used in the present model refers to the phenomenon where the neural, neuroendocrine, and endocrine constituents of the stress response, just enumerated, either: (1) activate, (2) increase or (3) inhibit normal activation, or (4) catabolize some organ system in the human body. Potential target-organ systems for the stress response include the cardiovascular system, the gastrointestinal system, the skin, the immune system, even the brain and its mental status, to mention only a few. It is from activation of the target organs and the subsequent emergence of various clinical signs and symptoms that we often deduce the presence of excessive stress arousal.

As for which target organs are most likely to manifest stress-related

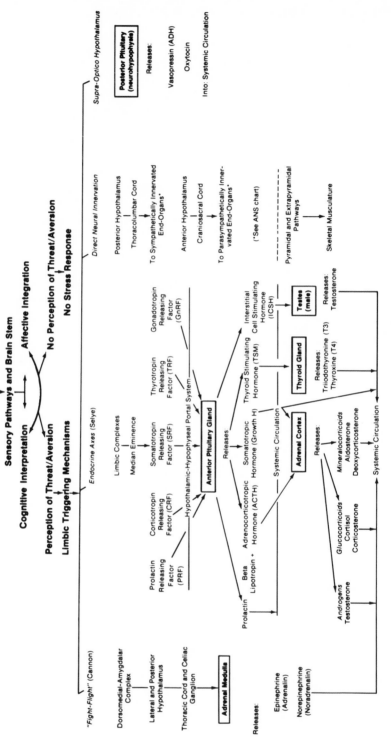

Figure 2.9. The multiaxial nature of the stress response.

disease or dysfunction, it appears as if two major biogenic factors assist in that determination (Everly, 1986): response mechanism stereotypy (Sternbach, 1966) and target-organ specificity (Everly, 1978). *Response mechanism stereotypy* refers to a preferential pattern of stress-related neural, neuroendocrine, or endocrine activation. The more consistent such activation, the greater the likelihood of a stress-related disease (Stoyva, 1977). Target-organ specificity refers to a predisposing vulnerability of the target organ to experience pathogenic arousal (Everly, 1986). Genetic, prenatal, neonatal, and traumatic stimuli may all play a role in such a determination.

Finally, feedback loop IV (in Figure 2.6) indicates that target-organ activation and subsequent signs and symptoms of disease may affect the patient's cognitive/affective behavior and therefore may also affect further neurological triggering and continued stress-response activity. In some cases (e.g., agoraphobic patients, obsessive patients, and hysterically prone patients), a hypersensitive awareness to target-organ symptoms can create a self-sustaining pathogenic feedback loop.

The issue of target-organ disease will be elaborated upon in the next chapter.

COPING

The preceding two sections went into great detail in an attempt to describe what many phenomenologists have called the "missing link" in psychosomatic phenomena, that is, the physiological mechanisms of mediation by which cognitive/affective discord could result in physical disease and dysfunction. It is an understanding of these physiological mechanisms of mediation that allows us to see stress-related disorders as the quintessential intertwining of "mind and body" as opposed to some hysterical anomaly. Yet we know that the manifestations of human stress are highly varied and individualistic. Whereas biological predisposition certainly plays a role in this process, a major factor in determining the impact of stress on the patient is his or her perceived ability to cope. *Coping* is defined as

> efforts, both action-oriented and intrapsychic, to manage (that is master, tolerate, reduce, minimize) environmental and internal demands, and conflicts among them, which tax or exceed a person's resources. Coping can occur prior to a stressful confrontation, in which case it is called anticipatory coping, as well as in reaction to a present or past confrontation with harm. (Cohen & Lazarus, 1979, p. 219)

More recently, coping has been defined as "constantly changing cognitive and behavioral efforts to manage specific . . . demands that are appraised as taxing or exceeding the resources of the person" (Lazarus & Folkman, 1984, p. 141).

From the perspective of the current model (Figure 2.6), coping may be thought of as environmental or cognitive tactics designed to attenuate the stress response. The present model views coping as residing subsequent to the physiological stress response and target-organ activation. Thus, coping is seen as an attempt to reestablish homeostasis. Anticipatory coping, as mentioned by Lazarus and other theorists, is subsumed, in the present model, in the complex interactions of the cognitive/affective domain.

To further refine the notion of coping, it may be suggested that coping strategies can be either adaptive or maladaptive (Girando & Everly, 1986). Adaptive coping strategies reduce stress while at the same time promoting long-term health (for example, exercise, relaxation, proper nutrition). Maladaptive coping strategies, on the other hand, do indeed reduce stress in the short term, but serve to erode health in the long term (alcohol/drug abuse, cigarette smoking, interpersonal withdrawal) (see Everly, 1979a).

Figure 2.6 reflects the belief that when coping is successful, extraordinary target-organ activation is reduced or eliminated and homeostasis is reestablished. If coping strategies are unsuccessful, target-organ activation is maintained and the chances of target-organ disease are increased.

Feedback loops V and VI once again reflect the interrelatedness of all components included in Figure 2.6.

The model depicted in Figure 2.6 reflects an integration of recent research and critical thought concerning human stress. It is presented as nothing more than a pedagogical tool designed to facilitate the clinician's understanding of the phenomenology of the stress response. If it has sensitized the clinician to the major components of the stress response and shown their interrelatedness, it has served its purpose. The phenomenological model in Figure 2.6 will be used as a common reference in subsequent chapters to facilitate better understanding of the topics of measurement and treatment of the human stress response.

SUMMARY

The purpose of this chapter has been to provide a somewhat detailed analysis of the psychophysiological nature of the human stress response. Let us review the main points of this chapter.

1. The nervous systems serve as the foundation of the stress response. The neuron is the smallest functional unit within any given nervous system. Communications between neurons, and therefore within nervous systems, are based upon electrical (ionic transport) and chemical (neurotransmitter mobilization) processes.

Nervous systems are anatomically arranged in the following schema:

  I. Central nervous system
    A. Brain
    B. Spinal

    II. Peripheral nervous systems
      A. Somatic (to skeletal musculature)
      B. Autonomic (to glands, organs, viscera)
        1. Sympathetic
        2. Parasympathetic

    2. Figure 2.6 represents an integrative epiphenomenological model of the stress response. Figure 2.6 is reproduced once again here as Figure 2.10 for review purposes. Let us summarize its components.

    3. Environmental events (stressors) may either "cause" the activation of the stress response (as in the case of sympathomimetic stressors) or, as is usually the case, simply "set the stage" for the mobilization of the stress response.

    4. The cognitive–affective domain is the critical "causal" phase in most stress reactions. Stress, like beauty, appears to be in the eye of the beholder. One's interpretation of the environmental event is what creates most stressors and subsequent stress responses.

    5. The locus ceruleus, limbic complexes, and the hypothalamic nuclei trigger efferent neurological, neuroendocrine, and endocrine reactions in response to higher cognitive–affective interactions.

    6. The actual stress response itself is the next step in the system's analysis. Possessing at least three major efferent axes—neurological, neuroendocrine, and endocrine—this "physiological mechanism of mediation" represents numerous combinations and permutations of efferent activity directed toward numerous and diverse target organs (see Figure 2.9).

The most rapid of the physiological stress axes are the neurological axes. They consist of mobilization of the sympathetic, parasympathetic, and neuromuscular nervous systems. The neuroendocrine axis, sometimes called the sympathoadrenal medullary axis (SAM), but better known as Cannon's "fight or flight" response, is next to be mobilized. Activation leads to the extraordinary release of epinephrine and norepinephrine. Finally, the endocrine axes, researched primarily by Hans Selye, are potential response mechanisms. Consisting of the adrenal cortical axis (HPAC system), the somatotropic axis, the thyroid axis, and the posterior pituitary axis, these axes play a major role in chronic disease and dysfunction. Selye's notion of the General Adaptation Syndrome is an attempt to unify these axes (see Table 2.6).

    7. As a result of the stress response axes being extraordinarily mobilized, target-organ activation is realized.

    8. The final step before pathogenic target-organ activation is coping. Here, the patient has the opportunity to act environmentally or cognitively, or both, so as to reduce or mitigate the overall amplitude and level of activation that reaches the target organs.

    9. Should stress arousal be excessive either in acute intensity or in chronicity, target-organ dysfunction and/or pathology will result.

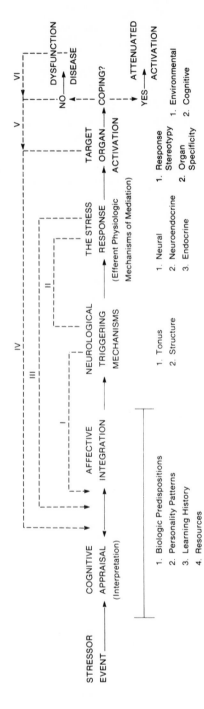

Figure 2.10 A systems model of the human stress response.

10. As a final note, it should be remembered that the aforementioned axes are always activated at some level of functioning. Inclusion in this chapter simply reflects their potential for pathogenic arousal in response to stressor stimuli and thus their aggregate designation as the physiologic mechanisms of the stress response.

11. In sum, this chapter was designed to provide the reader with a reasonable approximation of the mechanisms that serve to link the stressor stimulus with target-organ activation. The next chapter will extend this examination into the link between stress arousal and subsequent disease.

The Link from Stress Arousal to Disease

The notion that one's psychosocial environment, life style, and attitudes are linked to disease is by no means a new idea, as discussed in Chapter 1. In a scholarly meta-analysis, Tower (1984) reviewed 523 published reports investigating the relationship between psychosocial factors and disease. Ultimately selecting 60 of those studies on the basis of design considerations, she then submitted the data to a meta-analysis. The results supported the conclusion that there exists a strong relationship between psychosocial factors and illness. She notes, "Psychological well-being appeared to be most strongly associated with coronary heart disease and infectious processes . . . although it was significantly associated with all diseases [investigated] except complications of pregnancy" (Tower, 1984, p. 51). To assess the power of her findings, Tower calculated the number of fugitive studies required to reject the findings of her meta-analysis. The results of this analysis of outcome tolerance revealed that over 28,000 fugitive studies would be required to reject the conclusion that psychosocial factors are related to disease.

In the tradition of Pasteur, however, in order for a stimulus to be recognized as being a credible cause or contributor to disease, the pathophysiological processes that culminate in target-organ disease and dysfunction (sometimes called *mechanisms of mediation*) must be understood. Chapter 2 reviewed a model by which a *stressor* may activate *stress-response mechanisms*. That chapter further detailed potential stress-response effector mechanisms that might undergird such pathogenic relationships as confirmed by Tower (1984). The chapter offered evidence that an aggregation of neural, neuroendocrine, and endocrine response axes, collectively referred to as the *stress response,* were indeed vulnerable to extraordinary activation upon exposure to psychosocial stimuli. This chapter examines the logical extension of stress physiology by reviewing several noteworthy models of target-organ pathogenesis, that is, those proposed factors that link *stress arousal* mechanisms, once they are activated, to *target-organ disease.*

Although the literature in psychosomatic phenomenology as a global concept is voluminous, relatively few models exist that concern themselves more directly with the link between extraordinary arousal of the stress axes and the ultimate manifestations of stress-related disease. Let us take this opportunity to review several of those models.

SELYE'S "GENERAL ADAPTATION SYNDROME"

In Chapter 2, Selye's General Adaptation Syndrome (GAS) was introduced as a means of integrating the manifestations of the stress response as a sequential series of physiologic events. Its triphasic constituency was described at that point: (1) the alarm stage, (2) the stage of resistance (adaptation), and (3) the exhaustion stage. The GAS is mentioned in the present chapter because, not only does it serve to integrate, from a temporal perspective, many of the stress axes described earlier, but it also serves to explain the link from stress arousal to disease. As described by Selye (1956), stage 1 of the GAS involves a somatic "shock" and initial "alarm reaction" for biological sources within the body following exposure to a stressor. The insult to the bodily tissues during this acute alarm phase could be so great as to deprive the target organ of its ability to compensate. If this happens, as might occur in cases of burns, electrical shock, or acute psychological trauma, the target organ may simply cease to function (e.g., in the case of cardiac fibrillation). Thus the target organ will have been traumatically exhausted and rendered incapable of further functioning. Serious illness or death may then result.

If, however, the resources of the body are not completely compromised as a result of the "alarm" phase, then the stage of resistance is entered. Here the body's resources are mobilized to reestablish homeostasis. This is what usually occurs in most stress-related conditions. Yet, in order to maintain homeostasis in the face of a persistent stressor, there is a chronic drain of "adaptive energy," that is, physiological resources. Should the stressor persist indefinitely (even in the form of cognitive rumination) or should stages 1 and 2 recycle themselves too frequently, eventual exhaustion of the target organ is predicted. This is the third and final stage in Selye's schema, the exhaustion phase. Thus stress-related disease manifestation would occur as a result of a depletion of adaptive physiological resources and the subsequent target-organ exhaustion would be considered a result of excessive "wear and tear" (Selye, 1974). This then is the GAS as it attempts to define the stress-to-disease process. The GAS has been criticized for its global generality and lack of sensitivity for physiologic response specificity (Mason, 1971).

LACHMAN'S MODEL

In a "behavioral interpretation" of psychosomatic disease, Lachman (1972) proposes an "autonomic learning theory" that emphasizes:

> . . . the role of learning in the development of psychosomatic aberrations without minimizing the role of genetic factors or of nongenetic predisposing factors. The essence of the theory proposed is that psychosomatic manifestations result from frequent or prolonged or intense . . . reactions elicited via stimulation of receptors. (pp. 62–63)

Lachman argues that a major source of frequent, prolonged, or intense emotional and physiological reactions is a *learned* pattern of emotional and autonomic responsiveness. More specifically, he notes with regard to the stress-to-disease phenomenon, "In order for emotional reactions to assume pathological significance such reactions must be intense or chronic or both" (p. 70). He goes on to state that which end-organ structure will be affected pathologically depends on:

1. Genetic factors that biologically predispose the organ to harm from psychophysiological arousal
2. Environmental factors that predispose the organ to harm from psychophysiological arousal. These would include such things as nutritional influences, infectious disease influences, physical trauma influences, etc.
3. The specific structures involved in the physiological reactivity
4. The magnitude of involvement during the physiological response, which he has defined in terms of intensity, frequency, and duration of involvement of the organ

Lachman (1972) concludes that the determination of which structure is ultimately affected in the psychosomatic reaction depends on "the biological condition of the structure" (whether a function of genetic or environmental influences), "on the initial reactivity threshold of the organ, and on . . . learning factors," which affect the activation of the organ. He goes on to note that the "magnitude of the psychosomatic phenomenon" appears to be a function of the frequency, intensity, and chronicity of the organ's activation.

STERNBACH'S MODEL

In a somewhat more psychophysiologically oriented model, Sternbach (1966) provides another perspective on the stress-to-disease issue, which is considered a variation on the "diathesis" stress model of Levi and Andersson (1975).

The first step in Sternbach's model is *response stereotypy*. This term generally refers to the tendency of an individual to exhibit characteristically similar patterns of psychophysiological reactivity to a variety of stressful stimuli. Sternbach views it as a "predisposed response set." That such a response stereotypy phenomenon does indeed exist has been clearly demonstrated in patient and normal populations (Lacey & Lacey, 1958, 1962; Malmo & Shagass, 1949; Moos & Engel, 1962; Schnore, 1959).

Response stereotypy may be generally thought of as a form of the "weak-link" or "weak-organ" theory of psychosomatic disease. Whether the weak organ is genetically determined, a function of conditioning, or acquired through disease or physical trauma is unclear.

The second step in the Sternbach model entails the frequent activation of the psychophysiological stress response within the stereotypic organ. As Stoyva (1977) notes, the mere existence of response stereotypy is not enough to cause disease. It is obvious that the organ must be involved in frequent activation in order to be adversely affected.

Finally, Sternbach's model includes the requirement that homeostatic mechanisms fail; that is, once the stereotypic organ has undergone psychophysiological arousal, that stress-responsive organ must now be slow to return to its baseline level of activity. In effect, a slow recovery to baseline is evidenced. Such homeostatic failure has been implicated in the onset of disease since the work of Freeman (1939). Freeman advanced the theory that autonomic excitation that is slow to deactivate from an organ system does increase the strain on that system. Malmo, Shagass, and Davis (1950) empirically demonstrated that such a phenomenon exists. Lader's (1969) review on this issue implicates it as a potential precursor to disease.

Sternbach (1966) has then put forward these conditions as prerequisites for the development of a stress-related disorder. The reader is referred to the work of Stoyva for further commentary on the Sternbach model, as well as other theories of psychosomatic illness (Stoyva, 1976, 1977; Stoyva & Budzynski, 1974).

KRAUS AND RAAB'S "HYPOKINETIC DISEASE" MODEL

In their treatise on exercise and health, Kraus and Raab (1961) argue that many stress-related diseases are induced not so much by the direct physiology of the stress response, but by the lack of subsequent somatomotor expression of that physiology. They argue that little over 100 years ago vigorous physical labor was a way of life that actually served as a protective mechanism against diseases commonly referred to today as "diseases of civilization." These authors suggest that modern sedentary life-styles have put that protective mechanism "all but out of commission." Kraus and Raab (1961) conclude:

> The system that has been put all but out of commission, the striated musculature . . . has an important role which exceeds the mere function of locomotion. Action of the striated muscle influences directly and indirectly circulation, metabolism, and endocrine balance. . . . Last but not least the striated muscle serves as an outlet for our emotions and nervous responses . . . . Obliteration of [this] important safety valve . . . might well upset the original balance to which the bodies of primitive man have been adapted. (p. 4)

Therefore Kraus and Raab coined the term "hypokinetic disease" (hypo = under; kinetic = motion/exercise) to refer to a wide array of diseases that as a result of the lack of healthful expression/utilization of the physiological mechanisms of the stress response. The notion of the lack of physical activity serving as a risk factor for disease and dysfunction has been supported by the World Health Organization (Chavat et al., 1964), which conclude that suppression of somatomotor activity in response to stress arousal is likely to lead to increased cardiovascular strain.

SCHWARTZ'S "DISREGULATION" MODEL

Gary Schwartz working at Yale University (1977, 1979) has devised a general systems model of stress-related pathogenesis that revolves around homeostatic disregulation as its pathogenic core (see Figure 3.1). He notes,

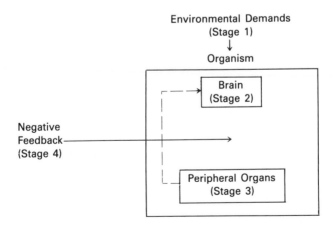

Figure 3.1. Schwartz's model.

"It follows directly from cybernetic and systems theory that a normally self regulatory system can become disordered when communication . . . between specific parts of the system is . . . disrupted" (Schwartz, 1979, p. 563).

Schwartz describes his model (Schwartz, 1977):

> When the environment (Stage 1) places demands on a person, the brain (Stage 2) performs the regulatory functions necessary to meet the specific demands. Depending on the nature of the environmental demand on stress, certain bodily systems (Stage 3) will be activated, while others may be simultaneously inhibited. However, if this process is sustained to the point where the tissue suffers deterioration or injury, the negative feedback loops (Stage 4) of the homeostatic mechanism will normally come into play forcing the brain to modify its directives to aid the afflicted organ. (p. 76)

Thus the negative feedback loops described by Schwartz dominate the normal physiological milieu and are necessary to effective, adaptive functioning. Yet Schwartz argues that it is a *disregulation* in Stage 4 homeostatic mechanisms that may lead to a host of stress-related diseases through target-organ overstimulation. Overstimulation may occur by the creation of positive, self-sustaining feedback mechanisms or the blockage of natural inhibitory processes. Schwartz argues that disconnection of any feedback mechanism, from a systems view, is capable of leading to disregulation and thus to disease.

Congruent with the aforementioned model, therapeutic interventions would entail reestablishing homeostasis (homeostatic regulation). Consistent with this is Greengard's (1978) perspective based on the observation of physiological systems: "It seems probable that derangements of homeostatic processes are responsible for many disease states. Conversely, it seems likely that the effects of many therapeutic . . . agents are exerted on such homeostatic systems" (p. 146). Therefore, as one might expect, Schwartz sees biofeedback and other autoregulatory therapies as useful agents for the treatment of stress-related disorders.

EVERLY AND BENSON'S "DISORDERS OF AROUSAL" MODEL

The "disorders of arousal" model of pathogenesis (Everly & Benson, 1989) is a direct result of an integration of efforts from Harvard University to understand the mechanisms of pathogenesis in psychosomatic disorders (Everly, 1985b, 1986) and the mechanisms active in the amelioration of such psychosomatic disorders (Benson, 1975, 1987).

It has been observed for over four decades that various technologies that could be used to induce a hypoarousal relaxation response were able to ameliorate, or at least diminish, the severity of a wide and diverse variety of diseases. Yet no one has reliably shown any single relaxation technology to be superior in its clinical efficacy; nor has research reliably shown any single disease to be maximally responsive to such an intervention (Lehrer & Woolfolk, 1984). It seems as if the initiation of what Herbert Benson (1975) has called the "relaxation response" has virtually a generic applicability across a wide spectrum of stress-related, psychosomatic diseases. That observation led to an investigation of the source of the broad-spectrum therapeutic effect of the relaxation response as a way of understanding the disorders it was useful in treating. The investigation culminated in an analysis of common phenomenological mechanisms, that is, common denominators (latent), occurring across anxiety and stress-related diseases that would serve to homogenize such disorders.

Based upon an integration of the work of Goddard on "kindling" (Goddard & Douglas, 1976), Post on "sensitisation" (Post & Ballenger, 1981), Gellhorn on "ergotropic tuning" (Gellhorn, 1967), and Gray (1982) on the limbic system, it has been proposed by Everly that the phenomenology of many chronic anxiety and stress-related diseases is undergirded by the existence of a latent, yet common denominator, existing in the form of a neurological hypersensitivity for excitation (or arousal) residing within the subcortical limbic circuitry (Everly, 1985b). This limbic hypersensitivity phenomenon (LHP) may be understood as an unusually high propensity for neurologic arousal/excitation with the potential to lead to, or exist as, a pathognomonic state of excessive arousal within the limbic system. Terms such as "hyperstartle reaction," "autonomic hyperfunction," and "autonomic lability" are diagnostic terms commonly used to capture such a notion. The LHP is believed to develop as a result of either acutely traumatic or repeated extraordinary limbic excitation and is credited with the potential to ignite a cascade of extraordinary arousal of numerous and varied neurologic, neuroendocrine, and endocrine efferent mechanisms (as discussed in Chapter 2) and, therefore, the potential to give rise to a host of varied psychiatric and somatic disorders. The subsequent disorders are then referred to as "disorders of arousal." This concept is captured in Figure 3.2.

Figure 3.2 depicts the notion that, responsive to a host of widely disparate etiologic factors (stressors) including environmental events, cognitive–affective dynamics, personologic predispositions, and the like, there exists a subtle, latent mechanism of pathogenesis: a neurologic hypersensitivity for pathogenic arousal located within the limbic circuitry. Such arousal is believed to be capable of triggering a subsequent variety of physiological effector mechanisms (stress-response axes), within existing patterns of response predisposition (response stereotypy), so as to ultimately give rise to a wide and diverse spectrum of target-organ disorders (disorders of arousal). Included in the disorders of arousal taxonomy would be most anxiety and adjustment disorders including some forms of depression, as well as virtually any and all stress-related physical disor-

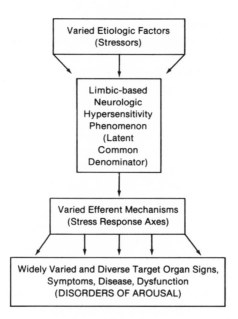

Figure 3.2. Limbic hypersensitivity phenomenon: the latent taxon in stress-related "disorders of arousal."

ders. The disorders of arousal will be enumerated in greater detail later in this volume. The reader may also refer to Everly and Benson (1989), Doane (1986), and Post (1986).

The natural corollary of the disorders of arousal model of pathogenesis is the notion that effective treatment of such disorders is highly related to reducing the subcortical hypersensitivity through the use of some "anti-arousal" therapy. In addition to various pharmacologic interventions, Benson's concept of the relaxation response represents a natural antiarousal phenomenon that appears antithetical to the mechanisms that undergird the disorders of arousal. Thus it may well be that a major source of the broad-spectrum therapeutic effect exhibited by the relaxation response resides in the homeostasis-seeking, antiarousal phenomenology of the relaxation response, which serves to inhibit the mechanism of limbic hypersensitivity believed to exist as a common denominator among the various disorders of arousal.

In sum, the disorders of arousal model of stress-induced pathology recognizes the influences of environmental factors, cognitive–affective dynamics, patterns of previous learning, and patterns of preferential psychophysiologic excitation as described in previous models and summarized elsewhere (Everly, 1986). Yet it focuses upon the limbic system proper, its efferent influences on cognitive processes, and its effector mechanisms through the hypothalamus. More specifically, it focuses upon a proposed limbic hypersensitivity phenomenon, developed as a result of extraordinary limbic excitation, as key constituents in linking the stress response to stress-related disease formation, especially chronic manifestations of such diseases.

Several different theories have been enumerated here to explain how psychophysiological arousal can be channeled to affect target organs adversely. Despite the disparity between the theories mentioned, there does appear to be one element, either directly stated or implied, that is common to all. That commonality pertains to how the target organs ultimately become dysfunctional or pathological—simply stated, if any given target organ is subjected to psychophysiological overload (overstimulation) for a long enough period, that organ will eventually manifest symptoms of dysfunction or pathology due to excessive "wear and tear," be it biochemically induced trauma or toxicity or actual visceromotor fatigue or exhaustion. According to Stoyva (1976) in his review of stress-related disorders, "A number of investigators have hypothesized that if the stress response is evoked too often, or sustained for too long, then disorders are likely to develop" (p. 370). In a "behavioristic interpretation" of psychosomatic disorders, Lachman (1972) states, "The longer a given structure is involved in an on-going emotional reaction pattern, the greater is the likelihood of it being involved in a psychosomatic disorder" (pp. 69–70). Lachman (1972) concludes, "Theoretically, any bodily structure or function can become the end focus of psychosomatic phenomena–but especially those directly innervated and regulated by the autonomic nervous system" (p. 71).

Perhaps of greater interest to the clinician than the theory concerning what causes a target-organ symptom to be overloaded is the widely accepted conclusion that target-organ stress-related diseases result from excessively frequent, intense, and/or prolonged activation, that is, overstimulation (see Everly, 1986; Everly and Benson, 1989; Kraus & Raab, 1961; Lachman, 1972; Sternbach, 1966; Stoyva, 1976; Stoyva & Budzynski, 1974). See Table 3.1.

SUMMARY

Chapter 2 described a mechanism by which psychosocial factors could serve to ignite extraordinary arousal of the physiological stress-response axes through cognitive–affective integrations and limbic–hypothalamic neurologic mechanisms. This chapter pursued the logical extension of stress-axis arousal by reviewing the pathogenic mechanisms that are postulated to link the stress response to subsequent target-organ disease. Let us review the main points covered in this review.

1. All major theories agree that target-organ pathology ultimately re-

Table 3.1. From Stress to Disease: Theories of Psychosomatic Pathogenesis

Theory	Pathogenic mechanisms	Result
Selye's "General Adaption Syndrome"	Triphasic fluctuation of neuroendocrine and endocrine mechanisms, especially ACTH. The chronic maintenance of the stage of resistance yields a depletion of adaptive energy.	Depletion of adaptive physiologic energy → exhaustion → disease, due to excessive wear and tear.
Lachman's "behavioral" model	Biological and learned factors interact to establish predisposing patterns of target-organ arousal and disease from excessively frequent stress arousal. Emotional and autonomic learning play a major role in repeated target-organ excitation.	Excessively intense or excessively chronic activation of target organs → stress-related disease (excessive wear and tear).
Sternbach's model	Response stereotypy. Frequent stress arousal. Homeostatic recovery failure.	Frequent target-organ activation → organ fatigue and pathology.
Kraus and Raab's "hypokinetic disease" model	Suppression of somatomotor behavior. Failure to ventilate and utilize the stress response once activated. Increased pathogenic risk.	Target-organ overload and pathology.
Schwartz's "disregulation" model	Failure in homeostatic feedback mechanisms following stressor exposure.	Target-organ overload and pathology.
Everly and Benson's "disorders of arousal" model	Limbic hypersensitivity phenomenon causing extraordinary arousal of stress response axes.	Excessively intense and/or excessively frequent or chronic activation of stress response axes → target-organ overstimulation and pathology.

sults when the specific target organ is overstimulated. Overstimulation may occur as a result of excessively frequent, excessively chronic, or excessively intense stimulation. Pathological states emerge from excessive "wear and tear" on the target organ and can be caused by biochemical toxicity or trauma (e.g., necrosis) as well as structural alteration and visceromotor fatigue or exhaustion.

2. The GAS of Selye presents a triaphasic model by which acute "shock" or chronic excitation could ultimately deplete the physiological constituents that normally allow target organs to continue to function in

the face of stress arousals. The results would be target-organ exhaustion and perhaps even death.

3. Lachman's behavioral model emphasizes that the point that emotional and autonomic responses could be learned. Interacting with other biological factors that are not learned, emotional and autonomic learning can cause repeated target-organ excitation. Excessively prolonged, frequent, or intense target-organ stimulation may then lead to disease.

4. Sternbach's psychophysiological model cites response stereotypy, frequent arousal of stress-response axes, and homeostatic recovery delay as factors that serve to exhaust target organs and lead to disease. Once again, the theme of overutilization emerges as the key pathogenic constituent.

5. Kraus and Raab's model emphasizes the role of suppressed somatomotor expression in the etiology of stress-related pathology. Such suppression leads to target-organ overstimulation, exhaustion, and ultimately disease.

6. Schwartz's "disregulation" model also accepts the overload/ overstimulation concept, but emphasizes the role of faulty negative feedback mechanisms in the pathological etiology.

7. Finally, Everly and Benson propose a model that serves to unite stress-related illnesses on the basis of a limbic hypersensitivity phenomenon, that is, a sensitization (increased propensity for activation) of cognitive, affective, and stress-response efferents in the formulation of stress-related disease. It is proposed that excessively frequent, chronic, or intense activation of target organs based upon the limbic hypersensitivity could ultimately exhaust the target organ and lead to a stress-related disease.

8. Thus, we see that all theories of pathogenesis, while emphasizing different phenomenological aspects as to why target-organ overstimulation occurs, agree that indeed overstimulation and excessive wear of target organs lead to stress-related dysfunction and disease.

Chapter 4 will review specific stress-related diseases commonly encountered in clinical practice.

Stress-Related Disease: A Review

I'm at the mercy of any rogue who cares to annoy and tease me.

—John Hunter, 18th-century physician

There has been skepticism that emotions aroused in a social context can so
seriously affect the body as to lead to long-term disease or death. But the work,
such as that of Wolf, shows that machinery of the human body is very much at
the disposal of the higher centers of the brain . . . . Given the right circumstances, these higher controls can drive it mercilessly, often without awareness
on the part of the individual of how close he is to the fine edge. (Henry &
Stephens, 1977, p. 11)

To review so far, Chapter 2 proposed a model of how psychosocial
factors can activate a complex myriad of neurological, neuroendocrine, and
endocrine response axes. Similarly, Chapter 2 reviewed the physiologic
constituents of these stress axes in considerable detail. Chapter 3 reviewed
the link from stress arousal to disease by summarizing several noteworthy
models constructed to elucidate how stress arousal can lead to disease and
dysfunction. That is, Chapter 3 reviewed mechanisms of pathogenesis that
serve to causally link stress arousal to target-organ pathology. The goal of
this chapter is to review some of the most common clinical manifestations
of excessive stress. More specifically, Chapter 4 is designed to familiarize
the clinician with some of the most frequently encountered target-organ
disorders believed to be related to excessive stress arousal.

GASTROINTESTINAL DISORDERS

Excessive stress and the diseases of the gastrointestinal system have been thought to be related for decades. The most commonly encountered stress-related gastrointestinal disorders are peptic ulcers, ulcerative colitis, irritable bowel syndrome, and esophageal reflux.

Gastrointestinal Physiology

Before reviewing specific gastrointestinal disorders, let us briefly review the basic physiology of the gastrointestinal system. As described by Weinstock and Clouse (1987), the gastrointestinal system involves a series of sequentially arranged tubular organs separated by sphincters. This system includes the esophagus, the stomach, the duodenum, the small intestine, and the large intestine (colon). See Figure 4.1 below.

The esophagus provides a tubular canal for the connection of the

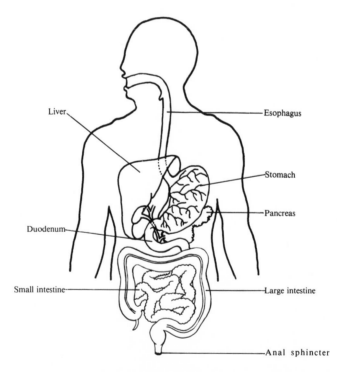

Figure 4.1. The gastrointestinal system. From Daniel A. Girdano & George S. Everly, Jr., *Controlling Stress and Tension: A Holistic Approach*, 2nd ed., pp. 36, 39. ©1986. Reprinted by permission of Prentice-Hall, Inc., Englewood Cliffs, New Jersey.

mouth and the stomach. The activity of the esophagus is primarily under vagal control and neural mechanisms are primarily responsible for esophageal motility. The upper border of the esophagus is the cricopharyngeus (upper esophageal sphincter). The lower border is the lower esophageal sphincter. This latter sphincter is the gateway to the stomach.

The basic functions of the stomach are to receive, pulverize, nutritionally regulate, and temporarily store the food one consumes. The stomach is lined with a mucosal tissue that serves to protect the stomach from its own digestive processes. Under the influence of factors such as gastrin, histamine, vagal stimulation and sympathetic stimulation, intragastric dynamics involving the release of hydrochloric acid, pepsin, and mucus as well as muscular contractions act upon food that has been delivered to the stomach from the esophagus.

From the stomach, the food passes through the pyloric sphincter to the duodenum. The gallbladder is responsible for releasing bile into the duodenum.

The small intestine and its specialized mucosal lining serves as the primary location for digestion and nutrient absorption.

Finally, the large intestine is designed for the absorption and orderly evacuation of concentrated waste products (Weinstock & Clouse, 1987).

Let us now review several common stress-related gastrointestinal disorders.

Peptic Ulcers

Peptic ulcers are usually further classified by their location in the gastrointestinal system: gastric, or stomach, ulcers, and duodenal ulcers. The incidence of peptic ulcer disease is about 18 in 10,000 with duodendal ulcers accounting for about 75% of those cases.

It was demonstrated many years ago that emotions of anger and rage were related to increased secretion of acid and pepsin by the stomach and that this secretion decreased with depression (Mahl & Brody, 1954; Mittelman & Wolff, 1942; Wolf & Glass, 1950). Although it might be concluded that what one sees in gastric ulcer, that is, an erosion of the wall of the stomach by the acid and enzyme it produces, is simply an exaggeration of a normal physiological response; actually it is not quite so simple. Certainly, emotions can raise gastric acid secretion and exacerbate an already-existing ulcer, but normally the stomach wall is protected from the acid within it by a lining of mucus secreted by other cells in its wall. How this protective system breaks down and what predisposes a person to such an event remain elusive.

There seems to be a combination of emotional and genetic factors involved in the pathogenesis of gastric ulcer, and such studies as that of

Weiner, Thaler, Reiser, and Mirsky (1957) have demonstrated this quite well. These investigators were able to predict in a group of recruits in basic training in the army which ones would develop gastric ulcers on the basis of serum pepsinogen levels—a genetic trait that is apparently a necessary but not sufficient factor in the formation of gastric ulcers. Gastric ulcer was also of interest to Selye (1951), who described ulcers apparently in response to chronic arousal of the endocrine stress axes in the general adaptation syndrome. One could thus conceive of a mechanism whereby stress through the intermediation of neural or hormonal mechanisms could result in significant irritation. In individuals who are so predisposed, ulceration of the stomach would occur given sufficient time and continued exposure to the stress. The picture is less clearcut, however, in that it has been suggested that the duodenal ulcer results from changes in the mucosal wall "associated with sustained activation and a feeling of being deprived" (Backus & Dudley, 1977, p. 199).

Therefore, strongly implicated in the stress response, the specific causal mechanisms involved in peptic-ulcer formation are probably multifactorial. Vagus-stimulated gastric hypersecretion as well as glucocorticoid anti-inflammatory activity on the mucous lining have been implicated. Yet conclusive data are lacking at present with regard to the selective activation of each mechanism.

Ulcerative Colitis

Ulcerative colitis is an inflammation and ulceration of the lining of the colon. Research by Grace, Seton, Wolf, and Wolff (1949), Almy, Kern, and Tulin (1949), and Grace, Wolf, and Wolff (1950) produced evidence that the colon becomes hyperactive and hyperemic with an increase in lysozyme levels (a proteolytic enzyme that can dissolve mucus) under stress. The emotions of anger and resentment are reported to create observable ulcerations of the bowel (Grace, Wolf, & Wolff, 1950). "Sustained feelings of this sort might be sufficient to produce enough reduction in bowel wall defenses to the point that the condition becomes self-sustaining" (Backus & Dudley, 1977, p. 199).

The predominant symptom of ulcerative colitis is rectal bleeding, although diarrhea, abdominal cramping and pain, and weight loss may also be present. Ulcerative colitis is sometimes associated with disorders of the spine, liver, and immune system. Rosenbaum (1985) has stated, "The frequency with which emotional precipitating-factors are identified varies, being as high as 74% in adults and 95% in children" (p. 79). Personologic investigations of colitis patients commonly find them to possess an immature personality structure often demonstrating extreme compulsive traits.

Irritable Bowel Syndrome

Mitchell and Drossman (1987) refer to irritable bowel syndrome (IBS) as the most common of the functional disorders. It is viewed as a syndrome of dysfunctional colonic motility; that is, the colon proves to be overreactive to psychological as well as physiological stimuli.

The diagnostic criteria for IBS includes atypical abdominal pain, altered bowel habits, symptomatic duration of 3 months or more, and disruption of normal life style (Latimer, 1985). Abdominal distention, mucus in the stools, fecal urgency, nausea, loss of appetite and even vomiting are other IBS symptoms.

The pathophysiology of IBS is clearly multifactorial with abnormal myoelectric phenomena, altered gut opiate receptors, abnormal calcium channel activity, and increased alpha-adrenergic activity. Personality characteristics of IBS patients often include compulsiveness, overly conscientious behavior, interpersonal sensitivity, and nonassertiveness (Latimer, 1985).

Esophageal Reflux

Before leaving this section on gastrointestinal disorders it would be prudent to mention gastroesophageal reflux and its frequent corollary, esophagitis. Dotevall (1985) has indicated that these syndromes are common stress-related disorders. According to Young *et al.* (1987):

> Heartburn, a common GI symptom, generally is experienced as a painful substernal burning sensation. However, sensations can radiate into the arms or jaw and mimic pain associated with coronary artery disease. Heartburn [esophageal reflux] symptoms typically occur after eating, when lying down, or during bending or straining. The symptoms result from frequent irritation of the sensitive mucosal lining of the esophagus by the usually acidic gastric contents. (p. 8)

Although the primary physiological cause of esophageal reflux and esophagitis is a weakened lower esophageal sphincter, psychological factors are known to contribute to the reflux phenomenon (Dotevall, 1985).

In his superb review of gastrointestinal physiology and stress, Dotevall (1985) listed the known effects of varied emotional reactions on gastrointestinal activity. These are summarized in Table 4.1.

CARDIOVASCULAR DISORDERS

The cardiovascular system is thought by many researchers and clinicians to be the prime target end organ for the stress response. The cardiovascular disorders most often associated with excessive stress are essential hypertension, migraine headache, and Raynaud's disease.

Table 4.1. Psychological Stimuli and Gastrointestinal Responses

Psychological state	GI response
Anxiety	Increased esophageal motility
	Increased colonic contractions
	Increased intraluminal pressure of the colon
Hostility, resentment, aggression (without somatomotor expression)	Increased colonic contractions
	Increased gastric acid
	Increased contractile activity of stomach
Depression	Decreased gastric acid
	Decreased colonic contractions
Wish to be rid of trouble	Rapid colonic transit with diarrhea

Cardiovascular Physiology

Before reviewing those specific disorders, a brief review of cardiovascular physiology is appropriate. Figure 4.2 details the cardiovascular system.

The heart is the key component in the cardiovascular system. It pumps nutrient-rich, oxygenated arterial blood to the cells of the body while at the same time pumping venous blood, which carries the various metabolic waste products.

The heart is divided into two halves: a right heart and a left heart. The circulatory cycle begins with blood entering the right heart. This blood supply is waste-filled venous blood. It has traveled throughout the venules and veins once it left the capillary beds, where the nutrient and gaseous exchanges initially took place within the body. The venous blood enters the resting heart and fills a small feeder chamber called the right atrium. Blood then passively moves through the tricuspid value into the pumping chamber of the right heart, the right ventricle. Once the right ventricle is almost completely filled, an electrical impulse begins in the sinoatrial conducting node so as to contract the right atrium. This action forces any remaining blood into the right ventricle.

More specifically, the electrical impulse transverses the atrium until it reaches the atrioventricular node, where there is a fraction-of-a-second delay completing the filling of the right ventricle. Then the electrical impulse is sent through the ventricle forcing it to contract and pump the venous blood through the pulmonary valve toward the lungs via the pulmonary artery. Once the blood arrives in the lungs, waste products such as carbon dioxide are exchanged for oxygen and the blood is returned to the heart.

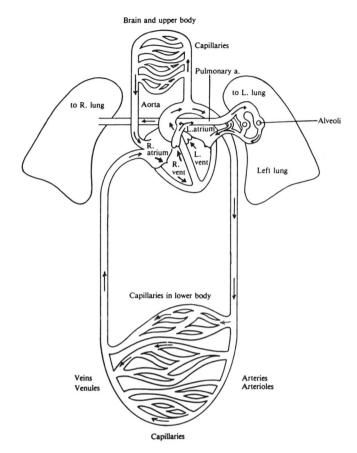

Figure 4.2. The cardiovascular system. From Daniel A. Girdano & George S. Everly, Jr., *Controlling Stress and Tension: A Holistic Approach*, 2nd ed., pp. 36, 39. ©1986. Reprinted by permission of Prentice-Hall, Inc. Englewood Cliffs, New Jersey.

The left heart receives the fresh, oxygenated blood from the lungs via the pulmonary vein. This blood enters the left heart at the point of the left atrium. From here the blood is moved through the mitral valve into the left heart's pumping chamber, the left ventricle. Once again, when the heart beats, it sends the electrical impulse from the sinoatrial node through the left atrium to the atrioventricular node, ultimately culminating in the contraction of the left ventricle. Blood pumped from the left ventricle passes through the aortic valve through the aorta into the arterial system, including the coronary arteries. The arteries narrow into arterioles, which feed the capillary beds where the cells exchange gases and nutrients. Then the capillaries feed the venules, which feed the veins, and the cycle is repeated.

Both the right and left hearts pump simultaneously; therefore blood is being pumped to the lungs at the same time blood is being pumped out to the body.

The cardiovascular system is a closed-loop system. As such, pressure within the system is a necessary driving force. The arterial system, including the left heart, is a high-pressure system driven by the contraction of the left ventricle. The venous system, including the right heart, is a low-pressure system, assisted in venous return by the contraction of the skeletal muscles during movement. Blood pressure, as it is typically measured and expressed, relates to the arterial system pressures. Blood pressure is measured in millimeters of mercury (mm Hg) and is expressed in terms equivalent to the amount of pressure required to raise a column of mercury so many millimeters. Blood pressure is expressed in terms of the systolic pressure (the pressure within the arteries during the contraction of the ventricles—called *systole*) and the diastolic pressure (the pressure within the arteries when the ventricles are filling at rest—called *diastole*).

Essential Hypertension

According to current estimations, 36 million adult Americans suffer from "the silent killer," cardiovascular hypertension. Cardiovascular hypertension is usually defined as arterial pressures over 140 mm Hg systolic pressure and/or 90 mm Hg diastolic pressure, although many authorities will adjust these figures upward (especially the systolic pressure) if the patient is advanced in age.

There are basically two types of cardiovascular hypertension: secondary and essential. Secondary cardiovascular hypertension represents a status of elevated blood pressure due to some organic dysfunction, for example, a pheochromocytoma (tumor of the adrenal gland). Essential hypertension has been loosely interpreted as being related to stress and such factors as diet. The term "essential" reflects the once-held notion that with advancing age one always acquired elevated blood pressure. This notion has been refuted (Henry & Stephens, 1977).

In a review of the pathophysiology of hypertension, Eliot (1979) states that in less than 10% of the cases organic disorders be found to explain hypertension. However, he suggests that both the sympathetic–adrenal medullary and the anterior pituitary–adrenal cortical stress axes are capable of increasing blood pressure in response to psychosocial factors alone. This may occur through a wide range of diverse mechanisms (see also Selye, 1976). With chronic activation, he concludes, the deterioration of the cardiovascular system may be irreversible.

Henry and Stephens (1977), in a useful review of psychosocial stimulation and hypertension, present evidence similar to that of Eliot. In their review of animal and human studies, they point to the ability of the psychophysiological stress mechanisms to effect an increase in blood pressure.

They point to the role of medullary norepinephrine as a vasoconstrictive force capable of increasing blood pressure. In addition, they point to the notion that increased sympathetic tonus (apparently regardless of origin) will lead to further increased sympathetic discharge. The end result may well be the tendency for the carotid sinus and aortic baroreceptors to "reset" themselves at a higher level of blood pressure. The normal effect of the baroreceptors is to act to moderate blood-pressure elevations. However, if they are reset at higher levels, they will tolerate greater blood pressure before intervening. Therefore, resting blood pressure may be allowed to rise slowly over time. Finally, these authors point to the role of the adrenal cortical response in the elevation of blood pressure, perhaps through some arterial narrowing or sodium-retaining mechanism. They suggest that psychosocial disturbance can play a major role in blood-pressure elevations that could become chronic in nature (see Steptoe, 1981).

Weiner (1977), however, states that "psychosocial factors do not by themselves 'cause' essential hypertension" (p. 183). They do however, "interact with other predispositions" to produce high blood pressure (p. 185). He concludes that the available data point toward the conclusion that essentially hypertension can be caused by a wide variety of influences and that psychological and sociological factors "may play a different etiological, pathogenetic, and sustaining role in its different forms" (p. 185).

Vasospastic Phenomena

Stress-related vasospastic phenomena include migraine headaches and Raynaud's disease. These disorders involve vascular spasms, more specifically, their phenomenology involves spasms of the arterial vasculature induced by excessive neurological tone (usually sympathetic nervous system activity) (see Guyton, 1982).

Migraine headaches may affect as many as 17 million Americans. There are two basic subtypes: classical migraine and common migraine. Although both are characterized by vasomotor spasms, the classical migraine is accompanied by a prodrome. The prodrome is often manifest in the form of visual disturbances, hearing dysfunction, expressive aphasia, and/or gastrointestinal dysfunction. The most common form of prodrome is the visual prodrome, for example, the development of an acute visual scotoma. The prodrome is a symptom of severe arterial vasoconstriction. The pain that accompanies migraine headaches occurs on the "rebound," that is, the point at which the arterial vasculature vasodilates in response to the original vasoconstriction. It is unclear whether the pain actually results from the physical dystension of the arterial vasculature or from associated biochemical processes (see Raskins, 1985; Wolff, 1963).

Raynaud's disease is another vasospastic disorder characterized by episodic pallor and cyanosis of the fingers and/or toes. Upon rebound vasodialation, there can be extreme pain characterized by sensations of aching and throbbing. Both exposure to cold and psychosocially induced stress can induce an attack of Raynaud's (Taub & Stroebel, 1978) (see Appendices C and D).

RESPIRATORY DISORDERS

Allergy

An allergy is a hypersensitivity that some people develop to a particular agent. The patient's body reacts with an exaggerated immunodefensive response when it encounters the agent (antigen).

One of the most familiar forms of allergy is hay fever. In this condition, the individual is sensitive to some forms of plant pollen, and when these are inhaled in the air, mucous membranes swell, nasal secretion becomes excessive, and nasal obstruction can occur. Because other particles in the air do not seem to elicit such a response, this is clearly an overreaction to a stimulus. However, hay fever has been generally thought to be a phenomenon related only to the body, as opposed to the mind. Yet the mind–body dualism is once again to be questioned by the finding that some subject with hay fever may respond minimally, if at all, when challenged with the allergenic substance in an environment in which he or she feels secure and comfortable, whereas in other, more stressful situations, the same challenge is met with by the usual nasal hypersecretion, congestion, and the like (Holmes, Trenting, & Wolff, 1951).

Bronchial Asthma

Although sharing some similarities with allergy, asthma is a more complex and potentially serious disorder. In asthmatic patients, bronchial secretions increase, mucosal swelling takes place, and finally smooth muscle surrounding the bronchioles contracts leading to a great difficulty in expiring air from the lungs. This "inability to breath" is, of course, anxiety-producing, and this stress itself leads to a need for more oxygen, thus exacerbating the stress response caused by the original stimulus no matter what its nature. That bronchial asthmatic attacks can be caused by or at least exacerbated by psychosocial stimulation is no longer in question. Research reviewed by Lachman (1972) warrants such a conclusion, as does the work of Knapp (1982).

Hyperventilation

Hyperventilation may be considered an example of an acute stress response. However, episodic hyperventilation can become a long-standing problem that goes undiagnosed for long periods of time in patients presenting vague problems that do not fit any particular pattern, such as vague aches and pains, nausea, vomiting, chest pains, and the like. The clinician must be on guard for this particular manifestation of the stress response, in order to protect the individual from unnecessary suffering and expense while searching for the cause. This, again, is a part of the fight–flight response in which the body is readied for action by increasing O_2 and decreasing CO_2; however, no action takes place. It has been suggested that any time a patient presents such vague problems that seem elusive to the clinician, he or she should maintain a high degree of suspicion regarding hyperventilation. Consideration may then be given to asking the patient to hyperventilate in the office. If the symptoms are reproduced, much time and effort of both physician and patient may be saved. For methods and cautions, refer to articles by Campernolle, Kees, and Leen (1979) and Lum (1975); see also Knapp (1982).

MUSCULOSKELETAL DISORDERS

This system comprises, as its name implies, all the body's muscles and bony support. It is thus the system that is responsible for the body's mobility and therefore plays one of the more obvious roles in a fight-or-flight type of response. At such a time, the muscles tense, blood flow is increased to them, and the very word "tension" associated with emotions such as anger or anxiety relates to this state of the musculoskeletal system (Tomita, 1975).

The stress-related disorders here are quite predictable. Low back pain may often be produced in a situation in which there is contraction of the back muscles as if to keep the body erect for fleeing a situation. If the contraction continues but there is no associated action (and therefore the stress situation remains), blood flow to the muscles decreases, metabolites increase, and pain is produced (Dorpat & Holmes, 1955; Holmes & Wolff, 1952).

Tension headache is a situation similar to that above, the muscles of the head and neck being kept in prolonged contraction, resulting in pain by the same mechanism. This is to be differentiated from the pain of vascular headaches, which seems to begin in periods *following* tension.

There have even been some studies that indicate a possible role for stress in the development or influence of the course of the inflammatory joint disease, rheumatoid arthritis (Amkraut & Solomon, 1974; Heisel, 1972; Selye, 1956).

SKIN DISORDERS

The skin is thought to be a common target end organ for excessive arousal (Musaph, 1977). Common stress-related disorders include eczema, acne, urticaria, psoriasis, and alopecia areata (patchy hair loss), according to Lachman (1972) and Engels (1985). According to Medansky (1971), 80% of dermatological patients have a psychological overlay. Supporting such a conclusion is empirical evidence that various neurodermatological syndromes have either been initiated or exacerbated through the controlled manipulation of psychosocial variables (Engles, 1985; Lachman, 1972). The specific mechanisms of pathogenesis have yet to be satisfactorily detailed in most instances, however.

THE IMMUNE SYSTEM

Before leaving the topic of organic manifestations of excessive stress, mention should be made of the effects of excessive stress on the immunological system. Selye (1976) and Amkraut and Solomon (1974) presented early reviews that support the conclusion that excessive stress can exert a generalized immunosuppresive effect. Selye (1976) states, "The immunosuppressive effect of stress and glucocorticoids is probably one of the characteristic consequences of thymicolymphatic involution and lymphopenia which have long been recognized as typical stress effects" (p. 712). If, indeed, excessive stress can exert generalized immunosuppressive effects, then it must be considered as a potential influence in the initiation and propagation, not only of psychosomatic diseases, but of infectious and degenerative diseases as well.

Let us take a closer look.

The immune system consists of two major divisions: cell-mediated immunity and humoral immunity. Both are initiated by macrophage stimulation.

Cell-mediated immunity consists of activation of the T-lymphocytes, the central character in this form of immunity. T-lymphocytes represent 70% of the circulating lymphocytes. These lymphocytes are derived from the bone marrow and thymus gland and come in several major variations: helper cells (T-4), suppressor cells (T-8), and cytotoxic cells (Borysenko, 1987). There are also natural killer cells (NK).

As was mentioned above, cell-mediated immunity is initiated by macrophage stimulation. Macrophages attack and devour antigens as well. Once the T-lymphocytes have been turned on, the activated, or sensitized, cells migrate to the lymph nodes, where they divide into memory cells. Sensitized T-cells then migrate to the source of the invading antigen, where they release chemicals known as *lymphokines*. The lymphokines are toxic to the antigen and also enlist the aid of larger macrophages to attach the antigen (Borysenko, 1984).

In *humoral immunity*, the antigen activates the B-lymphocyte. These sensitized B-cells proliferate into special antibody-producing plasma cells that create protein antibodies to attack the antigen as well as make the antigen more vulnerable to the macrophages. Examples of antibodies would be the five major immunoglobulins (Ig): IgG, IgM, IgA, IgD, and IgE (Borysenko, 1984).

As summarized by Borysenko (1987), "Upon interaction with antigens, macrophages initiate the immune response by producing interleukin −1, which in turn stimulates helper T-cells to proliferate and to produce interleukin −2. Elevated levels of this . . . result in the clonal expansion of effector T-cells or B-cells. Suppressor T-cells modulate the immune response by blocking helper T-cell activity . . . ." (p. 6).

Since the early research of Amkraut and Solomon (1974), major efforts have been put forth in the field of psychoneuroimmunology. Based upon the research and reviews of Borysenko (1984), Calabrese, Kling, and Gold (1987), and Jemmott and Locke (1984), the following conclusions seem warranted:

1. Stress, bereavement, and depression have been shown to be clinically significant immunosupressors.

2. The stress response serves to inhibit immunocompetence by at least three mechanisms: (a) cellular inhibition by circulating glucocorticoid hormones, (b) catecholamine-stimulated release of splanchnic marginated suppressor T-cells, and (c) noradrenergic neural inhibition of lymphoid tissue.

3. Stress suppresses immunity in proportion to the intensity of the stressor.

4. Prolonged stress may be more of an immunosuppressor than is acute, intense stress.

5. The ability to exert a sense of "control" over the stressor serves to mitigate immunosupression (see also Laudenslager *et al.*, 1983).

PSYCHOLOGICAL MANIFESTATIONS OF THE STRESS RESPONSE

The final category of disease to be discussed in this chapter is the psychological manifestations of the stress response. The psychological disturbances most associated with excessive stress are diverse, and for the first time are in some instances being officially recognized as resulting from excessive stress.

Acute and chronic stress episodes are both implicated in the development of diffuse anxiety, as well as in that of manic behavior patterns that are without defined direction or purpose. Gellhorn (1969) argues that high levels of sympathetic activity can result in anxiety reactions. This anxiety may occur as a result of sympathetic nervous system and proprioceptive discharges at the cerebral cortical level. Thus generalized ergotropic tone may then lead to conditions of chronic and diffuse anxiety. Guyton (1982), in apparent agreement with Gellhorn, notes that general sympathetic discharge and proprioceptive feedback may contribute to arousal states such as mania, anxiety, and insomnia. Greden (1974) and Stephenson (1977) have both found that the consumption of methylated xanthines (primarily caffeine) can create signs of diffuse anxiety as well as insomnia and may lead to a diagnosis of anxiety neurosis. The action of the methylated xanthines rests on their ability to stimulate a psychophysiological stress response primarily through sympathetic activation. Finally, Jacobson (1938, 1978) has argued that proprioceptive impulses as such would be found in conditions of high musculoskeletal tension and can contribute to anxiety reactions (see also Everly, 1985b).

Physiologically, in each of the cases just cited, it may be suggested that an ascending neural overload via the reticular activating system to the limbic and neocortical areas may be responsible for creating unorganized and dysfunctional discharges of neural activity that is manifested in the client's presenting symptoms of insomnia, undefined anxiety, and in some cases manic behavior patterns lacking direction or apparent purpose (see Everly, 1985b; Guyton, 1982).

In each of the three examples cited, activation of the psychophysiological stress response preceded the manifestation of diffuse, undefined anxiety, often diagnosed as generalized anxiety disorder or atypical anxiety disorder.

It is interesting to note that one link between anxiety and sympathetic stress arousal, specifically striate muscle tension (Gellhorn, 1969; Jacobson, 1938, 1978), has prompted the development of techniques designed to reduce anxiety through the reduction of muscle tension. We shall review such techniques later in this text.

Another psychological manifestation of excessive stress is thought to be depressive reactions. Stressor events that lead the patient to the interpretation that his or her efforts are useless, that is, that he or she is in a helpless situation, are clearly associated with arousal of the psychophysiological stress response (Henry & Stephens, 1977). The affective manifestation that typically follows is depression. Henry and Stephens have compiled an impressive review that points to the reactivity of the anterior pituitary–adrenal cortical axis during depressive episodes.

In addition to physiological evidence, there is psychological evidence to support the notion that excessive stress can precipitate a depressive reaction. Sociobehavioral research with depressed patients (see Brown, 1972; Paykel et al., 1969) produced somewhat similar evidence that social stressors can lead to major affective syndromes. Rabkin (1982) in her review of stress and affective disorders concludes, "Overall, it seems justifiable to conclude that life events do play a role in the genesis of depressive disorders" (p. 578). Indeed, depressed patients report more stressful life events than do normal controls. This was especially true for a 3-week period immediately preceding the onset of the depression (Rabkin, 1982). Evidence supports a link between stress and schizophrenia as well. One behavioral interpretation of schizophrenia views the illness as a maladaptive avoidance mechanism in the face of an anxiety-producing environment (Epstein & Coleman, 1970). Serban (1975) found in a study of 125 acute and 516 chronic schizophrenics that excessive stress did play a role in the precipitation of hospital readmission. A more far-reaching view of psychopathology and stress is presented by Eisler and Polak (1971). In a study of 172 psychiatric patients, they concluded that excessive stress could contribute to a wide range of psychiatric disorders, including depression and schizophrenia, as well as personality disturbance—depending on the predisposing characteristics of the individual (see Millon & Everly, 1985; see also Chapter 6 of this volume). Rabkin (1982) concludes that stress may well be associated with schizophrenic relapse and subsequent hospitalization.

Most important, however, with the advent of the DSM–III and DMS–III,R came the identification of psychiatric disorders that were, by definition, as result of stressful life events. Thus, for such categories mental status, that is, the mind, need no longer be seen as a viable target organ only by inference. Both the diagnoses of *brief reactive psychosis* and *posttraumatic stress disorder* are diagnostically viewed as being a *direct* consequence of a "recognizable stressor." So, too, would be the diagnostic categories of *adjustment disorders*. Diagnoses such as adjustment disorder with anxious mood, adjustment disorder with depressed mood, and adjustment disorder with mixed emotional features demonstrate an official nosological acceptance of the wide spectrum of psychiatric manifestations that can result directly from stress.

Thus, we see that in the last several years the "mind" has been officially recognized as a potential target organ for pathogenic stress arousal. Table 4.2 summarizes diagnostic categories that serve as psychological target-organ manifestations of excessive stress.

Table 4.2. Psychological Disorders and Excessive Stress

Brief reactive psychosis
Post-traumatic stress disorder
Adjustment disorders
Various anxiety disorders
Various affective disorders
Some forms of schizophrenia

SUMMARY

The purpose of this chapter has been to briefly review some of the more common disorders seen in clinical practice that have the potential to possess a significant stress-related component. Let us review some of the main points addressed in this chapter:

1. There is a well-established literature linking the gastrointestinal system to the stress response. The most commonly encountered stress-related gastrointestinal disorders are peptic ulcers (gastric and duodenal), ulcerative colitis, irritable bowel syndrome, and esophageal reflux. There appear to be two major pathogenic mechanisms in these disorders: vagus-induced hypersecretion of digestive acids and glucocorticoid (cortisol)-induced diminution of the protective mucosal lining of the GI system. Gastric acid hypersecretion has been shown to be related to anger and rage (Wolfe & Glass, 1950), whereas alterations in mucosal integrity have been shown to be related to depression and feelings of deprivation (Backus & Dudley, 1977).

2. The cardiovascular system is believed by many to be the prime target organ of the stress response, especially in males (Humphrey & Everly, 1980). The cardiovascular disorders most commonly associated with excessive stress are essential hypertension, migraine headaches, and Raynaud's disease. Essential hypertension is clearly a multifactorial phenomenon. Although stress may not be the solitary etiological factor in the majority of cases of essential hypertension, it appears to be a contributory factor in the majority of cases in a nonobese population. Mechanisms within the stress response that may contribute to the acute and chronic elevation of blood pressure include sympathetic nervous system activity and adrenal medullary activity, as well as cortisol and aldosterone hyperactivity (refer to Chapter 2).

3. Vasospastic phenomena such as migraine headaches and Raynaud's disease seem to be primarily a function of excessive sympathetic nervous system activity.

4. There is evidence that the respiratory system can also be a target organ for the stress response. Bronchial asthma, hyperventilation syndrome, and even some forms of allergies may be stress related. Mechanisms of mediation may include excessive parasympathetic activation, excessive sympathetic activation, and extraordinary adrenal medullary activity, respectively.

5. According to Jacobson (1938, 1970), Gellhorn (1967), and Tomita (1975), the striated neuromuscular system is an underestimated yet prime target for excessive stress arousal. Stress-response efferent mechanisms of mediation include alpha motoneuron innervation, adrenal medullary activity, and perhaps even sympathetic nervous system activity.

6. The skin serves as a target for excessive stress. Disorders such as eczema, acne, psoriasis, and alopecia areata have been implicated as stress-related disorders. Specific mechanisms of mediation are unclear.

7. Recent evidence from the newly emerged field of psychoneuroimmunology strongly implicates excessive stress in the formation of many bacteriological and viral disorders through a general inhibition of the immune system. Recent data suggest that the human immune system can be enhanced and suppressed on the basis of psychologic stimulation. Possible mechanisms of immunosuppression include inhibition of the cellular immune system by circulating cortisol and circulating medullary catecholamines. Noradrenergic activity may also serve to inhibit lymphoid responsiveness as well as increase suppressor cell release.

8. A final yet important target organ for the stress response must be the "mind," that is, psychological status. Mental disorders such as brief reactive psychosis, post-traumatic stress disorder, adjustment disorders, certain anxiety and affective disorders, and even some forms of schizophrenia may possess significant stress-related components.

9. In closing this chapter, it should be noted that the concept of stress-related psychosomatic diseases has been far broadened with the advent of the DMS-III and DSM-III-R. Now, via such diagnostic perspectives, the clinician can indicate the degree to which stress may have contributed to the primary Axis I diagnosis through the use of Axis III, Axis IV, and Axis V. Finally, data from the field of psychoneuroimmunology cogently suggest that even infectious and degenerative diseases may have significant stress-related components in their initiation or exacerbation.

CHAPTER 5

The Measurement of the Human Stress Response

In the final analysis, the empirical foundation of epistemology is measurement.

When an unexplained phenomenon, such as a stress-related disease, is first observed, it is common to search for possible etiologic factors. This search often culminates in a phenomenological theory; in this case, perhaps a theory of stress arousal and subsequent pathogenesis. On the basis of the formulated theory, for example, of stress arousal, it is then a useful next step to design an experiment in order to test the theory and any proposed relationships critical to the theory. Inherent in the design of the experiment is the designation of key variables and some means of measuring, recording, or otherwise quantifying those relevant variables. Relevant to the present discussion, this would typically involve a means of measuring the stress response and perhaps its pathological effects.

As one reviews the literature concerning human stress, it is obvious that in addition to the lack of a universal definition of stress, the field has also been plagued by a plethora of inconsistencies and potential phenomenological errors in the measurement of the human stress response. If one cannot reliably and validly measure the human stress response, what degree of credibility do we place upon investigations into its phenomenology? Indeed, meta-analytic research has suggested that the measurement of independent and dependent variables may be the single most important aspect of research design—even more important than the structure of the research design itself (Cohen, 1984; Fiske, 1983; Smith, Glass, &

Miller, 1980). With regard to stress research, it may be argued that the confounded or inappropriate measurement process has the greatest ability to limit the generation of useful data regarding this important public health phenomenon (Cattell & Scheier, 1961; Everly & Sobelman, 1987). Thus the purpose of this chapter is to discuss the measurement of the human stress response.

In Chapter 2, a systems model of the nature of the human stress response was constructed (Figure 2.6). As a means of integrating the following measurement-based discussions, that basic model is reproduced here with the addition of key measurement technologies having been superimposed (see Figure 5.1). Let us take this opportunity to examine, more closely, the measurement of the human stress response.

STRESSOR SCALES

The most widely used measurement tool for the assessment of human stress, in reality, doesn't measure stress at all—it measures stressors. The Social Readjustment Rating Scale (SRRS) is the "grandfather" of attempts at measuring stress. The SRRS was developed by Thomas Holmes and Richard Rahe (1967) and was based upon the theory that "life change" was causally associated with subsequent illness. This notion was by no means a new idea. Adolph Meyer pioneered empirical investigations into the relationship between psychosocial events and illness with the advent of his "life chart" as a means of creating a medical history.

The SRRS contains 43 items consisting of commonly experienced "life events." Each life event is weighted with a life change unit score (LCU). Respondents are simply asked to check each of the items they have experienced within the last 12 months. The arithmatic summation of LCUs represents the total LCU score. The total LCU score can then be converted to a relative health risk statement, that is, the risk of becoming ill within a stipulated time period. The association between high LCU scores and risk of subsequent illness is assumed to be a function of the fact that organisms must adapt to novel stimuli and otherwise new life events. The physiology of adaptation has long been known to be the same physiology as the stress response. Thus, stress may be seen as the linking pin between life events and illness as conceived of and measured by the SRRS.

The SRRS is not without its critics, however. Two major issues have been raised:

1. Life events scales should be modified so as to assess the perceived desirability of the life event. It has been suggested that negative life events are potentially more pathogenic than positive life events (Sarason, Johnson, & Siegel, 1978).

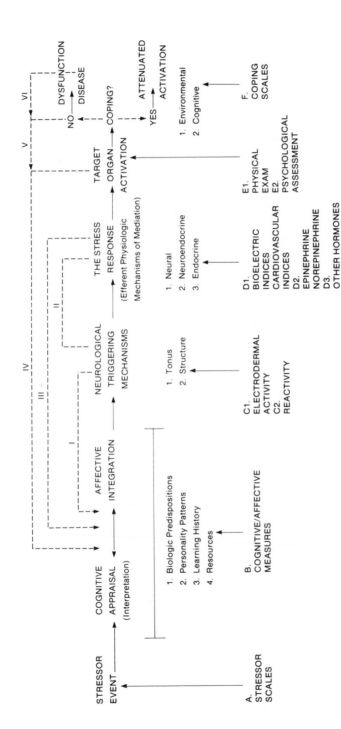

Figure 5.1. Measurement of the human stress response.

2. It has also been suggested that "minor hassles" are more important
predictors of illness than major life events (Kanner, Coyne, Schaefer,
& Lazarus, 1981).

Two other noteworthy efforts in the assessment of stressor stimuli
should be mentioned. In an attempt to improve the SRRS with regard to
the issue of event desirability, Sarason and his colleagues (Sarason, Johnson, & Siegel, 1978) created the Life Experiences Survey (LES). The LES not
only lists a series of life events, but inquires into the desirability of each of
the events. In a far more ingenious approach to the life events issue,
Lazarus and his colleagues investigated the daily hassles versus major life
events issue as it pertains to the prediction of subsequent illness (Kanner,
Coyne, Schaefer, & Lazarus, 1981). The Hassles Scale lists a series of minor
daily hassles, that is, sources of frustration that commonly recur to many
individuals. The scale also includes an "uplifts" assessment that theoretically serves to mitigate the adverse impact of negative life events.

The LES and the Hassles Scale are creative and alternative approaches
to the assessment of stressors, but the SRRS continues to enjoy the greatest
frequency of use, both clinically and for research purposes.

As for the genre of stressor scales, Monroe (1983) notes, "Although
findings of event–illness associations appear to be consistent in that increased life events predict dysfunction in both retrospective and prospective studies, the magnitude of the association reported typically has been
low . . ." (p. 190). The recognized consistency in the life events research
combined with its low-effect size leads one to believe that life events scales
such as the SRRS do indeed tap some domain that has meaning in stress
phenomenology, however, there appear to be other mediating variables
that need to be better understood. From the view of the present model, life
events scales tap the stressor domain and therefore cannot be said to assess
either the stress response itself or the causal mechanisms that undergird
stress arousal. Nevertheless, scales such as the SRRS can be of value,
especially in stress research when the researcher wishes to obtain valid and
reliable assessments of the "background noise," that is, intervening or
other otherwise confounding variables in psychosocial stressor research
(see Everly & Sobelman, 1987).

COGNITIVE/AFFECTIVE CORRELATE SCALES

Whereas the preceding section discussed the assessment of stressor
stimuli, the reader will recall from Chapter 2 that there is agreement among
most stress researchers that in order for psychosocial life events to engender a stress response and subsequent illness, they must first be processed via cognitive/affective mechanisms. It seems theoretically viable,

therefore, that one might assess the cognitive/affective domain of respondents as an indirect assessment of the human stress response (Everly & Sobelmen, 1987). Derogatis (1977) has argued that such a "self-report mode of psychological measurement contains much to recommend it" (p. 2). Further, Everly has argued that assessment of this domain may be the most practical, efficient, and cost-effective way of measuring the human stress response (Everly & Sobelman, 1987).

There are several scales that assess the cognitive/affective correlates of the stress response. The Derogatis Stress Scale (Derogatis, 1980) is a 77-item self-report inventory derived from interactional stress theory. It purports to assess not only emotional responses and personality mediators, but environmental events as well.

The Everly Stress and Symptom Inventory (ESSI) is a self-report inventory that assesses 20 cognitive/affective states that are known to be highly correlated with activation of the stress-response axes described in Chapter 2. These items were empirically selected on the basis of item analyses from a pool of over 120 original items. Coefficient alphas consistently emerge in the .93 to .95 range, and the standard error of measure for these 20 items is consistently in the 2.5 range. The ESSI also assesses the patient's use of 20 selected coping strategies (10 adaptive and 10 maladaptive). Finally, the ESSI provides a 38-item symptom scale that allows the respondent to indicate the frequency that he or she suffers from a selected series of symptoms highly correlated with excessive stress arousal (Everly et al., 1986; Everly, Sherman, & Smith, in press). A revised version of the ESSI adds a depression scale and is currently under development.

The final inventory worthy of note within this genre is the Millon Behavioral Health Inventory (MBHI) developed by Theodore Millon and his colleagues (Millon, Green, & Meagher, 1982). The MBHI is a 150-item self-report inventory that has been normed on medical patients. "Its intent is to aid in the psychological understanding of these patients and facilitate the steps required to formulate a comprehensive treatment plan" (Millon, Green, & Meagher, 1982, p. 2). The true–false inventory includes scales grouped into four categories: basic characterologic coping styles, psychogenic attitudes, psychosomatic correlates, and prognostic indices. Rigorously developed yet practical in its applicability, the MBHI is the best of the broad-spectrum inventories of its kind (Everly & Sobelman, 1987). The MBHI also profits from having its theoretical foundations firmly entrenched in the personality theory of Theodore Millon.

NEUROLOGICAL TRIGGERING MECHANISMS

The assessment of the sensitivity of neurologic triggering mechanisms is by no means an easy task. Aberrant evoked potentials emerging from the subcortical limbic system would be one indication of an existing hypersensitivity phenomenon within the limbic system. The accurate assessment of subcortical activity via electroencephalography is very difficult and may be considered a gross assessment at best, however. False negative findings are a common problem with such assessment and EEGs in general.

Electrodermal responsiveness as assessed via galvanic skin response (GSR) would be another way of assessing the reactivity of neurologic triggering mechanisms (Everly & Sobelman, 1987).

Finally, the general assessment of psychophysiologic reactivity is believed to be a viable process for assessing the efferent-discharge propensity of the limbic system (Everly & Sobelman, 1987). The phenomenology of this process is based upon the theories of Lacy, Malmo, and Sternbach discussed in Chapter 3.

MEASURING THE PHYSIOLOGY OF THE STRESS RESPONSE

It will be recalled from Chapter 2 that the stress response can be divided into three broad categories: (1) the neural axes, (2) the neuroendocrine axis, and (3) the endocrine axes. Let us briefly review several of the more common assessment technologies used to tap these phenomenological domains.

Assessment of the Neural Axes

Assessment of the neural axes of the human stress response is for the most part an attempt to capture a transitory state measurement phenomenon, as opposed to a more consistent trait. Technologies used for such assessment include (1) electrodermal techniques, (2) electromyographic techniques, and (3) cardiovascular measures.

Electrodermal Measures

The physiological basis of the electrodermal assessment of the stress response is the eccrine sweat gland. Located primarily in the soles of the feet and the palms of the hands, these sweat glands respond to psychologic stimuli rather than heat and emerge on the terminal efferent ends of sympathetic neurons. Although the neurotransmitter at the sweat gland itself is ACh, as opposed to NE, the assessment of this activity provides useful insight into the activity of the sympathetic nervous system. Electrodermal activity may be assessed via active GSR techniques or through passive techniques such as skin potentials (SP), according to Edelberg (1972). Andreassi (1980) has stated that electrodermal techniques are useful indices of somatic arousal.

Electromyographic Measurement

The physiological basis of electromyographic measurement of the stress response is the neurological innervation of the striated skeletal muscles. Electromyography, although an indirect measure of muscle "tension," is a direct measure of the action potentials originating from the neurons that innervate the muscles.

Skeletal muscles receive their neural innervation primarily as a result of alpha motoneuron presence, on the efferent limb, and secondarily as a result of gamma motoneuron activity as well. From the afferent perspective, proprioceptive neurons arising from the muscle spindles contribute to the overall electrical activity that originates from the skeletal musculature. In a relaxed state, skeletal muscle tone serves as a very useful general index of arousal (Gellhorn, 1964; Gellhorn & Loofbourrow, 1963; Jacobson, 1929, 1970; Malmo, 1975; Weil, 1974), yet in a contracted state this utility appears to disappear. Thus, when using skeletal muscles as general indices of arousal and stress responsiveness, it becomes of critical importance to teach patients to first relax those muscles (Everly et al., 1989).

There has been considerable debate for about a decade on the utility of a particular set of muscles as an index of arousal. That set of muscles is the group known as the *frontalis*.

Jacobson (1970) and Shagass and Malmo (1954) first recognized that the frontalis and related facial muscles were prime targets of the stress-arousal process. It was Budzynski and Stoyva (1969) and Stoyva (1979) who explored and refined the clinical utility of these muscles in the treatment of stress-related disorders. Similar work was undertaken by Schwartz et al. (1978) who found the corrugator muscles of similar utility in relation to depression.

It may be argued that the frontalis muscles of the forehead provide a useful site for the assessment of stress arousal. These muscles have been termed "quasi-voluntary" muscles because of their autonomic-like properties manifest during emotional states. In support of such a view is the recent series of studies that indicate that when simple facial expressions are mimicked, an alteration in heart rate and skin temperature can be observed, even when the subjects were simply asked to mimic the expression without any consideration for the cognitive or affective state that might be associated with it. Similarly, Rubin (1977) suggests that the frontalis muscles, in particular, may possess properties of dual innervation: skeletal alpha motoneuron and autonomic nervous system innervation.

Although, clearly, the frontalis musculature is predominately striated in nature (thus receiving efferent innervation from the alpha motoneuron assemblies), Rubin (1977) has argued that the frontalis also possesses thin nonstriated layers of musculature. These nonstriated muscles apparently receive their innervation (directly or indirectly) from the sympathetic nervous system (Miehlke, 1973). Thus, assessment of the frontalis muscles through electromyographic procedures may well provide insight into alpha motoneuron activity, sympathetic neural activity, as well as neuroendocrine activity (Everly & Sobelman, 1987). Although there is not total agreement on the utility of the frontalis musculature (Alexander, 1975), Stoyva (1979) provides useful guidelines for the use of that measurement variable.

Clinical biofeedback experience shows the frontalis muscles are useful in the treatment of a wide range of stress-related disorders including essential hypertension and disorders of the gastrointestinal system. Most clinicians, over the years, have reported use of the frontalis muscle in electromyographic assessment; however, the trapezius, brachioradialis, and sternocleidomastoid muscle groups have also been utilized.

In sum, most evidence suggests that the electromyographic assessment yields insight into the activity of other major muscle groups (Freedman & Papsdorf, 1976; Glaus & Kotses, 1977, 1978) as well as the generalized activity of the sympathetic nervous system (Arnarson & Sheffield, 1980; Budzynski, 1979; Jacobson, 1970; Malmo, 1966; Rubin, 1977; Everly *et al.*, 1989).

Cardiovascular Measurement

Cardiovascular measurement of the stress response entails the assessment of the stress response upon the heart and vascular systems. Common cardiovascular measures include heart rate, peripheral blood flow, and blood pressure.

Heart rate activity as a function of the stress response is a result of direct neural innervation as well as neuroendocrine activity of epinephrine and norepinephrine. During psychosocially induced stress, epinephrine is preferentially released from the adrenal medullae. The ventricles of the heart are maximally responsive to circulating epinephrine and will respond with increased speed and force of ventricular contraction. Of course, direct sympathetic neural activation drives heart rate to increase as well. The measurement of heart rate is most commonly achieved through the use of audiometric or oscillometric techniques during the normal assessment of blood pressure. Occasionally, heart rate will be measured from electrocardiographic techniques via the use of passive electrodes or even through plethysmography.

Plethysmography focuses upon the volume of blood in a selected anatomical site. The most common areas for such assessment of the stress response are the fingers, toes, calves, and forearms. During the stress response, most patients will suffer a reduction of blood flow from these areas. This vasoconstrictive effect is a result of direct sympathetic activity to the arteries and arterioles, as well as of circulating norepinephrine (Guyton, 1982). A decline of blood flow to these areas will also result in a reduction of skin temperature. Therefore, skin temperature is also sometimes utilized, although it is not as reliable as plethysmography. So we see that the assessment of peripheral blood flow can be accomplished via the use of plethysmography as well as skin temperature.

Finally, blood pressure is sometimes used as an *acute* index of the stress response. The assessment of blood pressure is generally achieved through the quantification of systolic blood pressure and diastolic blood pressure and may be considered highly state-dependent.

Systolic blood pressure is the hemodynamic pressure exerted within the arterial system during systole (the ventricular contraction phase). Diastolic blood pressure is the hemodynamic pressure exerted within the arterial system during diastole (relaxation and filling of the ventricular chambers).

Blood pressure is a function of several variables revealed in the following equation:

$$BP = CO \times TPR$$

where
  BP = blood pressure
  CO = cardiac output = stroke volume times heart rate
  TPR = total hemodynamic peripheral resistance

Blood pressure can be measured noninvasively through auscultation, audiometry, or oscillometry. In noninvasive paradigms, a sampled artery (usually the brachial) is compressed through the use of an inflatable rubber tube or bladder. The bladder is inflated until it totally blocks the passage of blood through the artery. Air pressure, measured in millimeters of mercury (mm Hg) is slowly released from the bladder until a sound is heard or a distension sensed. This sound and distension (called a Korotkoff sound) is indicative of blood being allowed to pass through the once blocked artery. Korotkoff sounds continue until the artery is fully opened and returned back to its natural status. The first Korotkoff sound is indicative of the systolic blood pressure. The passing of the last Korotkoff sound is indicative of the diastolic blood pressure.

The technique of audiometry measures blood pressure by the use of a microphone to sense the Korotkoff sounds. Oscillometry detects the Korotkoff phenomenon via a pressure-sensitive device placed on the outside of the artery. Finally, auscultation is the sensing of the Korotkoff sound via stethoscope. Audiometric and oscillometric techniques are far more reliable than is manual auscultation.

In sum, the measurement of cardiovascular phenomena can be seen to tap both neural and neuroendocrine domains; thus there is an overlap in phenomenology. Also, when using the cardiovascular domain to measure stress arousal, the clinician is interested only in the *acute* fluctuations, as opposed to chronic levels. This is due to the fact that stress exerts its most measurable effect upon the acute status of the cardiovascular system. A multitude of other factors enter into, and otherwise confound, the measurement process when examining cardiovascular indices such as chronic blood pressure and peripheral blood flow, for example.

Assessment of the Neuroendocrine Axis

Assessment of the neuroendocrine axis of the stress response entails measurement of the adrenal medullary catecholamines: epinephrine (adrenalin) and norepinephrine (noradrenalin).

Aggregated medullary catecholamines may be sampled from blood or urine and assayed via fluorometric methods. Reference values range for random sampling up to 18 μg/100 ml urine, for a 24-hour urine sample up to 135 μg, and for timed samples 1.4 to 7.3 μg/hour during daylight hours (Bio-Science, 1982). For aggregated catecholamines sampled from plasma, values range from 140 to 165 pg/ml via radioenzymatic procedures (Bio-Science, 1982).

Various fluorimetric (Anderson *et al.*, 1974; Bio-Science, 1982; Euler & Lishajko, 1961); chromatographic (Bio-Science, 1982; Lake, Siegler, & Kopin, 1976; Mason, 1972), and radioimmunoassay (Bio-Science, 1982, Mason, 1972) methods are available for the assessment of catecholamines. The most useful of all methods may be the High Pressure Liquid Chromatography (HPLC) with electrochemical detection as described in Hegstrand and Eichelman (1981) and McClelland, Ross, and Patel (1985). HPLC allows multiple catecholamines to be derived from sampled plasma, urine, and saliva with superior ease and sensitivity.

Epinephrine can be sampled from urine, plasma, or saliva. When sampled from urine a typical distribution is as follows (Harper, 1975):

Unchanged epinephrine	6%
Metanephrine	40%
Vanillylmandellic Acid	41%
4-Hydroxy-3-methoxy-phenylglycol	7%
3,4-Dihydroxymandelic Acid	2%
Other	4%
	100%

Norepinephrine can also be sampled from urine, plasma, and saliva. Table 5.1 provides a range of epinephrine and norepinephrine values when sampled from urine.

Despite the availability of methods such as HPLC, some researchers prefer the assessment of catecholamines by indirect routes, for example, through the assessment of urinary metabolites. Metanephrines and vanillylmandellic acid (VMA) are two popular choices.

Table 5.1. Value Ranges for Urinary Epinephrine
and Norepinephrine

	Epinephrine	Norepinephrine
Basal levels	4–5 µg/day	28–30 µg/day
Aroused	10–15 µg /day	50–70 µg/day
Significant stress	> 15 µg/day	> 70 µg/day

In the case of the metanephrines, one of the major deactivating substances acting upon epinephrine and norepinephrine is the enzyme cate-
cholamine-o-methyl-trasferase (COMT). Metabolites of this deactivation
process are metanephrine and normetanephine. Aggregated metanephrines range from 0.3 to 0.9 mg/day in urine. VMA levels range from 0.7 to
6.8 mg/day. VMA is the urinary metabolite of COMT and monoamine
oxidase.

Assessment of the Endocrine Axes

According to Hans Selye (1976), the most direct way of measuring the
stress response is via ACTH, the corticosteroids, and the catecholamines.
The catecholamines have already been discussed. The most commonly
used index of ACTH and corticosteroid activity is the measurement of the
hormone cortisol. Cortisol is secreted by the adrenal cortices activated by
ACTH. Cortisol is secreted at a rate of about 25 to 30 mg/day and accounts
for about 90% of glucocorticoid activity.

Cortisol may be sampled from either plasma or urine. Radioimmunoassay plasma levels for a normal adult may range from 5 to 20 µg/ 100
ml plasma (8 A.M. sample). The normal diurnal decline may result in a level
of plasma cortisol at 4 P.M. about one half of the 8 A.M. level. Normal
urinary free cortisol may range from 20 to 90 µg/24 hours (see Bio-Science,
1982). It has been suggested that urinary free cortisol is the most sensitive
and reliable indicator of adrenal cortical hyperfunction, followed by plasma
cortisol and finally 17-hydroxycorticosteroid, a cortisol metabolite (Damon,
1981). Normal values for 17-hydroxycorticosteroid (17-OHCS) measured
from urine typically range from 2.5 to 10 mg/24 hours in the female to 4.5 to
12 mg/24 hours in the male adult (Porter-Silber method). Slight increases in
17-OHCS are evidenced in the first trimester of pregnancy and in severe
hypertension. Moderate increases can be observed in the third trimester of
pregnancy and as a result of infectious disease, burns, surgery, and stress
(Bio-Science, 1982). In conditions of extreme stress, urinary 17-OHCS may
exceed 15 mg/24 hours. Plasma assessments of 17-OHCS range from 10 to
14 µg % at 8 A.M. basal levels to 18 to 24 µg % under moderate stress, to an
excess of 24 µg % in extremely stressful situations (Mason, 1972).

This section has discussed the assessment of the physiological constit- uents of the stress response. It should be noted that the assessment of this domain represents a challenging and potentially frustrating exercise. One major factor that confounds the assessment of most physiological variables is the fact that most physiological phenomena used to assess stress arousal are state-dependent variables that wax and wane throughout the course of a day as well as with acute situational demands. Normal diurnal fluctua- tions as well as acute situational variability can serve to yield false-positive findings or false-negative findings in the absence of meaningful baseline data. There has even been some question as to the predictive validity of acute physiological indices. Another issue that confounds the overall util- ity of many physiological measures is that such measures usually require special training, special equipment, or both. The difficulties associated with physiological assessment of the human stress response have been summarized by Everly and Sobelman (1987). Other issues, such as re- sponse specificity and organ reactivity, are also reviewed.

ASSESSMENT OF TARGET-ORGAN EFFECTS

Once the stress response has been activated to pathogenic propor- tions, there emerges another possible assessment strategy for measuring human stress—the assessment of the target-organ effects of the stress response. The assessment of target-organ effects can consist of measuring physical as well as psychological variables.

Physical Diagnosis

The assessment of the physical effects of stress would involve the use of standard diagnostic techniques common to the practice of physical med- icine. The goal of such assessments is to measure the integrity of the target organ's structural and functional status. An in-depth discussion of such procedures is far beyond the scope of this volume, however.

It should be mentioned that such assessments are never clearly assess- ments of stress. One never really knows to what degree pathogenic stress arousal has contributed to the manifestation of target-organ pathology. For this reason, the diagnosis of stress-related target-organ disease is typically a diagnosis by exclusion. That is, one systematically excludes nonstress- related etiologic factors while at the same time looking for evidence of pathogenic stress arousal through the assessment of other measurement domains as well. The stress-related diagnosis then emerges from a con- vergence of these data sets. There are also self-report scales that have proven to be valid and reliable indices of experienced physical illness. The Seriousness of Illness Rating Scale (Wyler, Masuda, & Holmes, 1968;

Rosenberg, Hayes, & Peterson, 1987) is one useful self-report tool for measuring illness and weighting its impact. The Stress Audit Questionnaire (Miller & Smith, 1982) is another. It is important still to keep in mind that there is still no certainty as to the extent of the role of stress arousal in the formation of the emergent illnesses/reactions.

Psychological Diagnosis

The psychological diagnosis of the stress response refers to the measurement of the "psychological" effects of the stress response. There currently exist numerous and diverse methods for the measurement of psychological states and traits. To cover this topic fully would require a volume of its own. Therefore, what we shall do in this section is merely highlight the paper-and-pencil questionnaires that a clinician might find most useful in measuring the psychological effects of the stress response.

Minnesota Multiphasic Personality Inventory (MMPI)

The Minnesota Multiphasic Personality Inventory (Hathaway & McKinley, 1967) is perhaps one of the most valid and reliable inventories for the assessment of long-term stress on the personality structure of the patient. The numerous clinical and content scales of the MMPI yield a wealth of valuable information. These numerous scales sample a wide range of "abnormal" or maladjusted personality traits (a personality trait is a rather chronic and consistent pattern of thinking and behavior).

The MMPI consists of 10 basic clinical scales developed on the basis of actuarial data:

1. Hs: Hypochondriasis
2. D: Depression
3. Hy: Conversion Hysteria
4. Pd: Psychopathic Deviate
5. Mf: Masculinity–Femininity
6. Pa: Paranoia
7. Pt: Psychasthenia (trait anxiety)
8. Sc: Schizophrenia
9. Ma: Hypomania (manifest energy)
10. Si: Social Introversion (preference for being alone)

In addition to the highly researched clinical scales, the MMPI has four validity scales that give the clinician a general idea of how valid any given set of test scores is for the patient. This unique feature of the MMPI increases its desirability to many clinicians.

Over the years, the MMPI items have given rise to numerous other scales in varying stages of validation (see Dahlstrom, Welsh, & Dahlstrom, 1975).

The MMPI offers a virtual wealth of information to the trained clinician; its only major drawback appears to be its length (550 items), although a shortened version (366 items) is available.

The Sixteen Personality Factor (16 P–F)

The Sixteen Personality Factor (Cattell, 1972) does much the same thing that the MMPI does by assessing a wide range of personality traits. The 16 P–F measures 16 "functionally independent and psychologically meaningful dimensions isolated and replicated in more than 30 years of factor-analytic research on normal and clinical groups" (Cattell, 1972, p. 5).

The 16 P–F consists of 187 items distributed across the following 16 scales:

- Reserved–Outgoing
- Less Intelligent–More Intelligent
- Affected by Feelings–Emotionally Stable
- Humble–Assertive
- Sober–Happy-Go-Lucky
- Expedient–Conscientious
- Shy–Venturesome
- Tough-minded–Tenderminded

- Trusting–Suspicious
- Practical–Imaginative
- Forthright–Astute
- Self-Assured–Apprehensive
- Conservative–Experimenting
- Group-Dependent–Self-Sufficient
- Undisciplined Self-Conflict–Controlled
- Relaxed–Tense

Millon Clinical Multiaxial Inventory-II (MCMI-II)

The Millon Clinical Multiaxial Inventory (MCMI) is a 175-item self-report, true–false questionnaire. The MCMI-II is not a widely utilized as the MMPI in the diagnosis of major psychiatric disorders. Yet the MCMI-II is clearly the instrument of choice when the clinician is primarily interested in personologic variables and their relationship to excessive stress. Further, the MCMI-II offers valuable insight into treatment planning. Another major advantage of the MCMI-II over the MMPI and 16 P–F is that it consists of only 175 items. The MCMI-II includes 22 clinical scales broken down into three broad categories; ten basic personality scales reflective of the personality theory of Theodore Millon (1981), three pathological personality syndromes, and nine major clinical psychiatric syndromes (Millon, 1983). From a psychometric perspective, the MCMI-II offers the best of both worlds: an inventory founded in a practical, clinically useful theory as well as an inventory featuring rigorous empirical development. The scales of the MCMI-II are listed below:

- Schizoid
- Avoidant
- Antisocial
- Narcissism
- Passive-aggression
- Compulsive
- Dependent
- Histrionic
- Schizotypal
- Borderline
- Sadistic

- Paranoid
- Anxiety
- Somatoform
- Hypomania
- Dysthymia
- Alcohol abuse
- Drug abuse
- Psychotic thinking
- Psychotic depression
- Psychotic delusions
- Self-defeating

Taylor Manifest Anxiety Scale (TAS)

The Taylor Manifest Anxiety Scale (Taylor, 1953), unlike the inventories described above, measures only one trait—anxiety. Its 50 items are derived from the MMPI. The TAS measures how generally anxious the patient is and has little ability to reflect situational fluctuations in anxiety.

State–Trait Anxiety Inventory (STAI)

The State–Trait Anxiety Inventory (Spielberg, Gorsuch, & Luchene, 1970) is a highly unique inventory in that it is two scales in one. The first 20 items measure state anxiety (a psychological state is an acute, usually situationally dependent condition of psychological functioning). The second 20 items measure trait anxiety. This is the same basic phenomenon as that measured by the TAS. The STAI can be administered in full form (40 items) or can be used to measure only state anxiety or trait anxiety.

Affect Adjective Checklist (AACL)

Another unusual measuring device is the Affect Adjective Checklist (Zuckerman, 1960). Like the STAI, the AACL can be used to measure a psychological state or trait. The AACL achieves this by using the same items (21 adjectives) and merely changing the instructions. The client may use the checklist of adjectives to describe how he or she feels in general or under a specific set of conditions—"now" for instance. Zuckerman and Lubin (1965) later expanded the AACL by adding specific items to assess hostility and depression. The new scale is called the Multiple Affect Adjective Checklist (MAACL).

Subjective Stress Scale (SSS)

The Subjective Stress Scale (Berkun, 1962) is a scale designed to measure situational (state) effects of stress on the individual. The scale consists of 14 descriptors that the patient can use to identify his or her subjective reactions during a stressful situation. Each of the 14 descriptors comes with an empirically derived numerical weight, which the clinician then uses to generate a subjective stress score.

Profile of Mood States (POMS)

The Profile of Mood States (McNair, Lorr, & Droppleman, 1971) is a factor-analytically derived self-report inventory that measures six identifiable mood or affective states (McNair, Lorr, & Droppleman, 1971, p. 5):

• Tension–Anxiety
• Depression–Dejection
• Anger–Hostility
• Vigor–Activity
• Fatigue–Inertia
• Confusion–Bewilderment

The POMS consists of 65 adjectives. Each adjective is followed by a five-point rating scale that the patient uses to indicate the subjective presence of that condition. The instructions ask the patient to use the 65 adjectives to indicate "How you have been feeling during the past week including today." Other time states have been used, for example: "right now," "today," and for "the past three minutes."

The POMS offers a broader range of state measures for the subjective assessment of stress when compared with the STAI, the AACL-MAACL, and the SSS.

THE ASSESSMENT OF COPING

It was mentioned earlier that the ESSI provided a measure of coping behavior within a larger stress and symptom inventory, yet other options are available to assess coping. The MBHI assesses the patient's characterologic coping style as opposed to the ESSI's assessment of specific coping behaviors. The Hassles Scale measures an indirect form of coping within its "uplifts" subscale. Everly created a simple coping inventory for use in conjunction with the National Health Fair (Everly, 1979a; Girdano & Everly, 1986). This checklist can be found in Appendix H.

Finally, perhaps the most popular of the recently designed coping indices is the Ways of Coping Checklist developed by Lazarus and Folkman. This is a 67-item checklist that assesses an individual's preference for various styles of coping patterns (e.g., defensive coping, information seeking, problem solving). This checklist enjoys a considerable empirical foundation and can be found in their 1984 textbook on stress, appraisal, and coping (Lazarus & Folkman, 1984). In the broadest sense, coping may be viewed as any effort to reduce or mitigate the aversive effects of stress. These efforts may be psychological or behavioral. The scales mentioned above sample both domains.

LAW OF INITIAL VALUES

A final point should be mentioned regarding the role of individual differences in the process of measurement. No two patients are exactly alike in their manifestations of the stress response. When measuring psychophysiological reactivity, or any physiological index, the clinician must understand that the patient's baseline level of functioning on any physiologic variable affects any subsequent degree of activity or reactivity in that same physiological parameter. This is Wilder's Law of Initial Values (Wilder, 1950). In order to compare an individual's stress reactivity (assuming variant baselines), a statistical correction must be made in order to assure that the correlation between baseline activity and stressful reactivity is equal to zero. Such a correction must be made in order to compare groups as well. Benjamin (1963) has written a very useful paper that addresses the necessary statistical corrections that must be made. She concludes that a covariance model must be adopted in order to correct for the law of initial values, though specific calculations will differ when comparing groups or individuals.* It must be remembered that the Law of Initial Values will affect not only the measurement of stress arousal but stress reduction as well.

SUMMARY

In this chapter we have described briefly some of the most commonly used methods of measuring the effects of the stress response. The methods described have included physiological and psychological criteria.

---

*One useful formula for correcting for the Law of Initial Values when comparing individuals is the Autonomic Lability Score (ALS) (Lacey & Lacey, 1962). The ALS is form of covariance and therefore consistent with Benjamin's recommendation. The ALS is expressed as

$$ALS = 50 + 10 \left[\frac{Y_z - X_z r_{xy}}{(1 - r_{xy}^2)^{0.5}} \right]$$

where X_z = client's standardized prestressor autonomic level, Y_z = client's standardized poststressor autonomic level, and r_{xy} = correlation for sample between pre- and poststressor levels.

The most important question surrounding the measurement of the stress response is "How do you select the most appropriate measurement criterion?" The answer to this question is in no way clear-cut. Generally speaking, to begin with you should consider the state versus trait measurement criterion issue. Basically, state criteria should be used to measure immediate and/or short-lived phenomena. Trait criteria should be used to measure phenomena that take a longer term to manifest themselves and/or have greater stability and duration. The psychological criteria discussed in this chapter are fairly straightforward as to their state or trait nature. The physiological criteria are somewhat less clear. Some physiological criteria possess both state and trait characteristics. Furthermore, normal values for blood and urinary stress indicators may vary somewhat from lab to lab. Therefore, the clinician should familiarize himself or herself with the lab's standard values. Before using physiological measurement criteria in the assessment of the stress response, the reader who has no background in physiology would benefit from consulting any useful physiology or psychophysiology text (see, for example Everly & Sobelman, 1987; Greenfield & Sternbach, 1972; Levi, 1975; Selye, 1976; Stern, Ray, & Davis, 1980). Finally, because no two patients are alike in their response to stressors, the clinician might consider measuring multiple and diverse response mechanisms (or stress axes) in order to increase the sensitivity of any given assessment procedure designed to measure the stress response (see Figure 5.1).

Having provided these closing points, let us review the major issues discussed within this chapter:

1. It has been argued that the single most important aspect of empirical investigation is the process of the *measurement* of relevant variables. This is true of investigations into the nature of human stress as well.

2. The Social Readjustment Rating Scale (Holmes & Rahe, 1967), the Life Experiences Survey (Sarason, Johnsonson, & Siegel, 1978), and the Hassles Scale (Kanner *et al.*, 1981) are all self-report inventories that assess the patient's exposure to critical "life events." Collectively, these scales do not measure stress; rather, they assess the patient's exposure to stressors. Stressor scales are correlated with stress arousal because the physiology of adaptation to novel or challenging stimuli is also the physiology of the stress response.

3. The Derogatis Stress Scale (Derogatis, 1980), the Everly Stress and Symptom Inventory (Everly *et al.*, 1986; Everly, Sherman, & Smith, in press), and the Millon Behavioral Health Inventory (Millon, Green, & Meagher, 1982) all represent scales designed to assess the patient's cognitive/ affective status. The stress response is thus assessed indirectly through the measurement of cognitive/affective states known to be highly associated with stress arousal. It has been argued that such assessments

may well be the most efficient, practical, and cost-effective way of assessing stress arousal. All of these scales also include symptom indices.

4. Albeit an important clinical phenomenon, the assessment of propensities for limbic efferent discharge (limbic hypersensitivity phenomenon) is extremely difficult. Subcortical electroencephalography is a crude measure at best. Electrodermal and general psychophysiological reactivity may be the best options currently available for the assessment of neurological triggering mechanisms of the human stress response.

5. Numerous measurement options exist for the assessment of the physiological stress response itself (if deemed appropriate).

5a. The neural stress axes may be assessed via electrodermal measures, electromyographic measures, as well as cardiovascular measures (heart rate, peripheral blood flow, blood pressures).

5b. The neuroendocrine stress axis can be measured via the assessment adrenal medullary catecholamines.

5c. The assessment of the endocrine stress axes is most commonly conducted via the assessment of cortisol.

6. The assessment of target-organ effects of pathogenic stress arousal can be conducted via standard physical medicine examination or the use of self-report inventories such as the Seriousness of Illness Rating Scale (Wyler, Masuda, & Holmes, 1968) to measure *physical effects*. *Psychological effects* may be assessed via self-report scales such as the MMPI, the MCMI, the 16 P-F, the TAS, the STAI, the AACL, the SSS, and the POMS.

7. Coping is an important potential mediating variable. It may be assessed via the MBHI, the Hassles Scale, a coping scale developed by Everly (Everly, 1979a) for the U.S. Public Health Service, via the ESSI, or via the Ways of Coping Checklist (Lazarus & Folkman, 1984).

The Treatment of the Human Stress Response

Part II is the second of three parts that constitute this volume. It is dedicated to the presentation of a treatment model for excessive stress arousal, with subsequent discussions of its therapeutic constituents.

In Part I, Chapter 2 presented an epiphenomenological systems model of the human stress response (Figure 2.6). Each of its components was described within that chapter so as to convey the notion that the human stress response is an active, dynamic, multifaceted process. In Chapter 5, the same model was again used, but this time to demonstrate how *measurement* technologies may be superimposed on the same phenomenological process and model (Figure 5.1). We will now once again call upon the phenomenological model first introduced in Chapter 2 as a means of presenting an integrated overview of the *treatment* of the human stress response.

The purpose of the first chapter in Part II, Chapter 6, is to not only briefly review the relationship between personality and human health, but more important to provide a rationale for the consideration of personality factors in the cause and treatment of stress-related disorders. A personologic diathesis (personality-based susceptibility to stress arousal) model will be constructed so as to facilitate the integration of personality factors in treatment planning. Chapter 6 is entitled "Personologic Diathesis and Human Stress."

Chapter 7, entitled "Control and the Human Stress Response," serves as preamble to all of the remaining chapters that concern themselves with specific technologies for therapeutic intervention. The perception of con-

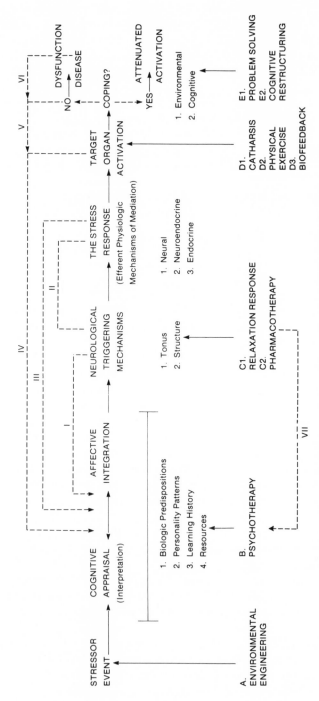

Figure II.1. A multidimensional treatment model for the human stress response.

trol, or self-efficacy, has been argued to be the most powerful single therapeutic force in the treatment of excessive stress and other syndromes of dyscontrol. Chapter 7 details some of the research that serves as the basis for such an argument.

In a review of the treatment model, the first technologies for therapeutic intervention to be listed are "environmental engineering" and "psychotherapy." The term "environmental engineering" is borrowed from the work of Girdano and Everly (1986) and refers to efforts to "act artfully upon" one's environment to reduce stress arousal through the alteration of one's exposure to stressors. Such strategies may be thought of as "preventive" or "reactive" problem solving through the manipulation of environmental variables. The concept of psychotherapy as used herein refers to any efforts that result in a more adaptive and health-promoting cognitive–affective style and expression as they pertain to the stress response. With this in mind, Chapter 8 is entitled "Psychotherapy: A Cognitive Perspective." It briefly reviews cognitive therapy from several perspectives, while providing a framework for integrating problem solving within a cognitive therapeutic framework.

Chapter 9, entitled "A Neurophysiological Rationale for the Use of the Relaxation Response," provides the reader with a cogent reason for employing strategies that engender the relaxation response in any treatment protocol designed to attend to pathogenic stress arousal or its target-organ effects. This chapter argues that the relaxation response may be used, not only as a secondary intervention, but in many cases as a primary therapeutic agent. Thus, Chapter 9 can serve as an introduction for the subsequent chapters that discuss specific technologies for engendering the relaxation response.

Chapters 10 through 13 address the topics of meditation, neuromuscular relaxation, respiratory control, and hypnosis, respectively. As prefaced by Chapter 9, these technologies are standard methods by which the clinician can teach the patient to elicit the relaxation response, thereby reducing manifest arousal as well as propensities for overreactivity. These chapters provide a brief introduction to the conceptual and research foundations upon which these techniques are based. More important, these chapters provide the clinician with a practical "boilerplate" protocol for employing these techniques, though it is designed to serve as a working foundation that the clinician will alter as need dictates.

Chapter 13, which addresses hypnosis, goes beyond the elicitation of the relaxation response and discusses behavior change technologies as well.

Chapter 14 discusses biofeedback as a therapeutic intervention. The reader will discover that biofeedback can be used to reduce pathogenic arousal as an aid in relaxation or it can actually be used to treat the target-organ manifestations of excessive stress.

Chapter 15, entitled "The Pharmacological Treatment of Excessive Stress," reviews the role that psychotropic medication may play in stress and stress-related disorders. This chapter discusses several drug classes, how they work, and their basic clinical effects and dosages.

The final chapter in Part II is entitled "Physical Exercise and the Human Stress Response." This chapter, as noted in the treatment diagram, can be used to release or ventilate the stress response once it has been engendered.

To summarize Part II, let us return to the multidimensional treatment model contained within this introduction.

Chapters 6 and 7 introduce topics that serve as clinical prefaces to the treatment of excessive stress arousal.

Chapter 8 addresses the topic of psychotherapy from a cognitive perspective and in doing so also addresses the topic of environmental engineering.

Chapter 9 provides the reader with a rationale for the utilization of the relaxation response and demonstrates its central phenomenological role in any treatment paradigm for excessive arousal or its target-organ effects. Chapters 10 through 13 serve as practical guides for the use of the relaxation response in clinical practice.

Chapters 14 and 15 continue that discussion into machine-assisted and drugs-assisted technologies.

Chapters 13, 14, and 16 address the issues of how one can intervene at the level of the target organ once the pathogenic stress response has been initiated.

Finally, Chapter 8 can once again be used to as a guide for problem solving and cognitive restructuring.

CHAPTER 6

Personologic Diathesis and Human Stress

Where malignant disease is concerned it may be more important to understand what kind of patient has the disease rather than what kind of disease the patient has.

—Sir William Osler, M.D.

The purpose of Part II is to review options that have proven useful in the treatment of excessive stress arousal. This chapter begins that discussion with an issue relevant to treatment planning—the role of personality in the etiology and treatment of the human stress response.

It will be recalled from Chapter 2 that the manner in which an individual chooses to perceive and interpret his or her environment (cognitive interpretation) serves as the single most important determinant of whether or not the stress response will be elicited in response to a psychosocial stressor. It may then be argued that the *consistent* manner in which an individual perceives and interprets the environment, in addition to the aggregation of consistent attitudes, values, and behavior patterns, serves as an operational definition of the construct of "personality." If one accepts such a proposition, it becomes reasonable to assume that there may well exist individuals whose consistent personality traits, including cognitive interpretations regarding their environment, may predispose them to excessive elicitation of the stress response and therefore, increased risk of stress-related disease. Such personality-based predispositions for stress may exist in the form of personologic diatheses, such as cognitive distortions, persistent irrational expectations, "ego" vulnerabilities, and/or consistent stress-producing overt behavior patterns.

If indeed one's personologic idiosyncrasies can predispose to excessive stress arousal, it behooves the clinician to familiarize himself or herself with the common manifestations of such personologic predispositions. Investigations into such relationships between personality factors and stress arousal have typically taken one of two perspectives.

1. Historically, investigations into the relationship between personality and stress have focused upon highly *specific* personality traits that appear to predispose individuals to highly *specific* diseases, without consideration of the global personality structure within which those traits reside (Alexander, 1950; Dunbar,1935).

2. More recent investigations have pursued the proposition that there exist consistent, personality-based predispositions, that is, "vulnerabilities" unique to and inherent within each and every basic personality pattern (Millon, 1981). Collectively, these characterological susceptibilities serve as a form of Achilles' heel, referred to here as a *personologic diathesis*, serving, under the right set of circumstances, to predispose one to the elicitation of the stress response and a host of subsequent stress-related disorders (Frances, 1982; Millon & Everly, 1985; Everly, 1987). These characterologic vulnerabilities may exist in the form of "ego" vulnerabilities, consistent cognitive distortions, expectations, and repeated stress-producing behaviors. Such an approach tends not to focus on specific traits and their association with specific diseases, but rather sees each different personality style or pattern as possessing a personologic diathesis consisting of an aggregation of personality-based susceptibilities to stress. Let us pursue these notions further.

HISTORICAL FOUNDATIONS

When one first thinks of the relationship between personality and stress, the Type A coronary-prone behavior pattern invariably comes to mind (Friedman & Rosenman, 1974). Yet the search for the stress-prone personality far predates the discovery of the Type A pattern.

The work of Dunbar (1935) represents one of the earliest and most noteworthy efforts at formulating psychosomatic theory based upon personality profiles. Dunbar described various personality profiles that seemed to be predisposed to specific stress-related diseases. For example, from her perspective, the hypertensive patient was one who could be seen as characterologically shy, reserved, rigid, yet possessing the propensity for "volcanic eruptions of feelings." The migraine patient, on the other hand, could be seen as perfectionistic and overachievement oriented.

The nuclear conflict theory of French and Alexander (Alexander, 1950) argued that persons prone to repeated characterological conflicts are prone to specific stress-related disorders; for example:

Frustration . . . Colitis
Unresolved maternal dependency . . . Asthma
Feelings of inferiority . . . Essential hypertension
Suppressed hostility . . . Essential hypertension
Oral dependency . . . Duodenal ulcer

In addition to the work of Dunbar and Alexander, there were other early contributions from the analytically oriented theorists, yet early interest waned with rather low reliability among the findings of the various theorists. Similarly, even when there were reliable findings, they contributed only minimal variation to the overall disease process. Thus research into the relationship between personality and disease significantly diminished for over a decade until interest was rekindled by cardiologists Friedman and Rosenman (1974) with their investigations into the Type A coronary-prone behavior pattern.

Friedman (1969) described the Type A pattern as a characteristic "action–emotion complex" exhibited by individuals engaged in a chronic struggle to "obtain an unlimited number of poorly defined things from their environment in the shortest period of time." Originally, the Type A pattern was believed to constitute chronic time urgency, competitiveness, polyphasic behavior, and poorly planned, often impulsive behavior (Friedman & Rosenman, 1974). The Type A pattern has also been described as consisting of primary traits of time urgency, hostility, ambition, and immoderation. They also described secondary traits of impatience, aggression, competitiveness, and denial.

The original search for the Type A pattern was, indeed, a search for a consistent behavior pattern that predisposed to premature coronary artery disease. When diagnosed via the standardized structured interview technique, the Type A pattern has consistently shown a relationship with coronary artery disease (see Powell, 1984; Shepherd & Weiss, 1987; Williams, 1984; Williams et al., 1980). Major investigations that have failed to uncover a relationship between coronary heart disease and the Type A pattern have generally used techniques other than the structured interview to assess the pattern (Everly & Sobelman, 1987; Shephard & Weiss, 1987). The use of diverse measurement technologies may have inadvertently added to the confusion surrounding the nature of the Type A pattern (Everly & Sobelman, 1987). Indeed, the pursuit of the Type A pattern has taken on a life of its own, so much so that individuals invariably ask if there is such a thing as a "good" Type A pattern. By definition, the answer to such a question must be "no," if one only remembers that the original quest for the Type A pattern was actually a search for a behavior pattern that predisposes to premature coronary heart disease. Considering this point, how could there be a "good" Type A?

The relationship between Type A behavior and coronary heart disease has prompted researchers to conduct various components analyses in search of the pathogenic core of the Type A pattern (Powell, 1984; Williams, 1984; Williams *et al.*, 1980). Such endeavors have uncovered a myriad of Type A constituents that serve to further clarify the nature of the pattern. Figure 6.1 represents an integrative model of Type A constituents.

Figure 6.1 represents an integration of findings reported as part of the "second generation" of Type A research designed to better understand the constituents of coronary-prone behavior (Powell, 1984; Williams, 1984, 1986; Williams *et al.*, 1980). The figure portrays a deeply rooted personologic insecurity as the foundation of the Type A pattern. That characterologic insecurity is thought to give rise to an extraordinary need for power and achievement, perhaps as a means of compensating for or contradicting the feelings of insecurity. Power and achievement are related to control, and it has been found that Type A individuals possess not only high achievement motives but also an extraordinary need for control. The need for control and the fear of the loss of control may then account for the observed impatience, time urgency, polyphasic behavior, competitiveness, and related traits that Type A persons exhibit. Studies by Williams and his colleagues have suggested that chronic hostility and cynicism may be an important psychological factor in the increased coronary risk that Type A individuals exhibit. Dembroski and Costa (1988) having reviewed the assessment of the Type A pattern note that the "global" Type A pattern is not a good predictor of heart disease, but that the hostility component may play a critical pathogenic role.

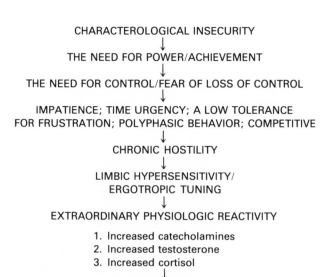

CHARACTEROLOGICAL INSECURITY
↓
THE NEED FOR POWER/ACHIEVEMENT
↓
THE NEED FOR CONTROL/FEAR OF LOSS OF CONTROL
↓
IMPATIENCE; TIME URGENCY; A LOW TOLERANCE
FOR FRUSTRATION; POLYPHASIC BEHAVIOR; COMPETITIVE
↓
CHRONIC HOSTILITY
↓
LIMBIC HYPERSENSITIVITY/
ERGOTROPIC TUNING
↓
EXTRAORDINARY PHYSIOLOGIC REACTIVITY

1. Increased catecholamines
2. Increased testosterone
3. Increased cortisol
↓
INCREASED RISK OF CORONARY HEART DISEASE

Figure 6.1. An integrative model of Type A characteristics.

Research has also shown that Type A individuals exhibit extraordinary physiologic reactivity when confronted with a psychosocial challenge. That reactivity has been shown to be manifest in increased release of catecholamines, increased testosterone, and increased cortisol release—all well-known atherogenic agents. The physiologic reactivity, according to the work of Everly (1985b) may well be based upon some form of limbic system hypersensitivity, or what Gellhorn (1967) has called the "ergotropic tuning phenomenon." Finally, the unusually high levels of circulating catecholamine, cortisol, and testosterone appear to be directly related to the increased risk of coronary artery disease manifest by Type A males. It should be noted that, at rest, the Type A manifests no significant differences in catecholamine, testosterone, or cortisol secretion when compared with non–Type A individuals. Only upon psychosocial challenge are the aforementioned differences seen to emerge.

The Type A pattern remains a promising area for continued research into the relationship between personality and disease, especially stress-related disease. It will be recalled that the catecholamines, testosterone, and cortisol are all key stress-responding hormones. The interested reader should refer to Shepherd and Weiss (1987) for an important review.

The next major contribution to the stress and personality phenomenon comes from Suzanne Kobasa. Kobasa investigated personality characteristics that seemed to act as a buffer between individuals and the pathogenic mechanisms of excessive stress. Her research investigated the domain of "hardiness," that is, characterologic factors that appear to mitigate the stress response. Kobasa (Kobasa, 1979; Kobasa & Puccetti, 1983) defined hardiness as the aggregation of three factors:

1. Commitment, that is, the tendency to involve oneself in experiences in meaningful ways
2. Control, that is, the tendency to believe and act as if one has some influence over one's life
3. Challenge, that is, the belief that change is a positive and normal characteristic of life.

The hardiness research has shown that individuals who demonstrate a commitment to self, family, work, and/or other important values; a sense of control over one's life; and the ability to see life change as an opportunity will experience fewer stress-related diseases/illnesses even though they may find themselves in environments laden with stressor stimuli.

The hardiness construct is indeed a tempting concept to entertain. This formulation has received a serious challenge from Lazarus and Folkman (1984), however. Lazarus and Folkman argue that there is a paucity of systematic studies that examine the relationship between antecedent variables and health. Conclusions, they suggest, are typically formulated on the basis of inference with regard to coping mechanisms. They argue that Kobasa's conclusions about hardiness are based on tenuous inferences about coping mechanisms generated through the use of questionable measurement technologies.

It seems clear that factors such as those described in the hardiness research may indeed play an important role in mitigating otherwise pathogenic circumstances. Nevertheless, it may be useful to better operationalize these factors before employing such notions in psychotherapeutic formulations.

No review of historical foundations in personality and stress research would be complete without mentioning what is the oldest longitudinal research investigation specifically of the relationship between personality and disease. The Johns Hopkins Precursors Study (see Thomas and McCabe, 1980) seeks to answer the question "Do individuals have distinctive personal characteristics in youth that precede premature disease and death?" The Precursors Study cohort consisted of 1,337 graduates of the Johns Hopkins School of Medicine between the years of 1948 and 1964. Thomas and McCabe (1980) investigated, via self-report, consistent "habits of nervous tension" (HNT) and subsequent disease. They conclude:

> Compared with those of the healthy group, the overall HNT patterns were significantly different for the cancer, coronary occlusion, mental illness and suicide groups. . . . It therefore appears that youthful reactions to stress as self-reported in a checklist of habits of nervous tension reflect individual psycho-biological differences that are linked with future health or disease. (p. 137)

Thus, in the most liberal interpretation of personality, the Precursors Study continues to reveal links between what may be argued to be characterological traits and the subsequent formation of disease.

Indeed, in a meta-analytic investigation in search of the "disease-prone personality," Friedman and Booth-Kewley (1987) reviewed a research base including *Psychological Abstracts* and *Index Medicus*. Focusing upon psychosomatic disease processes, the authors found 229 studies, of which 101 were ultimately used in the meta-analysis. They conclude: "The results point to the probable existence of a generic 'disease-prone' personality that involves depression, anger/hostility, anxiety, and possibly other aspects of personality" (p. 539).

Let us now turn to a discussion of more recent trends in personality research as it pertains to excessive stress arousal.

THE PRINCIPLE OF PERSONOLOGIC PRIMACY

Should the patient with passive–dependent traits presenting with a stress-induced chronic migraine headache syndrome be treated in the same manner as the patient with histrionic traits and a migraine syndrome of equal severity? Should the patient with avoidant traits and a panic disorder be treated in the same manner as a patient with compulsive traits and a diagnosed panic disorder of equal intensity? A growing body of evidence argues that the answer to both questions is "no" (Frances, 1982).

Theoretic (Everly, 1987; Millon, 1981; Widiger & Frances, 1985), as well as empirical evidence (Strupp, 1980; Taylor & Abrams, 1975; Kayser et al., 1987; Everly et al., 1987) suggests that clinical and subclinical personality patterns may be a uniquely important factor in the diagnosis and treatment of many psychiatric and stress-related disorders. More specifically, the "principle of personologic primacy" as proposed by Everly (1987) denotes that personologic style plays a uniquely important role in

1. The consistent propensity to create psychosocial stressors (via some diathesis)
2. The phenomenological course of psychiatric and stress-related disorders
3. Diagnostic refinement of major psychiatric syndromes
4. Psychotherapeutic, as well as psychopharmacologic, treatment responsiveness
5. The long-term prognosis for many psychiatric and stress-related disorders

The "principle of personologic primacy" further argues that basic personality patterns and their respective hosts of idiosyncratic interpretational predispositions (i.e., personologic diatheses) for stress and other clinical syndromes serve as phenomenological foundations from which major stress-related illnesses and psychiatric syndromes may emerge. Thus, such syndromes are best understood as pathological extensions of potentially malignant personologic undergirdings, for example, consistent cognitive distortions, irrational expectations, "ego" vulnerabilities, unfounded assumptions, and the like (Everly, 1987; Millon, 1981; Millon & Everly, 1985). Adverse environmental events, psychoactive drug reactions, and physical and/or psychological trauma may serve as sufficient impetus to cause the personologic substructure to express itself in pathological clinical manifestations such as headaches, panic attacks, hypertensive episodes, and acute tachycardic episodes, mediated through the physiological stress response (Chapter 2).

In sum, with regard to stress-related disorders, the "principle of personologic primacy" may be understood as suggesting that (1) a patient's *chronic* propensity to cognitively interpret the environment in such a manner as to engender the stress response with extraordinary frequency is more likely than not to be a function of a personality-based predisposition (diathesis); similarly, (2) a chronic and consistent pattern of elicitation of the stress response is perhaps best viewed more as a manifestation of a dysfunctional characterological predisposition, rather than merely one's exposure to a series of consistently hostile environments. This brings us to the natural corollary of the "principle of personologic primacy:" personality-based psychotherapy.

PERSONOLOGIC PSYCHOTHERAPY
AND STRESS-RELATED DISORDERS

If one does indeed accept personality as playing an important role in the etiology of stress-related disease, then one might logically assume that it must play some role in the treatment of such disease as well. Everly (1987) has introduced the concept of "personologic psychotherapy" as one way of recognizing the role that personality may play in treatment formulation. According to Everly, personologic psychotherapy represents a metatherapeutic approach to the treatment of psychiatric as well as stress-related disorders. More specifically, it is the embodiment of the belief that in most chronic psychiatric and stress-related syndromes, a dysfunctional personologic style supports these syndromes and, therefore, must also become a target for therapeutic intervention, if the chronic nature of the problem is to be addressed. Similarly, the concept of "personologic psychotherapy" embodies the belief that treating only the symptoms of *chronic, recurrent* clinical syndromes may in many cases be analogous to palliatively attending to a clinical veneer while ignoring an important aspect of the etiological malignancy (see also Millon, 1988).

The theoretical basis for "personologic psychotherapy" is Millon's biosocial learning theory (Millon, 1981, 1988). It is referred to as a metatherapy because the specific manner in which the personologic dysfunction is treated is left to the discretion of the treating therapist.

With specific attention to stress-related disorders, personologic psychotherapy is broadly interpreted to suggest that in addition to treating the florid symptoms of *chronic* stress-related disorders, it is necessary to direct some aspect of therapeutic effort toward the personologic predispositions (diatheses) that may be serving to sustain the chronic stress-related disorder.

Let us examine one example of how these concepts may be used in treatment planning with a patient who can be said to possess a dependent characterologic style while manifesting a chronic and more florid stress-related gastrointestinal (GI) dysfunction. According to the theoretical basis (Millon, 1981; Millon & Everly, 1985), a major sustaining mechanism in a chronic dependent character structure is an extraordinary need for interpersonal affection, affiliation, and support. Such an individual is most vulnerable to chronic stress when this critical need is being denied or perhaps only jeopardized. In such a scenario, alleviation of the stress-related GI symptomatology may serve to address only the immediate medical concern. If indeed symptom removal has been the only outcome achieved in treatment, then nothing has been done to preclude recurrent gastrointestinal dysfunction. On the other hand, therapy directed with personologic considerations in mind would certainly consider the potentially self-sustaining mechanisms of extraordinary dependency needs and would target the dependent pattern as an additional focus for therapy. Once again, the specific therapeutic technology employed remains at the discretion of the therapist.

The principle of personologic primacy and its therapeutic corollary by no means dictates that formal psychotherapy needs to be conducted in all stress-related disorders. Certainly, there are acute stress-related manifestations that may have little or no etiological basis in personality-related dysfunction. Similarly, "psychotherapeutic" change may well be realized on the basis of therapies not traditionally seen as being "psychotherapeutic" in nature, such as relaxation training and biofeedback therapy (Adler & Morrissey-Adler, 1983; Green & Green, 1983; Murphy & Donovan, 1984). Such therapies commonly yield outcome such as an improved sense of self-efficacy, a more internal locus of control, improved self-esteem, and what has been called by some a state of "cultivated low arousal" (Adler & Morrissey-Adler, 1983; Green & Green, 1983; Sarnoff, 1982; Stoyva & Budzynski, 1974). Chapter 8 will, however, discuss psychotherapy in greater detail.

MILLON'S PERSONALITY THEORY AND STRESS

Preceding sections in this chapter have argued basically two points: (1) that personality type is related to disease, including stress-related disease, (2) that treatment planning for stress-related diseases should take into consideration the undergirding personality structure if treatment is to be considered complete. It has also been argued that different personalities possess relatively unique characterologic "vulnerabilities," or personologic diatheses, which serve as characterological "weak points" for the initiation of pathogenic stress mechanisms should environmental conditions support such development. Yet, one factor that has served to limit the progression of the field of research related to personality and stress is the lack of a coherent superordinate theory of personality from which to extend relational investigations. This is in contrast to the traditional search for unique and specific independent personality factors, such as the Type A pattern.

The biosocial learning theory of personality is a theoretically sound but, more important, clinically useful perspective from which to examine the role that personality plays in the initiation and prolongation of the human stress response (Millon, 1981). A comprehensive review of Millon's theory is beyond the scope of this chapter. Interested readers should refer to Millon (1981). A brief description of his basic personality styles will be presented below.

Considering the realm of "normal" personologic styles, Millon (Millon & Everly, 1985) suggests that there exist eight basic and theoretically pure styles. These normal styles are fundamentally adaptive under most circumstances. Yet, each one of these styles will be considered to possess, as part of their intrinsic constituency, idiosyncratic "vulnerabilities" or uniqueness that can serve to predispose to excessive stress arousal under the proper set of environmental circumstances.

A brief review of these eight normal styles seems appropriate at this point. I shall label each of the styles (with one exception) with the traditional diagnostic terms most commonly associated. The reader must keep in mind, however, that although the terms used will be those most commonly associated with personality "disorders," the present discussion refers NOT to personality disorders but to the "normal" personologic variants.

The individual with an *aggressive* personality is one that has difficulty trusting others. He or she tends to usurp the rights of others and to be defensively self-centered. Action-oriented and highly independent, the behavioral style of the personality is forceful. The individual often displays intimidating interpersonal conduct and angry affective expressions, yet the self-perception is one of assertiveness. There is a significant need to control and dominate the environment. The basic sustaining reinforcement pattern is that of negative reinforcement where the individual strives to avoid a loss of control, humiliation, and any position or status that is perceived as being inferior.

The individual with a *narcissistic* personality, even in its normal variation, has difficulty postponing gratification. Passively independent, a poised behavioral appearance is usually manifest. Interpersonal conduct is usually seen as being unempathic, and the affective expression may be seen as serene. The self-perception of the narcissist is one of confidence. Narcissistic individuals seem preoccupied with being seen as unique or special. Such persons often resort to creating illusions of extraordinary competence or influence. They usually are so self-absorbed as to be incapable of seeing any point of view other than their own. This lack of empathy often leads to poor interpersonal communications and shallow relationships. The basic reinforcement pattern is that of positive reinforcement, whereas these individuals act to secure for themselves a position of "entitlement."

The *histrionic* personality is one driven by a need for approval, affection, affiliation, and support. Histrionic individuals project an animated, sociable, sometimes dramatic, appearance. An exaggerated affective expression is often present. These individuals are often seen as superficial, however, Boredom, especially interpersonal boredom, often plagues the personality with histrionic traits. With a flair for the drama in life, the histrionic personality moves about searching for approval, yet it seems as if this search is never-ending. Thus these individuals tend to pursue activities that make them the center of attention. The basic sustaining reinforcement pattern is positive reinforcement where support, approval, and affiliation are the rewards.

The *schizoid* personality style is described as a characterological pattern typified by a passive behavioral appearance and detached, unobtrusive interpersonal conduct, manifesting a rather bland affective expression. The self-perception of the character style is one of placidity. The individual with a schizoid personality style, juxtaposed to the histrionic style, expresses virtually no desire for interpersonal affiliation or support. The classic prototype of the "lone wolf," this individual appears to view interpersonal exchange as a burdensome process. The schizoid seeks isolation as a defense against excess stimulus bombardment and a sense of being overwhelmed. Thus the reinforcement pattern of the schizoid can be said to be negative reinforcement.

The *compulsive* personality is a highly respectful personologic style. Driven by the need to behave in a socially acceptable manner, and to avoid making mistakes, individuals with a compulsive personality walk the "straight and narrow." They consistently adhere to foredrawn rules and regulations, ethics and mores. They often appear as rigid and inflexible, tending to suppress emotions and any signs of distress. These people are most comfortable with the concrete things in life. The abstract and ambiguous are to be avoided as sources of distress. The sustaining pattern of reinforcement is negative reinforcement; that is, their behavior is driven by the need to avoid making mistakes and being perceived as socially inappropriate.

The *avoidant* personality is one that desires social affiliation and support yet is so afraid of social rejection that social avoidance becomes a way of life. Shy and withdrawing, individuals with an avoidant personality remain extraordinarily sensitive and vigilant to anything that resembles interpersonal rejection. The sustaining pattern of reinforcement appears to be negative reinforcement, that is, the avoidance of interpersonal rejection and/or humiliation.

The *dependent* personality is one driven by the search for support. Unlike the histrionic style, which actively attracts approval and support, the dependent personality acquiesces to gain affection and support. The chronic pattern of submissiveness and passivity often prohibits the natural development of independent skills and autonomous behaviors. The sustaining pattern of reinforcement is a dual pattern, that is, both positive and negative reinforcement. The pattern of positive reinforcement is revealed as a pattern where submissiveness "earns" the affection and support of others, thereby, through a negative reinforcement pattern, avoiding the penultimate stressor—rejection, abandonment, and interpersonal isolation.

The *passive–aggressive* personality, in its pure form, is an ambivalent personality. In many ways it represents an adolescent, from a maturational perspective, in an adult's body. The individual with a passive–aggressive personality desires interpersonal independence but lacks the skills required to function in such a manner. This causes the individual to resort to a dependent reinforcement pattern, yet not without considerable dissonance. Such individuals tend to behave aggressively, but, lacking the "adult" skills of assertiveness, cannot risk rejection, so they are aggressive in a hidden, cloaked, or "passive" manner. The sustaining reinforcement pattern for these individuals is that of negative reinforcement. Their chronic pessimism, negativism, and interpersonal "game playing" seems to provide rewards of some kind, especially when they can see others fail, compromise, or become as negative or cynical about the world as they are. Indeed, perhaps misery does love company. More important, the passive–aggressive manipulation allows the person to avoid a sense of interpersonal impotence and dependence.

These, then, are the theoretically "pure" personologic styles as described by Millon (Millon & Everly, 1985). In reality, it should be noted that most people are combinations of two or three of these styles. Further, to reiterate, each of the aforementioned personality styles can be said to be fundamentally "normal" and *not* to be considered a personality disorder, despite the use of descriptive labels usually used in conjunction with a personality disorder.

Returning to the issue of the human stress response, the notion of personologic psychotherapy as it pertains to the treatment of stress arousal argues that some degree of therapeutic effort needs to be directed toward the unique qualities and/or sustaining reinforcement patterns of the personality being treated; this, because it is felt that some idiosyncratic qualities or vulnerabilities may play a significant role in the etiology of chronic stress syndromes. Using Millon's schema, it may be argued that each of the eight basic personality styles possesses its own intrinsic personologic diathesis, that is, factors inherent in the personality that may serve to contribute to extraordinary stress arousal. These factors are listed in Table 6.1. From a clinical perspective, it is hoped that enumeration of these factors will assist the clinician in (1) understanding how personologic factors may contribute to chronic stress arousal syndromes and (2) targeting psychotherapeutic efforts toward the personologic foundations of excessive stress, that is, the unique vulnerabilities and/or sustaining mechanisms as described in the text above or in Table 6.1.

Table 6.1. Personologic Diatheses and Stress

Personality style	Sustaining reinforcement pattern	Consistent personality factors that contribute to extraordinary arousal
Aggressive	R−	1. Need to exert control of, and to vigilantly monitor, the environment 2. Being placed in a position having to rely on, or trust, other individuals 3. Fear of being taken advantage of and efforts to avoid that 4. Fear of being humiliated, and efforts to avoid that. 5. Assumption that "only the strong survive" and the persistent efforts to be "strong"
Narcissistic	R+	1. Inability to postpone gratification 2. Fear of not being seen as "special" 3. Need to create illusions of extraordinary competence 4. Inability to empathize with others leading to consistently poor communications 5. Assumption that others will recognize him/her as "special"
Histrionic	R+, R−	1. Interpersonal instability 2. Fear of a loss of affection 3. Fear of a loss of support or actual rejection 4. Frequent changes in life events 5. Need for interpersonal approval 6. Belief that he/she must earn, or "perform" for interpersonal affection, approval, and support
Dependent	R+, R−	1. Fear of the loss of interpersonal support 2. Fear of the loss of affection or actual rejection 3. Chronic submissiveness and inability to be assertive when desired 4. Fear and avoidance of interpersonal confrontation
Passive-aggressive	R−	1. Desire to behave in a manner contrary to previous learning history 2. Inability to act assertively 3. Chronic tendency to compare self to others

(continued)

Table 6.1. (*Continued*)

Personality style	Sustaining reinforcement pattern	Consistent personality factors that contribute to extraordinary arousal
		4. Chronic negativism 5. "Successes" of peer group 6. Actual failure or rejection
Compulsive	R−	1. Efforts to maintain rigid self-control 2. Change 3. Coping with abstract or ambiguous situations 4. Decision making when options are not clear 5. Unclear directions 6. The "gray areas" of rules and policies 7. Fear of making a mistake 8. Need for, and excessive efforts to, earn approval 9. Fear of social disapproval 10. Belief that emotions should be suppressed 11. Assumption that others share compulsive traits and will act accordingly 12. Waste (e.g., of time, money, effort) 13. Risk taking
Avoidant	R−	1. Interpersonal intrusion 2. Fear of interpersonal rejection 3. Need to remain highly vigilant 4. Lack of interpersonal support 5. Actual rejection 6. Interpersonal hypersensitivity
Schizoid	R−	1. Interpersonal intrusion 2. Lack of interpersonal support 3. Hyperstimulation

SUMMARY

In this chapter, the focus has been upon the role that personality plays in the initiation, prolongation, and ultimate treatment of the human stress response. Let us review the main points:

1. There is a commonly held belief that in the case of *chronic* stress

arousal and stress-related diseases, one's personality serves to play a significant role from an etiologic, as well as therapeutic, perspective.

2. Historically, investigations have focused upon *specific* personality traits and *specific* disease formation (Alexander, 1950; Dunbar, 1935).

3. More contemporary perspectives have chosen to look within the global personality for characterological vulnerabilities, that is, personologic diathesis, for extraordinary stress arousal and a subsequent host of stress-related diseases (Everly, 1987; Frances, 1982; Millon, 1981).

4. The principle of personologic primacy argues that consistent characterological traits serve to undergird, and therefore play a unique role in, the patient's propensity to create psychosocial stressors. Such factors play a major role in treatment planning and responsiveness (Frances & Hale, 1984; Everly, 1987) as well.

5. The notion of "personologic psychotherapy is the natural corollary of the principle of personologic primacy and basically argues that even in chronic stress-related disorders, characterologic traits require therapeutic attention and therefore should be considered in treatment planning (Everly, 1987; Millon, 1988).

6. When attempting to better understand and concretize the role that personologic vulnerabilities play as factors that predispose to extraordinary stress arousal, Millon's biosocial learning theory of personality serves as a theoretically cogent and clinically practical framework from which to operate. Table 6.1 describes common personologic factors that serve to contribute to extraordinary stress arousal within each of Millon's basic eight "normal" personality formulations. An understanding of these factors serves to foster a better understanding of *chronic* stress arousal and its subsequent disorders. Such understanding also serves to facilitate treatment planning and intervention when one looks beyond the florid symptoms of excessive stress arousal.

7. A final point needs to be reiterated before this chapter is brought to a close. This chapter has indeed attempted to sensitize the reader to the belief that personality traits play an important role in the nature and treatment of the human stress response. That is *not* to say, however, that formal psychotherapy needs to be an integral aspect of all stress treatment/stress management paradigms. Processes such as relaxation training, biofeedback, and even health education practices are clearly capable, in some instances, of altering dysfunctional practices. Yet, there are instances where chronic stress-related diseases are a direct function of personologic disturbances such as dysfunctional self-esteem, persistent cognitive distortions, irrational assumptions, inappropriate expectations of self and others, and so on. In such cases, some concerted psychotherapeutic effort would clearly be indicated. The most effective "mix" of therapeutic technologies (e.g., relaxation training, psychotherapy, hypnosis) remains to be

determined by the therapist on a case-by-case basis. It is clearly beyond the scope of this volume to dictate such guidelines.

Consistent, then, with the belief that the treatment of excessive stress is a multidimensional enterprise, we will now proceed to address a myriad of therapeutic technologies that have been found useful in the treatment of excessive human stress.

The discussion of specific therapeutic interventions begins in the next two chapters with an exploration of a "psychotherapeutic" genre that has shown special relevance to the treatment of excessive stress arousal.

Control and the Human Stress Response

Eileen R. Potocki and George S. Everly, Jr.

. . . grant me the strength to change what I can, the courage to bear what I cannot change, and the wisdom to know the difference.
— Reinhold Niebuhr, 1934

It was the purpose of the preceding chapter to sensitize the reader to the notion that the patient's personologic style (personality) serves as a critical epiphenomenological factor in the etiology and treatment of stress-related disorders. In concert with this view, Lazarus (1975) has stated that personality-based idiosyncrasies determine the manner in which an individual appraises and interprets his/or her environment. Further, Lazarus argues that personologic variations determine the subsequent experienced emotion, as well as influence the target-organ arousal that is ultimately experienced by the individual. Thus, it may be argued that personologic factors serve as a critical form of "filtering mechanism" that serves to shape one's idiosyncratic reality.

The present chapter attempts to address one specific aspect of the perceptual filtering process in psychosomatic processes. The main theme

Eileen R. Potocki • Department of Psychology, Florida State University, Tallahassee, Florida 32306-1051.

of this chapter is perhaps best summarized by Albert Bandura (1982), who cogently argues "To the extent to which one can prevent, terminate, or lessen the severity of aversive events, there is little reason to fear them" (p. 36). More specifically, the main theme of this chapter is the issue of *control* as it may affect human health.

Within the confines of this chapter we will examine an operationalization of the control construct. We will briefly overview several theories of control and consider the role that control may play in illness, recovery, aging, and the psychotherapeutic process. We will go into greater detail within this chapter as we describe the extant literature so as to provide a more in-depth analysis of the complexities inherent in this line of research.

Finally, it should be noted that the issue of control, although a more specific personality-based variable, is one that transcends all personality styles, regardless of one's theoretic orientation vis-à-vis personologic typologies.

A DEFINITION OF CONTROL

Control will be operationally defined here as existing within five domains:

1. The demonstrated ability to change or manipulate an environmental transaction (Bandura, 1977, 1982b; Thompson, 1981)
2. The perceived ability to change or manipulate an environmental transaction (Bandura, 1977, 1982; Krantz, 1980)
3. The ability to predict an environmental transaction (Seligman, 1975)
4. The ability to understand an environmental transaction (Averill, 1973; Krantz, 1980; Thompson, 1981)
5. The ability to *accept* the environmental transaction within some meaningful cognitive framework or belief system. Some authors refer to this as "relinquishing" of control.

THEORIES OF CONTROL

The maturation of Seligman's learned helplessness theory heralds the cognitive focus of other control theorists. Overmier and Seligman (1967) and Seligman and Maier (1967) originally demonstrated in dogs a replicable phenomenon of deficit in three distinct domains: motivation, cognition, and emotion. Subject to the typical learned helplessness triadic design in which one group receives controllable events, a second group yoked to the first receives uncontrollable events of the same intensity and duration, and a third control group receives neither controllable nor uncontrollable stimuli, dogs exposed to inescapable electric shock demonstrated deficits 24 hours later when placed in a shuttlebox in which crossing a barrier would have been the simple operant necessary for terminating the aversive stimulus. The yoked animals initiated few escape attempts (motivational deficit), failed to systematize occasional successful responses by following them with a series of effective operants (cognitive deficit), and did not react with overt emotionality while being shocked (emotional deficit). Naive dogs, unlike those exposed to uncontrollable stimuli, quickly acquired the instrumental escape response.

In a reexamination of Seligman's paradigm with an eye toward human responses such as depression, Abramson *et al.* (1978) perceived noncontingency between response and outcome as leading to future expectations that one has no control or limited control over internal or external situational demands. This perception of helplessness leads to a cognitive or associative deficit in which the organism anticipates lack of control in subsequent challenges. In addition, an emotional deficit characterized by sadness or depression and a dearth of motivational energy result in failure to enact coping responses since previous responses and outcomes were perceived as noncontingent.

Inability to account for the boundary conditions of learned helplessness and depression emerged as a lacuna in the theoretical explanation of helplessness and hopelessness and led to the postulation of cognitive factors intervening in the future response–outcome expectation. The cognitive component, or better stated, a subjective cognitive imperative, was defined as the necessary predecessor of learned helplessness. Thus, the cognitive imperative of perceived control emerged as the principal feature mitigating the environmental event and behavioral, or physiological, outcome relationship.

Langer (1983) recognizes the pervasive character of control in everyday life. Human beings are motivated to master their environment not only to demonstrate competence but also to allay the pernicious consequences of having no control. People strive to order their universe, often in objectively indeterminable situations. Langer introduces the notion of the illusion of control, that is, a cognitive error resulting in one's spurious perception of a chance event as a controllable skill event. Skill-relevant behaviors as choice, passive and active involvement (e.g., thinking about the task and possible strategies to be employed), stimulus and response familiarity (e.g., practice), and competition, when imposed upon a random situation induce a factitious sense of control.

This illusion of control is reminiscent of a higher order reasoning analogue of Wertheimer's perceptual organization laws—proximity, similarity, good continuation and closure—primarily unlearned basic human brain activity compelling one to organize sensory input. Langer's brilliantly subtle experimental exposition of the viability and function of illusory control has repercussions not only for manipulating chance events but also for maximizing coping, performance, and comfort in less than ideal living environments such as nursing homes.

Bandura (1977, 1982a,b) identified the augmentation of perceived efficacy as the executive mechanism common to diverse but effective treatment modalities. Like Seligman and Langer, Bandura focuses on a cognitive locus of determination in order to better understand behavior and treatment in maladapative stimulus–response sequences. Perceived self-efficacy refers to subjective judgments of one's ability to cope with prospective or hypothetical situations. Self-appraisals of competence and control influence behavior, thought patterns, and emotional reactions. Those acknowledging self-referent inefficacy mull over personal deficiencies, anticipate unrealistically threatening opponents, and create stress, thereby diverting potential problem-solving energy. Expectations of mastery (self-efficacy) encourage initiation and persistence of coping, whereas those of failure induce reticence.

What are the sources of efficacy expectations? (1) Performance accomplishments (participant modeling, performance desensitization, exposure) provide information of greatest import because mastery is based on actual success. (2) Vicarious experience via live or symbolic modeling increases confidence of adequacy especially when model and subject are characteristically similar. (3) Verbal persuasion (suggestion, self-instruction) of competence has a most profound impact when applied in combination with vicarious or enactive techniques. Interactives as well as independent strategies may be employed. (4) Finally, physiological arousal affords self-referent knowledge. Anxiety and anticipatory arousal signals an impending threat and cultivates avoidance. Physiological placidity alters the focus of perception from deficiency to potency. Success engendered by individual or combined techniques creates a reciprocal and spiraling relationship between positive self-referent thought and action.

Seligman, Langer and Bandura, reacting to stark environmental-action covariation as validation of theories of causation, introjected the cognition of control as the supreme mediator and process guide in human action. Although Seligman, Langer, and Bandura propose unique constructs, major concepts of each theory can be interpreted laterally. For example, Langer and Bandura consider Seligman's idea of learned helplessness to be an instance of the illusion of no control and a profound sense of personal inefficacy. The paramount common feature is a cognitive residue elevated to the status of an imperative, the explicit essence of which is the perception of control plurally defined and measured. In the following sections, we will stray from the study of theory in order to examine more concrete effects of control on stress and other health-related factors

CONTROL AND ILLNESS

Historically, medical personnel have noted an association between problems of perceived control and genesis or exacerbation of illness in their patients. Although distant literature does not detail physiological mechanisms directly linking perceptions of control and disease, it is worthy of cursory review as an initial attempt to define empirically the process relating cognition and sickness.

Engel (1968) introduced the "giving-up-given-up" complex in an interesting although anecdotal article. Engel described a general consensus among his colleagues and himself that 70% to 80% of physical illness seen in their medical practice occurred after the clinical manifestation of the following psychological state involving five characteristics: (1) a feeling of giving up experienced as helplessness or hopelessness, (2) a depreciated self-image, (3) a sense of loss of gratification from relationships or roles in life, (4) a feeling of disruption from the sense of continuity between past, present, and future, and (5) reactivation of memories of earlier periods of giving up. Engel noted that the complex was neither a coincidence nor a consequence of illness but a modifier of the capacity of the organism to cope with a pathogen.

Although the science of neurophysiology and neuroendocrinology at the time were relatively immature, Engel speculated that an individual's perception of inability to control or to cope stimulated the hypothalamus's chemical mobilization of the body's emergency systems, which eventually led to illness.

Difficulty in coping and feelings of helplessness were described in a cross-cultural study of the psychological processes of multiple sclerosis (MS) patients (Mei-tal, Meyerowitz, & Engel, 1970). A total of 32 clinic patients (17 from New York and 15 from Israel) diagnosed with MS were interviewed in order to examine the emotional setting during the transitional period between health and the onset or relapse of illness. Every patient was interviewed one to four times using a technique that explored simultaneously the somatic and psychosocial aspects of the patient's illness experience and life history. Of the 32 patients 28 indicated that illness occurred in conjunction with a psychologically stressful situation. The patients experienced difficulty in coping and feelings of helplessness and reported such an emotional reaction in response to events as sudden threats to the patient's life or to that of an important object, recent object loss by death, removal of body parts, significant events in the family, family conflicts, graduation or promotion, planned or actual marriage, and parenthood. Cross-cultural descriptions consistently revealed a final psychic state of giving up with pronounced feelings of helplessness and/or compensatory behaviors to overcome such feelings. The emergence of helplessness as the primary emotion at the onset of illness was universal in the 28 patients.

Paull and Hislop (1974) examined the etiologic factors in ulcerative colitis. A total of (20 males and 30 females) patients with diagnosed colitis were interviewed in order to document environmental factors preceding and surrounding the onset of the illness with particular emphasis on changes in life setting and interpersonal relationships within the family. A control group matched for age, sex, and marital status with the patients was interviewed confining inquiry to occurrence in the past 12 months of family bereavement, marriage, divorce or broken engagement, pregnancy, childbirth, and migration. The incidence of these factors was compared with that of the patient group. Life crises occurred more than twice as frequently in the patients, 38%, as in controls, 18%, a significant difference. Most important, Paull and Hislop pointed out that illness that followed a particular event such as bereavement might not be exacerbated during stress of a different nature such as pregnancy and, therefore, saw patient interpretation of events as stressful as the superior etiologic factor. Paull and Hislop related the onset of colitis to patient perception of helplessness and prolonged psychological decompensation.

Suls and Mullen (1981) examined the relationship between the perceived controllability and desirability of life events and health change in 119 (60 males and 59 females) college undergraduates. Students completed an illness questionnaire and a life-event scale modified in two significant ways–for each event acknowledged, subjects indicated (1) if the event was controllable, uncontrollable, or of uncertain control and (2) if desirable, undesirable, or of uncertain desirability. Factorially crossing the alternatives for desirability with those for controllability, nine classes of events were established. Pearson product-moment correlations calculated between the life events indices and the number of days ill yielded two significant relationships, that between days ill and undesirable, uncontrollable events and that between days ill and undesirable and ambiguously controllable events. Curiously, the life events–illness relationship was stronger for undesirable events of uncertain controllability than for undesirable, uncontrollable events. Perhaps the category including ambiguous control demonstrates the recalcitrance of extinction of behavior (autonomic hyperactivity) under a variable schedule of reinforcement (perceived uncertain controllability and capricious impact on the environment), which would lead to illness.

Although intriguing, the aforementioned studies failed to address the issue of the immunological mechanisms active in the observed phenomena. Visintainer et al. (1982) measured tumor rejection as a function of the controllability of shock by using a dose of tumor cells reported to induce tumors in 50% of unshocked rats. Ninety-three syngeneic healthy adult male rats were injected with growing Walker 256 sarcoma tumor preparation. Twenty-four hours later, the rats were divided into three groups: escapable shock (n = 30), inescapable shock (n = 30) and no shock (n =33). The rats that received inescapable shock were only half as likely to reject tumor and twice as likely to die as rats receiving escapable shock or no shock. Of the rats in the inescapable shock condition 27% as compared with 63% of the rats in the escapable shock condition and 54% of the rats in the control group rejected the tumor. The experimenters concluded that the inescapable and uncontrollable condition of the shock increased the probability that an animal would die by decreasing the rate of tumor rejection. In addition, the methodological advantage of the prospective design of this study supported uncontrollability as a causal agent in tumor rejection.

Noting that tumor growth and rejection could be affected by nonimmune system functions as vascular flow and steroid production, Laudenslager, Ryan, Druger, Hyson, and Maier (1983) compared *in vitro* the effects of equal amount and distribution of escapable and inescapable shock on antigen-induced proliferation of T-lymphocytes, a direct measure of immune function. A total of 12 rats received escapable shock that could be terminated by rotating a wheel in a wheel-turn box. A second group of 12 rats, each paired with an escapable shock rat with shocks beginning at the same time and ending when the pair escapable-condition rat responded, received inescapable shock. A third group of 13, serving as a control, was restrained in the apparatus for an equivalent time and was not shocked. Twenty-four hours later, all three groups were reexposed to footshocks. After shock reexposure, blood was collected from which lymphocyles were separated and adjusted to final equivalent concentrations. The T-cell mitogens, concanavalin (ConA) and phytohemagglutinin (PHA) were used to stimulate T-cell proliferation; 5.0 mcg/ml PHA produced maximum stimulation in all groups.

Exposure to neither escapable shock nor restraint affected lymphocyte proliferation. Inescapable shock, in contrast, was associated with suppression of lymphocyte proliferation. Significant differences in lymphocyte proliferation to ConA at 5.0 and 10.0 mcg/ml were obtained. Laudenslager *et al.* (1983) demonstrated inhibition of T-lymphocyte proliferation to ConA and PHA *in vitro* if the rat had no control over the shocks. This study supported the hypothesis that the controllability of stressors could modulate immune functions in rats.

The nuclear mishap at Three Mile Island (TMI) provided Davidson, Baum, and Collins (1982) the opportunity to compare the effects of altered perceptions of control induced by technological disaster on the stress response. A total of 75 participants (44 experimental subjects—residents of the TMI neighborhood—and 31 controls—residents living 80 miles from TMI) were interviewed to assess perceptions of control. Multidimensional stress indices included self-report, behavioral, and biochemical measures. TMI residents reported less perceived ability to control their environment and performed more poorly and less persistently on figure tasks than controls. Davidson *et al.* (1982) interpreted these results as indicators of the emotional, cognitive, and motivational deficits associated with learned helplessness. TMI residents exhibited greater symptom distress, specifically more somatic distress, anxiety, and depression than the comparison group. A median split was performed for both experimental and control samples regarding subjects' expectations for future control. Urinary norepinephrine levels yielded a significant interaction between residence and expectation for control, with TMI subjects reporting low expectations for future control producing higher levels of the catecholamine than any other subjects. Urinary epinephrine levels were similar across groups.

Bandura, Taylor, Williams, Mefford, and Barchas (1985) examined the effects of perceived coping efficacy on stress reactions by correlating strength of perceived self-efficacy with catecholamine secretion at a micro-level. Twelve women, severely phobic of spiders, rated the strength of their perceived self-efficacy in hypothetical performance situations. Modeling, which emphasized predictability and controllability, was used to elevate perceptions of efficacy until subjects reported imagined success with three tasks in weak, medium, and strong coping ranges. Epinephrine, norepinephrine, and dopac plasma levels were obtained as subjects were administered their individually selected performance tasks. Catecholamine levels were analyzed as a function of the differential strength of perceived self-efficacy. Epinephrine and norepinephrine secretion was highest for the tasks at medium perceived self-efficacy. Tasks eliciting judgments of strong or weak self-efficacy, the latter triggering avoidance of the performance measure, generated low levels of epinephrine and norepinephrine secretion. The pattern for dopac was linear, with secretion levels decreasing from weak to medium to strong perceptions of efficacy. In the final phase of the experiment, 11 subjects received participant modeling treatment until they judged themselves maximally efficacious in all three coping tasks. Their performance tasks were then administered in the original order, and catecholamine secretion was measured and compared across tasks. At this maximal strength of perceived self-efficacy, no significant difference appeared in epinephrine, norepinephrine, and dopac.

CONTROL AND RECOVERY

Laboratory studies with uncontrollable shock and experimentally defined response options sometimes yield results with limited applicability to natural settings. Thus clinical investigations can add to our knowledge. Myocardial infarction (MI) and surgery represent for most either uncontrollable or stressful disturbances of homeostasis in several domains. For example, an MI with its unpredictable onset and cardiac complication entails complex psychological, physiological, and social adjustment for the patient and his or her family. Manipulating aspects of control in a patient's recovery from either an MI or surgery provides information obtained in a field study with clinically relevant and useful results. This particular research harvest includes theoretical validation of categorical definitions of control with subtypes demonstrated to be differentially effective or ineffective in recuperation.

Krantz (1980) hypothesized that MI patients typically experience adverse prolonged reactions after the acute episode due in part to feelings of helplessness induced by the MI itself. Krantz's theoretical orientation is cognitive, with etiology and treatment explicitly grounded in understanding and fostering the perception of control and predictability. The model links cognitive appraisal with behavioral and physiological responses such that individuals feeling the most competent, least depressed, and least threatened during the acute phase of the illness demonstrate the most progressive recovery. Procedures facilitating recovery from MI must enhance the patient's behavioral control (e.g., providing choices) or cognitive control (e.g., providing information). Most important, procedures must be implemented in a manner that ensures patient perception of increased personal control.

Cromwell, Butterfield, Brayfield, and Curry (1977) conducted an intricate prospective study of recovery from accute attacks of MI. The nursing care substudy involved the relationship of patient care procedures to recovery. A total of 131 MI patients were randomly assigned to a factorial combination of high or low nursing treatment procedures termed information, participation, and diversion. High-information patients heard a recording and read literature explaining etiology and treatment of MI. Low-information subjects received a brief recording and general physician comments limited to support and reassurance. Participation in self-treatment was dichotomized such that high subjects were given access to a switch that would activate cardiac monitors providing EKG tracings upon the experiencing of symptoms. High-participation patients also received training in mild isometric and foot-pedaling exercises. Low-participation subjects received typical instructions regarding bed rest and self-feeding. High- diversion treatment involved liberal visitor privileges and access to television and reading materials. Low-diversion subjects were not provided with television and books and were permitted only limited visitor privileges.

The three nursing care factors interacted with one another in determining length of hospital stay. Specifically, the major finding was that high-information subjects were discharged quickly from coronary care and the hospital if they were also given high levels of diversion or participation. In contrast, high-information subjects had slow discharges if their generous information was paired with low levels of diversion and participation.

Cromwell *et al.* (1977) termed this effect "information coupling" to describe how a patient was given information about his or her cardiac condition. If knowledge was coupled with actual opportunities to foster recovery, coronary care and hospital stays were abbreviated. However, knowledge in the absence of participation or diversion procedures resulted in protracted recovery and hospital stays. Information coupling demonstrated the necessity of delineating subtypes of control, which, in turn, must be delicately balanced in order to induce in a recipient a salutary and not a deleterious effect. It is clear in this study that the control afforded through information to MI patients was not beneficial unless accompanied by active participation in the recovery process. Sheer rumination upon facts in isolation does not appear to instill a sense of control with recuperative benefits.

Although myocardial infarct and elective surgery differ in their predictability, that is, the former is almost always unpredictable and uncontrollable, both possess a common feature in their nature as stressful, threatening events. Recovery from surgery, therefore, is a clinical scenario parallel to recovery from MI from which one may evaluate the salubrious effects of control. Cohen and Lazarus (1973), seeking to explain non-uniform rates of postoperative recovery after medical problems of relatively equivalent severity, studied the active coping and coping dispositions of 61 (22 male and 39 female) patients undergoing elective operations for hernia, gallbladder, and thyroid conditions. Cohen and Lazarus distinguished between coping disposition, the tendency to use one or another coping process, and active coping, the actual type of coping employed. Subjects were interviewed before surgery and assessed for recent life changes, anxiety, and avoidant or vigilant modes of coping with the surgical process. Avoiders tended to deny the emotional threat and demonstrated restriction of procedure and personal knowledge as to surgical experience and postsurgical outlook. Vigilant patients, highly alert and in tune to the impending threat, actively pursued procedural and personal knowledge. Pencil-and-paper tests for coping dispositions tapped similar dimensions, repression and sensitization. Five outcome measures assessed recovery—number of days in the hospital, number of pain medications, number of minor complications, number of negative psychological reactions, and a final variable, the recovery index, defined as the sum of the previous four variables.

Results indicated that avoiders showed a faster rate of recovery on four of the five dependent measures than patients using vigilant modes of coping. This trend reached significance in only two instances: number of days in the hospital and frequency of complications. Coping dispositions, anxiety, and life stress were not related to recovery indices. Again, curious results surfaced. Information, considered either to be a genuine type or provider of control, failed to enhance recovery by enabling efficacious management of a threatening event. Cohen and Lazarus suggested that stressful situations may demand particular and not universal coping modes. Surgery, a stressful experience carrying potential but few threats that actually materialize, may be dealt with most effectively by avoidant–denial strategies.

Langer, Janis, and Wolfer (1975) specifically compared the roles of information and an active cognitive coping device as mediators of psychological stress in surgical patients. A total of 60 patients about to undergo elective surgery all with generally favorable prognoses were administered one of four standardized interviews. The interviewer in the coping device only condition, elaborating upon the basic premise that interpretation of events and often not the events themselves create stress, presented a strategy that encouraged reappraisal, calming self-talk, and cognitive control through selective attention to positive gains rather than negative experiences anticipated as results of the procedure. Subjects receiving the second stress-reducing strategy, preparatory information, were supplied with reassurance and factual information regarding the surgery with the intent of producing emotional innoculation. Preparatory information did not include explicit coping suggestions. A third interactive experimental procedure combined both the preparatory information and the cognitive coping strategy. In order to control for the effect of the presence and interest of psychologists, a final group was interviewed with the focus diverted from the imminent surgery to typical hospital routines.

Dependent measures included nurses' behavioral ratings and direct behavioral measures. The admitting nurses were asked to complete a questionnaire evaluating the patients' stress level in comparison with that of most other elective preoperative patients. Ratings were obtained before and 15 minutes after the experimental interviews. Thus, positive change scores reflected improvement in coping. In addition, overt behavioral postoperative indices of stress, including the total number of pain relievers and sedatives requested and length of hospital stay, were obtained. Physiological dependent measures, blood pressure and pulse readings recorded before and 15 minutes after the interview and again immediately before and 1 hour after the surgery, were obtained.

Results from the nurses' behavioral observations of stress assessment indicated main effects for the coping and combination coping–information groups. Unlike the control and information only communication, both coping and coping-information appeared to reduce preoperative stress. A significant main effect was also obtained for the coping device on number of pain relievers requested and percentage of patients requesting sedatives. Multivariate analysis of blood pressure and pulse rate failed to reveal any systematic variation. In general, preparatory information alone produced no significant effects on any pre- or postoperative measures.

Krantz (1980) emphasized in his controllability and predictability model that procedures facilitating recovery must be presented to the patient such that he or she perceives augmented personal control. The results of the surgery studies indicate the minimal effects of information in the absence of defined cognitive coping strategies on recovery. One may suppose that patients provided with information excluding functional solution alternatives apprehend perhaps a decrease in personal control. Again, the efficacy of control may be situation-specific. The surgery studies lend support to the categorization of control and its differential application based on the inherent character of the situation to be encountered.

CONTROL AND AGING

Can control affect the process of functional aging? Seligman (1975) described the learned helplessness phenomenon characterized by cognitive, motivational, and emotional deficits stemming from perceived response–outcome noncontingency. Langer and Benevento (1978) reported a similar behavioral display based not upon history with uncontrollable outcomes but upon more subtle contextual factors surrounding activities in which one is engaged. For example, assigning one an inferiority-laden label or merely helping another instead of encouraging independence may communicate an insidious although potent message of incompetence. Langer and Benevento termed the process in which an individual erroneously infers incompetence from interpersonal situational factors "self-induced dependence." Given the actual physical and emotional losses encountered by the elderly and the false but pervasive assumption in American society that old age necessarily demands deterioration and a one-way gravitational decline, the elderly may be especially susceptible to self-induced dependence. Rodin (1986) likewise noted that the relation between health and a sense of control may intensify with age.

Control-relevant experiences such as loss of family or friends, retirement, and deprivation of interpersonal feedback concerning competence simply increase with age. The association between health and control may be magnified via compromised immunologic function in the elderly and the medical care system itself, which traditionally has fostered conformity, dependency, and deferential obedience thus restricting active participation in health maintenance. The following discussion may enlighten the reader as to the dramatic noxious effect of quietly active innuendoes and may disabuse us of the notion that age equals inevitable decay.

The elderly, bearing negative labels, would be expected to be vulnerable to self-induced dependence and helplessness. Avorn and Langer (1982) studied changes in performance on a simple puzzle task in elderly residents of an intermediate-care facility. A total of 72 residents were randomly assigned to one of three groups: (1) helped—at each of four 20-minute sessions, an examiner sat with the subject, encouraged working on the puzzle, and actually selected pieces and solved the puzzle with the subject; (2) encouraged only—at each of four 20-minute sessions, an examiner sat with the subject and encouraged completion of the puzzle with minimal assistance; and (3) no contact—no participation in any sessions with an examiner.

Preexperimental testing on all subjects revealed no differences between groups with respect to performance on the puzzle task, interest in puzzles, cooperativeness, alertness, and age. Postexperimental puzzle testing yielded several performance deficits. Subjects in the helped group on average completed fewer pieces and did so more slowly on the posttest than subjects in the encouraged-only group. The no contact group performed intermediately. Interestingly, helped subjects performed less well on the posttest than pretest despite the intervening practice, whereas encouraged-only and no-contact subjects improved, the latter again intermediately. Self-report measures of confidence and independence were obtained on the posttest for subjects in the two experimental groups. Helped subjects rated themselves less confident with respect to anticipated ability to complete similar puzzles successfully than did encouraged-only subjects. Helped subjects also rated the puzzle as more difficult than encouraged-only subjects. These data indicate the ease with which a benign and often gratuitously convenient helping behavior can induce symptoms of helplessness.

Avorn and Langer (1982) demonstrated the facile induction of a helplessness behavior. Langer and Rodin (1976), attempting to reverse the outcome by introducing control, conducted an experiment to evaluate the effects of enhanced personal responsibility and choice on a group of nursing home residents. A total of 91 ambulatory adults, separated by floor in order to prevent communication contamination, were presented a specific lecture by the administrator. Some subjects ($n = 47$) received communication emphasizing responsibility and decision making. Subjects in this responsibility-induced group were also given the choice of accepting and caring for a plant and the opportunity to decide on which of two nights to view a movie. Subjects ($n = 44$) in the comparison group received a friendly communication that stressed the staff's responsibility for them and were implicitly denied choice by being given a plant to be cared for by a nurse and by being assigned a movie night.

Two types of questionnaires, each administered 1 week prior to and 3 weeks after the communication, assessed the effects of induced responsibility. The first was administered directly to the residents and addressed how much control they perceived over general events in their lives and how happy and active they felt. After this initial self-report data was collected, a research assistant rated the participants for alertness. The second questionnaire was completed by the nurses and assessed residents' happiness, alertness, dependence, sociability, activity level, and eating and sleeping habits. In addition, two behavioral measures were obtained—movie attendance and involvement in a competition in which all participants had to guess the amount of jelly beans in a jar. No differences were obtained on pretest ratings made by the subjects, nurses, and research assistant indicating initial comparability between groups. Statistical tests, based upon data of 52 subjects (24 responsibility-induced and 28 comparison) for whom two nurses provided ratings thus enhancing reliability, compared change scores (posttest minus pretest) of the experimental and comparison groups.

Self-report data indicated that the responsibility-induced group reported greater increases in happiness and activity after the experimental treatment than the comparison subjects. The interviewer's ratings of alertness also showed significantly greater increases for the experimental group. Nurses' ratings yielded significant differences between groups in change scores of general improvement and time spent visiting patients, visiting others, talking to and watching staff, with responsibility-induced subjects faring better than the comparison subjects in all measures. The behavioral measures showed a pattern of differences between groups consistent with the predicted effects of the experimental manipulation. Movie attendance and contest participation were significantly higher in the responsibility-induced group than in the comparison group after the experimental lecture.

Rodin and Langer (1977) returned to the nursing home 18 months later in order to compare health indices for subjects. The follow-up population consisted of 20 responsibility-induced, 14 comparison subjects, and 9 controls who had not participated in the initial study. Dependent measures included nurses' ratings of mood, awareness, sociability, mental attitude and physical activity, physician ratings of overall health, mortality statistics, and lecture attendance. Nurses judged patients in the responsibility-induced group to be significantly more actively interested in their environment, more sociable and self-initiating, and more vigorous than patients in the comparison and control groups. Health rating change scores between preintervention (1974) and follow-up (1976) were compared. The responsibility-induced group showed a significantly greater increase in general health than either the comparison and control subjects. There were no reliable differences in lecture attendance between groups.

Interesting mortality statistics emerged. Rodin and Langer selected the 18 months prior to the original intervention as an arbitrary comparison period for mortality. During that time the mortality rate for the entire nursing home was 25%. In the subsequent postintervention 18-month period, 15% of the responsibility-induced as compared with 30% of the comparison group had died, a significant difference. Rodin and Langer suggested that increasing choice and self-control in a nursing home may slow or even reverse the decline typically witnessed in these settings. Increasing the perception of effectiveness in the institutionalized appears to be conducive to robustness and better living. It should be noted, however, that the results obtained by Rodin and Langer have not been universally replicated. This may be owing to the presence of other variables exerting mediational effects or simply the inability of other researchers to truly replicate the conditions established by the original researchers.

CONTROL AND PSYCHOTHERAPY

In reviewing theoretical schools of psychotherapy, one finds that the control issue transcends treatment paradigms and theoretical orientations. For example, the analytic and behavioral treatment of phobias involves the phobic's testing himself or herself in the dreaded situation at the impetus of the therapists. The patient or client, trusting the therapist's recommendations and authority, transforms from a passive into an active agent and hopefully experiences success that generalizes to mastery of other problems. The personal metamorphosis in both situations demands the evolution of control from an unbalanced egodystonic perception to a balanced egosyntonic perception in the individual.

Strupp (1970) integrated control across models of psychotherapy. According to Strupp, the basic goal of all psychotherapies is to help the patient achieve greater control or mastery. Paradoxically, the patient must first subordinate himself or herself to someone else's control in a trusting interpersonal relationship before he or she can acquire self-control, mastery, competence, or autonomy. This self-abdication is exemplified most extremely in the transference situation developed in psychoanalysis. The patient must trust the therapist who in turn judiciously capitalizes upon his or her ascendency to spur the patient's development. Before becoming his or her own agent, the patient must submit to the control and judgment of another.

The acquisition of control in psychotherapy is a process. It is therefore wise to meter control throughout the course of therapy and not selectively at termination. Peterson and Seligman (1984) blindly rated the transcripts of individual psychotherapy sessions for causal explanations for bad events of four persons suffering depression following loss. Transcripts were available from the beginning, middle, and end of treatment. For each patient, causal explanations shifted from the most internal, stable, and global in the beginning session to the least internal, stable, and global in the final session. Examination of explanatory style indicated that depression as a symptom of helplessness was alleviated as subjects concurrently regained control by reinterpreting problems as transient, situation-specific, and manageable.

Bandura's control-relevant term is efficacy. Management of phobias, germane to applications of social learning theory, is described comprehensively in terms of incremental and process mastery in the phobia study previously discussed (Bandura *et al.*, 1985). Personal expectations of efficacy determine whether coping behavior will be initiated and maintained. Reduction in defensive behavior and a self-efficacy crescendo motivating approach behavior are derived from four principal sources of information—performance accomplishments, vicarious experience, verbal persuasion, and physiological states. Through enactive modeling, 11 spider phobics quickly were able to perform coping tasks, previously judged as either weak, medium, or strong threats, in the absence of autonomic hyperreactivity symptomatic of the stress response. In the social learning model, resolution of phobic behavior clearly demands the augmentation of the perception of control.

Foon (1985) conducted an interesting study concerning the possible influence of therapist and client locus of control on the therapeutic process and outcome. The previous studies described control as the instrument effecting change. Foon, in contrast, studied control as a factor behind the scenes affecting the actual therapeutic process. Here, control is not considered an agent of psychotherapy but an attribute variable mediating the process. Perhaps the two ultimately cannot be distinguished.

Nonetheless, researchers attempted to match clients' locus of control and success with certain types of therapy. Inconsistent interaction has been reported. Foon alternately matched therapists' and clients' locus of control and investigated the influence of such a match on therapeutic expectation and outcome. Foon reasoned that a congruent match might lead to successful outcome because client and therapist perceptions of response–outcome contingencies could be related to their actual behavior in therapy.

The sample consisted of 21 therapists and 78 clients presenting with mild or moderate neurotic symptomatology. Therapists initially were assessed for locus of control (via Rotter's scale), social class, and expectations of therapy in terms of effectiveness, satisfaction, and reward. At the termination of therapy, therapists completed a questionnaire evaluating outcome for each client. Client measures at the outset included locus of control, social class, and a self-report of anticipation of another therapy session and expected gain from therapy. At the completion of therapy, clients were asked to comment on their perceived degree of change and benefit from and satisfaction as a result of therapy. In addition, clients repeated the locus of control scale.

Intercorrelations between therapists' and clients' characteristics revealed that therapists had more favorable expectations of internal clients than of externals and clients had more positive expectations of therapy with internal than external therapists. Therapy outcome intercorrelations using repeat client locus of control measures revealed that therapists evaluated internal clients more positively than externals and internal clients rated therapy more favorably than did externals. Initial similarity in locus of control between client and therapists significantly influènced clinical expectations, and posttest locus of control similarity influenced evaluations of therapy outcome. Foon did not find that an initial match on locus of control produced favorable therapy evaluations. This latter result is intuitively sensible because we would expect a dimensional transition in client locus of control from external to internal to accompany successful therapy. Foon noted that contemporaneous matching of locus of control appears to be significant at certain stages of therapy and thus can serve as an important predictor of positive outcome.

The influence of control in psychotherapy at best and most humbly can be described as complex. Much of the literature reviews the systematic effects of the manipulation of control, an active and not an attribute variable. Future research should address the relationship between control as a more subtle attribute variable and the process of psychotherapy.

Before closing this chapter on the discussion of control and human health, two other psychotherapeutic issues come to mind.

According to Jerome Frank (1974), it may well be that all psychotherapeutic technologies, despite their seeming differences, derive their therapeutic effectiveness from a common ability to render an "antidemoralization effect." Through generic factors such as general information, predictability, objective successes, and emotional control, obtained through the process of psychotherapy, patients are given a means of combating demoralization that, according to Frank, serves as the foundation of the majority of psychopathological conditions. To Frank, the common therapeutic denominator in psychotherapy is antidemoralization, yet as operationalized by Frank, his antidemoralization effect sounds remarkably similar to the construct of control as described in the present chapter. Could Frank's antidemoralization effect actually be a form of greater perceived self-efficacy and control?

Last, this section has focused upon psychotherapeutic technologies and the issue of control. Yet, earlier in this volume it was mentioned that technologies such as biofeedback and other self-regulatory therapies were well known to impart a greater sense of self-efficacy and internal locus of control (Green & Green, 1977, 1983; Murphy & Donovan, 1984; Romano, 1982). Could the primary therapeutic effect emerging from biofeedback and related therapies actually be an improved sense of control and the unique ability to measure one's acquisition of self-efficacy?

SUMMARY

The majority of research reviewed in this chapter cogently argues the ubiquity of control as a mediating "filter" in psychosomatic processes.

Research into the realm of control's impingement upon psychosomatic activity is no longer based upon remote inferential deduction. Neuroendocrine and immunological assays combine with psychological and behavioral indices to paint a clearer picture regarding the phenomenology of such mechanisms. Indeed, the variable of control may be so intertwined in our perception of the world as to render its complete description ineffable. Nevertheless, this chapter has presented research that clearly argues that the variable of control as defined earlier is an important factor in the determination of psychosomatic realities. Let us review several of the main points:

1. Control has been operationalized as the ability to change an environmental transaction, the perceived ability to do so, the ability to predict environmental transactions, the ability to understand those transactions, and/or the ability to accept such transactions within some meaningful cognitive framework or belief system.

2. Seligman, Langer, and Bandura offer variant yet overlapping theories of control. Convergence is seen in their acceptance of control as a powerful mediator in stimulus-response paradigms.

3. Engel (1968) noted a "giving up-given up" complex in the onset of illness.

4. Illnesses such as multiple sclerosis, ulcerative colitis, and general illness patterns have been shown to be related to issues of control.

5. Visintainer et al. (1982) and Laudenslager et al. (1983) demonstrated a relationship between controllability and immune function.

6. Bandura and his colleagues (1985) demonstrated that the *perception* of control was an important aspect of the control variable.

7. Control has been demonstrated to play an important role in the recovery process from illness by Krantz (1980), Cromwell et al. (1977), Cohen and Lazarus (1973), and Langer et al. (1975).

8. Research by Langer, Rodin, and others have yielded results that support the conclusion that the perception of control may play an important role in the inhibition of the functional aging process.

9. Finally, the issue of control pervades even the process of psychotherapy. Such is the conclusion that one might reach reviewing the research and theoretical offerings of Strupp (1970) and Frank (1974). Could the latent therapeutic mechanism of action in all psychotherapies actually be rendering to the patient some aspect of enhanced control or improved self-efficacy? With this thought in mind, it seems the next reasonable step to investigate is the domain of psychotherapy as it pertains to the treatment of the human stress response. That is the task to be undertaken in the next chapter.

CHAPTER 8

Psychotherapy
A Cognitive Perspective

I'm an old man and have known a great many troubles, but most of them never happened.

—Mark Twain

Like beauty, a stressor resides in the eye of the beholder. It should be clear by now that the patient's cognitive interpretation of the environment leads to the formation of a psychosocial stressor from an otherwise neutral stimulus. This concept has given birth to more eloquent phrasing such as, "There are no things good or bad, but thinking makes them so" (Shakespeare); "It is not what happens to you that matters, but how you take it" (Hans Selye); "Men are disturbed not by things, but by the views which they take of them" (Epictetus); "No one can make you feel inferior without your consent" (Eleanor Roosevelt).

If one accepts the concept that the primary determinant of any given psychosocial stressor is the cognitive interpretation or appraisal of that stimulus (as argued in Chapter 2), then it seems reasonable to assume that a therapy useful in treating stress-related disorders might be a psychotherapeutic effort directed toward the cognitive interpretational domain. Although clearly not the only psychotherapeutic technology of value in treating excessive stress, psychotherapy directed with cognitive restructuring or reinterpretation as a goal seems particularly applicable to the treatment of pathogenic stress-response syndromes. The purpose of this chapter, therefore, is to review several cognitively based psychotherapeutic approaches that can be employed in the treatment of excessive stress arousal. This chapter will also serve as a forum to integrate the first stress-management technique listed in the therapeutic model ("environmental engineering") described in the introduction.

It is not the goal of this chapter to provide a "how to" manual for cognitively based therapies. Excellent practitioner-oriented guides are available elsewhere (see Beck & Emory, 1984; Meichenbaum, 1985; Meichenbaum & Jaremko, 1983). Rather, it is hoped that this chapter will sensitize the reader to the critical role that cognition plays in the initiation and prolongation of human stress and to the important role that cognitively based therapies can play in the treatment of stress-related problems.

COGNITIVE PRIMACY

That cognitive primacy postulation is the perspective accepted within this volume became apparent in Chapter 2, where it was noted that the patient's interpretation of the environment was the primary determinant in the elicitation of the stress response reactive to a psychosocial stressor. A similar yet more extensive view is nicely summarized by Roseman (1984), who states, "A cognitive approach to the causation of emotion assumes that it is the interpretation of events rather than events per se that determine which emotion will be felt" (p. 14).

Magda Arnold (1960) was the most explicit of the early theorists in support of a cognitive primacy. She concluded that emotions are caused by the "appraisal" of the stimuli that one encounters. Given the perception of some environmental stimulus, subsequent emotions are a function, not of the stimulus *per se* but of the cognitive interpretation (appraisal) of that stimulus.

Lazarus (1966, 1982) and his colleagues extended Arnold's work to recognize the role of initial appraisal of a given environmental stimulus, but added the notion of reappraisal, which entails the cognitive interpretation of one's perceived ability to handle, cope with, or benefit from exposure to the stimulus. As Coyne and Holroyd (1982) describe this transactional model,

> The Lazarus group applies the concept of appraisal to the person's continually reevaluated judgments about demands and constraints in transactions with the environment and options and resources for meeting them. A key assumption of the model is that these evaluations determine the person's stress reaction, the emotions experienced, and adaptational outcomes. (p. 108)

Thus the Lazarus group emphasizes first a primary appraisal ("Is this situation a threat, challenge, or aversion?") and then a secondary appraisal ("Can I cope or benefit from it?") in the origin of human adult emotions.

This basic position of the primacy of cognition in the cognitive-affective relationship is held by numerous theorists and researchers alike (Arnold, 1960, 1984; Averill, 1983; Cassel, 1974; Ellis, 1962; Lazarus, 1966, 1982; Mandler, 1975; Meichenbaum, 1977; Roseman, 1984; Selye, 1976; Taylor, 1983).

To reiterate, the cognitive primacy perspective argues "that cognitive activity is a 'necessary' as well as sufficient condition of emotion" (Lazarus, 1982, p. 1019). More specifically, cognitive activity refers to "cognitive appraisal," the role of which is to mediate the relationships between people and their environments (Lazarus, 1982). Furthermore, Lazarus (1982) adds, "The appraisal process gives rise to a particular emotion with greater or lesser intensity depending on how the relationship is evaluated with respect to the person's well-being. Cognitive appraisal means that the way one interprets one's plight at any given moment is crucial to emotional response" (p. 1012). This cognitive perspective is summarized well by Ray, Lindop, and Gibson (1982), who states that "it is the way in which a situation is perceived from the perspective of the individual's own history, values and expectations which is of central theoretical importance, rather than the set of characteristics ascribed to the situation on a consensual or normative basis" (pp. 387–388). Thus, cognitive theorists argue that conceptual clarity in the understanding of adult human emotions can be gained only through an analysis of interpretational responses.

Although the majority of the most prolific stress researchers support cognitive primacy, not all writers agree. Perhaps the most vehement defender of the position that affect need not follow cognition is Zajonc.

In a 1980 paper, Zajonc argued that an affective reaction can occur without cognitive participation under certain circumstances. Zajonc cites examples of extreme heat leading to affective expressions. As noted earlier, however, cognitive theorists feel that such stimuli trigger reflex responses that are not to be considered emotional until full integration occurs, which then leads to emotional expression.

In a chapter entitled "Independence and Interaction of Affect and Cognition," Zajonc et al. (1982) examine the question of whether affect and cognition are independent in order to promote an understanding of how they interact. Zajonc holds that the separation between affect and cognition has heuristic value and is primarily a theoretical distinction. If one assumes that cognitive appraisal is always a necessary precondition of emotion, then there would be no research on the matter. Zajonc would like to leave the question of cognitive appraisal open so that empirical studies can be done.

In a more cogent paper, Zajonc (1984, pp. 119–120) enumerated specific reasons for the independence of affect. They were as follows:

1. Affective reactions show phylogenetic and ontogenetic primacy.
2. Separate neuroanatomical structures can be identified for affect and cognition.
3. Appraisal and affect are often uncorrelated and disjoint.
4. New affective reactions can be established without an apparent participation of appraisal.
5. Affective states can be induced by noncognitive and nonperceptual procedures.

In a rebuttal, Lazarus (1984) effectively counters each of Zajonc's five points. He notes, for example, that not all developmental specialists hold with the view of the phylogenetic and ontogenetic primacy (Cicchette & Hesse, 1983). Furthermore, he notes that many functions that once held ontogenetic primacy (e.g., sucking) seem to recede into extinction or chronic latency as higher (e.g., neocortical) processes develop. Because anatomical separation in no way proves lack of a hierarchical transactional system, the notion of neuroanatomical separateness as a defense for the independence of affect seems rather weak. Such a hierarchy has been argued by Tucker (1981) in his review of lateral brain functions. Lazarus further argues that Zajonc's notion that affect and appraisal are often uncorrelated and disjoint is simply not supported by adequate research. In fact research indicates otherwise (Beck & Emery, 1984; Lazarus & Alfert, 1964). Lazarus goes on to suggest that a lack of "apparent" cognitive participation fails to demonstrate a "lack" of such participation or even a lack of primacy.

Zajonc's notion that affective states can be induced by noncognitive procedures reminds one of the Schachter and Singer (1962) experiments. Although these experiments were interesting and ingenious in their conception, when scrutinized they reveal little applicability to the dynamic transactional nature of normal human functioning and are functionally irrelevant to the present discussion (Reinsenzein, 1983). In other words, Cartesian, mechanistic, and reductionistic analyses such as those cited by Zajonc distort the normal process of human functioning. Systems theorists point to such analyses and condemn them for their tendencies to deny the existence of functional interrelationships and, thus, lead researchers to spuriously disparate conceptualizations of the phenomena under examination (Myer & Brady, 1979; von Bertalanffy, 1968).

In sum, after a review of several major contributions to the literature on the relationships between cognition and affect, it becomes clear that the cognitive primacy notion holds a dominant position. Although this debate may never be resolved to the satisfaction of all, it is important to note that the final test of a theory is the resultant development of a technology (Byrne, 1977). Health professionals should be aware that numerous psychotherapeutic technologies seem to be emerging from the theories of a cognitive imperative (see Beck, 1976; Ellis, 1962; and Meichenbaum, 1977). Let us review several of those cognitive-based psychotherapeutic technologies within the next section.

COGNITIVE-BASED PSYCHOTHERAPY

According to Bandura (1982), the primary factor in the determination of a stressful event is the individual's *perceived* inefficiency in coping with or controlling a potentially aversive event. Several models of cognitively based psychotherapeutic interventions may be employed to alter the patient's perception (cognitive interpretation) of an environmental transaction that might be seen as potentially aversive.

Ellis's Model

Ellis (1971, 1973) has proposed that individuals often acquire irrational or illogical cognitive interpretations (beliefs) about environmental transactions, or even about themselves. The degree to which these beliefs are irrational and important corresponds to the degree of emotional upset and subsequent distress experienced by the individual. Ellis summarizes his A-B-C theory of emotional disturbance in the following model:

$$A \longrightarrow B \longrightarrow C$$

| Activating | Belief | Emotional |
| experience | | consequence |

In Condition A, some environmental transaction involving the patient takes place (i.e., he or she is late for an appointment). In Condition B, the patient generates some "irrational" or otherwise inappropriate belief about himself or herself because of the original experience (e.g., "I'm stupid, worthless, incompetent for being late"). Condition C represents the emotional consequence (e.g., shame, guilt, depression) that results, not from the experience (A), but directly from the irrational belief (B). Ellis then employs his rational-emotive psychotherapeutic model, which consists of adding a "D" to the A-B-C paradigm representing a conscious effort to "dispute" the irrational cognitive belief that resulted in the emotional distress. As Ellis has noted, "It is not the event, but rather it is our interpretation of it that causes our emotional reaction." Therefore, it seems only reasonable to focus psychotherapeutic efforts toward the goal of altering the interpretation. Ellis has delineated a series of questions to assist in the disputation of irrational beliefs (see Table 8.1).

Table 8.1. Disputing Irrational Beliefs

1. What irrational belief needs to be disputed?
2. Can this belief be rationally supported?
3. What evidence exists for the falseness of this belief?
4. Does any evidence exist for the truth of this belief?
5. What worst things could *actually* happen to me if my initial experience (activating experience) does not end favorably?
6. What good things could I make happen even if my initial experience does not end favorably?

Beck's Cognitive Therapy Model

The cognitive therapy process according to Beck (1976) consists largely of helping patients use objective, reality-based data in their constructions and interpretations of environmental transactions, rather than using biases, misconceptions, or meager databases with which to construct their idiosyncratic realities. Beck and Emory (1985) describe in elaborate detail how cognitive restructuring principles can be used in the treatment of anxiety and stress-related disorders. We shall review a few of the basic tenets at this point.

According to Beck and Emory (1985), three basic strategies make up cognitive restructuring. They state, "Anxious patients in the simplest terms believe, 'Something bad is going to happen that I won't be able to handle.' The cognitive therapist uses three basic strategies or questions to help the patient restructure this thinking" (p. 200):

1. What is the evidence supporting the conclusion currently held by the patient?
2. What is another way of looking at the same situation but reaching some other conclusion?
3. What will happen if, indeed, the currently held conclusion/opinion is correct?

Let us take a closer look at each of these three strategic questions, keeping in mind that because of factors such as individual differences, patients will respond differentially to each of the three question techniques enumerated above. The therapist should be prepared to employ all three strategies throughout therapy.

1. *What is the evidence?* One goal of this strategy is to analyze the patient's cognitive patterns and search for "faulty logic." Therapists may help patients in correcting faulty logic and ideas through questioning techniques, which also model a cognitive style that the patient may later adopt. Typical questions might include (from Beck & Emery, 1985):

• What is the evidence supporting this conclusion?
• What is the evidence against this conclusion?
• Are you oversimplifying causal relationships?
• Are you confusing habits or commonly held opinions with fact?
• Are your interpretations too far removed from your actual experiences?
• Are you thinking in "all-or-nothing" terms (i.e., black/white, either/or, on/off, all-or-nothing types of decisions and outcome)?
• Are your conclusions in any way extreme or exaggerated?
• Are you taking selected examples out of context and basing your conclusion on such information?

- Is the source of your information reliable?
- Is your thinking in terms of certainties rather than probabilities?
- Are you confusing a low-probability event with a high-probability event?
- Are you basing your conclusions on feelings or values rather than facts?
- Are you focusing on irrelevant factors in forming your conclusion?

Through the use of such questions, patterns of faulty reasoning may be discovered and corrected.

2. *What is another way of looking at it?* The goal of this strategy is to help the patient generate alternative interpretations in lieu of the interpretation currently held. Such alternative interpretations can include reattribution, diminishing the significance of the environmental transaction, or even restructuring the transaction to find the positive side of the event.

3. *So what if it happens?* The goal of this strategy is to help the patient "decatastrophize" the environmental transaction as well as develop coping strategies and problem-solving skills. It will be recalled from the multidimensional treatment model that "environmental engineering" (Girdano & Everly, 1986) and "problem solving" are merely terms that describe the therapeutic processes of this third strategic phase of therapy as described by Beck and Emery (1985). These authors suggest that "therapist and patient collaboratively develop a variety of strategies that the person can use" (p. 208). Ultimately, the goal of therapy is to allow the patient to develop autonomous skills in each of the three strategic areas mentioned above. The notions of "environmental engineering" and "problem solving" will be more formally integrated in the next model, Meichenbaum's stress inoculation training model.

Meichenbaum's Stress Inoculation Training

Using the principles contained in his classic text, *Cognitive Behavior Modification* (Meichenbaum, 1977), Meichenbaum developed a specialized cognitively based therapy for the treatment of excessive stress. Meichenbaum's therapeutic formulation is called "stress inoculation training" (SIT).

According to Meichenbaum (1985):

> SIT is not a single technique. It is a generic term referring to a treatment paradigm consisting of a semistructured, clinically sensitive training regimen. The specific training operations . . . vary, depending upon the population treated. SIT combines elements of didactic teaching, Socratic discussion, cognitive restructuring, problem-solving and relaxation training, behavioral and imaginal rehearsal, self-monitoring, self-instruction and self-reinforcement, and efforts at environmental change. (p. 21)

The SIT paradigm consists of three phases. The first includes the development of a conceptual framework for understanding how the patient responds to stressors. The primary activities are data collection and patient education. In the second phase, coping and problem-solving skills are taught and rehearsed. Table 8.2 provides examples of self-statements that may be used as coping techniques. Skill acquisition in this phase is not limited to self-statements, however. Assertion training, communications

Table 8.2. Examples of Coping Self-Statements Rehearsed in Stress-Inoculation Training

Preparing for a stressor
>   What is it you have to do?
>   You can develop a plan to deal with it.
>   Just think about what you can do about it. That's better than getting anxious.
>   No negative self-statements: Just think rationally.
>   Don't worry: Worry won't help anything.
>   Maybe what you think is anxiety is eagerness to confront the stressor.

Confronting and handling a stressor
>   Just "psych" yourself up—you can meet this challenge.
>   You can convince yourself to do it. You can reason your fear away.
>   One step at a time: You can handle the situation.
>   Don't think about fear; just think about what you have to do. Stay relevant.
>   This anxiety is what the doctor said you would feel. It's a reminder to use your coping exercises.
>   This tenseness can be an ally; a cue to cope.
>   Relax; you're in control. Take a slow deep breath.
>   Ah, good.

Coping with the feeling of being overwhelmed
>   When fear comes, just pause.
>   Keep the focus on the present; what is it you have to do?
>   Label your fear from 0 to 10 and watch it change.
>   You should expect your fear to rise.
>   Don't try to eliminate fear totally; just keep it manageable.

Reinforcing self-statements
>   It worked; you did it.
>   Wait until you tell your therapist (or group) about this.
>   It wasn't as bad as you expected.
>   You made more out of your fear than it was worth.
>   Your damn ideas—that's the problem. When you control them, you control your fear.
>   It's getting better each time you use the procedures.
>   You can be pleased with progress you're making.
>   You did it!

From D. Meichenbaum (1977). *Cognitive-Behavior Modification*. Copyright by Plenum Press. Reprinted by permission.

skills, relaxation training, and other skills may be taught at this point. In the third phase, the skills acquired in the preceding phase are used in situations containing actual stressors. This phase also contains a follow-up component.

These three phases of SIT are enumerated in greater detail in Table 8.3. (A valuable guide for practitioners on the use of SIT is also available; see Meichenbaum, 1985.)

Meichenbaum's SIT training is of special interest in this volume because it manifests the belief that stress management is most effective when it is flexible and multidimensional. Similarly, SIT allows us to integrate the concept of "environmental engineering" as delineated in the treatment model described in the introduction of Part II. The term *environmental engineering*, it will be recalled, is borrowed from the work of Girdano and Everly (1986) as it was first described in 1979. The term refers to any conscious attempts at manipulating environmental factors to reduce one's exposure to stressor events. Both proactive, environmental change as well as reactive problem solving must be included under this heading. The reader will observe that within the model there are different points wherein problem solving, or any other form of environmental engineering, is obviously applicable.

As implied earlier, one of the real strengths of SIT is its inherent flexibility, structured as it is around a cognitive foundation. SIT has been demonstrated to be of value in the control of anger, test anxiety, phobias, pain, surgical preparation, essential hypertension, and general arousal-related syndromes of dysfunction (see Meichenbaum, 1985).

SUMMARY

Within this chapter, we have reviewed the first of the specific therapeutic interventions to be discussed in this volume for the treatment of pathogenic human stress. Previous chapters within this section have discussed issues of personality styles and personologic idiosyncrasies as they might relate to the cause and treatment of the stress response as well as the issue of "control" as it pervades all personality styles and looms as a major mediating factor in the etiology and treatment of excessive human stress.

This chapter has focused on the role that psychotherapy can play in treating excessive stress. More specifically (reflecting the biases of the epiphenomenological model of human stress constructed in Chapter 2), this chapter has chosen to review cognitive-based psychotherapeutic interventions. Let us review the main points contained within the chapter:

1. Referring back to Figure 2.6, this chapter recognizes the superordinate role that cognition plays in the creation of a psychosocially induced stress response.

Table 8.3. Flowchart of Stress-Inoculation Training

Phase One: Conceptualization
(a) Data collection–integration
   • Identify determinants of problem via interview, image-based reconstruction, self-monitoring, and behavioral observance.
   • Distinguish between performance failure and skill deficit.
   • Formulate treatment plan—task analysis.
   • Introduce integrative conceptual model.
(b) Assessment skills training
   • Train clients to analyze problems independently (e.g., to conduct situational analyses and to seek disconfirmatory data)
Phase Two: Skills Acquisition and Rehearsal
(a) Skills training
   • Training instrumental coping skills (e.g., communication, assertion, problem solving, parenting, study skills).
   • Train palliative coping skills as indicated (e.g., perspective-taking, attention diversion, use of social supports, adaptive affect expression, relaxation).
   • Aim to develop an extensive repertoire of coping responses to faciliate flexible responding.
(b) Skills Rehearsal
   • Promote smooth integration and execution of coping responses via imagery and role play.
   • Self-instructional training to develop mediators to regulate coping responses.
Phase Three: Application and Follow-Through
(a) Induce application of skills
   • Prepare for application using coping imagery, using early stress cues as signals to cope.
   • Role play (a) anticipated stressful situations and (b) client coaching someone with a similar problem.
   • "Role play" attitude may be adopted in real world.
   • Exposure to in-session graded stressors.
   • Use of graded exposure and other response induction aids to foster *in vivo* responding and build self-efficacy.
(b) Maintenance and generalization
   • Build sense of coping self-efficacy in relation to situations client sees as high risk.
   • Develop strategies for recovering from failure and relapse.
   • Arrange follow-up review.
General Guidelines for Training
   • Attend to referral and intake process.
   • Consider training peers of clients to conduct treatment. Develop collaborative relationship and project approachability.
   • Establish realistic expectations regarding course and outcome of therapy.
   • Foster optimism and confidence by structuring incremental success experiences.
   • Respond to stalled progress with problem solving versus labeling client resistant.
   • Include family members in treatment when this is indicated.

From "Stress Inoculation Training: Toward a Paradigm for Training Coping Skills" by D. Meichenbaum and R. Cameron in *Stress Reduction and Prevention* (p. 121) edited by D. Meichenbaum and M. E. Jaremko. Copyright 1983 by Plenum Press. Reprinted by permission.

2. The issue of "cognitive primacy" (the notion that affect is subsequent to cognition) is reviewed, and the Lazarus–Zajonc exchange is highlighted. The conclusion is that cognition is clearly the superordinate factor in the determination of a psychosocial stressor.

3. The rational-emotive therapy of Ellis (1971, 1973) is introduced as one cognitive-based psychotherapy that can serve to alter dysfunctional cognitions. Its core assumption is that individuals who suffer excessive stress may have a propensity, albeit pathogenic, to accept irrational or otherwise inappropriate beliefs about important environmental transactions. This propensity can be corrected by teaching the patient to "dispute" his or her irrational beliefs as they give rise to excessive stress arousal.

4. Beck's cognitive therapy is reviewed as a broader spectrum cognitive intervention that not only focuses on inappropriate cognitive patterns but assists the patient in developing other coping and problem-solving activities, as well. Three basic therapeutic strategies are employed to assist in cognitive restructuring: (1) analyzing the nature of any evidence that affected the individual's cognitive interpretation, (2) generating alternative interpretations via cognitive reattribution and searching for positive aspects inherent in the environmental transaction ("the silver lining"), (3) developing environmental engineering, adaptive coping strategies, and useful problem-solving techniques.

5. The broadest spectrum cognitive-based stress-management intervention extends well beyond just psychotherapy and is referred to as "stress inoculation training." The paradigm was developed by Meichenbaum (1977, 1985). The intervention consists of three basic stages: (1) education, (2) skill acquisition, and (3) application to a real-world setting. The multiple components of this approach are delineated in Table 8.2.

6. Cognitive-based interventions have proved useful in the treatment of a wide variety of problems, including anger, pain, phobias, anxiety, general stress reactions, headaches, and even victimization (see Meichenbaum, 1985, Table 3.1).

A Neurophysiological Rationale for the Use of the Relaxation Response

Since the original applications of behavioral technologies to the treatment of disease, it has been observed that the elicitation of what Benson (1975) has called the "relaxation response" has proved useful in the treatment of a wide variety of psychiatric and stress-related somatic disease (Benson, 1985; Kutz, Borysenko, & Benson, 1985; Lavey & Taylor, 1985; Shapiro & Giber, 1978). The relaxation response is perhaps best understood as a psychophysiological state of hypoarousal engendered by a multitude of diverse technologies (e.g., meditation, neuromuscular relaxation, hypnosis). Research into the relaxation response as a therapeutic mechanism and its clinical proliferation have been hampered, however, by a lack of conceptual clarity regarding its therapeutic foundations and/or its mechanisms of action. This chapter will explore the physiological and psychological foundations of the relaxation response to set the stage for discussions in subsequent chapters of specific therapeutic technologies (e.g., meditation, neuromuscular relaxation) used to elicit the relaxation response for the treatment of stress-related diseases.

Portions of this chapter were adopted from Everly, G. S., & Benson, H. (1988, September) *Disorders of arousal: A reformulation of the nature and treatment of stress-related disease.* Paper presented to the IVth International Conference on Psychophysiology, Prague, Czechoslovakia.

The specific aims of this chapter are (1) to explore the psycho-physiologic foundations of the relaxation response as a possible rationale for the use of the relaxation response as a primary therapy as well as an adjunctive therapy in the treatment of pathogenic stress arousal (while remaining aware of the fact that in some cases specific end-organ symptoms may initially require medical stabilization or amelioration); (2) to gain insight into the counterintuitive and antireductionistic observation that a single therapeutic mechanism (i.e., the relaxation response) can be of value in treating a wide and disparate variety of psychiatric and stress-related somatic disorders; and (3) to consider the relaxation response as a natural treatment for anxiety and excessive stress arousal—a treatment intrinsically antithetical to the very nature of pathogenic stress arousal.

In order to formulate such a view of the relaxation response as a therapeutic mechanism, it first becomes necessary to reformulate the common perspective on psychiatric and stress-related somatic disorders.

DISORDERS OF AROUSAL

Traditionally, science has classified diseases on the basis of their cause or their end-organ symptoms or signs. The American Psychiatric Association's *Diagnostic and Statistical Manual of Mental Disorders* (DSM-III-R, 1987) is replete with examples of both. Regarding classification by "cause," for example, adjustment disorders are "caused" by the inability to adjust to new situations; viral disorders are caused by viruses; and bacteriological disorders are caused by bacteria. Regarding classification by symptoms, on the other hand, mood disorders are characterized by affective symptom complexes, and anxiety disorders are characterized by anxious symptomatology. The posttraumatic stress disorder is classified by both its cause (trauma) *and* its symptoms (stress). Seldom in our nosological quests, however, do we bother to consider other, less obvious, taxonomic criteria, even though these "latent taxa" might be far more utilitarian. Such a taxonomic consideration is derived from the work of Meehl (1973).

Based on an integration of the work of Selye (1976), Gellhorn (1967), Gray (1982), and Post (Post & Ballenger, 1981), it has been proposed that various anxiety and stress-related diseases be viewed in light of a new taxonomic perspective (Everly, 1985b; Everly & Benson, 1989). Evidence indicates that numerous psychiatric and somatic stress-related diseases possess a latent yet common denominator that serves nosologically as a latent taxonomic criterion—"latent taxon" for short. It has been proposed that this latent taxon is pathognomonic arousal. Thus, such disorders may be referred to collectively as "disorders of arousal." Despite a wide variety of etiologic stimuli, and an even wider variety of symptom complexes, these disorders are best seen as but variations on a theme of a pathognomonic hypersensitivity for, or an overall characteristic of, arousal.

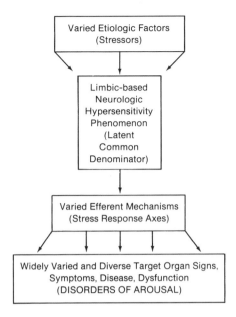

Figure 9.1. Limbic hypersensitivity phenomenon: The latent taxon in stress-related "disorders of arousal."

More specifically, the "disorders of arousal" concept is based on a corpus of evidence indicating that a major homogenizing phenomenological constituent of these disorders is a limbic-system-based neurologic hypersensitivity; that is, a lowered threshold for excitation and/or a pathognomonic status of excess arousal within the limbic circuitry or its neurological, neuroendocrine, and/or endocrine efferent limbs. This neurologic hypersensitivity is then capable of giving rise to a host of psychiatric and stress-related somatic disorders as noted in Chapters 3 and 4 (see Figure 9.1). These disorders are referred to collectively as "disorders of arousal."

PSYCHIATRIC DISORDERS OF AROUSAL

Over the years, clinical psychiatry anecdotes have well documented the notion that anxiety disorders and stress-related syndromes seem to be characterized by what appears to be an increased vulnerability to frustrating, challenging, or sympathomimetic stimuli. This phenomenon is best thought of as a hypersensitivity for stimulation; a sort of neurologic sensitization combined with a lowered activation threshold for emotional arousal. Such reports of sensitization or hyperreactivity are consistent with the well-documented activity and function of the limbic system and its major neurologic, neuroendocrine, and endocrine efferents (Cannon, 1929; Gray, 1982; MacLean, 1949; Nauta & Domesick, 1982).

In a seminal paper, Papez (1937) boldly discussed the rhinencephalon as the anatomical basis for emotional arousal. He considered the mammillary bodies, fornix, hippocampus, cingulate cortex, and anterior thalamic nuclei as key elements in a then-proposed mechanism of emotion. In a description of Papez's model, Isaacson (1982) notes:

> Neural activity representing the emotional processes originating in the cortex would be passed along into the hippocampus, the fornix, the mammillary bodies, and the anterior nuclei of the thalamus and would finally be projected onto the receptive region of the "emotional cortex" (i.e., the cingulate cortex). From the cingulate cortex, activity representing emotional processes could pass into other regions of the cerebral cortex and add emotional coloring to psychic processes occurring elsewhere. (p. 55)

The "Papez Circuit," as it came to be called, was modified as a contributor to human emotional arousal by MacLean (1949), who developed the notion of a "limbic system" (the term *limbic* is derived from limbus, which means border and refers to the fact that this system serves to undergird the cerebral neocortices). MacLean hypothesized that in addition to the basic circuitry of Papez, the amygdala, septum, and associated areas were best understood as a "system" of integrated anatomical structures that were implicated not only in emotional expression but in the aggregation of all sensory stimulation with affect, and that ultimately provide for emotional expression, or "discharge." Such discharge would have profound potential to affect not only mental health but physical health as well. According to MacLean,

> This region of the brain appears to be so strategically situated as to be able to correlate every form of internal and external perception. And . . . has many strong connections with the hypothalamus for discharging its impressions. (p. 351)

It should be noted that the hypothalamus and hippocampus are still thought to be the prime sites of integration for visceral efferent arousal discharge (Van Hoesen, 1982; Reiman *et al.*, 1986).

Finally, the work of Nauta (Nauta, 1979; Nauta & Domesick, 1982) further refined and clarified our understanding of the vital role that the limbic system plays in emotional arousal, the integration of internal and external stimulation, and the process of hypothalamically mediated "psychosomatic" processes. His work supports the conclusion that sensory input is integrated and processed via limbic structures such as the amygdala, the hippocampus, and cingulate gyrus and that such limbic structures have the potential for upward and downward efferent projections. Such projections are likely to exert influence over neocortical as well as hypothalamic, neuroendocrine, and endocrine processes.

It is important to note at this juncture that the limbic system receives efferent impulses from, as well as sending afferent impulses to, brain-stem structures—more specifically the reticular activating system and the locus ceruleus. The reticular activating system (RAS) may be thought of as a system of projections with responsibility for nonspecific arousal of the entire cerebrum. The locus ceruleus (LC) represents an aggregation of 20,000 to 30,000 cells responsible for 50% to 70% of the norepinephrine in the human brain (Redmond, 1979). Its activity is highly associated with worry, threat, and flight behavior. The reciprocal connections that the LC has with prefrontal and limbic structures suggests cognitive, affective, and LC activity are intimately interwoven (Gellhorn, 1967; Redmond, 1979) and collectively may play key etiologic roles in psychiatric and somatic disorders (Doane, 1986; Gellhorn & Loofbourrow, 1963; Gloor, 1986; Post, 1986; Post & Ballenger, 1981).

The American Psychiatric Association's own DSM–III and DSM–III, R have included references to criteria such as hyperalertness, hypersensitivity, and autonomic nervous system hyperactivity in the diagnosis of anxiety-related disorders. Considerable evidence that these symptoms arise from the limbic circuitry comes from benzodiazepine and other behavior pharmacological research (Carr & Sheehan, 1984; Gray, 1982) as well as neurotransmitter research (Mefferd 1979). Even major reviews of the etiology, diagnosis, and treatment of anxiety disorders implicate subcortically initiated arousal and reactivity as core features of anxiety disorders (Barlow & Beck, 1984; Carr & Sheehan, 1984; Gorman et al., 1985; Shader, 1984).

Anxiety disorders are not the only psychiatric disorders wherein arousal plays a significant role. Post and his co-workers (Post, 1985; Post & Ballenger, 1981; Post et al., 1982) have cogently argued that limbic hypersensitivity ("sensitisation") underlies various primary and secondary affective disorders. They conclude that "sensitisation models provide a conceptual approach to previously inexplicable clinical phenomena in the longitudinal course of affective illness" (p. 191). Neurologic sensitization is also believed to underlie various functional psychoses, personality disorders, posttraumatic reactions, addictive disorders, and withdrawal syndromes (Monroe, 1970, 1982; Post, 1985; Post & Ballenger, 1981; van der Kolk, Greenberg, Boyd, & Krystal, 1985). Similarly, Gellhorn and Loufburrow (1963) implicated propensities for excessive limbic excitation in a host of emotional disorders (see Table 9.1).

SOMATIC DISORDERS OF AROUSAL

The psychiatric domain is not the only arena within which pathogenic arousal may manifest itself. Many stress-related "medical" syndromes contain a core arousal constituent. Reviews by Lown et al. (1976) and Verrier and Lown (1984) concluded that ventricular fibrillation in the absence of coronary heart disease may be related to increased sympathetic tone or activity. Similarly, evidence indicates that increased sympathetic tone and sympathetic hyperreactivity may be key etiologic factors in the develop-

Table 9.1. Psychiatric Disorders Related to Arousal

1. Anxiety disorders (posttraumatic stress disorder, panic disorders, and diffuse generalized anxiety disorders)
2. Adjustment disorders (with anxious mood and with mixed emotional features)
3. Various primary and secondary affective disorders (especially fast cycling bipolar disorders and secondary reactive depression)
4. Addictive disorders (cocaine, amphetamine, nicotine)
5. Temporal lobe disorders
6. Acute atypical psychotic decompensation
7. Alcohol withdrawal ($X > 6$ years alcoholism)

ment of psychophysiologic essential hypertension (Eliot, 1979; Gellhorn, 1964a; Henry & Stephens, 1977; Steptoe, 1981; Suter, 1986). Other cardiovascular diseases implicated as having pathogenic arousal as a key etiologic factor include nonischemic myofibrillar degeneration (Corley, (1985; Eliot, 1979), coronary artery disease (Corley, 1985; Eliot, 1979; Henry & Stephens, 1977; Manuck & Krantz, 1984, for a more conservative interpretation), sudden death (Corley, 1985; Eliot, 1979; Steptoe, 1981), migraine headaches and Raynaud's disease (Suter, 1986). Gellhorn (1967), Weil (1974), and Malmo (1975) have implicated excessive sympathetic tone as a major etiologic factor in a host of muscle contraction syndromes and dysfunctions including muscle contraction headaches. Finally, there is some evidence that peptic ulcers (Wolf, 1985), irritable bowel syndrome (Latimer, 1985), and other gastrointestinal disorders may be related to an excessive propensity for arousal (Dotevall, 1985) (see Table 9.2).

In sum, pathognomonic hypersensitivity within the limbic circuitry as

Table 9.2. Somatic Disorders Related to Arousal

1. Hypertension
2. Stress-related ventricular fibrillation
3. Nonischemic myofibrillar degeneration
4. Stress-related coronary artery disease
5. Migraine headaches
6. Raynaud's disease
7. Muscle contraction headaches
8. Non-head-related muscle contraction dysfunctions
9. Peptic ulcer
10. Irritable bowel syndrome

a common denominator within a host of otherwise widely disparate disorders seems to warrant the proposed taxonomic reconsideration, that is, the disorders of arousal taxonomy. It may well be that research will ultimately show that disorders of arousal actually include all stress-related psychosomatic disorders.

THE NEUROLOGICAL FOUNDATIONS OF LIMBIC HYPERSENSITIVITY AND THE DISORDERS OF AROUSAL

Ergotropic Tuning

Within this chapter, it has been argued that a limbic-system-based neurologic hypersensitivity to stimulation and a propensity for sustained arousal undergirds a host of psychiatric and stress-related somatic disorders, herein called "disorders of arousal." The work of Gellhorn not only documented the existence of complex autonomic nervous system–neocortical–limbic–somatic integration (Gellhorn, 1957, 1967) but later served as one of the most coherent and cogent explanations of the pathognomonic arousal described in this chapter. Over two decades ago, Gellhorn described a hypothalamically based "ergotropic tuning" process as the neurophysiological basis for affective lability, autonomic nervous system hyperfunction, anxiety, stress arousal, and related emotional disorders (Gellhorn, 1965, 1967; Gellhorn & Loofbourrow, 1963). Gellhorn has stated:

> It is a matter of everyday experience that a person's reaction to a given situation depends very much upon his own mental, physical, and emotional state. One might be said to be "set" to respond in a given manner. In the same fashion the autonomic response to a given stimulus may at one time be predominantly sympathetic and may at another time be predominantly parasympathetic . . . The sensitization of autonomic centers has been designated "tuning" and we speak of sympathetic tuning and parasympathetic tuning . . . and refers merely to the sensitization" or "facilitation" of particular centers of the brain. (Gellhorn & Loofbourrow, 1963, pp. 90–91)

Gellhorn chose the term *ergotropic tuning* to describe a preferential pattern of sympathetic nervous system responsiveness. Such a neurologic status could then serve as the basis for a host of psychiatric and stress-related somatic disorders.

From an etiological perspective, Gellhorn (1965) states: "in the waking state the ergotropic division of the autonomic is dominant and responds primarily to environmental stimuli. If these stimuli are very strong or follow each other at short intervals, the tone and reactivity of the sympathetic system increases" (pp. 494–495). Thus, either extremely intense, acute (traumatic) sympathetic stimulation or chronically repeated, intermittent lower level sympathetic stimulation, both of which can be environmental in origin, can lead to sympathetic nervous system hyperfunction. Such sympathetic activity, according to Gellhorn, creates a condition of sympathetic neurological hypersensitivity, called ergotropic tuning, which serves as the neurological predisposition, or even etiological factor, associated with the psychophysiological sequelae observed in anxiety, stress, and related disorders of arousal.

Several mechanisms may sustain the ergotropically tuned status. Gellhorn (1964) has provided cogent documentation that discharge from limbic centers sends neural impulses in two simultaneous directions: (1) to neocortical targets and (2) to the skeletal musculature via pyramidal and extra pyramidal projections (see also Gellhorn & Loofbourrow, 1963). The neocortical centers then send impulses back to the limbic areas and to the locus ceruleus by way of noradrenergic and other pathways, thus sustaining limbic activity. Simultaneously, neuromuscular proprioceptive impulses (indicative of neuromuscular status) from afferent muscle spindle projections ascend primarily via the dorsal root and reticular activating system, ultimately projecting not only to cerebellar targets but to limbic and neocortical targets as well. Such proprioceptive bombardment further excites target areas and sets into motion a complex mechanism of positive neurological feedback, sustaining and potentially intensifying ergotropic tone (Gellhorn, 1964, 1965, 1967).

Thus, we see that Gellhorn has proposed a model and empirically demonstrated that intimate neocortical hypothalamic somatic relationships exist that use the limbic system as a central "hub" for efferent projections to the neocortex and somatic musculature as well as an afferent target for neocortical, proprioceptive, interoceptive, and brain-stem impulses. This configuration creates a functional, potentially self-sustaining mechanism of affective and ergotropic arousal. It certainly seems reasonable that such a mechanism could play a major role in chronic anxiety and stress-related disorders of arousal.

Neurologic Reverberation and Charging

Weil (1974) has developed a model somewhat similar to that of Gellhorn. In fact, Weil makes brief reference to the work of Gellhorn in his construction of a neurophysiological model of emotional behavior.

Weil notes, in agreement with Gellhorn, that the activation thresholds of the autonomic nervous system (particularly hypothalamic nuclei), as well as limbic centers, can be altered. Instead of the concepts of sympathetic and parasympathetic systems, Weil uses a parallel but broader construction, that of arousal and tranquilizing systems, respectively. He calls the facilitation of activation within these systems, "charging." With regard to the concept of neurological hypersensitivity, Weil notes that two major processes can be effective in "charging the arousal system" in the human organism: (1) high-intensity stimulation and/or (2) increased rate of repeated stimulation. The processes that appear to underlie the charging of the arousal system as well as the mechanisms that could serve to sustain such a neurological status seem to be (1) the neuromuscular proprioceptive system, as described earlier and (2) intrinsic neuronal reverberation. Regarding the latter, Weil (1974) notes:

> The reciprocal association of the hypothalamus with the midbrain and the thalamic reticular formation makes possible the establishment of intrinsic reverberating circuits. Such hypothalamic reticular circuits are in a position to be set into motion by extrinsic impulses reaching the reticular formation. They provide a neuroanatomical basis for the maintenance of a reverberating supply of impulses to reticular non-specific activation even during a momentary reduction or deficiency of extrinsic input. (p. 37)

Thus, we see that Weil's notion of charging is similar to Gellhorn's notion of tuning. Weil's formulation seems somewhat broader in the neurological mechanisms it encompasses, yet narrower in its implications for emotional and behavioral disorders. Points of agreement can be found, however, in the recognition of the fact that neurological hypersensitivity (i.e., a lowered threshold for activating limbic, autonomic, and hypothalamic effector systems) can be achieved through environmental stimulation and proprioceptive stimulation when presented in either an acute and intense (traumalike) manner or in a lower level yet chronically repeated exposure pattern. Once achieved, such a status of lowered activation threshold could serve as a self-sustaining neurological basis for emotional and psychophysiological dysfunction.

Neuromuscular Set-Point Theory

In reviewing Gellhorn's and Weil's notions of tuning and charging theory, respectively, and the neurological mechanisms that support them, one is impressed with the central role that the striate musculature plays in sensitizing and maintaining hypersensitivity (ergotropic status). The work of Malmo seems appropriate to introduce at this juncture, for it deals directly with the role of striate muscles in psychophysiological and anxiety disorders. In a brief but cogent treatise, Malmo (1975) summarizes his classic studies on the prolonged activation of the striate musculature of anxiety patients following stressor presentation, compared with nonanxiety patients exposed to the same stressor. The work of Gellhorn clearly demonstrated that the striate muscles were target organs for limbic arousal. Malmo and his colleagues found that select groups of individuals who processed arousal disorders, such as anxiety, seemed to demonstrate somewhat higher baseline levels of muscle tension when compared with nonpatients. More important, however, upon the presentation of a stressor stimulus, the muscle tension of the patient population reached higher levels of peak amplitude and subsequently took significantly longer to return to baseline levels once the stressor was removed. This phenomenon was interpreted by Malmo as being indicative of a defect in homeostatic mechanisms following arousal in such patients.

Malmo offered two possible mechanisms that might explain the observed homeostatic dysfunction: one neural, one biochemical. He cites the research of Jasper (1949), who discovered that direct stimulation of the motor cortex created not only the expected electromyographic activity in the target muscle but also an "after discharge" in that muscle. The after discharge may be thought of as a residual depolarization of the neurons in the absence of direct exogenous stimulation. However, when Jasper simultaneously stimulated the thalamic-reticular system, the after discharge was eliminated. These data suggest that the thalamic-reticular system may play a role in dampening, or inhibiting, excess neuromuscular activation. Malmo then extended Jasper's work to his own and used it as a model to explain the homeostatic dysfunction observed in his own studies. Malmo saw Jasper's discovery as the homeostatic mechanism that was most likely dysfunctional in anxiety patients (i.e., a mechanism protracting neuromuscular excitation in stressful situations). More specifically, he argues that this neural inhibitory system represents a "set point" similar to that of a thermostat. This neural set point may be designed to dampen excessive muscular activity, thus preventing excessive strain. He notes that in cases where muscles are extremely tense and corresponding proprioceptive activity is sufficiently strong (i.e., exceeding the tolerances of the set point), the inhibitory neurons would be activated, thus reducing lingering peripheral muscular aftercharge activity. He further notes:

> Such a system as this would work well in providing for extra muscular exertion to meet emergencies; and by the return of the set point to normal afterwards, the motor system would have a built-in protection against excessive strain. If, however, extremely demanding life situations are prolonged . . . it seems the set-point "sticks" at the higher (above normal) level even when the individual is removed to a quiet environment.
>
> This then would be a neural mechanism that could account for the "persistence" of anxiety and the accompanying increase in muscular activity. (Malmo, 1975, pp. 152–153)

Malmo places the most emphasis on this neural mechanism in explaining the homeostatic dysfunction seen in anxiety patients, yet he does briefly mention a biochemical–neurological process that has played a central role in the formulation of current thinking on arousal disorders. Malmo notes that muscle tension leads to increased levels of lactic acid (a byproduct of anerobic metabolism). Furthermore, he notes research by Pitts and McClure (1967) clearly demonstrating that lactate infusions had panicogenic properties for panic anxiety patients but had none for nonanxiety patients. It has been postulated that panic patients metabolize lactate normally, thus suggesting a neural receptor hypersensitivity existing somewhere in their central nervous system as the etiologic site for this dysfunction. The lactate infusion data are similar to those obtained by inhalation of 5% CO_2, thus demonstrating panicogenic properties for this agent as well. The specific mechanism by which these agents induce panic attacks is unclear at this time. Interested readers should refer to Carr and Sheehan (1984), Gorman et al. (1985), and Liebowitz et al. (1985). The major point of clinical interest, however, is that Gellhorn and Weil, as well as Malmo, have shown mechanisms by which anxiety and stress may lead to chronically contracted muscles and that these muscles (while under chronic anerobic contraction) may produce a byproduct (lactic acid) that may have anxiogenic properties of a biochemical nature in addition to the anxiogenic properties of excessive proprioceptive bombardment of the brain stem, limbic system, and neocortex. Thus, there appears to be remarkable agreement from researchers in diverse fields as to the probability that neurologic hypersensitivity underlies anxiety and stress-related disorders of a chronic nature.

Models of Neuronal Plasticity

In an attempt to understand the phenomenon of neurological hypersensitivity at the most basic structural levels, this section will briefly review popular models of neuronal plasticity.

The concept of *kindling* represents one of the most popular models of plasticity and neurological hypersensitivity in clinical literature. *Kindling* is a term originally conceived of to identify the process by which repeated stimulation of limbic structures leads to a lowered convulsive threshold (limbic ictus) and to a propensity for spontaneous activation of such structures, with resultant affective lability, autonomic nervous system hyperfunction, and behavioral disturbances (Goddard, McIntyre, & Leech, 1969; Joy, 1985; Post, 1985; Post, Uhde, Putnam, Ballenger, & Berrettini, 1982). Kindling-like processes have been implicated in a host of behavioral and psychopathological conditions (Post & Ballenger, 1981; Monroe, 1970, 1982).

Shader (1984) has stated, "with regard to anxiety disorders, one might speculate that kindling processes . . . could increase attack-like firing from a source such as the locus ceruleus" (p. 14). Redmond and Huang (1979) support such a conclusion by suggesting that panic disorders are predicated on a lowered firing threshold at the locus ceruleus. Such discharge could then arouse limbic and cortical structures on the basis of ventral and dorsal adrenergic efferent projections arising from the locus ceruleus. Monroe (1982) has provided evidence that certain episodic behavioral disorders may be based on a kindling-like limbic ictus. He notes, "as it is known that environmental events can induce synchronized electrical activity within the limbic system, this also provides an explanation of why environmental stress might sensitize patients to acute exacerbations of an ictal illness" (p. 713). Monroe (1970, 1982) implicates explosive behavioral tirades, impulsively destructive behavior, extreme affective lability, and episodic psychotic behavior in such a neurologic dysfunction. According to van der Kolk, Greenberg Boyd, and Krystal (1985), "long-term augmentation of LC (locus ceruleus) pathways following trauma underlies the repetitive intrusive recollections and nightmares that plague patients with PTSD (posttraumatic stress disorder)" (p. 318).

Post *et al.* (1982) have taken the kindling model and extrapolated from it, stating, "kindling and related sensitization models may also be useful conceptual approaches to understanding the development of psychopathology in the absence of seizure discharges" (p. 719). They report data that demonstrate the ability of adrenergic and dopaminergic agonists to sensitize animals and humans to behavioral hyperactivity and especially affective disorders. They refer to this phenomenon as "behavioral senitisation" rather than kindling because no ictal status is obtained as an end point. Rather, the achieved end point represents a lowered depolarization threshold and an increased propensity for spontaneous activation of limbic and related circuitry.

According to Racine, Tuff, and Zaide (1976), "Except for neural development and learning, the kindling phenomenon may be the most robust example of neural plasticity in the mammalian nervous system" (p. 19). Indeed, models of learning and memory may serve as tools for understanding the biology of kindling-like phenomena. Goddard and Douglas (1976) conducted a series of investigations designed to see if the "engram" model of memory had applicability in the understanding of the kindling phenomenon. They concluded:

> Thus it would appear that kindling is caused, in part, by a lasting potentiation of excitatory synapses. More work is needed to decide whether the changes are pre-synaptic or in the post-synaptic membrane, whether they are accompanied by alteration in synaptic morphology . . .
> Our answer to the question: does the engram of kindling model the engram of normal long term memory? is yes. (pp. 14–15)

Lynch and his colleagues at the University of California have sought to clarify this mechanism and have identified postsynaptic processes as the likely target area. Their research in long-term neuronal potentiation revealed a functional augmentation in the dendritic spines of stimulated neuronal pathways. More specifically, such changes included a 33% increase in synaptic contacts, as well as a decrease in the length and width variation of the dendritic spines (Deadwyler, Gribkoff, Cotman, & Lynch, 1976; Fifkova & van Harreveld, 1977; Lee, Schottler, Oliver, & Lynch, 1980). Rosenzweig & Leiman (1982) have suggested that the number of dendritic spines as well as the postsynaptic membrane area may be increased in such neural plasticity. Delanoy, Tucci, and Gold (1983) pharmacologically stimulated the dentate granule cells in rats and found a kindling-like neurolgic hypersensitivity to result. Similar agonists have been shown to enhance state-dependent learning.

Joy's superb review of the nature and effects of kindling (Joy, 1985) summarizes the potential alterations in biologic substrata that may be involved in the kindling phenomenon. He notes that "kindling produces important changes in neuronal function and connectivity" (p. 46) and continues:

> One would expect that these changes would have morphological or neurochemical correlates. Increased connectivity could result from a morphological rearrangement of neuronal circuits, perhaps from collateral sprouting and new synapse formation. Alternatively, it could result from a modification of existing synapses, perhaps by the growth of presynaptic terminals or by an increase in the postsynaptic receptive surface or number of receptors. (p. 49)

Whatever the biological alteration underlying the neuronal plasticity associated with limbic system neurological hypersensitivity, the phenomenon: (1) appears to be inducible on the basis of repeated, intermittent stimulation (Delanoy *et al.*, 1983), with the optimal interval between stimulations to induce kindling being about 24 hours (Monroe, 1982); (2) appears to last for hours, days, and even months (Monroe 1982; Deadwyler *et al.*, 1976; Fifkova & van Harreveld, 1977; Goddard & Douglas, 1976); (3) appears to show at least some tendency to decay over a period of days or months in the absence of continued stimulation if the initial stimulation was insufficient to cause permanent alteration (Fifkova & van Harreveld, 1977; Joy 1985); and (4) appears to be inducible on the basis of environmental, psychosocial, pharmacological, and/or electrical stimulation (Black *et al.*, 1987; Doane, 1986; Monroe, 1970; Post, 1986).

In sum, the preceding sections have argued for the existence of a group of disorders that share a latent yet common denominator of limbic-based neurological hypersensitivity and arousal. The neurology of this "common thread" has been discussed in some detail. Figure 9.2 graphically depicts the hypersensitivity phenomenon.

The etiological and/or sustaining mechanisms of the limbic-system-based neurological hypersensitivity that serves to undergird the disorders of arousal may be summarized into three basic categories:

1. Increased catecholamine activity within the limbic circuitry (Black *et al.*, 1987; Mefferd, 1979; Post, 1985; Post & Ballenger, 1981; Post, Rubinow, & Ballenger, 1986)
2. Increased arousal of neuromuscular efferents with resultant increased proprioceptive bombardment of the limbic system (Gellhorn, 1964, 1968, 1958a; Malmo, 1975; Weil, 1974)

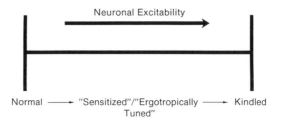

Figure 9.2. Limbic hypersensitivity phenomenon (LHP).

3. Repetitive cognitive excitation (Gellhorn 1964, 1968; Gellhorn & Loofbourrow, 1963; Post, Rubinow, & Ballenger, 1986)

The important point to keep in mind here is that these mechanisms appear to be inducible and responsive to environmental, psychosocial, pharmacological, and/or electrical stimulation. If, indeed, a group of psychiatric and somatic diseases exist that differ in their end-organ symptoms yet share a common pathogenic thread of neurological hypersensitivity and arousal, a therapy for the etiological and sustaining mechanisms of such disorders of arousal seems almost too obvious. If we look beyond the multitude of varied symptoms and signs that characterize these numerous disorders to the common yet latent taxonomic criterion of limbic-based neural hypersensitivity, it becomes obvious that, at least in theory, antiarousal therapies are "ideal" for achieving a neurological desensitization and amelioration of the core mechanism of pathogenesis in all of these disorders. Any such therapy, therefore, should prove of value in treating not only the *symptoms* of these varied disorders (assuming the symptoms have not become self-perpetuating) but the *causal mechanisms* of neurological hypersensitivity and psychophysiological arousal as well. Ironically, Gellhorn and Loofbourrow (1963) noted a quarter of a century ago, "If it were possible to alter the autonomic reactivity at the hypothalamic level important therapeutic results might be obtained" (p. 90).

THE RELAXATION RESPONSE

The preceding sections have argued that there exists a host of psychiatric and stress-related somatic disorders that, although diverse in their end-organ symptomatology, share a latent common thread of limbicogenic hypersensitivity (i.e., a propensity for hyperreactivity and/or sustained psychophysiological activation). These disorders have been referred to as "disorders of arousal." The available data suggest that these disorders may possess the following key etiological or sustaining constituents: (1) increased catecholaminergic (especially adrenergic) activity, (2) increased neuromuscular arousal, and (3) repetitive cognitive excitation. It would seem reasonable that in order for a therapeutic intervention to work effectively to ameliorate these disorders, it should work in such a way as to neurologically desensitize and reduce overall activity within the limbic circuitry. This can be achieved by (1) reducing catecholaminergic, especially adrenergic, responsivity, (2) reducing neuromuscular arousal, and (3) reducing cognitive excitation. Just such an antiarousal therapy has been uniquely captured in Benson's concept of the "relaxation response," a natural antiarousal psychophysiological phenomenon intrinsically antithetical to the mechanisms that undergird the "disorders of arousal" (Benson, 1975; Benson, 1985; Benson, Beary, & Carol, 1974).

Current evidence fails to reliably indicate that there is a best way of eliciting the relaxation response; furthermore, there is no reliable evidence that only one or two specific diseases may show superior therapeutic improvement from its application (Lehrer & Woolfolk, 1984). Indeed, many technologies are available to elicit the relaxation response, such as mantra meditation, progressive relaxation, presuggestion hypnosis, and prayer (Benson, 1983, 1985), and a wide variety of diverse diseases seem amenable to its therapeutic effect (Benson, 1985; Lavey & Taylor, 1985; Murphy & Donovan, 1986; Shapiro & Giber, 1978).

The Physiology of the Relaxation Response

The physiology of the relaxation response is fundamentally a physiology of hypoarousal, and much of its therapeutic effect derives from this quality. According to Gellhorn, relaxation is a result of a "loss in ergotropic tone of the hypothalamus, [and] a diminution of hypothalamic-cortical discharges" (Gellhorn & Kiely, 1972, p. 404). In agreement with Gellhorn, Taylor (1978) has suggested that relaxation involves a decrease in the arousability of the central nervous system. According to Benson (1983), "the relaxation response results in physiological changes which are thought to characterize an integrated hypothalamic function. These physiological changes are consistent with generalized decreased sympathetic nervous system activity" (p. 282). A more current reinterpretation might be that the relaxation response represents a neurological "desensitization" of the limbic system and/or its sympathetic efferents.

Specific empirical investigations have traditionally shown the elicitation of the relaxation response to result in decreases in oxygen consumption and carbon dioxide elimination, with no change in the respiratory quotient. Other similar changes include a reduction in heart and respiratory rates with a similar reduction in arterial blood lactate (Benson, 1983, 1985). All of these alterations are consistent with a decrease in central and peripheral adrenergic excitation (Benson, 1985; Delmonte, 1984). Yet the actual mechanisms appear more complex. Research has failed to show reductions consistently in circulating adrenergic catecholamines (Michaels, Haber, & McCann, 1976). In fact, it has been observed that plasma norepinephrine may actually increase as a result of the elicitation of the relaxation response (Lang, Dehof, Meurer, & Kaufmann, 1979; Hoffman, et al., 1982). Yet more recent investigations into this seeming paradox reveal that although there may be more norepinephrine available, a diminished adrenergic responsivity actually occurs at the end organ itself (Hoffman et al., 1982; Lehmann et al., 1986). In effect, the relaxation response has shown evidence of exerting effects consistent with those of an adrenergic end-organ blocking agent (Benson, 1983, 1985; Lehmann et al., 1986).

Behavioral psychophysiological studies support the notion that the relaxation response is capable of dampening a form of adrenergic responsivity. In one study, Allen (1981) used a 2,7000-Hz tone at 90 dB for a duration of 0.7s to trigger what was assumed to be posterior hypothalamically mediated arousal in 653 subjects. He found that after training in the relaxation response for a period of approximately 10 weeks, subjects demonstrated a dampened psychophysiological responsivity to the auditory stressor. The results of Allen's (1981) study are basically in concert with those of Goleman and Schwartz (1976), who compared the stress reactivity of 30 experienced meditators with that of 30 control subjects. Results indicated that recovery from a 12-min video stressor was more rapid among the experienced meditators when compared with the control subjects. A study English and Baker (1983) used a cold pressor to induce arousal and then measured blood pressure recovery time among 36 subjects. All subjects participated in a 4-week progressive relaxation program and then were submitted to a repetition of the cold pressor. Results indicated that relaxation training did not reduce cardiovascular response during the stressor but did facilitate a more rapid recovery within the domain of measured blood pressure.

Similar results regarding facilitated psychophysiologic recovery as described in this section have been found by Praeger-Decker and Decker (1980) and by Michaels, Parra, McCann, and Vander (1979). Although not totally concordant, these studies in the aggregate still suggest that the elicitation of the relaxation response serves to reduce forms of excessive arousal (Benson & Friedman, 1985; Delmonte, 1984). Complete agreement among observers remains entangled, however, in methodological and phenomenological complexities. The interested reader is referred to Holmes (1984), Suler (1985), Delmonte (1984), Shapiro (1985), and Benson and Friedman (1985) for a useful debate of this topic.

Having addressed the notion of arousal responsivity and the relaxation response, we will now consider the issue of neuromuscular arousal. Gellhorn (1964b) notes that "states of abnormal emotional tension are alleviated in various 'relaxation' therapies through reducing proprioceptive impulses which impinge on the posterior hypothalamus and maintain the cerebral cortex in an abnormal state of excitation" (p. 457). Gellhorn (1958a, 1958b, 1964) and Weil (1974) have clearly documented the existing interconnections between the neuromuscular system and the limbic circuitry. Similarly, they have argued that reductions of neuromuscular tone achieved by the elicitation of the relaxation response would be of value in reducing abnormal states of limbic sensitivity and excitation. The primary mechanism of mediation used to achieve such a neurological desensitization, Gellhorn and Weil argue, is the reduction of proprioceptive stimulation to the limbic system.

Finally, Averill (1973), Benson (1983, 1985), Gellhorn (1958b, 1967, Gellhorn & Kiely, 1972), and Lazarus and Folkman (1984) all agree that cognitive distortion, rumination, and overall cognitive excitation can give rise to states of ergotropic and generalized psychophysiological arousal. Similarly, evidence shows that a reduction in cognitive arousal via the relaxation response contributes to a reduction in ergotropic tone and a neurological desensitization effect as well as a reduction in dysphoric psychological states (Benson, 1985; Klajner, Hartman, & Sobell, 1984; Kutz, Borysenko, & Benson, 1985; Lavey & Taylor, 1985; Shapiro & Giber, 1978).

The "psychotherapeutic effect" of the relaxation response has been hypothesized to be derived from a sense of "mental calmness" (Rachman, 1968), a sense of "control" (Klajner, Hartman, & Sobell, 1984; Stoyva & Anderson, 1982), and a reduction of cognitive–affective rumination (Gellhorn, 1964b; Gellhorn & Loofbourrow, 1963). In reviewing the evidence for the psychotherapeutic value of the relaxation response, one is struck by the recurrent theme of an increase in "self-efficacy" derived from consistent practice of the relaxation response, as well as the sense of control engendered by the physiological autoregulatory skills developed (Bandura, 1977; Romano, 1982; Sarnoff, 1982; Shapiro & Giber, 1978). This point is especially well made by Green and Green (1977), Hamberger and Lohr (1984), and Stoyva and Anderson (1982). Bandura (1982), however, has done the most to develop this theme. He notes that the most powerful tool for combating perceptions of low self-efficacy and helplessness appears to be experience. Furthermore, he has shown that perceptions of self-efficacy can actually influence sympathetic nervous system activity, as well as subsequent performance. He concludes, "Treatments that eliminate emotional arousal . . . heighten perceived efficacy with corresponding improvements in performance" (Bandura, 1982, p. 28). The relaxation response appears to be just such a treatment.

SELECTING A RELAXATION TECHNIQUE

As noted earlier in this chapter, many different techniques/strategies can engender the relaxation response. Such therapeutic technologies include meditation, neuromuscular relaxation, controlled breathing, imagery, and hypnosis. As Lehrer and Woolfolk (1984) point out, research has shown there to be no single best relaxation technology; nor has any one stress-related disorder proved to be the most responsive to therapeutic amelioration by any specific relaxation technique. Not all relaxation techniques, however, are equally efficacious. The answer to this seeming paradox resides in the concept of individual differences.

"Inadequate recognition of individual differences is a methodological deficiency that has seriously slowed psychological research" (Tart, 1975, p. 140). Indeed, few outcomes in the behavioral sciences are a result of "main effects"; rather, "interaction effects" usually explain far more clinical variation.

So how does the clinician know what relaxation technology to employ? What treatment will be the most useful? Rather than ascribe main effects to therapies, perhaps the individual patient should be given primary consideration, as discussed in Chapter 6. If, then, the relaxation response can be engendered via numerous techniques, with none showing generic superiority, then the clinician should select the relaxation technique that best meets the interacting needs of patient, therapist, setting, and disorder (Paul, 1967). Unfortunately, there are no algorithmic models to guide the clinician to this end. Nevertheless, a review of Chapter 6, or texts such as that of Millon and Everly (1985), will serve to give the clinician insight into personologic differences. For example, compulsive persons may respond well to structured, directive therapy interventions (e.g., biofeedback), whereas avoidant-defensive persons may respond better to less structured technologies.

CLINICAL PRECAUTIONS AND UNDESIRABLE SIDE EFFECTS

Until rather recently, it was assumed that the clinical use of the relaxation response was a totally harmless therapeutic intervention. Recent data have argued contrary to such a position.

Luthe (1969) was perhaps the first to point out that the relaxation response should be used with caution. A pioneer in self-regulatory therapies, Luthe has compiled an impressive list of precautions for such therapies. They include psychotic states, dissociative reactions, paranoid ideation, dysfunctional thyroid conditions, and "disagreeable cardiac and vasomotor reactions."

Stroebel (1979), another pioneer in self-regulatory therapies (especially biofeedback), has argued that fragile ego structures serve as precautions for self-regulatory interventions. Heide and Borkovec (1983) observed in 30.8% of their progressive neuromuscular relaxation patients and in 53.8% of their meditation patients clinical evidence of anxiety reactions during preliminary training. Edinger (1982), on the other hand, reported that undesirable side effects arose from relaxation training in 3% to 4% of the clinical cases they surveyed.

These disparate reports led Everly, Spollen, Hackman, and Kobran (1987) to conduct a survey analysis of clinical practitioners who use relaxation training as a major component of their practice. Data were obtained from a national survey of 133 clinicians reporting on over 71,000 patients and over 700,000 patient hours. The results indicated that anxiety reactions occurred about 1.0% of the time; muscle tension headaches resulted about 0.8% of the time; a freeing of repressed ideation resulted about 0.7% of the time; and undesirable depersonalization resulted about 0.7% of the time from the elicitation of the relaxation response or some other form of self-regulatory therapy.

Based on the research of Luthe (1969), Stroebel (1979), Emmons (1978), and Everly *et al.* (1987), five major areas of concern in the elicitation of the relaxation response are briefly discussed below.

Loss of Reality Contact

The loss of reality contact during the elicitation of the relaxation response includes dissociative states, hallucinations, delusions, and perhaps parasthesias. Care should be taken when treating patients who suffer from affective or thought-disturbance psychoses. Care should also be taken with patients who use nonpsychotic fantasy excessively. In such conditions, the use of deep relaxation may exacerbate the problem.

Drug Reactions

Clinical evidence has clearly indicated that the induction of the relaxation response may actually intensify the effects of any medication or other chemical substance that the patient may be taking. Of special concern would be patients taking insulin, sedatives/hypnotics, or cardiovascular medications. All such patients should be carefully monitored, medically (although in many cases chronic relaxation may ultimately result in long-term reductions in required use of medications).

Panic States

Panic-state reactions are characterized by high levels of anxiety concerning the loss of control, insecurity, and, in some cases, seduction, Diffuse, free-floating worry and apprehension have also been observed. With such patients it is generally more desirable to provide a more concrete relaxation paradigm (such as neuromuscular techniques or biofeedback), rather than the abstract relaxation paradigms (such as meditation). Similarly, it is important to assure the patient that it is he or she who is really always in control—even in the states of "passive attention," which will be discussed in the following chapter on meditation.

Premature Freeing of Repressed Ideation

It is not uncommon for deeply repressed thoughts and emotions to be released into the patient's consciousness in response to a deeply relaxed state. Although in some psychotherapeutic paradigms such reactions are considered desirable, they could be perceived as destructive by the patient if such reactions are unexpected and/or too intense to be dealt with constructively at that point in the therapeutic process. Before implementation of relaxation techniques, the clinician may wish to inform the patient of the possibility that such ideation may arise. Similarly, the clinician must be prepared to render support should such thoughts emerge (see Adler & Morrissey-Adler, 1983; Glueck & Stroebel, 1978).

Excessive Trophotropic States

In some instances, the use of relaxation techniques that were intended to be therapeutic may induce an excessively lowered state of psychophysiological functioning. If this occurs, several phenomena may result:

1. *Temporary Hypotensive State.* This is an acute state of lowered blood pressure, which may cause dizziness, headaches, or momentary fainting, particularly if the patient rushes to stand up following the relaxation session. The clinician should know the patient's history of resting blood pressure before employing relaxation techniques. Caution should be used if the patient's resting blood pressure is lower than 90 mm Hg systolic and 50 mm Hg diastolic. Dizziness and fainting can often be aborted if the patient is instructed to open his or her eyes and to stretch and look around the room at the first signs of uncomfortable lightheadedness. Similarly, the patient should be told to wait one to three minutes before standing up following the relaxation session.

2. *Temporary Hypoglycemic State.* This is a condition of low blood sugar that may follow the inducement of the trophotropic state. This condition is most likely to last until the patient eats. Deep relaxation, like exercise, appears to have in some patients an insulinlike action, and may induce such a condition if the patient has a tendency for such conditions, or has not eaten properly that day. The acute hypoglycemic state just described may result in symptoms similar to the hypotensive condition.

3. *Fatigue.* Although relaxation techniques are known to create a refreshed feeling of vigor in many patients, a very few have reported feeling tired after relaxation practice. This is a highly unusual result and may be linked to an overstriving to relax on the part of the patient. The clinician should inform the patient that the best outcome in any attempt at relaxa-

tion is achieved when the patient *allows* relaxation to occur, rather than making it happen.

SUMMARY

Earlier in this chapter, it was suggested that the disorders of arousal described earlier might be treated effectively if limbic hypersensitivity and related factors could be reduced. Operationally, this meant: (1) achieving a reduction in adrenergic catecholamine activity and responsiveness, (2) achieving a reduction in neuromuscular arousal, and (3) achieving a reduction in pathogenic cognitive processes, such as rumination and perceptions of powerlessness and a lack of control. This chapter has reviewed the concept of the relaxation response as described by Benson and found it to be capable of achieving all three of the aforementioned therapeutic goals necessary for the successful treatment of the stress-related psychiatric and somatic disorders of arousal. Thus it would appear as if a cogent rationale for the use of techniques that engender the relaxation response in the treatment of the human stress response has emerged. To briefly review, this chapter has suggested that:

1. Neuronal hypersensitivity for excitation residing within the limbic system (LHP) may be a latent common denominator serving to undergird a host of stress-related psychiatric and somatic disorders.

2. These disorders, in the aggregate, have been referred to as "disorders of arousal" by Everly and Benson (Everly, 1985b; Everly & Benson, 1989).

3. The relaxation response, as described by Benson, represents a broad-spectrum psychophysiological phenomenon antithetical to the stress-related disorders of arousal.

4. As such, the relaxation response may be a valuable tool in the treatment of all of the disorders of arousal, despite their wide varieties of etiologic mechanisms and their diverse target organ symptom complexes.

5. There is no best relaxation technology. Clinicians should consider the interaction of the needs of the patient, therapist, setting, and disorder in the selection of the technology for the elicitation of the relaxation response.

6. Contrary to popular opinion, the elicitation of the relaxation response is not without its precautions and its undesirable side effects. Precautions include psychotic disorders, major affective disorders, patients on pharmacotherapy, and those with dysfunctional thyroid conditions, fragile ego structure, and delusion conditions, Undesirable side effects appear to occur between 3% and 4% of the time (Everly et al., 1987; Edinger, 1982) and include depersonalization, excessive trophotropic states, anxiety reactions, freeing of repressed ideation, and headaches.

In sum, this chapter has reviewed in detail the neurophysiology of the limbic system and of the relaxation response. The notion of the disorders of arousal has also been introduced. In effect, we see the emergence of a rationale for using the relaxation response in the treatment of a multitude of diseases spanning a wide spectrum of traditional diagnostic boundaries—something counterintuitive to traditional linear Pasteurian conceptualization.

Thus, it is hoped that this chapter has given new therapeutic credibility and importance to therapeutic technologies such as meditation, controlled respiration, and especially progressive neuromuscular relaxation exercises (given the important role of proprioception in the prolongation of stress-related disorders). With these points in mind, let us now move to a discussion of techniques that engender the relaxation response and see how they can be used in the treatment of all stress-related disorders of arousal described in this chapter as well as in Chapter 4.

CHAPTER 10

Meditation

The preceding chapter provided a rationale for the use of the relaxation response in the treatment of stress-related disorders. Let us explore several techniques for creating the relaxation response. The purpose of this chapter is to provide a clinically useful introduction to meditation.

In our Western culture, *meditation* refers to the act of thinking, planning, pondering, or reflecting. Our Western definitions, however, are not representative of the essence of the Eastern world's notion of meditation. In the Eastern tradition, meditation is a process by which one attains "enlightenment." It is a growth-producing experience along intellectual, philosophical, and, most important, existential dimensions. Within the context of this book, I shall use the term "meditation" to mean, quite simply, the autogenic practice of a genre of techniques that have the potential for inducing the relaxation response in the practicer through the use of a repetitive focal device. Inherent in a high level of achievement using these procedures is a mental state characterized by a nonegocentered and nonintrusive mode of thought processing.

HISTORY OF MEDITATION

Some of the earliest of written records on the subject of meditation come from the Hindu traditions of around 1,500 B.C. These records consist of scriptures called the Vedas, which discuss the meditative traditions of ancient India.

The sixth century B.C. saw the rise of various forms of meditation–Taoist in China, Buddhist in India. Even the Greeks delved into meditation.

171

The earliest known Christian meditators were the desert hermits of Egypt in the fourth century A.D. Their generic meditative practices strongly resembled those of the Hindu and Buddhist traditions.

In the eleventh and twelfth centuries A.D. the Zen form of meditation, called "zazen," gained popularity in Japan.

Finally, in the 1960s a wave of meditative practice was begun in the United States in a form representing a "Westernized" style in the Hindu tradition. It was brought to this country by Maharishi Mahesh Yogi and is called "Transcendental Meditation" (TM).

TYPES OF MEDITATION

The practice of meditation represents the practice of a given technique or procedure that has the potential of inducing the relaxation response as mentioned earlier. Although there are many kinds of meditation, one element common to all forms of meditative technique is a stimulus, or thing, which the meditator will focus his or her awareness on. According to Naranjo and Ornstein (1971), it is something to "dwell upon," in effect, a focal device.

Meditative techniques may then be categorized by the nature of their focal devices. Using this criterion, there are four forms of meditative technique.

1. *Mental Repetition.* This form of focal device involves dwelling on some mental event. The classic example of a mentally repetitive focal device is the "mantra." A mantra is a word or phrase that is repeated over and over, usually silently to oneself. We would include chanting under this category as well. TM uses a mantra format. The TM mantra is chosen from several Sanskrit words. Benson (1975) employs the word "one" as a mantra for the hypertensive patients he treats. A Tibetan Buddhist mantra in verse form is "Om mani padme hum." The Christian prayer "Lord Jesus Christ, have mercy on me" is said to be a form of mantra as well.

2. *Physical Repetition.* This focal device involves the focusing of one's awareness on some physical act. An ancient Yogic (Hindu) style of repetitive meditation focuses on the physically repetitive act of breathing. Various forms of breath control and breath counting (called "pranayama") serve as the basis for one form of Hatha Yoga. The aspect of Hatha Yoga best known to the public involves the practice of postures (called "asanas"). The Moslem Sufis are known for their practice of continuous circular dancing, or whirling. The name "whirling dervishes" was given to the ancient practitioners of this style. Finally, the popularity of jogging in the United States has given rise to the study of the effects of such activity. One effect reported by some joggers is a meditativelike experience. This could be caused by the repetitive breathing or the repetitive sounds of the feet pounding the ground.

3. *Problem Contemplation.* This focal device involves attempting to solve a problem with paradoxical components. The Zen "koan" is the classic example. In this case, a seemingly paradoxical problem is presented for contemplation. "What is the sound of one hand clapping?" is one of the most commonly known koan.

4. *Visual Concentration.* This focal device involves visually focusing on an image. It could be a picture, a candle flame, a leaf, a relaxing scene, or anything else. The "mandala" is a geometric design that features a square within a circle, representing the union of humanity with the universe. This is often used in Eastern cultures for visual concentration.

MECHANISMS OF ACTION

Exactly how the meditative technique works, no one knows for sure. However, significant insight is yielded into this problem by examining the common link between all forms of meditation—the focal device. This stimulus to "dwell upon" appears to be the critical ingredient in the meditative procedure (Benson, 1975; Glueck & Stroebel, 1975, 1978; Naranjo & Ornstein, 1971; Ornstein, 1972; White, 1974).

The role of the focal device appears to be to allow the intuitive, non-egocentered mode of thought processing (thought to be activity of the brain's right neocortical hemisphere) to dominate consciousness in place of the normally dominant analytic, egocentered mode of thought processing (thought to be left-hemisphere activity). The focal device appears to set the stage for this shift to occur by sufficiently engaging the left hemisphere's neural circuitry to allow the right hemisphere to become dominant (see Davidson, 1976; Naranjo & Ornstein, 1971; Ornstein, 1972). The focal device may occupy the left hemisphere by engaging it in some monotonous task, such as attending to a mantra, focused breathing, or a set of postures. Or, the focal device may overload and frustrate the left hemisphere. This would be the case when the meditator dwells on seemingly paradoxical problems, as in Zen, or when the meditator engages in intense physical activity, as practiced by the Sufis (whirling dervishes), the Tantrics, or perhaps even the American jogging enthusiast.

When the focal device is successfully employed, the brain's order of processing appears to be altered. "When the rational (analytic) mind is silenced, the intuitive mode produces an extraordinary awareness" (Capra, 1975, p. 26). This awareness is the goal of all meditative techniques when practiced by the devoted practitioner.

This state of "extraordinary awareness" has been called many things. In the East, it is called "nirvana" or "satori." A liberal translation of these words yields the word "enlightenment." Similar translations for this state include "truth consciousness" or "Being-cognition." In the early Western world, those few individuals who understood it called it the "supracon-sciousness" or the "cosmic consciousness." Benson (1975) has called this state the "relaxation response," as described in the preceding chapter.

More modern research investigations have attempted to qualify the neurophysiology of this supraconscious state. To date, research investiga-tions in the neurophysiological domain have been inconclusive. Results of early studies point in the direction of lowered frequency of brain-wave production, with increased amplitude during the supraconscious state. More recent investigations in the neurophysiology of meditation point toward a shift from left-hemisphere dominance to right-hemisphere, as mentioned earlier (Pagano & Frumkin, 1977; see also Davidson, 1976, and Orme-Johnson & Farrow, 1978, for reviews). In the final analysis, we may find this state to result from some combination of lowered neocortical activity occurring in a dominant right hemisphere.

It is crucial at this point to emphasize that meditation and the achieve-ment of the supraconscious state are not always the same! It should be made clear to the patient that meditation is the process, or series of tech-niques, which the meditator employs to achieve the desired goal of the relaxation response and its supraconsciousness.

THERAPEUTIC HALLMARKS

As just mentioned, the "extraordinary awareness" of the relaxation response, or supraconscious state, is the desired goal of the devoted practi-tioners of all meditative styles. However, it is important for the clinician *and* patient alike to understand that achievement of this state is never assured, and that this state may not be achieved every time by even the very experienced meditator. Given this fact, the question must then arise, "Is the time spent in the meditative session wasted if the meditator is unable to achieve the supraconscious state?" The answer to this question is clearly No! Positive therapeutic growth can be achieved without reaching the ultimate supraconscious state. The rationale for this statement lies in the fact that there exist several "therapeutic hallmarks" inherent in the process of medi-tation as one approaches the supraconscious state. Whereas Shapiro (1978) discusses five steps in meditation: (1) difficulty in breathing, (2) wandering mind, (3) relaxation, (4) detached observation, and (5) higher state of con-sciousness, we will expand upon the hallmarks we see in the meditative process.

The first and most fundamental of these hallmarks resides in practice itself. Even the ancient Hindu and Zen scriptures on meditation point out that it is far more important to attempt to achieve the supraconscious state than it is to actually reach that state. It should be clear to the twentieth-century clinician that, simply by taking time out to meditate, the patient is making a conscious effort to improve health. This effect, by definition, is the antithesis of the behavior pattern that leads to excessive stress. Similarly, by emphasizing to the patient the importance of simply meditating, rather than achieving the supraconscious state, the clinician will remove much of the competitive, or success-versus-failure, component in this process.

The second hallmark is a noticeable increase in somatic relaxation. At this point, the patient begins autogenically to induce a state of somatic relaxation. This is the awakened state of hypometabolic functioning referred to in the literature. This state is therapeutic in that (1) the body is placed into a mode equal or superior to sleep with regard to the restorative functions performed (Orme-Johnson & Farrow, 1978) and (2) ergotropically stimulating afferent proprioceptive impulses are reduced (Davidson, 1976; Gellhorn & Kiely, 1972).

The third hallmark is that of detached observation (see Shapiro, 1978). In the Indian scriptures this hallmark is described as a state in which the meditator remains "a spectator, resting in himself" as he observes his environment. This state is an egoless, passive state of observation in which the meditator simply "coexists" with the environment, rather than confronting or attempting to master it. It is a nonanalytic, intuitive state. One similar experience that many individuals have had is that of "highway hypnosis." This state is often experienced by individuals driving on monotonous expressways. At one point they notice they are at Exit #6; a mere moment later they may notice they are at Exit #16 yet have no immediate memory of the 10 exits between. Many call this a "daydreaming state." It is important to note that the driver of the car was fully capable of driving; this is not a sleep state. If an emergency had arisen, the driver would have been able to react appropriately. Therefore, the clinician should explain that this state is not one of lethargy or total passivity (a major concern for many patients).

The final step in the meditative experience is the "supraconscious state." This state appears to be a summation of all the previous states except that it is more intense. Davidson (1976) has characterized its nature as:

1. A positive mood (tranquillity, peace of mind)
2. An experience of unity, or oneness, with the environment; what the ancients called the joining of microcosm (human) with macrocosm (universe)
3. A sense of ineffability
4 An alteration in time/space relationships
5. An enhanced sense of reality and meaning
6. Paradoxicality, that is, acceptance of things that seem paradoxical in ordinary consciousness

Figure 10.1. A meditative continuum.

Because the clinician will be bombarded with questions concerning the nature of the patient's meditative experiences, common experiences are placed on a continuum for better understanding (see Figure 10.1). This continuum of meditative experiences is not totally progressive from one discrete state to another. A meditator may jump from any one state to another and back again. On the other hand, varying degrees of depth within each state can be experienced. Note that boredom and distracting thoughts often precede more positive effects. The clinician should explain to the patient that this is natural, and that he or she should be tolerant of such occurrences and simply return concentration to the focal device.

The meditator should be discouraged from evaluating the meditative sessions, for this sets up a success–failure paradigm. Simple descriptive reports to the clinician are useful, so as to monitor the course of the activity for a period of two to three weeks. A daily log might be kept by the client, as long as it is descriptive and not evaluative.

RESEARCH ON THE CLINICAL APPLICATIONS AND EFFECTS OF MEDITATION

Well-controlled research studies on the clinical effectiveness of meditation are now abundant (see Benson, 1985; Lehrer & Woolfolk, 1984; Shapiro & Giber, 1978 for discussions and reviews). These studies point to a potentially wide range of stress-related therapeutic applications for meditation. Specifically, meditative techniques of the mantra type have been found useful:

1. In the treatment of generalized autonomic arousal and excessive ergotropic tone (Benson, 1985; Benson, Beary, & Carol, 1974; Hoffman *et al.*, 1982)
2. In the treatment of anxiety and anxiety neurosis (Benson *et al.*, 1974; Emmons, 1978; Girodo,1974; Lehrer & Woolfolk, 1984; Vahia, 1972)
3. In the treatment of phobias (Boudreau, 1972)
4. For increasing "self-actualization" and "positive mental health" (Benson, 1985; Emmons, 1978; Kutz, *et al.*, 1985; Nidich, 1973)

5. As an adjunct in the treatment of drug and alcohol abuse (Benson, 1969; Lazar, 1975)
6. As an adjunct in the treatment of essential hypertension (Benson *et al.*, 1974; Datey, 1969)
7. Murphy and Donovan (1984) have compiled an excellent review of research on meditative practices for a broad spectrum of health-related concerns.

Having provided a rationale for the clinical use of meditation, let us now examine its implementation.

HOW TO IMPLEMENT MEDITATION

The following discussion is provided as a guide to the clinical use of meditation.

Preparation for Implementation

In addition to the general precautions for relaxation mentioned in an earlier chapter:

1. Determine whether the patient has any contraindications specifically for the use of meditation. For example, affective or thought-disturbance psychoses may possibly be exacerbated by meditation. Similarly, the clinician should use care with patients who demonstrate a tendency to employ nonpsychotic fantasy, as in the schizoid personality. It should also be noted here that some compulsive or action-oriented individuals appear to have greater difficulty in learning to meditate effectively then do less compulsive individuals. Boredom and distracting thoughts appear to complete with the meditation.

2. Inquire into the patient's previous knowledge or experience in meditation. Pay particular attention to any mention of cultic or religious aspects. These are the most common misconceptions that patients find troublesome. Some will feel that if they meditate they will be performing a sacrilegious act.

3. Provide the patient with a basic explanation of meditation.

4. Describe to the patient the proper environment for the practice of meditation (see next section).

Components within Meditation

In his book *The Relaxation Response*, Benson describes four basic components in successful meditation:

1. A quiet environment
2. A mental device
3. A passive attitude
4. A comfortable position

Let us expand Benson's paradigm to some extent.

The first condition we would recommend is a *quiet environment*. The quiet environment is absent of external stimuli that would compete with the meditative process. Many patients will state that it is impossible to find such a place. If this is so, then some creativity may be needed. The patient may wish to use music or environmental recordings to "mask" distractions. In our laboratory experiments, we have found the steady hum of a fan or an air conditioner to be effective as a masking noise. Sounds of steady, low to moderate amplitude can actually be relaxing. In situations where this is not possible, the patient may elect to wear a blindfold and/or earplugs to reduce external stimulation.

The second condition (for physically passive meditation) is a *comfortable position*. Muscle tension can be disruptive to the meditative process. When first learning, the patient should have most of his or her weight supported. The notable exceptions would be the head and neck. By keeping the spine straight and the head and neck unsupported, there will be enough muscle tension to keep the patient from falling asleep. If the patient continually falls asleep during meditation, then a posture that requires greater muscle tension should be used.

The third condition is a *focal device*. This is the link between all forms of meditation, even the physically active forms, as discussed earlier. The focal device appears to act by allowing the brain to alter its normal mode of processing.

The fourth condition is a *passive attitude*. This attitude has been called "passive volition" or "passive attention" by some. Benson (1975) states that this "passive attitude is perhaps the most important element" (p. 113). With this attitude, the patient "allows" the meditative act to occur, rather than striving to control the meditative process. As Greenspan (1979) has noted, "The patient can only begin to win by surrendering resistance and allowing the . . . process to proceed" (p. 18).

If the patient is unable to adopt this attitude, he or she will ask questions such as

"Am I doing this correctly?"–usually indicative of concern regarding performance.

"How long does this take?"–usually indicative of concern for time.

"What is a *good* level of proficiency?"–usually indicative of concern for performance outcome, rather than process.

"Should I try to remember everything I feel?"–usually indicative of overanalysis. The more the patient dwells on such thoughts, the less suc-

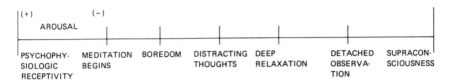

Figure 10.2. Arousal and the meditative continuum.

cessful he or she will be. Distracting thoughts are completely normal during the meditative process and are to be expected. However, adoption of a passive attitude allows the patient to recognize distracting thoughts and simply return concentration to the focal device. A fascinating discussion of the passive attitude may be found in a paper written by Peper (1976).

The fifth and final condition that we would recognize is a *receptive psychophysiological environment*. By this we mean a set of internal psychophysiological conditions that will allow the patient to meditate. It has been noted, for example, that patients who are psychophysiologically aroused when they attempt to meditate have a very low success rate. Therefore, it may be necessary to teach the patients to put themselves in a more "receptive condition" for meditating (this would apply to biofeedback, hypnosis, and guided imagery as well). To achieve this receptive condition, the patient may wish to use a few neuromuscular relaxation techniques before the meditation, in order to reduce excessive muscle tension. I have recommended that the patient take a hot bath before meditating. In some instances, patients have reported high levels of success if they meditated while sitting in a hot tub. I have found this seldom-mentioned concept of psychophysiological receptivity to be a critical variable in many clinical experiences. Therefore, the meditative continuum will be expanded (Figure 10.1) to include this variable (see Figure 10.2).

Example Protocol

Provided below is an example of a protocol for a physically passive mantra-like form of meditation. Examine it and make notes in the margins provided as to what changes you might make in order to make the protocol more effective for your specific needs and individual patients.

Background Information

The purpose of these instructions is to familiarize you with the use of meditation as a way of reducing the stress in your life. These instructions consist of background information and specific directions for the use of four techniques that you may choose from in order to meditate. Follow all the instructions closely. Later you may wish to modify a part of the technique to fit a personal preference or situation, but in the initial learning phase you should do all the exercises exactly as instructed. Once you have chosen one of the meditative techniques, employ that technique as instructed for 15 to 20 minutes of uninterrupted meditation once or twice a day.

Some people, not familiar with the nature and origins of meditation, confuse its pure form with its possible uses. There are important differences. The techniques of meditation presented here represent techniques derived from the ancient Eastern philosophies that have then been blended with modern relaxation and stress-reduction techniques. Although some of the techniques were used in the practice of specific religions, to say that meditation is a religious practice is like saying wine is a religious instrument simply because many religions use wine in their ceremonies. Meditation is a technique of quieting the mind, which, of course, is a necessary prerequisite for reducing anxiety and tension.

As taught here, a quiet mind is an end in itself. What you do with this valuable skill is, of course, up to you.

The fundamentals of meditation are often misunderstood, as meditation itself is difficult to define. Meditation is not a physiological state. Nor is it any specific psychological feeling. It is not a religion. Rather, as used here, meditation is a technique. Meditation is so basic that it has transcended time, cultures, races, religions, and ideologies. The physiological, psychological, and philosophical goals of meditation cannot be achieved without training, and mastery of technique cannot be achieved except through continued practice.

Although there are many types of meditation, the most popular meditative techniques in Western society are derived from specific practices of ancient Yoga and Zen. Each type of meditation represents a variation of purpose and technique. Those presented here are thought to be the best suited for stress reduction. The technique is the easiest to learn and the one most devoid of cultic, religious, and spiritual overtones. It is complete and can be all the meditation one will ever need; or, it may serve as an introduction to more specific types.

There are several essential steps you should follow when learning to meditate.

A first essential step is to find a quiet environment, both external and internal. A quiet room away from others who are not meditating is essential, especially while learning. Take the phone off the hook, or at least go into a room without one. Generally, do whatever can be done to reduce external noise. If you cannot completely eliminate the noise, which is often the case in busy households or in college dorms, etc., use ear plugs. Play a record or tape of some soft instrumental sounds, or use any of the numerous environmental sound recordings that are commercially available. Even the steady hum of a fan or an air conditioner can serve effectively to block out, or mask, external noise. You will also wish to turn down, or completely off, any lights in the room. Now that you have quieted your external environment, the next essential step is to work on quieting your internal environment. One way is to reduce muscle tension. Muscle tension represents one of the biggest obstacles to successful meditation. Spend some time relaxing your muscles. One way to reduce muscle tension is to sit comfortably, You may not feel like a real meditator unless you are sitting in the Eastern cross-legged lotus position, but that takes a great deal of flexibility and training. For now, sit comfortably on the floor, or, better yet, sit in a straight-backed, comfortable chair, feet on the floor, legs not crossed, hands resting on the thighs, fingers slightly opened, not interlocked. You should sit still, but remember, meditation is not a trance. If you are uncomfortable or feel too much pressure on any one spot, move. If you have an itch, scratch. Do not assume a tight inflexible position or attitude. Relax. It is best not to lie or support your head or you will tend to fall asleep. Keep the head, neck, and spine in a straight vertical line. A small but significant amount of muscle tension is needed to maintain this posture, and this effort helps prevent sleep from occurring, while at the same time it creates an optimal position for learning to meditate.

There are many types of meditation. Some focus on inner forces, inner power, or self-identity. Others focus on external things, like words, lights, or sounds. Meditation is a simply natural process. And though techniques may differ, the core experience is essentially the same. The basic meditative experience involves passively concentrating on some stimulus, whether it be a word, an image, your breath, or nothing at all. The stimulus acts as a vehicle to keep distracting thoughts out of your mind. And yet, the harder you concentrate on the stimulus, the harder it is to meditate. Although this sounds confusing, it is true, simply because meditation is a "passive" activity. You must allow the stimulus, whatever it is, to interact passively with you. You must learn to concentrate passively on your stimulus. The skill of passive concentration takes time to develop—so don't be discouraged if it seems difficult for the first few weeks. Just continue to practice.

Actual Instruction

You are now ready to begin the actual instruction. To begin with, close your eyes. Notice the quietness. Much of our sensory input comes in through our eyes. Just by closing your eyes, you can do much to quiet the mind.

The Use of Breath Concentration

What we are going to do now is clear our minds. Not of all thoughts, but of ongoing thoughts, which use the imagination to increase stress arousal. Focus on your breathing. Shift your awareness from the hectic external world to the quiet and relaxing internal world.

As you breathe in, think in. Let the air out. Think out. In and out. Concentrate on your breathing. Think in. Think out. Breath in through your nose and let the air out through the mouth very effortlessly. Just open your mouth and let the air flow out. Do not force it. Become involved with the breathing process. Concentrate on your breathing. In and out. Now, each time you breathe in, I want you to feel how cold the air is, and each time you breathe out, feel how warm and moist the air is. Do that now. (*Pause 30 seconds.*)

The Use of One

Now we would like to replace the concentration on breathing with the use of a mantra. A mantra is a vehicle that is often a word or phrase. It is merely a vehicle to help control your mind from wandering back to daydreams. An example of a mantra, suggested by Herbert Benson in his book *The Relaxation Response*, is simply the word "one" (o-n-e). This is a soft, noncultic word that has little meaning as a number. Every time you breathe out, say the word "one" to yourself. Say one. One. Say it softly. One. Say the word one without moving your lips. Say it more softly yet until it becomes just a mental thought. (*Pause 75 seconds here.*)

The Use of *OM*

The word "one" is an example of a mantra: a vehicle to help clear your mind. By concentrating on a word without emotion or significance, your mind's order of processing begins to change. The mind begins to wander, with a quieter, more subtle state of consciousness. Many people like to use words from the ancient Sanskrit language, feeling that they represent soft sounds with spiritual significances that can also be used as a focus for contemplation. The universal mantra is the word "om"; spelled o-m, it also means one. Each time you breathe out say the word om. Om. Om. Breathe softly and normally, but now do not concentrate on your breathing. Repeat the mantra in your mind. Just think of saying it. Do not actually move your lips. Just think of it. Do not concentrate on your breathing. Let the mantra repeat itself in your mind. Do not force it. Just let it flow. Gradually the mantra will fade. The mind will be quiet. Occasionally, the quiet will be broken by sporadic thoughts. Let them come. Experience them, then let them leave your mind as quickly as they entered, by simply going stronger to your mantra. Let us now use "om" as a mantra. Say the word om, om. (*Pause here 75 seconds.*) Remember, the mantra is a vehicle to help clear the mind when you cannot do so without it. Also remember, keep your movements to a minimum, but if you are uncomfortable, move. If you are worried about time, look at a clock. Discomfort or anxiety will prevent full attainment of the relaxed state.

The Use of Counting

A final mantra that you may select from, if you find your mind wandering too much, is a mantra that requires a little more concentration than the three previous meditation techniques.

As you breathe out, begin to count backward from 10 to 1. Say a single number to yourself each time you exhale. As you say the number, try to picture that number in your "mind's eye." When you reach 1, go back to 10 and start over. Let us do that now. (*Pause here 3 minutes.*)

Reawaken

Now I want to bring attention back to yourself and the world around you. I will count from 1 to 10. With each count you will feel your mind become more and more awake and your body become more and more refreshed. When I reach 10, open your eyes, and you will feel the best you've felt all day—you will feel alert, refreshed, full of energy, and eager to resume your activities. Let us begin: 1–2 you are beginning to feel more alert, 3–4–5 you are more and more awake, 6–7 now begin to stretch your hands and feet, 8– now begin to stretch your arms and legs, 9–10 open your eyes *now!* You feel alert, awake, your mind is clear and your body refreshed.

Having read the preceding example, one should note the following points:

1. In the example, the patient was given four different mantras to choose from. Such "freedom of choice" may increase clinical effectiveness. It is important to ask the patient which mantra was the best for him or her, and why. Such questions foster introspection and self-understanding.

2. The meditation example contains a *reawaken* step, as does the neuromuscular-relaxation example in the next chapter.

3. The clinician should indicate, at some point, when the patient should meditate. We have found once or twice a day to be sufficient, 15 to 20 minutes in duration for each session. As with neuromuscular relaxation, before lunch or before dinner are generally the best times to meditate, although practice in the morning may provide a relaxing start for the entire day.

SUMMARY

In this chapter the first of several techniques that can be used to engender the relaxation response was discussed. This chapter specifically addressed the meditative technology. Let us review several of the main points addressed:

1. The practice of meditation is but one way to engender a relaxation response. Other techniques will be reviewed in subsequent chapters (e.g., neuromuscular relaxation, controlled respiration).

2. The "supraconscious state" as described in this chapter may be considered as one of the end points on a meditative continuum within the realm of the relaxation response.

3. Research has now clearly shown the relaxation response, as engendered by the practice of meditation via a focal device, can be useful in the treatment of a wide variety of stress-related disorders.

4. Within this chapter, a protypical protocol for the teaching of meditation has been provided. The clinician should tailor it to the personal needs of each patient when practical.

5. As meditation is not the only way to create the relaxation response at clinically significant proportions, let us now turn our attention to another technology useful in helping the patient engender the relaxation response.

6. Last, but most important, never simply give the patient the homework assignment of practicing meditation, or any other relaxation technique, without first practicing in the office setting. This gives the clinician the opportunity to: (1) observe whether the technique is done properly, and (2) debrief the patient as to the results.

CHAPTER 11

Neuromuscular Relaxation

Chapter 9 presented a neurophysiological rationale for the use of the relaxation response in the treatment of stress-related disorders. In developing that rationale, the research efforts of Gellhorn (1958a, 1958b, 1964b, 1967), Weil (1974), and Malmo (1975) are reviewed. A reader of these respective literatures cannot help but be impressed by the convergence these independent authors reached as to the critically central role that the neuromuscular system plays in the determination of, not just intentional articulation, but emotional and stress-related manifestations as well. Yet it was Gellhorn (1958a, 1958b, 1964b) who demonstrated through a series of well-designed experiments that the nuclear origin of the sympathetic nervous system, the posterior hypothalamus, is dramatically affected by neuromuscular proprioceptive feedback from the skeletal musculature. Such findings led him (1964b) to conclude "that states of abnormal emotional tension are alleviated in various 'relaxation' therapies through reducing proprioceptive impulses which impinge on the posterior hypothalamus" (p. 457). This chapter will explore the clinical corollary of this notion.

The purpose of this chapter is to provide a clinically useful introduction to a genre of interventions termed *neuromuscular relaxation* (NMR). As used in this chapter, this term refers to a process by which an individual can perform a series of exercises to reduce the neural activity *(neuro)* and contractile tension in striate skeletal muscles *(muscular)*. This process usually consists of isotonic and/or isometric muscular contractions, which are performed by the patient with initial instruction from the clinician. The proper practice of NMR will ultimately lead to the elicitation of the relaxation response.

HISTORY OF NEUROMUSCULAR RELAXATION

The neuromuscular-relaxation procedure presented in this chapter comes from four primary sources: (1) the "Progressive Relaxation" procedures developed by Edmund Jacobson, (2) research protocols developed by the present author, (3) the research of Bernstein and Borkovec (1973), and (4) the clinical work of Vinod Bhalla applying neuromuscular interventions to the field of physical medicine and stress.

Research by Jacobson (1938) on the knee-jerk reflex led to the conclusion that striate muscle tension represented a contraction of muscle fibers. He further concluded that this striate muscle tension played a large role in anxiety states. By teaching individuals to reduce striate muscle tension, Jacobson reported success in reducing subjective reports of anxiety. Gellhorn (1958b, 1964b) later offered a neurophysiological rationale for the use of progressive relaxation in the treatment of stress-related disorders. After the 1940s Charles Atlas developed a program of muscular "dynamic tension" for general health, but the model developed by Jacobson gained greater popularity among practicing clinicians.

Jacobson called his system "progressive relaxation." This system consists of a series of exercises by which the subject tenses (contracts) and then relaxes selected muscles and muscle groups so as to achieve the desired state of deep relaxation. Jacobson considered his procedure "progressive" for the following reasons:

1. The subject learns progressively to relax the neuromuscular activity (tension) in the selected muscle. This process may require several minutes to achieve maximal neuromuscular relaxation in any selected muscle.

2. The subject tenses and then relaxes selected muscles in the body in such a manner as to progress through the principal muscle groups until the entire body, or selected body area, is relaxed.

3. With continued daily practice, the subject tends progressively to develop a "habit of repose" (p. 161)—a less stressful, less excitable attitude.

Progressive relaxation gained considerable popularity when Wolpe (1958) used the same basic relaxation system in his treatment for phobias called "systematic desensitization." This treatment paradigm has become a classic behavioral therapeutic intervention, which consists of relaxing the subject before and during exposure to a hierarchy of anxiety-evoking stimuli. Wolpe has successfully employed the principle that an individual cannot be relaxed and anxious at the same time; that is, relaxation acts to inhibit a stress response. An excellent review of Jacobson's approach is that of McGuigan (1984).

MECHANISMS OF ACTION

Jacobson (1978) argues that the main therapeutic actions of the neuromuscular-relaxation system reside in having the patient *learn* the difference between tension and relaxation. This learning is based on having the patient enhance his or her awareness of proprioceptive neuromuscular impulses that originate at the peripheral muscular levels and increase with striate muscle tension. These afferent proprioceptive impulses are major determiners of chronic diffuse anxiety and overall stressful sympathetic arousal, according to Jacobson. This conclusion is supported by the research of Gellhorn, who demonstrated the critical role that afferent proprioceptive impulses from the muscle spindles play in the determination of generalized ergotropic tone (Gellhorn, 1958a,1958b, 1964b, 1967). The neuromuscular mechanisms of action were discussed in detail in Chapter 9. Refer back to the work of Gellhorn, Malmo, and Weil as discussed in that chapter.

Once the patient learns adequate neuromuscular awareness, he or she may then effectively learn to reduce excessive muscle tension by consciously and progressively "letting go" or reducing the degree of contraction in the selected muscles. It has been argued that it is difficult for "unpracticed" individuals to achieve a similar degree of conscious relaxation because they are not learned in the sensations of tension versus conscious deep relaxation—as a result, measurable "residual tension" will remain during conscious efforts to relax.

More recent studies on progressive relaxation have suggested that there are two principal therapeutic components at work. Although it is generally accepted that the traditional Jacobsonian concept of *learned awareness* of the differences between the tension of contraction compared with the relaxation experienced on the release of contraction is an important therapeutic force, there may be more. It has been suggested that the actual procedure of *contracting* a muscle before attempting to relax it may yield some additional impetus to the total amount of relaxation achieved in that muscle, over and above the process of learned awareness (Borkovec, Grayson, & Cooper, 1978).

RESEARCH ON CLINICAL APPLICATIONS AND EFFECTS
OF NEUROMUSCULAR RELAXATION

A review of research and clinical literature on the genre of techniques that would fall under the heading of neuromuscular relaxation (including Jacobson's procedures) reveals a wide range of stress-related therapeutic applications. Specifically, neuromuscular relaxation has been concluded to be effective for:

1. Insomnia (Jacobson, 1938; Nicassio & Bootzin, 1974; Steinmark & Borkovec, 1973)
2. Essential hypertension (Deabler, 1973; Shoemaker & Tasto, 1975)
3. Tension headaches (Cox, Freundlick, & Meyer, 1975)
4. Subjective reports of anxiety (Jacobson, 1978; Paul 1969a)
5. General autonomic arousal and excessive ergotropic tone (Jacobson, 1978; Paul, 1969a,b)
6. Development of a calmer attitude, which may act as a prophylactic against excessive stress arousal (see Stoyva, 1977)
7. The most recent research compendium on neuromuscular relaxation is that of McGuigan, Sime, and Wallace (1984)

On the basis of these research findings, it may be concluded neuromuscular relaxation strategies may be an effective component of most treatment programs for chronic stress. Let us now examine a structure for clinical implementation.

HOW TO IMPLEMENT A PHYSICALLY ACTIVE FORM OF NEUROMUSCULAR RELAXATION: PREPARATION

To review, neuromuscular relaxation represents a series of exercises during which the subject tenses (contracts) and then releases (relaxes) selected muscles in a predetermined and orderly manner. Some preliminary activities that the clinician should undertake before implementing the procedure are as follows:

1. In addition to the general precautions for relaxation mentioned in an earlier chapter, determine whether the patient has any muscular or neuromuscular contraindications: for example, nerve problems, weak or damaged muscles, or skeletal problems that would be made worse through the neuromuscular exercises. When in doubt, avoid that specific muscle group until a qualified opinion can be obtained.

2. Inquire into the patient's previous knowledge or experience of neuromuscular techniques. The clinician must determine whether such knowledge or experience will be detrimental or facilitative in the present situation. It is often helpful to discuss in detail any previous exposure that the patient may have had to neuromuscular techniques.

3. Provide the patient with background and rationale for use of neuromuscular techniques.

4. Describe to the patient the proper environment for the practice of

neuromuscular techniques: (a) quiet, comfortable surroundings, darkened, if possible, in order to allow full concentration on bodily sensations; (b) loose clothing; remove contact lens, glasses, and shoes if desired; (c) body supported as much as possible (with exception of neck and head if client falls asleep unintentionally).

5. Instruct the patient in the differences between the desired muscle "tension" and undesirable muscle "strain." Tension is indicated by a tightened, somewhat uncomfortable sensation in the muscles being tensed. Strain is indicated by any pain in the muscle, joints, or tendons, as well as any uncontrolled trembling in the muscles. Strain is in actuality excessive muscle tension.

6. Instruct the patient in proper breathing. Do not hold the breath while tensing muscles. Rather, breathe normally, or inhale on tensing and exhale on relaxing the muscles.

7. Before beginning the actual protocol with the patient, informally demonstrate all the exercises that you will be employing. Take this opportunity to answer any questions that the patient may have.

8. Finally, explain to the patient exactly "how" you will give the instructions. For example: "In the case of each muscle group that we will focus upon, I will always carefully describe the relaxation exercise to you first, before you are actually to do the exercise. Therefore, don't begin the exercise described until I say, 'Ready? Begin.'"

The exact order of these steps may vary. In order to facilitate patient awareness of some of these preliminary points, the clinician may present them on a type of handout.

HOW TO IMPLEMENT NEUROMUSCULAR RELAXATION: PROCEDURE

Whenever possible, begin the total protocol with the lowest areas of the body to be relaxed and end with the face. This is done because once a muscle has been tensed and then relaxed, we attempt to insure that it is not inadvertently retensed. The quasivoluntary muscles of the face are the most susceptible to retensing, therefore we relax them last to eliminate the opportunity.

The Sequential Steps to Follow for Each Muscle Being Relaxed

Once the clinician is ready to initiate the actual protocol, he or she should be sure to follow a fundamental sequence of steps for *each* muscle group.

Step 1. Describe to the patient the specific muscle(s) to be tensed and how it/they will be contracted. "We are now going to tense the muscles in the calf. To begin I'd like you to leave your toes flat on the floor and raise both of your heels as high as you can."

Step 2. Have the patient initiate the response with some predetermined cue: "Ready? Begin."

Step 3. Have the patient hold the contraction for three to five seconds. During this time you may wish to encourage the patient to exert an even greater effort: "Raise your toes higher, higher, even higher."

Step 4. Signal to the patient to relax the contraction: "And now relax."

Step 5. Facilitate the patient's awareness of the muscles just relaxed by having him or her search for feelings of relaxation: "Now sense how the backs of your legs feel. Are they warm, tingling, do they feel heavy? Search for the feelings."

Step 6. The clinician may wish to encourage further relaxation: "Now let the muscles relax even more. They are heavier and heavier and heavier."

Step 7. Pause at least five to ten seconds after each exercise to allow the patient to experience relaxation. Pause 15 to 20 seconds after each major muscle group.

Step 8. When possible, go directly to the opposing set of muscles. In this case, it would involve leaving the heels flat on the floor and raising the toes as high as possible.

Example Protocol

Provided below is a brief protocol in which the previously discussed components have been included. See whether you can identify the major preliminary activities (only a few can be included in this example). See whether you can identify the sequenced steps (some sample muscle groups will have only six or seven of the steps to avoid monotony).

As you read the example, make notes in the margins provided as to what changes you might make in order to make the protocol more effective for your needs in teaching a general NMR protocol.

Background Information

As early as 1908, research conducted at Harvard University discovered that stress and anxiety are related to muscle tension. Muscle tension is created by a shortening or contraction of muscle fibers. The relationship between stress and anxiety on one hand, and muscle tension on the other, is such that if you are able to reduce muscle tension, stress and anxiety will be reduced as well.

Progressive neuromuscular relaxation is a tool that you can use to reduce muscle tension and, therefore, stress and anxiety. Progressive neuromuscular relaxation is a progressive system by which you can systematically tense and then relax major muscle groups in your body, in an orderly manner, so as to achieve a state of total relaxation. This total relaxation is made possible by two important processes.

First, by tensing a muscle and then relaxing it you will actually receive a sort of running start, in order to achieve a greater degree of muscular relaxation than would normally be obtainable. And, second, by tensing a muscle and then relaxing it, you are able to compare and contrast muscular tension and muscular relaxation. Therefore, we see that the basic premises underlying your muscular relaxation are as follows:

1. Stress and anxiety are related to muscular tension.
2. When you reduce muscular tension, a significant reduction in stress and anxiety will be achieved as well.
3. Neuromuscular relaxation provides you with the unique opportunity to compare and contrast tension with relaxation.

4. Neuromuscular relaxation has been proven to be a powerful tool that can be used to achieve relaxation and peace of mind. However, relaxation is an active skill and like any skill it must be practiced. The mistake that most individuals make is to rush through this relaxation procedure. Neuromuscular relaxation works, but it takes practice and patience to succeed. But, after all, isn't your health and well-being worth at least 15 minutes a day?

Preliminary Instructions

Before beginning the progressive neuromuscular relaxation procedure, let us review some basic considerations.

First, you should find a quiet place without interruptions or glaring lights. You should find a comfortable chair to relax in, though you will find progressive relaxation useful performed lying down in bed in order to help you fall asleep at night as well. You should loosen tight articles of clothing. Glasses, jewelry, and contact lenses should be removed.

Second, the progressive neuromuscular relaxation system requires you to tense each set of muscles for two periods, lasting about five seconds each. However, it is possible to tense each set of muscles up to several times if you continue to feel residual tension. Muscular tension is not equal to muscular strain. They are not the same. You will know that you have strained a muscle if you feel pain in the muscle or any of the joints around it, or if it begins to shiver or to tremble uncontrollably. In either case, these should be signs to you to employ a lesser degree of tension, or simply avoid that exercise. The entire neuromuscular relaxation procedure lasts about 20 to 30 minutes, should you wish to relax your entire body. The time may be less if you choose to relax only a few muscles groups.

Last, don't hold your breath during contractions. Breathe normally, or inhale as you tense and exhale as you release the tension.

Actual Instructions

You are now ready to relax progressively the major muscle groups in your body, in order to achieve a state of total relaxation. I would like you to settle back and get very, very comfortable. You may loosen or remove any tight articles of clothing, such as shoes or coats, ties or glasses. You should also remove contact lenses. You should try to get very, very comfortable. I would like you to close your eyes. Just sit back and close your eyes. And I would like to begin by directing your attention to your breathing. The breath is the body's metronome. So let us become aware of the metronome. Become aware of how the air comes in through your nostrils and down into your lungs, and as you inhale how your stomach and chest expand, as you exhale how they recede. Concentrate on your breathing. (*Provide 30 second pause here.*)

In the case of each muscle group that we shall focus on, I shall always carefully describe the relaxation exercise to you first, before you are actually to do the exercise. Therefore, do not begin the exercise described until I say, "Ready? Begin."

Chest

Let us begin with the chest. I would like you, at my request, and not before, to take a very, very deep breath. I would like you to breathe in all the air around you. Let's do that now. Ready? Begin. Take a very deep breath. A very deep breath; hold it . . . and relax. Just exhale all the air from your lungs and resume your normal breathing. Did you notice tension in your chest as you inhaled? Did you notice relaxation as you exhaled? If you had to, could you describe the difference between tension and relaxation? Let us keep that in mind as we repeat this exercise. Ready? Begin. Inhale very deeply, very deeply. Hold it, and relax. Just exhale and resume your normal breathing. Could you feel the tension that time? Could you feel the relaxation? Try to concentrate on that difference in all the muscle groups that we shall be attending to.

(*Always pause 5–10 seconds between exercises.*)

Lower Legs

Let us go now to the lower legs and the muscles in the calf. Before we begin, I should like you to place both your feet flat on the floor. Now, to engage in this exercise, I should like you simply to leave your toes flat on the floor, and raise both your heels at the same time as high as they will go. Ready? Begin. Raise your heels. Raise them both very high (see Figure 11.1). Hold it, and relax. Just

Figure 11.1

Figure 11.2

let them fall gently back to the floor. You should have felt some contraction in
the back of your calves. Let us repeat this exercise. Ready? Begin. Raise the heels
very high, higher this time. Hold it, and relax. As you relax, you may feel some
tingling, some warmth. Perhaps some heaviness as the muscle becomes loose
and relaxed. To work the opposite set of muscles, I should like you to leave both
your heels flat on the floor, point both sets of your toes very, very high. Point
them as high as you can toward the ceiling. This is the same motion that you
would make if you lifted your foot off the accelerator pedal in your car (see
Figure 11.2). Except that we shall do both feet at the same time. let us do that
now. Ready? Begin. Raise the toes very high. Hold it, and relax. Now let us
repeat this exercise. Ready? Begin. Raise the toes high. Higher this time. Hold it,
and relax. You should feel some tingling or heaviness in your lower legs. That
feeling is there. You must simply search for it. So take a moment and try to feel
that tingling, warmth, or perhaps that heaviness that tells you that your muscles
are now relaxed. Let those muscles become looser and heavier and even heavier.
(*Pause for 20 seconds.*)

Thighs and Stomach

The next set of muscles that we shall concentrate on are those of the thigh.
This exercise is a simple one. At my request, I should like you simply to extend
both your legs out in front of you as straight as you can (see Figure 11.3). (*If this
is uncomfortable for the patient, let him or her exercise one leg at a time.*) Remember to
leave your calves loose. Do not tense them. Let us do that now. Ready? Begin.
Straighten both your legs out in front of you. Very straight. Hold it, and relax.
Just let the feet fall gently to the floor. Did you feel tension in the top of your
thighs? Let us repeat this exercise. Ready? Begin. Straighten both your legs out.
Very straight. Straighter this time. Hold it, and relax. To work the opposite set of
muscles, I should like you to imagine that you are at the beach and are digging
your heels down into the sand (see Figure 11.4). Ready? Begin. Dig your feet
down into the floor. Harder. And relax. Now let us repeat this exercise. Ready?
Begin. Dig your heels down into the floor. Harder than that, and relax. Now the
top of your legs should feel relaxed. Let them become more and more relaxed—
more and more relaxed. Concentrate on that feeling now. (*Pause here 20 seconds.*)

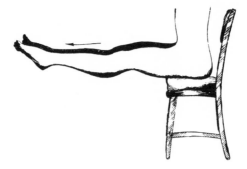

Figure 11.3

Figure 11.4

Hands and Arms

Let us move now to the hands. The first thing that I should like you to do, with both your hands at the same time, is make very tight fists (See Figure 11.5). Tighten your fists and arms together. Ready? Begin. Clench your fists very tightly. Tighter. Tighter than that. Hold it, and relax. This exercise is excellent if you type or do a lot of writing during the day. Now let us repeat. Ready? Begin. Clench both your fists very tightly. Very tightly. Tightest of all. Hold it, and relax. To work the opposing muscles, simply spread your fingers as wide as you can (see Figure 11.6). Ready? Begin. Spread your fingers very wide. Wider. Hold it, and relax. Now let us repeat this exercise. Ready? Begin. Spread the fingers wide. Wider. Widest of all. Hold it, and relax. Concentrate on the warmth or tingling in your hands and forearms. (*Pause here 20 seconds.*)

Shoulders

Now let us work on the shoulders. We tend to store a lot of our tension and stress in our shoulders. This exercise simply consists of shrugging your shoul-

Figure 11.5

Figure 11.6

ders vertically up toward your ears. Imagine trying to touch your ear lobes with the tops of your shoulders (see Figure 11.7). Let us do that now. Ready? Begin. Shrug your shoulders up high. Higher than that. Hold it, and relax. Now let us repeat. Ready? Begin. Shrug the shoulders high. Higher. Much higher. Hold it, and relax. Let us repeat this exercise one more time. Ready? Begin. Shrug the shoulders as high as you can. Hold it, and relax. Very good. Now just concentrate on the heaviness in your shoulders. Let your shoulders go, let them completely relax—heavier and heavier. (*Pause here 20 seconds.*)

Face

Let us move now into the facial region. We shall start with the mouth. The first thing I should like you to do is smile as widely as you possibly can (see Figure 11.8). An ear-to-ear grin. Ready? Begin. Very wide smile. Very wide. Hold it, and relax. Now let us repeat this exercise. Ready? Begin. Grin very

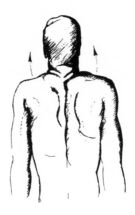

Figure 11.7

wide. Wide smile. Much wider. Hold it, and relax. The opposite set of muscles will be activated when you pucker or purse your lips together, as if you were trying to give someone a kiss (see Figure 11.9). Ready? Begin. Pucker the lips together. Purse them together very tightly. Hold it, and relax. Now let us repeat that exercise. Ready? Begin. Purse the lips together. Tightest of all. Hold it, and relax. Let your mouth relax. Let the muscles go—let them relax, more and more; even more.

Now let us move up to the eyes. (Be sure to remove contact lenses.) I should like you to keep your eyes closed, but to clench them even tighter. Imagine that you are trying to keep shampoo suds out of your eyes (see Figure 11.10). Ready? Begin. Clench the eyes very tightly. Tighter, and relax.

Let us repeat this exercise. Ready? Begin. Clench the eyes, tighter. Hold it, and relax.

The last exercise consists simply of raising your eyebrows as high as you can. Now, remember to keep your eyes closed, but raise your eyebrows as high as you can (see Figure 11.11). Ready? Begin. Raise the eyebrows high. Higher

Figure 11.8

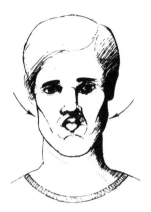

Figure 11.9

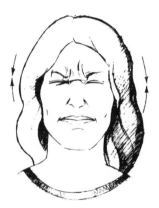

Figure 11.10

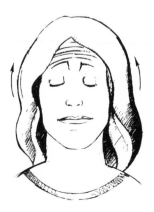

Figure 11.11

than that. Hold it, and relax. Now let us repeat this exercise. Ready? Begin.
Raise the eyebrows higher. Highest of all. Hold it, and relax. Let us pause for a
few moments to allow you to feel the relaxation in your face. (Pause 15 seconds.)

Closure

You have now relaxed most of the major muscles in your body. To make
sure that they are all relaxed, I shall go back and name the muscles that we have
just activated and just relaxed. And, as I name them, let them go even further
into relaxation. You will feel a sense of relaxation descend over your entire body
in a warm wave. You will feel the muscular relaxation now in your forehead,
and as it goes down into your eyes, down into your checks, you can feel the
heaviness of relaxation descend into your jaws, into your neck, down through
your shoulders, to the chest, and arms, to the stomach, into your hands. Relaxation is descending into your legs, into the thighs and calves, and down to the
feet. Your body now feels very heavy. Very relaxed. This is a good feeling. So
take a moment and enjoy this feeling of relaxation. (*Pause here 2 minutes.*)

Reawaken

Now I want you to bring your attention back to yourself and the world
around you. I shall count from 1 to 10. With each count you will feel your mind
become more and more awake, and your body more and more refreshed and
responsive. When I reach 10, open your eyes, and you will feel the *best* you've
felt all day—you will feel alert, refreshed, full of energy, and eager to resume
your activities. Let us begin: 1–2 you are beginning to feel more alert, 3–4–5 you
are more and more awake, 6–7 now begin to stretch your hands and feet, 8-now
begin to stretch your arms and legs, 9–10 open your eyes *now!* You feel alert,
awake, your mind is clear and your body refreshed.

Having read the example protocol, one should note the following
points:

1. Once the process is completed with desired groups of muscles, the
clinician should go back and provide the patient with a final opportunity to
achieve further relaxation, or "closure." Here the clinician simply goes
back and names the major muscles relaxed, and he instructs the patient to
release any residual tension. This is demonstrated in the example protocol
under the heading "Closure."

2. In cases where the entire body is relaxed, we have observed in
many patients a deeply relaxed state that carries over, or lingers, for several minutes to an hour or so. This can be highly desirable, if the goal of the
relaxation is to hasten sleep, or simply to act as a tranquilizing agent.
However, for patients who must go back to work or study within a brief
time after relaxation, it becomes desirable to show them how to "reawaken" or energize themselves. One such technique is provided in the
example protocol under the heading "Reawaken."

3. Inform the patient when to practice at home or at work. Inform the

patient that it is best to practice the technique twice a day—though once a day has been found to be effective for many. We have found the best times typically to be before lunch and before dinner, since digestive processes seem to interfere with effective concentration. In the treatment of insomnia, these techniques should be done while lying in bed at the end of the evening as the patient attempts to go to sleep.

4. Emphasize to the patient that a big advantage in the use of neuromuscular relaxation resides in its flexibility. That is, patients can elect to employ the entire system, relaxing the entire body, or select one or two muscle groups that seem to be the most tense. This obviously cuts down on the time needed to complete the exercises and creates a highly useful symptom-specific intervention role for NMR.

5. Finally, reemphasize that the technique of neuromuscular relaxation is a *skill,* that will be developed *only* through consistent practice.

SUMMARY

The series of exercises presented in the example represents a brief protocol. It is not a prescription for use with clients so much as an example of how such protocol may be created. Usually greater specificity is included

Table 11.1. Summary Checklist of Neuromuscular Relaxation Components

Preparation for implementation:

_____ 1. Identify contraindications and precautions.
_____ 2. Inquire as to previous knowledge/experience in techniques.
_____ 3. Provide patient with background/rationale for use of technique.
_____ 4. Describe proper environment for practice of technique.
_____ 5. Instruct patient in the difference between muscle "tension" and muscle "strain."
_____ 6. Instruct patient in proper breathing.
_____ 7. Informally demonstrate all specific msucular contractions to be used.
_____ 8. Describe "how" you will provide instruction and cues.

Implementation of sequential steps for *each* muscle being relaxed.

_____ 1. Describe the specific muscle and "how" it will be contracted.
_____ 2. Signal the patient to begin contraction.
_____ 3. Hold contraction and encourage greater contraction.
_____ 4. Signal the patient to release tension, that is, relax.
_____ 5. Facilitate the patient awareness of muscles just relaxed through verbal and intonational cues.
_____ 6. Encourage further relaxation.
_____ 7. Pause and allow patient to become aware of sensations.
_____ 8. Proceed with opposing muscle group, if applicable.

for muscle groups, and even individual muscles, depending on the requirements of the patient. It is important to mention that Jacobson clearly emphasizes the utility of relaxing the facial muscles, particularly the throat, mouth, and eyes, to obtain maximal relaxation. Therefore, far more specialization directed toward those muscle groups may be considered in developing a protocol:

1. The clinician may encourage the patient to develop his or her own personalized protocol. The clinician may further encourage or provide the patient with a home practice tape.

2. Jacobson's text *You Must Relax*, represents an excellent resource for additional and far more specific exercises. However, in the final analysis, it is up to the clinician to assess the clinical suitability of any form of neuromuscular relaxation on an individual basis.

3. Table 11.1 may be used as a checklist of important procedural points that should be covered when teaching clients neuromuscular relaxation. As each step is completed, simply check it off. This same table may be used to evaluate clinical student's mastery of these procedures. It is designed to be reprinted from this text and used clinically or in educational settings.

4. Finally, Appendix B contains a different version of neuromuscular relaxation. It consists of a physically passive form that uses focused sensory awareness and directed concentration for the reduction of striate muscle tension. The clinician may consider this as a potential clinical alternative to the form of neuromuscular relaxation just described.

CHAPTER 12

Voluntary Control of Respiration Patterns

The purpose of this chapter is to discuss using voluntary control of respiration patterns in the treatment of excessive stress. As used in this text, this term refers to the process by which the patient exerts voluntary control over his or her breathing pattern—in effect, breath control. There are hundreds of diverse patterns of controlled respiration; we shall examine several that we feel have particular introductory utility for the clinician concerned with the treatment of the stress response. The exercises presented here are by no means the only exercises that maybe used. I have simply chosen several patterns that are simple to learn, as well as being effective. Simply stated, the goal of voluntary controlled respiration in the treatment of excessive stress is to have the patient voluntarily alter his or her rhythmic pattern of breathing so as to create a more relaxed state.

HISTORY

Voluntary control of respiration patterns (breath control) is perhaps the oldest stress-reduction technique known. It has been used for thousands of years to reduce anxiety and to promote a generalized state of relaxation. The history of voluntary breath control dates back centuries before Christ. References to voluntary breath control for obtaining a relaxed state can be found in the Hindu tradition of Hatha Yoga. In fact, Hatha Yoga (the yoga of postures) is essentially built on various patterns of breathing. These patterns are called *pranayama*. The term *pranayama* means breath control, or breath restraint. According to Hewitt (1977), however, *pranayama* may be more loosely translated to mean relaxing breath control. As Hatha Yoga flourishes today, so does the practice of voluntary control of respiration.

While in ancient India breath control was developing in the Hindu tradition, the Chinese were practicing it as well. The development of the movement arts of T'ai Chi and Kung Fu saw the inclusion of controlled breathing as a basic component in both art forms. These "martial arts" have enjoyed a rebirth of popularity in the United States. Breath control remains an important component of both.

Perhaps the most widely used form of breath control today is the procedure for "natural" childbirth. In this form of childbirth, various types of controlled breathing are used to reduce pain for the mother during delivery and to facilitate the descent of the child through the birth canal.

In this chapter we shall concern ourselves only with the voluntary controlled breathing patterns that seem most useful as general aids to relaxation, without any specific goal other than common stress reduction.

BASIC PATTERNS OF BREATHING

In this section, we shall describe briefly the fundamentals involved in the breathing process by examining the four phases of the respiratory cycle and describing three basic types of breathing.

According to Hewitt (1977), four distinct phases of the breathing cycle are relevant in learning voluntary control of respiration patterns (the clinician will find this phasic division useful in teaching any form of deep-breathing technique):

1. Inhalation (inspiration). Inhalation occurs as air is taken into the nose or mouth, descends via the trachea, the bronchi, and bronchioles, and finally inflates the alveoli, which are the air sacs constituting the majority of the lobes of the lungs.

2. The pause that follows inhalation. During this pause, the lungs retain their inflated characteristic.

3. Exhalation (expiration). This occurs as the lungs are deflated, emptying the waste gases from the alveoli into the same system used for inhalation.

4. The pause that follows the exhalation phase. During this phase, the lungs are at rest in a deflated state.

Ballentine (1976) describes three basic types of breathing. These are named and differ primarily according to the nature of the inhalation initiating the breathing cycle: clavicular, thoracic, and diaphragmatic.

The clavicular breath is the shortest and shallowest of the three. It can be observed as a slight vertical elevation of the clavicles, combined with a slight expansion of the thoracic cage upon inhalation.

The thoracic breath represents (in varying degrees) a deeper breath—deeper in the sense that a greater amount of air is inhaled, more alveoli are inflated, and the lobes of the lungs are expanded to a greater degree. It is initiated by activation of the intercostal muscles, which expand the thoracic cage up and outward. The thoracic breath can be observed as a greater expansion of the thoracic cage, followed by an elevation of the clavicles on inhalation. Thoracic breathing is the most common breathing pattern.

Finally, the diaphragmatic breath represents the deepest of all the breaths. In this breath the most air is inhaled and the greatest number of alveoli are inflated. In addition, for the first time the lowest levels of the lungs are inflated. The lower third of the lungs contains the greater part of the blood when the individual stands vertically; therefore the diaphragmatic breath oxygenates a greater quantity of blood per breathing cycle than the other types. During the diaphragmatic breath, the diaphragm (a thin, musclelike structure that separates the thoracic and the abdominal cavities) flattens downward on inhalation. This forces air to descend into the lungs, while pushing the organs in the abdominal cavity down and forward. The movement of the diaphragm becomes the major cause of the deep inhalation. The full diaphragmatic breath may be observed as the abdominal cavity expands outward, followed by expansion of the thoracic cage, and finally elevation of the clavicles.

Variations of the diaphragmatic breath are considered by many to be the simplest and most effective form of controlled respiration in the reduction of excessive stress. Therefore, we shall limit ourselves to discussing the role of diaphragmatic patterns in reducing excessive stress. It would, however, be helpful to the clinician to learn to identify all three basic patterns of breathing.

MECHANISMS OF ACTION

Although the specific mechanisms involved in stress reduction via breath control may differ from technique to technique, a general therapeutic force is thought to be the ability of the diaphragmatic breath to induce a temporary trophotropic state.

Hymes (1980) notes that the tone of the sympathetic and of the parasympathetic nervous systems is greatly affected by the process of respiration. Harvey (1978) concludes that "diaphragmatic breathing stimulates both the solar plexus and the right vagus nerve in a manner that enervates the parasympathetic nervous system thus facilitating full relaxation" (p. 14). Finally, Pratap, Berrettini, and Smith (1978) have proposed a neural mechanism through which diaphragmatic breathing may reduce neocortical activity (as is useful in anxiety reduction):

It is clear from the description of this practice that it evokes a strong Hering-Breuer reflex. The afferent limb of the Hering-Breuer reflex consists of stretch receptors in the lung which are excited as inspiration proceeds. The resultant impulses ascend via the vagus nerve to the Pontine Apneustic Center. . . . The excessive stimuli (physiologically speaking) evoked by this practice may functionally alter some areas of the ascending reticular activating system, thereby suppressing sensory input to the cortex bringing about a steadying of the mind. (p. 174)

Ballentine (1976) notes that expiration increases parasympathetic tone. It is interesting to note that during most types of diaphragmatic breathing expiration is protracted, therefore a protracted period of parasympathetic relaxation is apparently created. In summary, Hymes (1980) states, "Autonomic functioning may be voluntarily shifted back to calm by exercising conscious breath control (with an associated reduction of anxiety and pain)" (p. 10).

Unfortunately, there is no substantial body of research literature directed specifically toward one type of therapeutic breath pattern, although research efforts (at the Eleanor N. Dana Laboratory of the Himalayan International Institute, for example) have been directed toward improving this condition. Until such research is undertaken, voluntary breath control may suffer from the stigma of an ancient forgotten remedy.

Finally, independent of any predominantly physiological mechanisms, voluntary breath control may prove therapeutic from a predominantly cognitive perspective as well. The rationale for this statement comes from the fact that concentration on respiration patterns acts to compete with obsessive thought patterns, and perhaps even compulsive behaviors. This point must be assessed on a patient-to-patient basis.

CLINICAL RESEARCH

1. Using psychophysiological indices of arousal, Morse, Cohen, Furst, & Martin (1984) found that respiratory patterns appeared to herald other alterations in autonomic nervous system activity. Although noting the difficulty in assuming causality, the authors suggest that respiratory control may be a means of gaining access to voluntary alteration of the autonomic nervous system.

2. In a study of 105 subjects waiting to receive electric shocks, McCaul, Solomon, and Holmes (1979) investigated the efficacy of paced respiration and expectational set upon autonomic nervous system arousal. Results indicated that slowing of respiration rate reduced physiological indices of arousal (skin resistance and finger pulse volume), as well as self-reports of anxiety. Expectation showed no effect on arousal.

3. Bainton, Richter, Ballantyne, and Klein (1985) found that respiratory influences on both sympathetic and parasympathetic autonomic nervous system activity appear to originate in the brain stem.

4. Grossman, de Swart, and Defares (1985), in a controlled study of 56 subjects, found that controlled respiration was an effective treatment for hyperventilation syndrome.

5. Everly (1979b,c) investigated the effects of a diaphragmatic breathing technique on physiological and psychological indices of arousal. Results of this study of asymptomatic individuals found that diaphragmatic breathing was capable of reducing electromyographically assessed muscle tension and self-reports of state anxiety within 60 seconds.

HOW TO IMPLEMENT

Voluntary breath control appears to be the most flexible of the interventions for the reduction of excessive stress. It can be used under a wide variety of environmental and behavioral conditions.

Despite its versatility, voluntary breath control should not be used without precaution. When breathing is used as a meditative device, the precautions discussed in the chapter on meditation would seem to apply. Apparently, the major precaution unique to voluntary breath control is one against hyperventilation. Hyperventilation may be simply defined as a condition where the patient "overbreathes." Overbreathing can quickly create a state of hypocapnia (diminished CO_2 levels in the blood) followed by an excess in the bicarbonate ion and an insufficiency in the hydrogen ion (Lum, 1975). The resultant symptoms can include palpitations, tachycardia, Raynaud's phenomenon, tunnel vision, dizziness, grand mal seizures, shortness of breath, chest pain, tingling in the lips, fingers, and/or toes, epigastric pain, tetany, anxiety, weakness, and loss of consciousness—to mention only a few. Many of these symptoms could appear after several minutes of prolonged hyperventilation. Dizziness and tingling appear to be among the earliest of warning signs that the client is beginning to hyperventilate. Hewitt (1977) adds to the list of precautions for breath control:

> No more than momentary pauses between inhalation and exhalation are safe for persons with lung, heart, eye, or ear troubles, or for persons with high blood pressure. . . . Persons with low blood pressure may pause briefly after breathing in, but should make no deliberate pause after breathing out. The breath should not be deliberately held during pregnancy. (pp. 79–80)

Unfortunately, Hewitt offers no clinical or physiological rationale for these statements. Therefore, the clinician reading this text must reach his or her own conclusions regarding this matter. It is interesting to note, however, that Lum (1975) states that one form of diagnosis of hyperventilation "rests on reproducing the patient's symptoms by voluntary hyperventilation in a form which the patient recognizes and on taking reasonable steps to exclude significant pathology" (p. 378).

Listed below are three diaphragmatic breathing exercises reported to be useful in promoting a more relaxed state. In teaching any form of diaphragmatic breathing, the clinician must monitor the activities of the patient to assure proper techniques. Hewitt (1977) offers the following guidelines, which we feel are appropriate for all forms of diaphragmatic breathing:

> You fill the lungs to a point of fullness without strain or discomfort (p. 90) If after retention [of the inhalation] the air bursts out noisely, the suspension has been overprolonged; the air should be released in a steady smooth stream. . . . Similarly, following the empty pause, the air should unhurriedly and quietly begin its ascent of the nostrils [as the new inhalation begins]. (p. 73)

I have found these general guidelines useful in having patients avoid overbreathing, as well as other inappropriate breathing practices. These guidelines should be followed when instructing a patient in each of the following three breathing exercises.

Breathing Exercise No. 1

This breathing technique may be thought of as a "complete breath." In fact, variations of this breath appear in the Yogic literature with similar names. The technique is extremely simple to complete. In order to assist the clinician in teaching the exercise to patients, it will be described according to the four phases of breath described by Hewitt (1977).

Inhalation   The inhalation should begin through the nose if possible. The nose is preferred to the mouth because of its ability to filter and warm the incoming air. On inhalation, the abdomen should begin to move outward, followed by expansion of the chest. The length of the inhalation should be two to three seconds (or to some point less than that where the lungs and chest expand without discomfort).

Pause after inhalation   There should be no pause. Inhalation should transfer smoothly into the beginning of exhalation.

Exhalation   Here the air is expired (through the mouth or the nose, whichever is more comfortable). The length of this exhalation should be two to three seconds.

Pause after exhalation   This pause should last only one second, then inhalation should begin again in a smooth manner. I have found that this exercise can be repeated by many patients for several minutes without the initiation of hyperventilation. However, the patient should usually be instructed to stop when light-headedness occurs.

Breathing Exercise No. 2

This breathing exercise may be thought of as a form of "counting breath," of which variations appear in the Yogic literature. The term *counting* is applied to this exercise because the patient is asked literally to count to himself or herself the number of seconds each of the four phases of the exercise will last. In order to assist the clinician in teaching this exercise, it will be described according to the four phases of breathing described by Hewitt (1977).

Inhalation   The inhalation should begin through the nose if possible. The abdomen should begin to move outward, followed by expansion of the chest. The length of the inhalation should be two seconds (or to some point less than that where the lungs and chest expand without discomfort). The length of the inhalation should be counted silently, as one thousand, two thousand.

Pause after inhalation   There should be a pause here, following the two-second inhalation. The counted pause here should be one second in duration.

Exhalation   Here the air is expelled. The counted exhalation should be three seconds in duration.

Pause after exhalation   This counted pause should last one second. The next inhalation should follow smoothly. I have found that this exercise can be repeated by many patients for several minutes without the occurrence of hyperventilation. However, the patient should usually be instructed to stop when light-headedness occurs.

Breathing Exercise No. 3

This technique, developed by G. S. Everly, is designed to rapidly induce (within 30 to 60 seconds) a state of relaxation. Research has shown it to be effective in reducing muscle tension and subjective reports of anxiety as well as having some potential for reducing heart rate (see Everly, 1979b,c; Vanderhoof, 1980). The following description is presented as if instructing a patient:

> During the course of an average day, many of us find ourselves in anxiety-producing situations. Our heart rates increase, our stomachs may become upset, and our thoughts may race uncontrollably through our minds. It is during such episodes that we require fast-acting relief from our stressful reactions. The brief exercise described below has been found effective in reducing most of the stress reaction that we suffer from during acute exposures to stressors—it is, in effect, a quick way to "calm down" in the face of a stressful situation.

The basic mechanism for stress reduction in this exercise involves deep breathing. The procedure is as follows:

Step 1. Assume a comfortable position. Rest your left hand (palm down) on top of your abdomen, over your navel. Now place your right hand so that it rests comfortably on your left. Your eyes can remain open. However, it is usually easier to complete Step 2 with your eyes closed (see Figure 12.1).

Step 2. Imagine a hollow bottle, or pouch, lying internally beneath the point at which your hands are resting. Begin to inhale. As you inhale imagine that the air is entering through your nose and descending to fill that internal pouch. Your hands will rise as you fill the pouch with air. As you continue to inhale, imagine the pouch being filled to the top. Your rib cage and upper chest will continue the wavelike rise that was begun at your navel. The total length of your inhalation should be two seconds for the first week or two, then possibly lengthening to two and a half or three seconds as you progress in skill development (see Figure 12.2).

Step 3. Hold your breath. Keep the air inside the pouch. Repeat to yourself the phrase, "My body is calm." This step should last no more than two seconds.

Step 4. Slowly begin to exhale—to empty the pouch. As you do, repeat to yourself the phrase, "My body is quiet." As you exhale, you will feel your raised abdomen and chest recede. This step should last as long as the two preceding steps, or may last one second longer, after a week or two of practice. (*Note:* Step 1 need only be used during the first week or so, as you learn to breathe deeply. Once you master that skill, you may omit that step.) Only repeat this four-step exercise three to five times in succession. Should you begin to feel light-headed, stop at that point. If light-headedness recurs with continued practice, simply

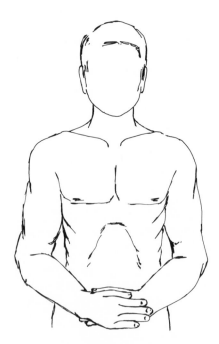

Figure 12.1

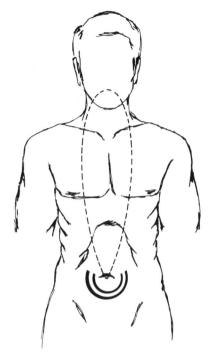

Figure 12.2

shorten the length of the inhalation and/or decrease the number of times you repeat the exercise in succession.

Practice this exercise 10 to 20 times a day. Make it a ritual in the morning, afternoon, and evening, as well as during stressful situations. Because this form of relaxation is a skill, it is important to practice at least 10 to 20 times a day. At first you may not notice any on-the-spot relaxation. However, after a week or two of regular practice, you will increase your capabilities to relax temporarily. Remember, you must *practice regularly* if you are to master this skill. Regular, consistent practice of these daily exercises will ultimately lead to the development of a more calm and relaxed attitude—a sort of antistress attitude—and when you do have stressful moments, they will be far less severe.

SUMMARY

This chapter has been presented a discussion of voluntary controlled patterns of respiration for use in reducing excessive stress. As mentioned earlier, the goal of voluntary controlled respiration in the treatment of excessive stress is to have the patient voluntarily alter his or her rhythmic pattern of breathing to create a more relaxed state.

1. Three basic types of breathing patterns—clavicular, thoracic, and diaphragmatic. The first two are associated with (and may stimulate) a sympathetic response. The latter is associated with (and may stimulate) a parasympathetic response (see Ballentine, 1976). It has been found useful for the clinician to learn to recognize these patterns in patients. It is also useful to teach patients how to recognize such patterns in themselves.

2. Although the literature (especially the Yogic) presents numerous and diverse respiratory techniques for relaxation, we have focused on diaphragmatic breath. This emphasis is based on the conclusion that variations of diaphragmatic breathing are the simplest to teach and are among the most effective for achieving a relaxed psychophysiological state in the patient. For these reasons, the clinician may find the variations of the diaphragmatic pattern most useful.

3. In the final analysis, the clinician must assess the suitability of using voluntary controlled respiration with each patient individually. The clinician may attempt to teach the several breathing exercises, in order to assess which may be of most utility to that individual. Presented here have been three variations of the diaphragmatic breath, not as prescription but as sample variations of a basic type of breath control (diaphragmatic breathing), which has been found useful in reducing excessive stress. Many other useful variations exist (see Hewitt, 1977; Jencks, 1977). The clinician must assess their utility on a case-by-case basis.

4. The major drawback mentioned to the use of breath control in stress reduction is the hyperventilation reaction. This is not a problem when the patient uses breathing exercises (such as those described in this chapter) for short periods of time and ceases when light-headedness ensues. The Yogic literature says that no more than 15 minutes of any hour should be spent in pranayama practice. Once again, however, this issue must be assessed on a case-to-case basis.

5. In conclusion, Hymes (1980) states that "control of the breath may be a major practical key to the smooth and balanced functioning of the autonomic nervous system [contributing] to a healthier body and a more tranquil mind" (p. 10). This analysis seems accurate. In addition, if nothing else, teaching the patient simply to pause and breathe more slowly may indeed be therapeutic in a life style that encompasses potentially pathogenic time urgency.

Hypnosis and Stress

Prevention and Treatment Applications

Joseph E. Mallet

Clinicians working in the area of stress prevention and treatment are likely to benefit from learning how hypnosis can increase their therapeutic effectiveness. This chapter will attempt to provide this learning experience with the following information: a brief history of clinical hypnosis; definitions and explanations of basic concepts; mechanisms of action in hypnotic treatment; clinical applications of hypnosis for prevention and treatment of the stress response; treatment precautions; and summary.

HISTORICAL BACKGROUND

Although hypnoticlike treatments of illness have been reported from the beginning of historical records, frequent use of hypnosis with psychophysiological disorders is generally believed to have begun at the time of Franz Anton Mesmer (1734–1815). A Viennese physician who practiced in Paris, Mesmer believed that hypnotic effects were brought about by the transmission of an invisible magnetic fluid from the hypnotist to the patient. He called this process animal magnetism. Although Mesmer report-

Joseph E. Mallet • Health Psychology Associates, Two Wisconsin Circle, Suite 700, Chevy Chase, Maryland 20815.

edly had many spectacular cures with his form of hypnosis, he fell into disfavor in 1784 after a negative report from a special commission of the French Academy (Crasilneck & Hall, 1985). They concluded that no evidence could be found of the existence of a magnetic fluid. The therapeutic effects were ascribed to imagination, suggestions, and imitation (Frankel, 1976). Nevertheless, Mesmerism, the name given to Mesmer's type of hypnosis, spread to other parts of the world, including the United States where one of its practitioners, Phineas Parkhurst Quimby (1802–1866), achieved fame for his successful treatment of a bedridden invalid later to become famous as Mary Baker Eddy (1821–1910), the founder of Christian Science (Hilgard & Hilgard, 1975).

Baird (c. 1793–1860), an English physician, has been called the father of modern hypnosis because he coined the term *hypnotism* from the Greek word for sleep. John Elliotson (1791–1868), an English surgeon who introduced the stethoscope into England, reported on numerous surgical operations performed painlessly under hypnotic conditions. A Scottish doctor, James Esdaile (1808–1859) recorded 345 major operations performed in India with hypnosis as the sole anesthetic. Later, when he demonstrated hypnotic anesthesia for amputation of a gangrenous limb before members of the Royal College of Physicians of England, one skeptical observer reported that Esdaile must have hired a "hardened rogue" to undergo the operation for a fee. A writer in the British medical journal, the *Lancet*, asserted that "the patient was an imposter who had been trained not to show pain" (Ornstein & Sobel, 1987, p. 99).

Meanwhile, back in France, two schools of thought concerning hypnosis were developing. The Salpetriere school was headed by Jean-Martin Charcot (1835–1893), the most famous neurologist of his day. Charcot believed that hypnosis was essentially hysterical behavior and that its major manifestations were limited to those who suffered some abnormality of the nervous system. The Nancy school, on the other hand, under the leadership of Auguste Ambroise Liebeault (1823–1904) and Hyppolyte Bernheim (1840–1919) regarded hypnosis as an entirely normal phenomenon and attributed it to the influence of suggestion. They defined suggestibility as the aptitude to transform an idea into an act (Frankel, 1976).

History reveals a veritable *Who's Who* of luminaries in psychology and medicine who were involved with hypnosis over the years. The American psychologist William James (along with Lombroso, the Italian psychiatrist and criminologist), attended the first International Congress for Experimental and Therapeutic Hypnotism held in Paris in 1889.

James included a chapter on hypnosis in his classic text *Principles of Psychology*, and Wilhelm Wundt, the father of modern experimental psychology, wrote a book on hypnosis. The Paris Congress was also attended by Sigmund Freud, who used hypnosis successfully for a while but later substituted his method of free association and psychoanalysis.

Pierre Janet (1859–1947), a student of Charcot, stressed the dissociative aspects of both hysteria and hypnosis. One of his followers in the United States was Morton Prince (1854–1919), founder of the psychological clinic at Harvard. The work of William McDougall (1871–1944) and others involved in treatment of soldiers with "shell shock" at the end of World War I increased public awareness of hypnosis. The experimental study of hypnosis was enhanced by the publication of Clark Hull's (1884–1952) *Hypnosis and Suggestibility* in 1933.

The term *hypnoanalysis* was coined during the war by J. A. Hadfield, who used hypnosis to facilitate abreactions of battlefield traumas (Crasilneck & Hall, 1985). Watkins (1949) reported the use of similar hypnotic techniques during World War II in his book *Hypnotherapy of Wartime Neurosis*.

In 1958, the American Medical Association issued a policy statement recognizing hypnosis as a legitimate treatment method. The American Psychological Association in 1969 established a division for psychologists who engage in hypnosis research and specialize in using it in their clinical practice.

The wider application of hypnosis in the areas of disease prevention and health maintenance is likely to be a significant health care trend in the coming years. A recent survey by Rodolpha *et al.* (1985) of 500 members of the American Society of Clinical Hypnosis revealed that they believed that behavioral medicine was "the general area with the most promising future for the application of hypnosis" (p. 24).

BASIC CONCEPTS

In simple terms, *hypnosis* refers both to the procedure for producing a hypnotic effect and to the hypnotic experience itself. Thus, hypnosis in one sense is a stimulus for the elicitation of a hypnotic response. The other meaning of hypnosis refers to the hypnotic effect or the individual's experience in response to a hypnotic stimulus. A stimulus intended to be hypnotic does not automatically lead to a hypnotic response. Whether such a stimulus elicits such a response depends on the hypnotic conditions. These conditions include such mediating variables as the individual's motivations, expectations, and trust as well as the individual's skill in responding to hypnotic communication (hypnotizability).

Any communication, whether through words or various nonverbal cues, can serve as a hypnotic stimulus or induction and can lead to a hypnotic response if the suggested effect is realistic and if the hypnotic conditions are favorable (i.e., good motivation, positive expectations, adequate trust, and hypnotic skill).

In general terms, the hypnotic process has three main components: an induction, a treatment strategy, and termination. The induction consists of any kind of procedure aimed at guiding the individual to become imaginatively caught up or engrossed in some focused awareness experience (absorption) while letting the surrounding reality or ordinary reality orientation fade away temporarily (detachment and dissociation). The resulting focused awareness experience, relatively free of peripheral distractions, produces an ideal learning or conditioning environment. Induction procedures to produce this absorption and concomitant dissociation can be fairly structured (as when instructing the individual to stare fixedly at a spot on the wall until peripheral awareness fades and the eyes close). A technique like progressive muscle relaxation can also be used. During such procedures, the therapist speaks slowly and calmly while matching or leading the subject's reactions and often tells the subject repeatedly that he or she is entering a relaxed and comfortable hypnotic state.

Less-structured and more improvised inductions can also be used by giving suggestions to focus on an immediate experience, such as a relaxed pattern of breathing, or simply asking the client to remember what it felt like to experience hypnosis in the past.

Once the focused awareness state has been achieved, individuals who are favorably oriented toward experiencing hypnosis (i.e., motivated, positively expectant, trusting) and who have some degree of hypnotic skill are then especially receptive and responsive to suggestions of altered experience. These suggestions make up the second component of the hypnotic process—the treatment strategy. Typical strategies consist of directing the individual to imagine and feel the effects of a relaxing experience, to remember something important, to mentally rehearse coping with a problem, or to anticipate a progressive experience of symptom alleviation. A genuine hypnotic effect occurs when the individual experiences the suggested effects as happening without conscious effort to make them happen. In fact, it may seem that special effort would be required to resist the suggestions. In other words, when a true hypnotic effect is experienced, the subject does not feel like he or she is purposely complying with the suggestions, nor is there any interference with their intended effect.

The third component of the hypnotic process is the exit or termination procedure, which serves to reorient the individual from the imaginatively engrossed, focused awareness state to the more analytic, diffuse, and widely oriented awareness of everyday experience. A typical exit instruction is to follow a count from 1 to 5, using the number 5 as a signal to return fully to one's ordinary awareness.

Self-hypnosis refers to the process by which the individual guides himself or herself into the experience by simply thinking about or imagining the intended effects. Hypnotic skill enables the individual to become so focally aware and imaginatively involved in goal-directed thinking and imaging that the self-suggested effects are experienced with a high degree of realism.

Hypnotizability refers to the individual's skill and ability to receive and respond to hypnotic communication in a hypnotic way (i.e., imaginatively involved, noncritical, or selectively attentive to awareness consistent with the suggestions and experiencing the effects as seemingly nonvolitional). Most people of normal intelligence can be hypnotized if they are motivated to some degree, expect a positive outcome, have sufficient trustful rapport with the therapist, and receive competent guidance in focusing their attention and allowing themselves to become imaginatively involved in the communication matched to them as an individual. Hypnotizability rating scales have been described elsewhere (e.g., Crasilneck & Hall, 1985; Hilgard & Hilgard, 1975). These scales are more frequently used in experimental studies, because many clinicians believe the best indication of hypnotic ability is a client's response to practice inductions of hypnosis in the clinical setting.

Several authors have noted that individuals may be more hypnotizable when under high stress (e.g., Bartlett, 1971; Frankenthal, 1969; Orne, 1965; Stone, 1986). This may be so for two reasons. First, individuals in distress are likely to be highly motivated to receive relief. This predisposes them to greater responsivity to therapeutic suggestions. Second, if the individual's mental state is characterized by an intense focused awareness of the distressing experience, this may be a hypnosis-equivalent state that can be used therapeutically.

MECHANISMS OF ACTION

It is important to realize that hypnosis is not a treatment by itself. Therefore, hypnosis denoted as a treatment or as hypnotherapy should be understood to refer to hypnosis combined with some independent treatment technique such as relaxation instructions, systematic desensitization, cognitive restructuring, or exploration for insight.

Hypnosis *per se* involves the elicitation of an absorbed state of mind characterized by receptivity to processing information in a hypnotic way (i.e., imaginative involvement, selective attention, and nonvolitional experiencing). The hypnotic induction produces a state of readiness to respond to a treatment strategy, which can involve any technique aimed at thought, feeling, or behavior change. Hypnosis has been likened to a syringe. The description is apt because like a syringe, hypnosis cannot produce a treatment effect until it is combined with some therapeutic ingredient (the strategy). Hypnosis can also be compared to an empty envelope into which strategic therapeutic information is placed before being transmitted to the individual. Thus, hypnosis *per se* is an ancillary technique that serves as a catalyst to facilitate or potentiate the effectiveness of a particular treatment procedure.

This facilitative function of hypnosis makes it extremely versatile. It can be combined with any psychological treatment for stress (e.g., breathing techniques, active progressive relaxation, imaginal progressive relaxation, guided imagery, systematic desensitization, cognitive restructuring, thought stopping and switching, suggestions or instructions to modify thoughts, images, or behaviors, cue conditioning, and mental rehearsals of stress reducing behavior). Hypnosis is also well-suited for combination with biofeedback-assisted relaxation training. All of these stress treatment methods can be sent "special delivery" in the hypnotic envelope to facilitate getting the message across faster and more effectively. The induction serves to absorb the subject's attention and make his or her hypnotic resources accessible. Then the treatment is delivered, frequently with the arrangement of posthypnotic cues to extend the treatment effect. Finally, the termination procedure reorients the subject.

It can be seen from the description above that it is meaningless to compare hypnosis to a standard treatment such as systematic desensitization without specifying what the hypnotic procedure consisted of. Sometimes when an unspecified hypnotic procedure is reported, it consisted of direct, repetitive, authoritative suggestions such as, "When you awaken, your headache will be gone." Such simplistic procedures are only rarely effective and fail to represent the creative versatility possible when the individual is guided in using his or her imagination in hypnosis to effect change.

The hypnotic state in itself or hypnosis in combination with various therapeutic techniques has the following characteristics, which may constitute the mechanisms of action in hypnotic prevention and treatment of the stress responses:

1. *Relaxation.* Many hypnotic inductions include relaxation suggestions. Most people who experience hypnotic relaxation describe it as one of the most relaxing experiences they have ever had. This relaxation is important to counteract the excessive psychophysiological arousal of the stress response. Hypnotically induced relaxation can also facilitate desensitization to stressors by producing a stronger association of relaxation with the previously stressful imagined event.

A further advantage of hypnotic relaxation is found in the fact that the simple suggestion to become relaxed and to become hypnotized seems to produce a lowering of the amount of corticosteroids circulating in the bloodstream (Sacher, Fishman, & Mason, 1965). These corticosteroids are harmful when they inhibit the immune system's ability to protect the body (Bowers & Kelly, 1979, p. 495).

2. *Imagery.* Hypnotically produced images are more subjectively compelling (Kihlstrom, 1979) and are clearer and more vivid (Glick, 1970; Lang, Lazovick, & Reynolds, 1965; Lazarus, 1971, 1977). Hypnotically enhanced imagery results in greater functional exposure in desensitization and facilitates a number of hypnotic strategies such as goal-directed imagining, "as if" thinking, and imagery rehearsals of coping with stressors.

3. *Concentration.* Hypnosis is characterized by heightened concentra-

tion, which can facilitate most therapeutic strategies. For example, an individual could use hypnotically enhanced concentration to be more aware of stress-inducing thoughts, images, and behaviors. Stress can inhibit concentration abilities, and hypnotic training can help to restore concentration, especially when combined with relaxation and creative problem solving.

4. *Increased Suggestibility. Suggestibility* refers to responsiveness to suggestions, which can be any communication—whether in the form of advice, instructions, interpretations, guided imagery, or even nonverbal cues. Hypnosis increases this responsiveness (Fromm, 1980; Spiegel, 1978) when the hypnotic conditions are favorable and the suggestions are appropriate. Hypnosis adds something to so-called "waking suggestibility" (Evans, 1967, 1968). The communication is received in an uncritical and imaginatively absorbed way, and suggested effects are experienced as nonvolitional or seemingly outside of conscious control. Hypnotically enhanced suggestibility can therefore be used to potentiate the effectiveness of therapeutic communication regarding stress, its prevention, and its treatment.

5. *Absorption.* The quality of being imaginatively involved or caught up in the hypnotic experience is referred to as *absorption.* Related characteristics common to hypnosis are heightened concentration, focused attention, and increased awareness. These cognitive experiences are helpful in stress management for such goals as increased awareness of potential and actual stressors, greater consciousness of thoughts, images, and behaviors related to stress and stress control, increased memory of critical incidents related to stress, and improved problem solving through focused attention.

6. *Dissociation.* This phenomenon is the complement of absorption. In the context of hypnosis it is an adaptive way of detaching or disconnecting oneself from ordinary reality orientation for the purpose of experiencing an altered sense of reality. A patient can be taught to dissociate from stressful experiences in a controlled way during office visits. During periods of high stress in everyday life, he or she can use self-hypnosis to engage in dissociative techniques such as coping imagery or calm scene visualizations.

Several other dissociative techniques are commonly used in the context of hypnosis. *Amnesia* may be suggested to temporarily block memories of an event with which the patient is not yet prepared to cope. *Hypnotic age regression* guides the subject to remember and perhaps reexperience a stressful event from an earlier period in order to gain insight or to have an emotionally corrective experience. Alternatively, age regression can be used to remind the patient of some earlier pleasant event or mastery experience. *Hypnotic time distortion* techniques can allow the client to experience a speeding up, slowing down, or halting of the passage of time in order to cope with some stressful experience. And *age progression* suggestions can give the patient a sense of experiencing some future time when a stressful experience is finally over or some therapeutic goal has been achieved.

7. *Selective attention and suspension of critical judgment.* The hypnotic

experience has several common characteristics. Hypnotized individuals are less analytical and critical in their appraisal of experience. Consequently, they are inclined to accept logical inconsistencies and to ignore evidence contrary to suggested experiences while selectively paying attention to data consistent with the suggestion. This aptitude will enable a stressed patient to ignore the implications of a telephone ringing when imagining the relaxing experience of lying on a remote sandy beach with only the sound of the waves and the seagulls.

8. *Nonvolitional experiencing.* This phenomenon refers to the absence of conscious effort, willpower, or mere compliance in producing hypnotic effects. Hypnotized persons in effect dissociate from awareness their role in the production of hypnotic effects. This characteristic, sometimes referred to as automaticity of response, is considered the classical hypnotic effect.

This experience often serves to dramatically impress hypnotic subjects with the power of their hypnotic talent. When stressed individuals can experience such hypnotic phenomena as a hand levitation (hand rises effortlessly) arm catalepsy (arm is experienced as rigid and immobile), or glove anesthesia (hand genuinely feels like it is in an anesthetizing glove) at the same time that they are instructed to notice the power of their mind to create such an extraordinary effect, they can be taught to generalize the experience to a sense of greater self-control in changing a stressful life style or alleviating stress-related symptoms.

9. *Alteration of consciousness or experience.* Such alterations through suggestion are another common characteristic of hypnosis. The experiences to be altered or modified can include behavior, thoughts, attitudes, beliefs, feelings, images, sensations, perceptions, and memories. It is evident that stress prevention and treatment is concerned with such alterations of experience, and hypnosis is well-suited for the task.

Standard stress management techniques often include instructions for alteration of sensations such as tension. When these instructions are given in the context of hypnosis, they become powerful hypnotic suggestions that are generally experienced as taking effect without the subject's conscious effort. This serves to enhance their effectiveness.

SELF-HYPNOSIS AND STRESS REDUCTION

Self-hypnosis in particular is well-suited to augmenting the effectiveness of standard stress prevention and treatment methods, and at times it offers improvements over heterohypnosis. Some of the advantages self-hypnosis offers are listed below:

1. A sense of self-control and the ability to achieve self-regulation is

very important, as described in Chapter Seven. The experience of self-initiated hypnotic effects serves to impress the clients with their personal power and self-efficacy. It is difficult for clients to feel as helpless or out of control when they recognize they are directly responsible for altered experience.

2. A feeling of being an active participant rather than a passive recipient in the treatment process is fostered by training in self-hypnosis skills. This experience also tends to improve compliance with treatment.

3. Untrusting, resistant, or skeptical patients may benefit from treatment sooner by learning to hypnotize themselves. When there is no longer an issue of mistrusting or resisting the hypnotist, skepticism soon fades, and impressive self-hypnotic effects are achieved.

4. Through self-hypnosis training, the overly dependent patient can learn to be aware of and rely on his or her own resources for stress control.

5. Self-hypnosis makes treatment effects more generalizable. The patient learns how to apply the same self-hypnotic skills to other situations.

6. Treatment effects are also more available on the spot and are longer lasting when the patient knows how to reactivate coping skills through self-hypnosis.

7. Self-hypnotic treatment strategies are, by definition, individualized and are therefore likely to be relevant to the patient's needs.

8. Stress-inducing cognitions (e.g., to fail a test is a catastrophe) that are resistant to change can be viewed as a form of negative self-hypnosis. Therefore it is appropriate to substitute more adaptive and helpful self-hypnosis. The very act and experience of self-hypnosis familiarizes and impresses individuals with the power of their thoughts and images either outside or inside the context of hypnosis.

Further advantages of combining hypnosis with standard stress prevention and treatment methods are:

1. Faster therapeutic effects are often reported with hypnosis. These faster results frequently occur because rapport usually develops more quickly, because clients expect more rapid change, and because hypnotic experiences are usually more intense. The results can be maintained through training in self-hypnosis and the emphasis in therapy on self-efficacy and self-control.

2. Positive expectations and experiences enhance the effectiveness of techniques augmented by hypnosis. Patients in clinical settings frequently seek hypnotic treatment because of the reputation of hyp-

nosis as a powerful, rapid-action technique. Sometimes there is some degree of magical thinking involved in these expectations, but a skillful clinician can educate the patient and use those expectations to the patient's advantage.

Usually hypnosis subjects report that their experience of hypnosis is very pleasant and impressive. Frequently, they will say they were reluctant to "come out of it" because the experience felt so good. They express how impressed they are by such exclamations as "that was amazing" or "that was really incredible." These favorable responses make the experience more rewarding, thus enhancing treatment effectiveness and compliance with any homework assignments.

The positive expectations of hypnosis sometimes lead to its being approached as a last resort. The clinician can very profitably capitalize on this reaction while being cautious of the fact that patients may try to prove that "even hypnosis doesn't work" if they are not yet prepared to be free of symptoms.

3. Specialized hypnotic techniques are particularly applicable to stress prevention and treatment. Through posthypnotic cues the patient can be conditioned to experience relaxation or some coping resource at the time of a stressful episode. Self-hypnosis can be used for reestablishing the hypnotic experience of stress control on the spot. In addition, other traditional hypnotic techniques such as age regression, age progression, and time distortion (described above) can be used to enhance the therapeutic benefits of stress treatments.

4. Therapist stress reduction is another advantage of hypnosis for stress control. Most experienced hypnotherapists would probably report that their access to the powerful tool of hypnosis makes their work more interesting, more creative, more enjoyable, more satisfying, and more effective. These experiences definitely make working with patients less stressful. This will certainly benefit the patient.

The advantages of combining hypnosis in general and self-hypnosis in particular with standard stress treatments have been outlined in the preceding sections. The next three sections will illustrate how these combined hypnotic techniques can be applied to bring about modification of stress-related behaviors, stressful cognitions, and stress-related symptoms themselves. Note that modification of stress-related behaviors and cognitions can help to prevent the stress response characterized by excessive psychophysiological arousal. Chronic or very intense exposure to the stress response can result in formation of stress symptoms. Hypnotic techniques for modification of stress-related behaviors are designed to help the patient increase or decrease behaviors that are linked to the initiation, exacerbation, or maintenance of the stress response and stress symptoms.

HYPNOSIS AND THE MODIFICATION OF STRESS-RELATED BEHAVIOR

Stress-related behaviors include engaging in stress-producing actions and failing to engage in stress-reducing activities that are linked to the initiation, exacerbation, or maintenance of the stress response or stress symptoms. In some cases, the individual needs to avoid, minimize, or modify exposure to stressors (e.g., leave an excessively stressful job, take some time off, or transfer to another department). In other cases, he or she needs to increase stress-reducing behaviors. A sample of stress-reducing behaviors would include acting assertively, utilizing time management, compartmentalizing problems, delegating of responsibility, building social supports, obtaining psychotherapy, reducing intake of stimulants (such as caffeine or alcohol), getting proper nutrition and exercise, and engaging in hobbies and pleasureful diversions.

Hypnotic techniques can be used to increase awareness of stressors or stress-related behaviors using a variety of exploratory techniques. Then hypnotic problem-solving techniques can be used to find solutions to these problematic behaviors, and various resource-accessing or ego-strengthening techniques, including posthypnotic suggestions, can be used to motivate patients and help them to continue using coping behaviors.

Standard techniques oriented toward modification of stress-related behaviors include such methods as systematic desensitization, mental rehearsals, flooding, and implosion. Hypnosis and self-hypnosis can improve the effectiveness of these techniques because of the advantages listed previously (e.g., increased relaxation, imagery, and suggestibility).

The following description of a coping behavior mental rehearsal illustrates a number of techniques used in hypnotic intervention. It will be outlined in terms of the three main components of the hypnotic process: induction, strategy, and termination.

1. *Induction.* The induction can consist of any instructions that serve to disconnect the subject's awareness from the multiple, diffuse stimuli in the surrounding environment and to narrow down the focus of attention to something more specific. A focus on breathing or any other body awareness can accomplish this purpose. Instructions to imagine a calm scene somewhere presumably distant from the present location further serve to distance subjects mentally from their immediate surroundings and contribute to a temporary fading of general reality orientation. Instructions to use as many perceptual senses as possible to amplify their imaginative involvement in a relaxing scene increases dissociation from general reality orientation, deepens or intensifies the imagined experience of relaxation and, in a sense, serves as a warm-up for focusing imaginatively on some therapeutic goal after the calm scene imagery. Individuals who would benefit from further relaxation training could be guided in relaxation scanning or imagin-

ing relaxation spreading slowly but surely through the body from the head to the toes. This downwardly progressive scanning led with suitable intonation can serve as a deepening procedure, that is, one that increases the intensity of the client's experience of hypnotic involvement. The time spent for this procedure (several minutes) and the narrow focus on some immediate awareness probably increase the degree of dissociation and further prepare the person for focused imagining. The following is a sample induction:

> Sit or lie in a comfortable position and let the closing of your eyes signal your readiness and willingness to shut out everyday cares and concerns for a while . . . prepare to go on a pleasant internal journey of discovery . . . feeling excited about discovering some solutions you seek . . . it's like shifting mental gears so you become so much more aware of some important things . . . and then focus your attention on your breathing . . . slowing down . . . so relaxed and regular . . . comfortable . . . relaxing a little bit more each time you exhale . . . just breathing out any tightness or tension, any stress or strain . . . that's right . . . and then imagine going away in your mind to some very calm nature scene . . . perhaps it's a favorite vacation spot or just a place you've dreamed of visiting . . . enjoy it completely, using as many of your senses as you can . . . see what there is to see (pause) . . . perhaps there are sounds connected with your calm scene or maybe it's just a quiet calm (pause) . . . notice any aromas you can smell or just enjoy the clean fresh air (pause) . . . be aware of how you feel both outside and inside . . . notice the temperature and the pleasant feelings in your body (pause) . . . feeling peaceful, serene . . . safe and secure . . . there might even be some pleasant tastes connected with your special place (pause) . . . your entire body relaxing completely . . . your forehead relaxing, just smoothed out and tension-free . . . like a calm pond . . . and your eyes relaxing, just lightly shut and so comfortable . . . you feel your entire face relaxing, your jaw slack, your teeth separated . . . imagine the experience of an inner smile . . . the facial features softening . . . a feeling of serenity . . . feeling your throat relaxing, your neck relaxing . . . notice your shoulders relaxing, lowering slightly as any unnecessary tension just drains out . . . you're aware of your right arm and hand relaxing completely, perhaps feeling heavy and warm . . . your left arm and hand relaxing likewise . . . relaxed and tension-free, heavy and warm . . . feeling your chest relax, and your upper back . . . loosening up, completely supported by the furniture, your abdomen relaxing, your lower back . . . warm and comfortable and tension-free . . . just settling down into the supporting furniture . . . both legs and feet relaxing, feeling heavy and warm . . . the entire body, relaxing completely.

2. *Strategy.* At this point, the subject is presumably in a hypnotic state—imaginatively absorbed, uncritically and selectively attending to suggested effects, and experiencing the effects occurring essentially without conscious effort. It should be noted here that the client is more likely to have these experience if he or she has been taught how to experience them by verbal and behavioral modeling as well as by direct instruction (Katz, 1979).

The next step is to use the hypnotic state to implement a treatment strategy. One technique to make the transition from calm scene imagery or relaxation scanning to problem-solving is to guide the subject in imagining discovering a trail nearby and deciding to follow it. This treatment strategy will be illustrated by the following sample verbalization.

Feeling very relaxed now . . . and you notice a path nearby . . . you decide to follow it and discover where it leads you . . . you feel yourself moving along easily and effortlessly . . . having a sense of expectation about finding something important . . . and then you notice ahead, a small building . . . maybe it is a cottage or a cabin . . . you decide to go up to it and find out what's inside . . . as you open the front door, you have a strong sense that there is something for you to find inside . . . you go in and see a hallway with doors on either side . . . you choose one and open it . . . inside is a room decorated in a special way you like . . . then you see a chair that looks very comfortable and inviting . . . you go over and sit down . . . it's such a relaxing comfortable chair . . . you close your eyes and just let your thoughts drift . . . it's like you're kind of experiencing your stream of consciousness . . . thoughts and images just flowing . . . and now you have a sense that this is a very special time and place to work on something important . . . just relaxing, and then you become aware of a problem solving technique . . . it has four steps: (1) become aware of a stressful behavior, (2) become aware of the imagined threat you are responding to, (3) become aware of a healthier response, and (4) imagine yourself experiencing the healthier response in the future . . . you are excited about trying it out . . . step 1, become aware of some stressful behavior . . . experience that behavior with as many senses as you can . . . (Sample behavior: getting excessively upset in traffic jams.) . . . just nod your head when you have become aware of it . . . (nods head) . . . good . . . Step 2, become aware of the imagined threat you are responding to . . . ask yourself, "What am I saying to myself and what am I imagining could go wrong?" . . . just nod your head when you are finished . . . (Sample self talk: "My supervisor will think I am irresponsible if I'm late"; "I'll be fired if I'm late one more time." Sample images: I can see that disapproving look on my supervisor's face; I can hear my supervisor asking me what happened in that critical tone.) . . . (nods head) . . . good . . . Step 3, become aware of a healthier response . . . notice how you could change your self-talk, images and behaviors in order to experience less stress . . . take all the time you need and when you are finished, just nod your head . . . (Sample self-talk change: "My supervisor knows I am a responsible person; it is highly improbable that I would be fired." Sample image/behavior change: picture myself going directly to my supervisor and assertively describing the traffic jam; I see and hear her responding with understanding) . . . (nods head) . . . fine . . . Step 4, imagine experiencing your healthier response in the future . . . just imagine being in a situation in which in the past you reacted in that stressful way . . . now things are different . . . at any hint of the old stress response it will occur to you to say to yourself, "There's my cue to cope" . . . then you flash an image of your calm scene and focus on your breathing, letting each of your next five calm breaths relax you more and more . . . you become aware of any imagined threat by asking yourself, "What am I saying to myself and what am I imagining could go wrong?" . . . then you substitute healthier thoughts and images and imagine coping successfully with the situation . . . that's fine . . . take a few more minutes to store this new thought and behavior pattern in your consciousness.

3. *Termination.* The following is a sample termination or exit procedure:

As you prepare now to return to your everyday awareness of your immediate surroundings . . . finding it easy to follow a count from one to five . . . each number guiding you to a wider awareness so that by the number five you will be alert, refreshed . . . with a full return of all of your natural sensations, perceptions, memories and experiences, but bringing along with you some special new learning . . . ready . . . one, two, three, four, five . . . alert and refreshed and feeling very good."'

HYPNOSIS AND THE MODIFICATION OF STRESS-RELATED COGNITIONS

Stressful cognitions include thoughts, images, attitudes, assumptions, beliefs, and even memories that lead the individual to interpret events and experiences as worthy of a stress response. Dreams are another category of cognitions that may be stressful, and they will be addressed here as well.

Traditional nonhypnotic treatments for modification of thought patterns include thought stopping and switching, cognitive restructuring, rational-emotive therapy, and cognitive-behavior modification. All of these treatments can easily be combined with hypnosis.

Hypnotic techniques are also well suited to helping the patient change stressful images, memories, and even dreams. Images refer to any mental representation of an experience involving any or all of the senses. Visual images are very familiar, but an individual could also be stressed by mental representations that are auditory, olfactory, gustatory, tactile, or kinesthetic.

Hypnosis as a technique characterized by selective attention and imaginative involvement is especially well suited for management of stressful images. For example, the hypnotherapist can teach the patient who became stressed by a plane crash at sea to mentally create less traumatic image substitutes for the sight of the bodies, the sound of the screaming, the smell of the smoke, the sense of falling, the taste of the salt water, and the cold feeling of the frigid water. The patient could be taught to use flashbacks as a cue to use a thought-stopping technique and then switch the thoughts and images to a safe calm scene. Hypnotic suggestions for amnesia could also be used.

Hypnotherapy is well suited to helping patients to forget, recall, or change stressful memories. Hypnotic recall of stressful memories may help in exploring the circumstances of a traumatic event. Once the memories are recalled, the hypnotist can teach the patient to imagine leaving the memories locked away, at least temporarily until he or she has the skills to deal with them. Memories can even be altered or purposely distorted in hypnosis. For this reason, forensic uses of memory enhancement require caution. But adaptive alterations can be made through techniques such as imagining that one is directing a play in which events are changed in order to give the individual greater peace of mind.

A commonly used technique for memory work involves hypnotic age regression, which consists of guiding the patient to experience going back through time to recall and perhaps reexperience certain critical incidents in order to learn something or to have an emotionally corrective experience. This technique is excellent for helping clients deal with stressful events that took place earlier in life.

Hypnotic age progression consists of guiding the individual to imagine a future event. A patient, for example, who is plagued by grief and doubts that he or she can get through an upcoming funeral can be taught to imagine having used various coping techniques along the way, to remember having had social supports that had been forgotten about, and even to have experienced some peace of mind when events were put in perspective.

Traumatic dreams or nightmares can be a very stressful experience and deprive the patient of adequate sleep time. There is some evidence that highly hypnotizable subjects can change the content of their night REM dreams by giving themselves instructions to do so before sleep (Belicki & Bowers, 1982; Stoyva, 1965; Tart, 1964). Eichelman (1985) reported the cases of two veterans with posttraumatic stress disorders whose recurrent and traumatic dreams were terminated following hypnotic treatment and a dream substitution technique. The hypnotherapist demonstrated to the patients that hypnotically rehearsed dreams could be incorporated into nocturnal dreams in order to convince them of their control over nocturnal dream content. After the dream substitutions were rehearsed in hypnosis and subsequently were dreamed at night, the veterans' original traumatic dreams ceased.

HYPNOSIS AND THE MODIFICATION OF STRESS-RELATED SYMPTOMS

Stress-disordered patients can experience the initiation, exacerbations, or maintenance of symptoms from chronic elicitation of the stress response for any of the following reasons: (1) he or she was unable to avoid or alter exposure to certain intrinsic stressors such as excessive noise or temperature; (2) when the stressor was avoidable or alterable, the patient failed to engage in stress-reducing behaviors such as avoidance (e.g., quit excessively stressful job) or direct problem solving (e.g., insist on working conditions being changed) or else engaged in stress-producing behaviors (e.g., abused alcohol and got fired); (3) he or she engaged in stress-producing cognitions (e.g., "I should try to please everyone") or failed to engage in stress-reducing cognitions (e.g., "One day at a time.") The end result can be end-organ damage or dysfunction as well as psychological dysfunction and distress. The good news is that some relief through hypnosis is available without harmful side effects or invasive procedures.

This section will list a sample of hypnotic treatment reports illustrating the wide applicability of hypnotic treatments to a variety of stress-related symptoms and disorders. Following that will be an outline of the multiple ways hypnosis can be applied to treatment of one of these disorders, essential hypertension.

Everly and Rosenfeld (1981) have noted that the psychological disturbances most associated with excessive stress are diffuse anxiety, manic behavior patterns, insomnia, and depression. They also cite evidence of a link between stress and schizophrenia (p. 44). The reader can get an idea of how these conditions have been treated with adjunctive hypnosis by referring to two recent texts (Wester, 1987; Wester & Smith, 1986), which cover hypnotic treatments of these and a wide range of other psychological and physiological disturbances.

The following is a list by category of some of the psychophysiological disorders and stressful reactions to them that have been treated using hypnosis: skin disorders, including psoriasis, acne, pruritis, eczema, neurodermatitis, and herpes (cf. Brown & Fromm, 1987; Chiasson, 1986; Frankel, 1976; Kroger & Fezler, 1976); gastrointestinal disorders, including gastritis, peptic ulcer, irritable bowel syndrome, inflammatory bowel disease, and ulcerative colitis (cf. Brown & Fromm, 1987; Byrne, 1973; Chiasson, 1987; Hunter, 1987; Kroger & Fezler, 1976; Pratt, Wood, & Allman, 1984); headaches (cf. Barnet, 1984; Brown & Fromm, 1987; Daniels, 1977; Greanleaf, 1974; Herbert & Gutman, 1980; Kroger & Fezler, 1976; Maher-Loughman, 1975; Pratt et al., 1984; Todd & Kelly, 1970); cancer and immune-related diseases (cf. Araoz, 1983; Brown & Fromm, 1987; LeBaron & Zeltzer, 1984; Spiegel & Bloom, 1983; Weitz, 1983); insomnia (cf. Barnet, 1984; Fabian & Manus, 1986; Herbert & Gutman, 1980; Todd & Kelly, 1970); asthma (cf. Brown & Fromm, 1987; Collison, 1968; Hunter, 1987; Kroger & Fezler, 1976; Maher-Loughnan, 1975; Moorefield, 1971; Pratt et al., 1984; Wadden & Anderton, 1982); posttraumatic stress syndrome (cf. Brende, 1980; Eichelman, 1985; MacHovec, 1985; Spiegel, 1981; Stutman & Bliss, 1985); and essential hypertension (cf. Brown & Fromm, 1987; Deabler, Fidel, Dillenkoffer, & Elder, 1973; Friedman & Taub, 1978; Kroger & Fezler, 1976; Pratt et al., 1984; Wester, 1986).

Brown and Fromm (1987) have cited the application of numerous hypnotic techniques to the treatment of hypertension, including the following: (1) Hypnotic exploration techniques can be used to discover or increase awareness of risk factors, for example, stress-producing behaviors and cognitions, excessive salt or alcohol use, and overeating. (2) Mental rehearsals in hypnosis can be used to facilitate stimulus control or modification of exposure to products that can raise blood pressure (e.g., salt, caffeine, tobacco, and alcohol) as well as stressful environmental stimuli such as excessive noise or temperature. (3) Hypnotic mental rehearsals combined with hypnotic relaxation can be used to facilitate compliance with treatment, including taking of medication and exercise. (4) Hypnotic relaxation can be used for lowering systolic and diastolic blood pressure (Deabler, Fidel, Dillen, Koffer, & Elder, 1973; Friedman & Taub, 1977, 1978).

Suggestions can be given to relax the musculoskeletal system as well as the internal organs such as the heart and blood vessels. Through relaxation training with hypnosis, the patient can learn control over sympathetic nervous system activity and possibly disrupt the feedback mechanism associated with maintaining the elevated blood pressure (Abboud, 1976). (5) Direct hypnotic suggestions to slow the heart rate plus heart rate feedback can be used to reduce cardiac output. Direct suggestions to lower pulse rate have been shown to be effective for certain patients (Collison, 1970; Van Pelt, 1958) but not for others (Jana, 1967). The patient can be taught self-hypnosis and can be given posthypnotic suggestions to sustain the lowered heart rate outside the clinical session. (6) Hypnotic suggestions combined with thermal biofeedback have been shown to decrease blood pressure (Roberts, Kewman, & MacDonald, 1973). Guided imagery (e.g., of warm sun baking down, hot sand, or heated glove) or open-ended suggestions can be used in the context of hypnosis to teach the patient voluntary control over peripheral vasodilation. Brown and Fromm (1987) point out that the hand-warming technique may be combined with the heart-rate reduction techniques to deal with both aspects of the fight-or-flight reaction implicated in elevated blood pressure, namely, increased cardiac output and peripheral vasoconstriction associated with increased peripheral resistance. (7) Hypnosis combined with cognitive-behavior therapy can help the client identify and change stressful thoughts, images, and behaviors. For example, perfectionistic thinking could be corrected through self-suggestions such as "I did my best," or "Let it go." (8) More dynamically oriented psychotherapy or hypnoanalysis can be used to explore and work through possible conflicts contributing to stressful emotions such as anger.

TREATMENT PRECAUTIONS

Hypnosis in itself is very safe, but like any tool it can be misused. There are two main guidelines for the use of hypnosis in the area of stress-related disorders. First, a thorough medical and/or neurological examination should be made whenever there is any doubt as to the origin of the symptoms. Second, clinicians should treat with hypnosis only problems that they are competent to treat without hypnosis, unless they receive direct supervision.

The following are some types of subjects with whom special caution is required when using hypnosis.

1. *Psychotic and other severely disturbed patients.* Hypnosis is generally intended to produce alterations in general reality orientation and an absorption in inner experiences, including alterations in perceptions, sensations, thoughts, images, and memories. Therefore, caution must be used when working with individuals who already have lost some contact with reality and who may experience hypnosis as a frightening further dissociation or out-of-control experience.

2. *Paranoid patients.* The hypnotherapist working with paranoid clients must be aware of issues of trust, possible ideas of influence, attribution of exaggerated powers to the therapist, and the potential for feeling out of control.

3. *Depressed patients.* Hypnosis and self-hypnosis could be used by depressed clients as a form of further withdrawal at times when they perhaps would benefit from further social contact or potentially reinforcing activities of daily living. During a depressive episode, they may use hypnosis to be too introspective and ruminative and at such times they may experience less control of suicidal ideation. Nevertheless, cautious use of hypnosis by a therapist competent to work with depressed patients may be very beneficial (Miller, 1986; Torem, 1987).

4. *Overly anxious patient.* Clients who are highly anxious and who fear "letting go" may experience hypnosis very negatively without special guidance. The therapist must be skilled and comfortable working with anxious patients and introduce hypnosis or self-hypnosis very gradually if the client is motivated enough to try it. With adequate preparation, even highly anxious patients can generally benefit from hypnotic treatment. It is likely that they are already negatively hypnotizing themselves quite successfully with catastrophical imagery and negative self-talk.

5. *Magical thinkers and excessive daydreamers.* Caution is required when using hypnosis with individuals who are looking for a magic pill or who excessively engage in fantasy to the neglect of coping behaviors. It is possible to take advantage of such tendencies by introducing these clients to the "magic" of self-control and the adaptive uses of fantasy for creative problem solving and mental rehearsals of coping.

6. *Overly dependent patients.* Skilled hypnotherapists can avoid fostering unhealthy dependence. They can educate clients with strong dependency needs about the collaborative nature of the therapeutic enterprise and the importance of experiencing self-efficacy through

self-control skills using self-hypnosis and other self-regulation techniques.

Caution is also required in the specific applications of hypnosis. The following is a list of some potentially problematic hypnotic effects.

1. *Removal of symptoms that signal physical dysfunction or damage.* It is possible with hypnosis to remove a symptom, such as headache pain, that serves as an alarm signal of a pathological condition such as a brain tumor. The competent hypnotherapist will obtain medical or neurological clearance before working on symptom alleviation or elimination of any suspect symptoms.

2. *Removal of symptoms masking psychological problems.* Anxiety, tension, and pain may be the body's reaction to the stress of psychological problems. Attempting symptom alleviation without attention to such underlying psychological conditions could delay necessary psychological treatment, and any symptom change may be slow, blocked, or subject to relapse. When such dynamics are suspected, a thorough psychological assessment and clincial interview should be conducted. If this is indicated, a psychotherapist trained in hypnosis can help the client solve the underlying problem while learning to control the symptoms.

3. *Suggestions that are too general or ambiguous.* Such suggestions can pose risks. For example, aversive suggestions to vomit at the smell of cigarette smoke could cause great distress if the client reacted as suggested everytime someone else lit up a cigarette.

4. *Neglect of required medical treatment.* A client in hypnotic treatment who is misinformed or who has unrealistic expectations of hypnosis may avoid or prematurely terminate necessary medical treatment or physical therapy.

5. *Overmedication.* Any medication should be closely monitored during hypnotic treatment of stress-related disorders because if symptoms are alleviated or eliminated while the medication level is maintained, the patient may be dangerously overmedicated. Deep relaxation as part of the hypnotic treatment may also result in excessive potentiation of the effects of the medication (Everly, 1981).

6. *Spontaneous age regression and abreaction.* Occasionally, the focused awareness of the hypnotic state results in the spontaneous elicitation of an age regression whereby the patient has a sense of returning to an experience earlier in life. If this event was traumatic, the patient may then experience a very dramatic abreaction or emotional catharsis. The hypnotherapist must be prepared to deal with the emotional reaction in a constructive way or arrange for a consultation with a mental health professional.

SUMMARY

This chapter has attempted to present the potentially valuable role of hypnosis in enhancing and accelerating treatments aimed at the prevention and treatment of excessive stress reactions. The information presented can be summarized as follows:

1. Hypnosis has been used since earliest times as part of the treatment of human illness. Many clinicians who use hypnosis in their practice believe that behavioral medicine is the general area with the most promising future for the application of hypnosis.

2. Any communication, whether through words or various nonverbal cues, can serve as a hypnotic stimulus or induction and can lead to a hypnotic response if the suggested effect is realistic and if the hypnotic conditions are favorable (i.e., good motivation, positive expectations, adequate trust, and hypnotic skill). The hypnotic response is an experience of being imaginatively involved, selectively attentive, and feeling as if the suggested effects are dissociated from conscious control. Hypnotizability refers to the individual's skill and ability to experience such a hypnotic response. Self-hypnosis involves creating this response through one's own goal-directed thinking and imaging.

3. The mechanisms of action by which hypnosis is believed to enhance the effectiveness of standard stress treatments are most likely a combination of the following: increased relaxation, improved imagery, heightened concentration, increased suggestibility, absorption with concomitant dissociation, selective attention with suspension of critical judgment, nonvolitional experiencing, and alteration of consciousness or experience. Self-hypnosis offers special advantages in this area, and both forms of hypnosis aim to promote accelerated change, capitalize on positive expectations and experience, and allow for use of specialized hypnotic techniques applicable to stress treatment, including posthypnotic cues, age regression, age progression, and time distortion. The facilitative function of hypnosis is also likely to reduce the therapist's stress, which will benefit the patient.

4. Hypnosis offers many advantages to clinicians involved in stress prevention and treatment programs. It can be combined with virtually any stress treatment that is aimed at thought, feeling, or behavior change to increase its effectiveness. Hypnotic techniques are well-suited for preventing and altering the stress response by helping the client to increase stress-reducing cognitions and behaviors and to decrease those that produce stress. Health risk behaviors (e.g., smoking, overeating, noncompliance with treatment) that can exacerbate stress-related disorders can also be modified with adjunctive hypnosis.

If the individual experiences chronic elicitation of the stress response and develops stress symptoms and disorders, many of these can be treated with ancillary hypnotic techniques. Clinicians working with symptom alleviation or elimination are cautioned to arrange for adequate medical and/or neurological screening of patients, as well as monitoring during treatment.

5. Hypnosis has the advantage of being a noninvasive treatment modality, and it has no harmful side effects when used properly. Caution in using this powerful tool must be exercised when working with certain patient populations, and care must be given to formulating suggestions that are safe and appropriate.

When competent clinicians with training in clinical hypnosis adhere to these safeguards, they are likely to make a significant contribution to the prevention and treatment of excessive stress arousal and stress-related disorders.

Biofeedback in the Treatment of the Stress Response

The purpose of this chapter is to provide a basic introduction to biofeedback in general and as it relates to the treatment of excessive stress. Biofeedback may be thought of as a unique "high technology" therapy that may be used to: (1) engender a relaxation response, thus treating the stress response itself, or (2) alter target-organ activity, thus treating the symptoms of excessive stress arousal.

Biofeedback may be conceptualized as a procedure in which data regarding an individual's biological activity are collected, processed, and conveyed back so that ultimately one can modify that activity. It is the construction of a "feedback loop," which may be envisioned as in Figure 14.1.

Feedback loops exist in almost all functions of the human body, from the rate-modifying feedback loops concerned with the most elementary biochemical reactions to the most complex human endeavors. Information regarding the result of any event is necessary at some level, if it is to be modified in any but random fashion.

Thus, the concept underlying biofeedback is an elementary one in all biology, yet one that has not yet been widely put to use in the therapeutic sciences. In the traditional medical model, the patient presents a physiological disturbance, and data regarding his or her physiological functioning are collected by the clinician, who draws conclusions and institutes appropriate therapy, the patient playing a passive role. This interaction as visualized below represents an indirect closed loop of information, starting and

Figure 14.1

ending with the patient and including information-gathering devices, the clinician, and therapeutic devices.

As can be seen from a comparison of Figures 14.1 and 14.2, the principle on which biofeedback is based involves the active participation of the patient in the modification of his or her condition.

Consider the case of a function like breathing, which, when one turns one's attention to it, one is aware of but which continues without conscious awareness. The question of awareness, of course, does not even enter into the picture in terms of visceral autonomic responses generally. It is as if there are priorities for the human brain, with many functions carried out at subcortical levels—especially those that must be maintained in an ongoing fashion, such as heartbeat and biochemical reactions. Although this may be the most efficient way for an organism to function, it keeps it from being able to monitor many of its autonomic functions consciously and thus consciously change them. This is what biofeedback provides for the individual—the potential to exert some control over autonomic biological activity.

Given the appropriate information, as in biofeedback, it is being increasingly found that we can learn to change bodily functions that were heretofore thought to be inaccessible. This includes greater finite control over the activities of both the voluntary and the autonomic nervous systems.

The purpose of this chapter is to amplify and elaborate on the principles on which biofeedback is based and outline how it may be of benefit in

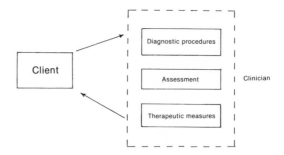

Figure 14.2

the treatment of the stress response. We will also describe some of the historical trends that have led to the present state of the art of biofeedback and then discuss some of the biofeedback modalities in current use. Finally, we will examine the role of the therapist in the biofeedback paradigm.

HISTORY

The term *biofeedback* is relatively new, reportedly having been coined at the first annual meeting of the Biofeedback Research Society in 1969 as a shortened version of "biological feedback." Although the term itself is new, the foundations are less so.

The historical development of biofeedback can be traced back to the early 1900s and the work of Pavlov and Watson on one hand and Thorndike on the other. Pavlov and Watson's research in the classical conditioning of the autonomic nervous system was thought to be discretely separate from the work of Thorndike in the operant conditioning of the musculoskeletal system. Early researchers were convinced that conditioning that affected the autonomic nervous system had to be accomplished through a classical conditioning paradigm (an S → R model involving conditioning on the basis of association rather than as a function of behavioral consequence as in an operant model). This idea persisted for many years. At the same time, according to a review by Gatchel and Price (1979), case reports were emerging of individuals who reportedly could voluntarily alter autonomic functioning (see Lindsley & Sassaman, 1938; Luria, 1958; McClure, 1959; Ogden & Shock, 1939). However, the mechanisms by which these changes were effected were unknown.

In the early 1960s, research reported the ability of subjects to alter heart rate (Frazier, 1966; Shearn, 1962; see Engel, 1972, for an early review).

At the same time, Basmajian (1963) was reporting the ability of patients to control single motor-unit activity. With the development of an electromyographic biofeedback system, Budzynski and Stoyva began delving into the applications of biofeedback in the facilitation of general relaxation and in the treatment of tension headaches (see Stoyva & Budzynski, 1974, for a review).

During this period, the Menninger group led by the Greens was delving into the application of thermal biofeedback to clinical conditions (see Green & Green, 1979).

Finally, the early work of Kamiya (1969) and Brown (1977) in electroencephalographic biofeedback gained widespread attention for applications in relaxation and alteration of consciousness, although it was Sterman's (1972, 1973) work in the clinical applications in the treatment of epilepsy that appeared to have the most clinical utility.

In recent years, biofeedback has shown even more potential applicability to a host of clinical problems including vasoconstrictive syndromes (Green & Green, 1983), gastrointestinal disorders (Schuster, 1983), muscle-contraction syndromes (Budzynski, 1983), and physical rehabilitation (Basmajian, 1983), to mention only a few.

Despite these advances, the question remains, "What is biofeedback?" Is it a type of operant paradigm or something else? What is the role, if any, of striate muscle activity on autonomic activity? These questions have yet to be answered in a definite manner.

Biofeedback in its present form is a new endeavor, the technology for which has become available only since the end of World War II. New methods are being made available almost daily for acquiring, storing, processing, and displaying data, and it is an area in which one can expect a great deal of new research and development in the coming years.

BIOFEEDBACK MODALITIES

In this section, we will briefly review several types of biofeedback, describing their nature and potential utility.

Electromyographic (EMG) Biofeedback

Description

The term EMG as applied to biofeedback stands for electromyograph. The EMG instrument that is used is one in which electrical impulses are picked up through special metal sensors (electrodes), which are applied to the skin with electrode jelly used as a conducting medium. The impulse is amplified and processed by the machine in such a way as to produce a display of lights, a deflection of a meter, a sound that correlates with the magnitude of the signal, or any combination of these. They are noted by the client, and the client is thus given the information that he or she needs in order to modify the function—in this case, muscle tension.

The words "stress" and "tension" are often used interchangeably, and the muscle tension itself is a very obvious component of the fight–flight response. When a threat is perceived, any muscle throughout the body may tense; however, some do so in a characteristic way. For example, the muscles in the back of the neck will characteristically become tense as if in an effort to keep the head erect to aid in vigilance. Back, shoulder, and jaw muscles tense when the individual perceives himself or herself as being threatened or when he or she is under stress.

Because we are describing striated muscle, it would seem that control would be voluntary, and therefore easily subject to learning. The difficulty arises when the contraction increases so slowly and imperceptibly that the individual is not aware of increased muscle tension until the muscles are already in spasm. The EMG apparatus allows the individual to become aware of small increments of change in muscle tension, thus allowing him or her to learn to relax the muscles involved.

One can place the EMG electrodes virtually over any striated muscle available to either skin or needle electrodes. Frontalis muscle biofeedback is frequently used for "cultivated low-arousal training" (Stoyva, 1983). Other placements may include wrist to wrist for upper body and ankle to ankle for lower body.

Indications

For the purposes of this chapter, EMG biofeedback is used to treat the stress response primarily in two ways. First, by allowing the patient to learn to relax a particular muscle or set of muscles (e.g., the masseter muscles in bruxism). Second, EMG biofeedback may be used to produce a more generalized state of relaxation and decreased arousal (e.g., frontalis muscle EMG biofeedback), thus affecting the stress response more centrally (see Stoyva, 1977, 1983; Stoyva & Budzynski, 1974; see also Chapter 9).

Perhaps the two most commonly encountered specific muscle-contraction problems are muscle-tension headaches and bruxism. Budzynski (1983) and Sharpley and Rogers (1984) conclude that EMG biofeedback can be highly useful in alleviating or eliminating muscle-contraction headache syndromes. Cannistraci (1975) argues that EMG biofeedback is useful in reducing the clenching and toothgrinding associated with bruxism.

As noted in Chapter 5, the frontalis muscles appear to have a unique value in the treatment of the human stress response because of their ability to serve as an indicator of generalized arousal, for example, sympathetic nervous system arousal (Rubin, 1977). This by virtue of what appears to be their dual neurological constituency, that is, alpha motoneuron innervation and sympathetic neural innervation (see Everly & Sobelman, 1987). Thus, not only can EMG biofeedback be useful in specific neuromuscular syndromes, but via the frontalis assemblies, it can serve as a means of engendering the relaxation response discussed in Chapter 9.

When using the frontalis muscles as a means of engendering the relaxation response, it is important to keep in mind that it may first be necessary to have the patient learn to specifically relax the frontalis before expecting that any generalizability to the autonomic nervous system will occur. That is say, the frontalis muscles may serve as indicators of sympathetic activity only when they are in a relatively relaxed state. Everly and Sobelman (1987) note other issues in the use of EMG biofeedback:

1. Be sure to employ reliable skin preparation procedures for electrode placements.
2. Be sure that comparable filter selections are employed when comparing intersession performance as well as intersubject or interstudy EMG levels.
3. Be sure that comparable amplitude quantification procedures are employed in intersession, intersubject, or interstudy comparisons. For example, 1 volt peak = 2 volts peak-to-peak = .707 volts RMS = .636 volts averaged.

The EMG biofeedback paradigm has clearly demonstrated its scientific integrity and clinical utility in the hands of competent professionals and should be viewed as a useful tool in the treatment of the human stress response (see Sharpley & Rogers, 1984, for a meta-analysis).

Temperature Biofeedback

Description

The use of temperature biofeedback is based on the fact that peripheral skin temperature is a function of vasodilatation and constriction. Thus, when the peripheral blood vessels are dilated, more blood is flowing through them, and the skin is warmer. By measuring the temperature in the extremities, one can get an indication of the amount of the constriction of the blood vessels, and because the constriction-dilation is controlled by the sympathetic portion of the autonomic nervous system, one can get a second, indirect measurement of the amount of sympathetic activity.

The equipment used in thermal biofeedback has the same basic function as the EMG-biofeedback equipment described above—that is, there is a sensor, a processor, and a display. The sensor in this case is a thermistor, a small thermal sensing device that is usually taped to the subject's finger. This is connected to a machine that transforms the electrical signal the thermistor produces into a signal that is amplified and processed in such a way that once again either lights are displayed, sounds are produced, or a change on a meter is produced to indicate raising or lowering of temperature in very small amounts. Typically, the width of the meter on the biofeedback instrument is plus or minus one degree Fahrenheit.

It seems obvious that skin temperature can be raised only to a theoretical high of core body temperature 98.6° Fahrenheit, although Fuller (1972) reports producing higher than core body temperature. If a patient has a baseline skin temperature of 70°, there is greater change possible in terms of warming than if a patient has a baseline temperature of 94°. The increase in temperature will not be as dramatic.

Indications

Temperature feedback has been useful in those instances in which one needs to be concerned with circulatory functions, such as in Raynaud's disease and peripheral vascular disease (Taub & Stroebel, 1978). It has been utilized in the treatment of migraine headaches and hypertension, in those instances in which one is seeking to control sympathetic activity such as in asthma, and in psychotherapy. In the latter case, it has been found to be useful in the determining of areas in which sympathetic discharges are prominent, and thus may relate to resistance on the patient's part in psychotherapy. One minor difficulty with the technology involved is that there is a short but significant delay of several seconds between the time of sympathetic discharge, vasoconstriction, and lowering of temperature in the extremity. This measurable lowering of temperature may be displayed several seconds after the passing of the event that caused the sympathetic discharge to occur.

Temperature biofeedback has a definite role in the treatment of the stress response in that it is a good indicator of sympathetic-nervous-system arousal. For this reason it is a useful tool in teaching general relaxation, the subject being instructed to try to raise skin temperature. This mode of therapy is often used alone, alternatively with EMG, or in combination with it. The reader should refer to Green and Green (1983) for a useful review of thermal biofeedback.

Electroencephalographic (EEG) Biofeedback

Description

The brain is known to discharge electrical activity continually. The electrical activity that arises in the brain appears to be the result of discharges at synapses. In 1924, Hans Berger developed a method for graphically recording that electrical brain-wave activity. What appears to be recorded by the EEG are those synapses closest to the surface of the brain. There are many ascending pathways to the cortex; however, it is felt that the area that is the most highly represented on the outermost surface of the cortex is the reticular activating system. This is a very difficult set of data to analyze, because a single neuron can have as many as a thousand branchings in the cortex. Therefore, although what is picked up on the EEG is very nonspecific, it is generally agreed that various wave forms do correlate with certain states of consciousness and do reflect activity, particularly in the reticular activating system.

Brain waves have been divided into four categories, depending on their predominant frequency and amplitude. The term "frequency" refers to the number of cycles produced per second or per minute and reflects the number of firings of neurons per unit of time. The amplitude refers to the amount of electricity generated and is a reflection of the number of neurons firing synchronously.

The brain waves may be described as follows. Beta waves have 14 or more cycles per second frequency and low amplitude. They are characteristic of the awake, attentive state. This is the state that one is in when one is focusing one's concentration or when one is aroused. Alpha waves are characterized by a frequency of 8 to 13 cycles per second and an amplitude of 20 to 100+ microvolts. This state is supposedly related to the relaxed state characterized by serenity, passive attention, and calm. Theta waves are 4 to 8 cycles per second in frequency and have a usual amplitude of 20 microvolts or less. They are often characterized as being a part of the daydreaming state. Last, delta waves are from .5 to 4 cycles per second in frequency and are associated with deep sleep.

There are standard electrode-placement sites; however, exact placement is not too critical from session to session because what is being measured is a very averaged measurement over a wide cortical area. One of the major problems in this kind of measurement is movement artifact and muscle artifact, as well as artifacts being introduced from electrical systems around the machinery. Typically, the subject is instructed to close his or her eyes to decrease the amount of arousal from visual stimuli. The instruments are generally equipped so that an upper and lower frequency can be set. Usually, the upper frequency is set at a point at which the person gets a feedback sound 50% of the time, with the lower-frequency threshold set at 4 cycles per second below baseline, thus producing a "window" for feedback. The amplitude levels are set so that the lower level is just below that average produced by the person, often about 20 microvolts, and the upper limit well above the highest brain-wave amplitude, that is, about 60 microvolts. This allows an amplitude "window" that excludes noise and most muscle artifact. This is the method described by Fuller in his book *Biofeedback: Methods and Procedures in Clinical Practice* (1972).

Feedback is provided to the subject when both amplitude and frequency are within the desired windows. The type of feedback best for learning will be a function of the preferences of the patient. If multiple options are available, it is usually wise to allow the client to select.

Of all the biofeedback modalities, EEG has probably found the fewest proven uses. To summarize a review by Barbara Brown (1977), attempts have been made to increase alpha in order to produce general relaxation. This is purportedly useful in people who exhibit obsessive compulsive patterns, as well as generally high stress/anxiety levels. It has also been used in facilitating sleep and in improving concentration and attention, the latter being particularly through the suppression of alpha in order to concentrate more easily. There has been some speculation as to increasing theta in order to increase creativity; however, reports seem to indicate that there is an ambiguous relationship between increased creativity and increased theta.

Another proposed use of EEG has been in reduction of chronic pain. The idea is to help the patient develop an ability to unfocus his or her awareness of the pain so that the cycle of pain, tensing up from the pain and thus producing more pain, is broken by focusing one's attention away from it. Some positive results have been reported for this particular use of EEG biofeedback. Biofeedback has also been mentioned in the treatment of epilepsy (Lubar, 1983).

As regards its use in the treatment of the stress response, its main function seems to be in training to increase alpha, decrease arousal, and generally to increase the individual's ability to attend passively; however, this particular area may have gotten more publicity and greater enthusiasm than it should have. At present, it seems to have found fewer uses than the other biofeedback modalities and is being studied in greater depth in the laboratory (Lubar, 1983).

Electrodermal (EDR) Biofeedback

Description

Electrodermal is a generic term that refers to the electrical characteristics of the skin. There are numerous measurement options available when considering this type of biofeedback. The oldest and most commonly used is the galvanic skin response (GSR). Generally speaking, variation of the skin's electrical characteristics appears to be a function of sympathetic neural activity; therefore when using EDR biofeedback the patient appears to be training to affect sympathetic neural arousal.

Indications

The major use for EDR is to reduce levels of sympathetic tone and reactivity. In addition, an attempt is being made to use the patterns of response in order to see if they can be paired with personality structure; however, this research is considered quite preliminary at present. One of the major uses in psychotherapy is for systematic desensitization, the theory being that one cannot be both relaxed and aroused at the same time and that phobias and anxiety are therefore amenable to treatment with this modality. Finally, it has been used as a tool for exploration in psychotherapy. In this case, the machine is used to demonstrate graphically to both therapist and patient areas of arousal that can be useful as another type of "body language" for interpretation (see Fair, 1986).

PRECAUTIONS

There are several adverse reactions that can occur as a result of biofeedback. The practitioner should be aware of the adverse conditions that may be produced or potentially exacerbated by its use (see Chapter 9; see also Schwartz, 1987). Let us review several of these issues.

First is the case of the patient who is taking medication for any purpose. Biofeedback may be considered a replacement for medication by some patients, and they prematurely or mistakenly stop taking medication prescribed for some other purpose. It is necessary to question patients closely regarding their medication history and to deal appropriately with this matter. Most dramatic are diabetic patients who are taking insulin. In these cases, the inducing of relaxation may reduce the need for insulin and the normal amount that the patient had been taking may now become a dose that could precipitate a hypoglycemic coma. Changes in blood pressure are also an area of potential difficulty in patients who are taking medication for hypertension or hypotension. In addition, it has been found that for those patients with epilepsy who are in training with biofeedback, especially for slow-wave EEG (6 to 9 Hz), seizure may be more likely to occur. Higher-frequency EEG training, however, may indeed hold more promise in the treatment of epilepsy.

Other problems may arise related to improper training of the patient by the therapist. An example might be treatment of bruxism with unilateral placement of EMG sensors, producing dislocation of the jaw through imbalance of the muscles. Improper muscle biofeedback in the treatment of torticollis may also result in a greater imbalance than before the biofeedback.

Treatment of cardiac arrhythmia should be undertaken by those who are well versed in cardiac physiology and have access to life-support equipment and personnel. Such training often takes place in cardiac-care units.

ROLE OF THE THERAPIST AND OTHER FACTORS

From what has been said thus far in this chapter, it would seem that the major element in biofeedback is the machinery. This really is not the case. A far more important element in this form of therapy is the clinician–patient dyad. This, more than many kinds of therapies, requires motivation on the patient's part to want to get better and to practice between sessions what he or she has learned. Because of this, his or her relationship with the clinician is quite important.

One determinant of success in biofeedback appears to be the extent to which cognitive restructuring takes place in patients so they can begin to see the ways in which mind and body interact. This again is dependent on the patient's relationship with his or her clinician, who is able to help with this process. In this framework, biofeedback can be seen as an adjunct to a more total therapeutic relationship. It is not unlike hypnosis, relaxation therapy, etc., in that it is a tool that can be brought to bear on a symptom or symptom complex, but only within the context of the total therapeutic relationship. In this sense, clinicians are like theatrical directors—they set the stage for change to take place. They give useful hints, pointers, feedback, and reinforcement, but they do not change patients themselves; they merely facilitate that change by making it easier for patients to change through the relationship that they have the clinicians with him. Our original diagram of the biofeedback situation (Figure 14.1) may now be modified as indicated in Figure 14.3.

Thus, the clinician receives information from both the instrument and the patient regarding the patient's functioning and feeds information to the patient, allowing the patient to better use the data that he or she acquires from the instrument alone (clarification, reinforcement, interpretation). In this context, then, the clinician is seen as an important part of the biofeedback loop, even though the responsibility for change and the change itself are carried out by the patient. It is possible that some divergent results of biofeedback efficacy by different authors may reflect such "nonspecific factors" as the effect of the clinicians. The reader should see Gaarder and Montgomery (1977) for a discussion of this topic. See also Shellenberger and Green (1986).

A review of the material in Chapters 6 and 7 is appropriate at this point. As Peper's (1976) useful treatise points out, the clinical biofeedback paradigm is replete with interaction effects. The office, the temperature, the clinician's demeanor, the empathic skills of the clinician, and perhaps even the ability of the clinician to serve as an effective health educator all serve to affect the outcome of clinical biofeedback. Recalling Chapter 6, at best it is naive to believe that personality factors do not affect biofeedback

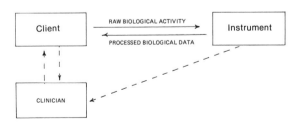

Figure 14.3

skill acquisition. As Chapter 6 argued, different individuals bring different strengths, vulnerabilities, and fears to the clinical situation. The clinician must be aware of these issues as they relate to therapy. As noted in Chapter 7, issues of mastery, self-control, and self-efficacy are especially germane to the biofeedback paradigm. Bandura (1977, 1982a, 1982b) has noted, however, that it is the perception of self-efficacy that is even more critical than the degree of actual self-efficacy manifest. Therefore, once again, the role of the clinician is paramount in helping the patient recognize meaningful skill acquisition in the face of what could be propensities for self-debasement, catastrophic ideation, or just general pessimism. Given the critical role of the clinician in the biofeedback paradigm, it may be useful to review other relevant issues.

In a practical treatise on biofeedback training, Shellenberger and Green (1986) discuss a series of the most common errors made in the utilization of biofeedback within both the research and clinical applications. Listed below are those that have applicability to the use of biofeedback in the treatment of excessive stress.

1. Failure to provide the patient with a sufficient number of training sessions—Biofeedback represents some form of learning. With regard to learning, it is clear that individual differences account for a major portion of the variation; therefore, no hard-and-fast rule governing the rate of skill acquisition exists. Nevertheless, it is clear that most people simply cannot acquire useful biofeedback skills in only two or three sessions.

2. Failure to provide the patient with sufficient time within any given training session—Once again, the aforementioned issue of individual differences governs skill acquisition.

3. Failure to provide the patient with homework exercises that reinforce and extend the skills acquired within the office or laboratory setting—Because biofeedback is learning, practice becomes an important aspect of skill acquisition.

4. Failure on the part of the clinician to recognize and nurture the critical formation of a sense of self-control, or self-efficacy, within the patient—As Chapter 7 discussed, the concept of perceived self-efficacy may be one of the most powerful therapeutic forces at work within the biofeedback paradigm (see Bandura, 1982a, 1982b).

5. Failure of the clinician to recognize and facilitate the social psychological and "clinical" aspects of biofeedback—Many clinicians erroneously believe that biofeedback is immune to the usual clinical variables that affect other aspects of clinical psychology or psychiatry. For this reason it is sometimes useful to conceptualize some forms of biofeedback as "biofeedback assisted psychotherapy."

6. Failure to take baseline measurements relevant to the biofeedback variables to be trained–To some degree, it is useful to see the clinical patient as the control within a single-subject research design and to structure the clinical paradigm with a similar notion in mind.

7. Failure on the part of the clinician to allow the patient to habituate to the physiological assessment process—Biofeedback, in addition to being a therapeutic intervention, is also an exercise in physiological measurement. In any such paradigm, the subject must be allowed to habituate to the novel stimuli represented by the biofeedback training environment. Habituation needs to occur within each and every training session.

8. Premature termination, that is, failure to train to "mastery" as opposed to initial skill acquisition—Too many patients are prematurely terminated by biofeedback clinicians who lose sight of the need to have patients "overlearn" the acquired skill in self-regulation.

A FINAL WORD OF CAUTION

The reader will undoubtedly detect a sense of optimism regarding the clinical utility of EMG, EDR, and temperature biofeedback. Such a positive view of biofeedback as a clinical technology is not universally shared by practicing clinicians, not to mention researchers. Perhaps one of the most recent papers that expresses serious doubt as to the clinical utility of biofeedback is that of Roberts (1985).

Roberts states, "There is absolutely no convincing evidence that biofeedback is an essential or specific technique for the treatment of any condition" (p. 940). How can a scientific endeavor, such as biofeedback, continue to grow in the laboratory and in the clinic in the presence of such scholarly contrary opinion? Or are such criticisms simply without merit? The issue can be resolved, not by an examination of research investigations, as much as by an examination of frames of reference within which research is conducted.

In his paper on biofeedback research, Peper (1976) seemed to anticipate the problems that would evolve in the quest to demonstrate the clinical efficacy of biofeedback technologies. Peper argues that in our effort to isolate the magnitude of effect contributed by clinical variables within a research investigation, we sometimes inadvertently alter, or even destroy, the phenomenon we are interested in observing. In what should be mandatory reading for every clinical student and practitioner, Shellenberger and Green (1986) directly address and resolve the critical epistemological issues that affect the conduct of inquiry as it pertains to the investigation of the clinical efficacy of biofeedback.

SUMMARY

This chapter has explored biofeedback, the creation and clinical utilization of psychophysiological feedback loops for the purpose of treating excessive stress and/or its target-organ effects. Let us review the main points:

1. Biofeedback gives the patient access to learning paradigms that involve physiological functions not previously accessible to conscious alteration.

2. Biofeedback can be used to directly modify the stress response itself, through the elicitation of the relaxation response or through the alteration of target-organ activity.

3. Temperature, EMG, and EDR biofeedback are the most commonly used forms of clinical biofeedback.

4. The clinician plays a critically important role in the overall biofeedback paradigm. So critical is this role that it can mean the difference between clinical success or failure. For this reason, the clinician should be trained not only in clinical psychophysiology but also in the fundamentals of counseling or clinical psychology as well.

5. In trying to understand the source of therapeutic effect, one of the most important aspects of clinical biofeedback may be the creation of the perception of self-efficacy, as discussed by Bandura (1977).

6. The use of biofeedback is not without its precautions. Refer to Chapter 9.

7. Useful reviews of clinical biofeedback are Schwartz (1987), Shellenberger and Green (1986), and Basmajian (1983).

CHAPTER 15

The Pharmacological Treatment of Excessive Stress

Robert Rosenfeld and George S. Everly, Jr.

Previous chapters have provided clinically relevant discussions of and protocols for the elicitation of the relaxation response. Not only is the relaxation response the natural antithesis of pathogenic stress arousal, but skill in its elicitation engenders in the patient an improved sense of self and a therapeutically useful increase in self-efficacy. Nevertheless, there do come instances where the stress arousal is so intense in magnitude or the target-organ effects are so discomforting that the autogenic elicitation of the relaxation response seems impossible. In such instances, the pharmacological treatment of the stress response warrants serious consideration. The purpose of this chapter is to provide a useful overview of the pharmacological treatment of excessive stress.

The discomfort associated with excessive stress arousal and its target-organ effects often brings patients to the desire for instant relief. The search for such relief has invariably led to the pursuit of psychopharmacotherapeutics. There is little question that psychotropic agents have contributed much to the treatment of excessive stress. Millions upon millions of dollars are spent every year in the development and promotion of antianxiety medications. The proliferation of these medications has created

Robert Rosenfeld • Formerly of the Department of Psychiatry, Walter Reed Army Hospital, Washington, D.C.

a generic familiarization with such drugs and the notion of a false pharmacological panacea in the minds of many individuals, a situation that has no doubt led to a major drug abuse problem in the United States. The fact that the minor tranquilizers remain among the most widely sold medications in the country potentiates problems of abuse.

Within this chapter we shall review the major pharmacological approaches to the treatment of excessive stress. The subsequent material regarding dosages should be used only for general edification and not for clinical prescription.

INTRODUCTION

Because this volume will be read by nonmedical clinicians, it may be of value to begin this chapter with a review of some basic concepts.

A drug may be thought of as any chemical that interacts with a biological system. A psychotropic drug may be thought of as any drug that affects cognition, affect, or perception, that is, any drug that affects the psychological domain.

Recalling Chapter 2, most psychotropic medications to be discussed within this chapter work by virtue of their effects upon the neuron. More specifically, most psychotropic drugs work by affecting either the presynaptic membrane or the postsynaptic membrane. Some drugs work by affecting the axonal membrane as well. Most drugs work by virtue of their effects upon drug receptors, which are also neurotransmitter receptors, that exist along the presynaptic and postsynaptic membranes. Another way of viewing the receptor concept is that the receptors serve as chemical target sites that either drugs or neurotransmitters can activate or inhibit. Thus, drugs serve either as agonists, which facilitate action, or as antagonists, which inhibit action.

There exist several mechanisms by which drugs can act as agonists or antagonists. They include:

1. Stimulation of the release of stored neurotransmitters
2. Simulation of the release of neurotransmitters by directly stimulating the synaptic receptors
3. Inhibition of biochemical deactivation of neurotransmitters
4. Inhibition of the biosynthesis of neurotransmitters
5. Inhibition of the reuptake of neurotransmitters into the presynaptic membrane
6. Inhibition of the storage of neurotransmitters
7. Inhibition of postsynaptic neurotransmitter binding
8. Inhibition or facilitation of the ability of the axonal membrane to depolarize

Strictly speaking, however, pharmacological treatment could also include the treatment of the most peripheral manifestations of the stress response, such as the use of antacids in the treatment of gastric ulcer or aspirin or other analgesics for the treatment of tension headache. Nevertheless, we will in this chapter primarily concentrate on the use of those medications whose purpose it is to relieve that subjective state of distress described as tension or anxiety and reduce psychophysiological overactivity (i.e., the psychotropic drugs).

Many clinicians agree that pharmacological intervention can play a useful role in the treatment of the stress response. Perhaps its greatest utility comes in its ability to relieve the symptoms of excessive stress that are acutely intense and/or that interfere with other forms of therapy. Therefore, the most constructive use of pharmacological interventions is generally felt to be limited to the short term with the main goal that of decreasing the symptoms enough to permit other, longer-lasting forms of treatment to have effect.

It must be kept in mind that, as in almost every other form of therapy discussed, the relationship with the clinician is certainly an important element in the success of the treatment. This is reflected in patient compliance in taking the medication regularly and reporting improvement, side effects, or fears and concerns. We shall not discuss here the element of the placebo effect in the use of medications; however, it must be kept in mind that the faith in the clinician and the expected effect of the medication have been shown by many authors to be as important as the medication itself (see Harlem, 1977; Jones, 1977).

In this chapter we will discuss several categories of medication used in the treatment of the stress response. We will review the mechanisms of action and their major indications, contraindications, and side effects. Furthermore, we will review examples of specific medications and dosages within each class. The intention is to provide a concise and practical guide for the understanding of such a treatment option.

SEDATIVE-HYPNOTICS—AN INTRODUCTORY HISTORY

"The term sedative-hypnotic is intended to denote the dose-dependency of the effect of these drugs" (Swonger & Constantine, 1976, p. 113). At low doses, these drugs produce a sedative effect, at high doses they can induce sleep. This is perhaps the oldest class of medications to be discussed in this chapter. One of its earliest representatives is ethyl alcohol, probably the oldest "tranquilizer" known. Another useful pharmacological agent (introduced around 1850) was bromide salts. These proved to be a fairly good central-nervous-system depressant; however, the possibility of intoxication made their usefulness somewhat limited. The use of chloral hydrate as a sedative was begun around 1869, and is still in limited use.

The next sedative-hypnotic medication that became available was the barbiturates, which are still being used by some practitioners for the treatment of anxiety. But because of the tendency to produce tolerance and their addictive potential, they are not very desirable in the treatment of chronic stress.

Following the barbiturates, the next major drug to be produced for the treatment of the syndrome was meprobamate, a propanediol, which was manufactured beginning in 1957. Its addictive properties also made it less than desirable, although this was not known at first.

Finally, in 1960, the "new age of anti-anxiety medications" began with the development of chlordiazepoxide (Librium) by the Hoffmann-LaRoche Company.

What all these substances seem to have in common is their ability to decrease anxiety and, in larger doses, to produce sleep. Though all these agents decrease anxiety and are often grouped together by authors, it may be useful in the context of this chapter to consider separately the barbiturate and the nonbarbiturate sedatives and hypnotics, followed by the anti-anxiety agents, which are more specific in dealing with anxiety and seem to work at a different level in the central nervous system.

BARBITURATES

Barbiturate sedative-hypnotic agents appear to have their major locus of action in the reticular formation and the cerebral cortex. They all produce depression of the central nervous system, and as the dosage is increased, the response progresses from sedation to respiratory depression and ultimately death. They can be used to reduce restlessness and agitation and must be administered in small doses for this purpose, in order not to interfere with alertness and psychomotor performance. They have been used by practitioners particularly in treating the psychogenic component of organic diseases, gastrointestinal, cardiovascular, or respiratory, reducing the anxiety resulting from the somatic symptoms. Their most common use now is in the treatment of insomnia, although, as mentioned before, some physicians still rely heavily on these medications for the treatment of anxiety.

The barbiturates have been classified as long-, intermediate-, and short-acting. The major disadvantage of the barbiturates is that they tend to induce liver enzymes, which means that they make the liver work faster to metabolize them as well as other substances. This is particularly dangerous when a patient is getting other medication along with a barbiturate.

A classic example is the patient who is taking barbiturates and dicumarin (a medication to decrease blood coagulability) simultaneously. While the patient is taking barbiturates, the amount of dicumarin needed to produce a therapeutic effect is greater than normal because it is being metabolized at a greater rate than normal by the liver enzyme induced by the barbiturate. If the patient were to stop the barbiturate, in one to two weeks the effect of the same amount of dicumarin would be dangerously increased, because the liver would no longer be metabolizing it at the rapid pace caused by the barbiturate induction of its enzymes. Because of this induction of enzymes, a tolerance is ultimately built up to the barbiturates themselves, and more medication has to be used to obtain the same effect as previously. Perhaps the major disadvantage of these medications is the addictive potential they have; and abrupt withdrawal from them may lead to delirium, convulsions, coma, and death. This type of withdrawal is also seen with alcohol.

Another disadvantage of barbiturates is that they are relatively nonspecific central-nervous-system depressant, and the only way to use them in treating the stress response is to use very small dosages, that is, dosages that do not produce drowsiness, and for a very brief period of time. However, in reality, as regards the stress response, there appears to be no advantage to using the barbiturates given other pharmacological options. Table 15.1 presents commonly prescribed barbiturates.

Overdosage of barbiturates will produce a picture similar to drunkenness with ataxia. Eventually, profound shock, hypotension, tachycardia, respiratory depression, coma, and death due to depression of medullary centers for respiration will occur.

Table 15.1. Commonly Prescribed Barbiturates

Generic name	Trade name	Common doses for adults
Phenobarbital (long-acting)	Luminal	As a sedative: 30–120 mg daily in 2–3 divided doses As a hypnotic: 100–320 mg at bedtime
Amobarbital (Intermediate-acting)	Amytal	As a sedative: 50–300 mg daily in a divided doses As a hypnotic: 65–200 mg at bedtime
Pentobarbital (short-acting)	Nembutal	As a sedative: 100–200 mg daily in 3 divided doses As a hypnotic: 100–200 mg at bedtime
Secobarbital (short-acting)	Seconal	As a sedative: 100–300 mg daily in divided doses As a hypnotic: 100–200 mg at bedtime

Table 15.2. Commonly Prescribed Nonbarbiturate Sedative Hypnotics

Generic name	Trade name	Common doses for adults
Ethchlorvynol	Placidyl	As a sedative: 200–600 mg in divided doses As a hypnotic: 500–1000 mlg at bedtime
Glutethimide	Doriden	As a sedative: 250–750 mg in divided doses As a hypnotic: 250–1000 mg at bedtime
Methaqualone	Quaalude	As a sedative: 300–450 mg in divided doses As a hypnotic: 150–400 mg at bedtime
Chloral hydrate		As a sedative: 300–1500 mg in divided doses As a hypnotic: 500–1000 mg at bedtime

NONBARBITURATES

Nonbarbiturate sedative hypnotics act in the same way as the barbiturates and though they were originally thought to be nonaddictive, we now know that dependence can result. They include such drugs as Placidyl, Doriden, and Quaalude. They are probably somewhat less potent, and also it is felt that they offer no advantage in the treatment of the stress response. Other sedative-hypnotics include chloral hydrate and paraldehyde, which again offer no advantage in the treatment of the stress response, the former being used primarily as a sleep aid and the latter as a treatment in alcohol withdrawal. Bromide salts are no longer in use at all for the treatment of the stress response, but they have in the past been available in over-the-counter preparations. The bromides came into use in the mid-1800s as antianxiety agents, but problems arose because of their relatively long half-lives and tendency to accumulate in the body causing a bromide psychosis. It should not be overlooked, however, that the bromide salts do sometimes find their way into people's bodies, often through the use of bromide-salt-containing substances. Table 15.2 presents the commonly used nonbarbiturate sedative-hypnotics.

ANTIANXIETY AGENTS

In this section, we will review numerous types of medications that are commonly prescribed with the primary intention of reducing anxiety and psychophysiological arousal without inducing a hypnotic effect.

Propanediols

When meprobamate (a compound of the propanediol group) was first introduced, it was hoped that it was an agent that would be a major advance from the barbiturates; however, it has been found that, though it is probably better at relieving anxiety than the barbiturates, it may have an almost equal potential for addiction and abuse. Interestingly, there is a member of this class of drugs named tybamate, which has an extremely short half-life, and in which very little addiction potential has been found. Both these drugs, however, are much less effective than the benzodiazepines and are not typically recommended for the treatment of stress. Their major disadvantages, as with the barbiturates, are impairment of motor function, development of drowsiness, and induction of hepatic enzymes. In conclusion, the propanediols, such as meprobamate and tybamate, may be classified in between the sedative-hypnotics and the next drug class to be discussed—the benzodiazepines.

Benzodiazepines

All the evidence gathered so far would indicate that the benzodiazepines as a class are extremely effective as antianxiety medications. Several generic compounds that belong to the benzodiazepine group, such as chlordiazepoxide (Librium), diazepam (Valium), alprazolam (Xanax), Flurazepam (Dalmane), and oxazepam (Serax) are considered less toxic and less addicitive than the sedative-hypnotic medications described thus far. The very popularity alluded to at the beginning of this chapter is a testimony to either their effectiveness or the belief in that effectiveness. It is generally felt that the benzodiazepines have their effect on the limbic system, and therefore do not interfere with cortical function in the same way as the other medications described. Several possible mechanisms have been described for the way in which the benzodiazepines may work pharmacologically. Stein, Wise, and Berger (1973), for example, offer the finding that oxazepam (a derivative of benzodiazepine) may somehow be related to serotonin (another neurotransmitter) turnover in terms of its antianxiety action; however, the significance of this finding is still somewhat unclear.

The major advantage in the use of the benzodiazepines for the treatment of the stress response is the fact that in the dosage ranges generally recommended, they do not significantly reduce cortical functioning and therefore impair ability to work or concentrate. They appear to enhance interaction in those people who are overly anxious, inhibited, and isolated, thus allowing them to become more amenable to therapy. The other main advantage is the large difference in the level of medication that it takes to be effective as compared with the level considered to be lethal. It is virtually impossible to commit suicide with the benzodiazepines without combining them with another drug that also acts as a depressant of the central nervous system.

The major disadvantage lies in the half-lives of the drugs. The half-life for Librium is 30 to 40 hours, for Valium and its active metabolites about 96 hours. Thus, with repeated dosages, blood levels rise over a period of days. This can potentially lead to more depression of the central nervous system than one had anticipated, a situation that can be especially troublesome in older people. Also, there can be a withdrawal syndrome from benzodiazepines, and though this may not be of the magnitude of the withdrawal syndrome from barbiturates, the psychological and physiological addictive properties of the benzodiazepines are becoming much more familiar to the physician, and they are being prescribed with much more caution. Another disadvantage of the benzodiazepines is their ability to compromise respiratory function through centrally mediated mechanisms. This can obviously be a problem with people with lung disease.

Antihistamines

There are several types of antihistamines that have been used in treating anxiety; however, the one that is most frequently used is hydroxyzine. The main reason for using antihistamines in the treatment of anxiety is not for their primary pharmacological property, which is to antagonize the peripheral effects of histamines, but for their side effect, which is sedation, and for this reason they can be used to treat anxiety and insomnia. This type of medication seems to be somewhat useful for this purpose, and patients do not seem to build up a tolerance to it. In low doses it does not seem to cause significant impairment of mental alertness or coordination, and it appears not to produce cortical depression. It, like the benzodiazepines, has a wide margin of safety between the therapeutic and the lethal doses. There have been no reported cases of addition or deaths related to its use. The commercial names for hydroxyzine are Vistaril and Atarax.

Beta-Adrenergic Blocking Agents

In those patients whose anxiety and psychophysiological stress arousal are manifested by peripheral autonomic symptoms primarily, it has been found helpful by some physicians to use propranolol. This is a medication that appears to act by blocking synaptic transmission to the beta group of adrenergic receptors. Because this is a peripheral and not a centrally acting phenomenon, it will reduce symptoms associated with anxiety and stress arousal, but does not alter consciousness in any way. This drug is not officially approved for this particular use. It must also be taken with care in patients who would be susceptible to beta adrenergic blockade, such as those with asthma. The trade name for propranolol is Inderal.

Phenothiazines

In those individuals in whom anxiety is part of a more hyperactive, distractible, obsessional, disorganized picture, the use of major tranquilizers is sometimes helpful. Major tranquilizers are purported to have their effect centrally in blockade of the neurotransmitter dopamine at its receptor site. Dopamine is another neurotransmitter in the central nervous system, and it has been speculated that it is a disorder of the dopamine system that is manifested by psychosis.

For the purpose of this discussion, the major tranquilizers are useful only in those cases in which the stress response reaches severe proportions, threatening to disorganize thought processes, and where it would be useful to help the individual reduce the psychomotor response to the stress and be able ultimately to integrate his or her thought processes in a more functional way. It is not a step that should be lightly taken by the practitioner, because it has been found that even small doses of phenothiazine can produce tardive dyskinesia, a syndrome manifested by abnormal movements, particularly of the face and tongue and sometimes of the body as a whole, which appears after a period of use of even small doses of phenothiazines, and for which there is as yet no cure known. However, this medication may be useful in those individuals described above, and therefore should not necessarily be withheld as long as therapeutic benefit has been properly weighed against possible risk factors. It is felt that the phenothiazine compounds chlorpromazine (Thorazine) and thioridazine (Mellaril), the more sedating phenothiazines, can be useful in small doses in the treatment of excessive stress. The side effects of these medications tend to be similar to those of the tricyclic antidepressants with common anticholinergic side effects.

In those clients in whom anticholinergic side effects would be most difficult, and those in whom cardiovascular factors would mitigate against using phenothiazine type drugs, another alternative is to use a butyrophenone, which is a drug class related to the phenothiazines. The butyrophenone compound haloperidol (Haldol) has somewhat less sedating effects and less anticholinergic side effects, but more extrapyramidal side effects, which would be manifested by a stiffness in gait, a decreased facial expressiveness, a feeling of restlessness, movement disorder, and so forth, all of which are reversible when the drug is withdrawn.

Buspirone

A new, atypical antianxiety agent that has recently emerged is buspirone. The trade name for buspirone hydrochloride is BuSpar. The mechanism of action for buspirone is currently unclear, although there appears to be no interaction with benzodiazepine receptor or with GABA receptors (Baldessarini, 1985). Some form of antidopaminergic action has been suggested for this drug, but clear evidence as to its action has not yet emerged (Baldessarini, 1985). According to information released by the manufacturer, Mead/Johnson, BuSpar shows no cross-tolerance with benzodiazepines, sedative/hypnotics, or alcohol. Further, no adverse age-related phenomena have been reported. The optimal daily dose, according to the manufacturer, is 20 to 30 mg in divided doses. The initial recommended dosage is 5 mg three times a day. For full therapeutic benefit to be achieved, the manufacturer recommends that treatment continue for at least 3 to 4 weeks.

The most commonly observed indications of overdose have been vertigo, nausea, headache, and nervousness. The manufacturer indicates that there is no evidence of abusive potential or tolerance development. There has emerged no evidence of the potential to cause dopaminergically mediated neurological dysfunction, such as tardive dyskinesia, dystonia, and the like. The manufacturer warns that BuSpar should not be used to block benzodiazepine or sedative/hypnotic withdrawal.

Table 15.3 lists the commonly used antianxiety drugs mentioned above.

Table 15.3. Medications Used to Treat Anxiety[a]

Generic name	Trade name	Doses
Alprazolam	Xanax	.75–4.0 mg/day in divided doses
Meprobamate	Miltown	1200–1600 mg/day in divided doses
Tybamate	Tybatran	750–2000 mg/day in divided doses
Diazepam	Valium	6–40 mg/day in divided doses
Chlordiazepoxide	Librium	15–100 mg/day in divided doses
Flurazepam	Dalmane	15–30 mg/day in divided doses
Oxazepam	Serax	30–120 mg/day in divided doses
Temazepam	Restoril	15–30 mg/at bedtime
Clonazepam	Clonopin	1–3 mg/day in divided doses
Clorazepate	Tranxene	15–90 mg/day in divided doses
Lorazepam	Ativan	1–6 mg/day in divided doses
Hydroxyzine	Atarax	50–400 mg/day in divided doses
Propranolol	Inderal	30–120 mg/day in divided doses
Chlorpromazine	Thorazine	10–100 mg/day in divided doses for stress
Thioridazine	Mellaril	10–100 mg/day in divided doses for stress
Haloperidol	Haldol	1–5 mg/day in divided doses

[a]Dosages are based on experience of authors and/or recommended by manufacturer.

Antidepressants

It may seem paradoxical that antidepressants can be used effectively in the treatment of anxiety and stress-related syndromes; nevertheless, this is indeed the case. Antidepressants appear to have their greatest applicability in two instances: (1) when the patient suffers from panic attacks and (2) when the patient suffers from a combination of anxiety and depression.

There are two major categories of antidepressants: (1) monoamine oxidase inhibitors (MAOI) and (2) tricyclic antidepressants.

Monoamine oxidase is a chemical that is present in the neuron itself and outside of the neuron in the synaptic cleft. Its job is to biochemically degrade catecholamines. MAOI medications serve to retard that natural degrading process, thus increasing the availability of catecholamines, such as norepinephrine, and thereby serving to ostensibly elevate mood. MAOIs also serve to inhibit panic attacks, via a mechanism not clearly understood, possibly by altering presynaptic autoreceptors. Phenylzine (Nardil) and tranylcypramine (Parnate) are commonly prescribed MAOIs. The major problem with MAOIs appears to be the potential for troublesome pressor effects through interaction with dietary pressor amines (e.g., tyramine). Thus, MAOI patients are warned to watch their diet for these substances, which are contained in many cheeses, red wines, fermented foods, and pickled foods, to name a few. Patients are also cautioned about the use of sympathomimetics.

Because of the dietary cautions associated with MAOIs, tricyclics are often a more popular antidepressant. These drugs have their mechanism of action in blocking reuptake of norepinephrine and serotonin at the synapses of the central nervous system. It will be recalled that norepinephrine and serotonin are neurotransmitters at synapses in the brain. It is hypothesized that the tricyclic antidepressant agents act by blocking the reuptake of these neurotransmitters at the presynaptic neurons, and thus produce a relief from depression. One of the side effects of the antidepressants is sedation. This is particularly true with the amitriptyline and doxepin tricyclics.

It has been found that the use of the tricyclic imipramine can also prevent panic attacks. This can be done with a dose as small as 10 mg a day, although in some patients it is necessary to increase the dosage to as high as one would normally use in treating depression. Typically, the sedative or antianxiety effect of the tricyclic antidepressants is seen soon after taking the medication, and sometimes the medication is given only at night, in order to take advantage of its rather shorter-acting sedative component.

The major disadvantage of the use of tricyclic antidepressants is their side effects, which can be particularly bothersome. These are generally anticholinergic in nature and present such symptoms as dry mouth, diffi-

Table 15.4. Antidepressants

Generic name	Trade name	Dose
Tricyclics		
Imipramine	Tofranil	75–300 mg/day divided
Desipramine	Norpramine	100–300 mg/day divided
Amitriptyline	Elavil	75–300 mg/day divided
Nortriptyline	Aventyl	50–150 mg/day divided
Doxepin	Sinequan	75–300 mg/day divided
Monoamine Oxidase Inhibitors		
Phenylzine	Nardil	45–75 mg/day divided
Tranylcypramine	Parnate	20–30 mg/day divided

culty with accommodation of vision, urinary retention, and a particular danger to patients with narrow-angle glaucoma. There are cardiovascular risks, particularly postural hypotension and cardiac arrhythmia. They have been known to cause psychomotor slowing and difficulties in concentration and planning. The margin of safety in dosage of the tricyclics as compared with the benzodiazepines is much less, and the possibility is present of paradoxical reaction with increased anxiety and depression. Finally, these antidepressants may also precipitate a psychosis in those individuals who have an underlying psychotic disorder. Table 15.4 lists commonly prescribed antidepressants.

SUMMARY

No medication is an answer in and of itself. Rather, medications work within a larger therapeutic context in most cases so as to facilitate other therapeutic mechanisms. Pharmacotherapy is as much an art as it is a science. It is as important to know one's patient as it is to know one's medicinal armamentarium. Let us review some of the main points covered in this chapter:

1. A psychotropic drug is a chemical that interacts with a biological system so as to cause an alteration in cognition, mood, or other aspects of the psychological domain.

2. The vast majority of the drugs discussed within this chapter yield a pharmacological action by virtue of the fact that they exert some effect upon neurotransmitter receptor sites located primarily at the presynaptic or postsynaptic membranes.

3. The drugs that are most commonly used to treat anxiety and stress-related syndromes are as follows:

• Barbiturate and nonbarbiturate sedative/hypnotics, which act at the brain stem to suppress all cerebral activity. They include Luminal, Amytal, Nembutal, and Seconal (barbiturates), and Placidyl, Doriden, and Quaalude (nonbarbiturates).

• Propanediols such as meprobamate and tybamate, developed to be a less addicting and global sedative when compared with the barbiturates. Although somewhat better for the treatment of anxiety, they appear to be equally addictive.

• Benzodiazepines, which have their locus of action within the limbic system. More specifically, they work by activating the GABA inhibitory neurotransmitter system within the limbic circuitry. Although superior for anxiety, they possess addictive potentials and the possibility of abuse. Drugs like Valium, Librium, Restoril, and Ativan are commonly prescribed benzodiazepines. A newer benzodiazepine, Xanax, seems useful not only for anxiety but panic as well.

• Antihistamines, beta blockers, and even neuroleptics, which can be used for treatment of arousal syndromes.

• Buspirone, the newest of the antianxiety drugs. Its mechanism is not clearly understood, but could be antidopaminergic.

• Antidepressant medications such as tricyclics and MAOIs, proven to be of value in the treatment of panic disorders, though they appear to do little for the more generalized anxieties. Examples would include Tofranil, Norpramine, and Elavil (tricyclics) and Nardil and Parnate (MAOIs).

CHAPTER 16

Physical Exercise and the Human Stress Response

It has been suggested (Chavat *et al.*, 1964; Kraus & Rabb, 1961) that the "wisdom of the body" dictates that the human stress response should lead to physical exertion or exercise. Indeed, physical exercise appears to be the most effective way of ventilating, or expressing, the stress response in a health-promoting manner, once it has been engendered.

Having read, in Part I, about the psychophysiologic nature of human stress, one cannot help but be impressed by the proposition that stress represents a psychophysiological process that prepares the body for physical action. The increased blood supply to the heart and skeletal muscles coupled with the increase in neuromuscular tension, the increase in circulating free fatty acids and glucose, as well as the diminished blood flow to the gastrointestinal system all lead one to conclude that the stress response is preparing the organism for action (Benson, 1975; Cannon, 1914, 1929; Chavat *et al.*, 1964; Kraus & Raab, 1961).

It is reasonable to assume that thousands of years ago the highly active life style that was led by primative humans afforded them ample opportunity to physically express the arousal that resulted from the frustrations and dangers they faced on a daily basis. Similarly, there was most likely sufficient opportunity for those ancient humans to develop many of the positive physical and psychological advantages known to accrue from regular physical exercise. Yet as we developed from "physical beings" to "thinking beings," we provided ourselves with fewer and fewer opportunities to ventilate our frustrations, failures, and challenges in healthful physical expression. So important is this need to ventilate and refresh our minds and bodies through exercise, that some have suggested (Chavat *et al.*, 1964; Kraus & Raab, 1961) that when the stress response does not lead to physically active somatomator expression, the risks of disease and dysfunction are greatly increased.

Based upon the World Health Organization's discussions, Chavat *et al.* (1964) concluded that when the body is aroused for physical action but that physical expression is suppressed, a condition of strain or psychophysiologic overload may be created. They note:

> When in civilized man . . . [stress] reactions are produced, the . . . [physically motivating] component is usually more or less suppressed . . . What is obvious is that often repeated incidents of . . . [suppressed somatomator activity] must imply an increased load on heart and blood vessels . . .

Similarly, Kraus and Raab (1961) gave such suppressed physical expression a preeminent role in the etiology of a host of anxiety and stress-related diseases. They referred to such diseases as "hypokinetic diseases." This notion is said to have influenced President John F. Kennedy to promote physical fitness as a major national priority during the early 1960s.

If, indeed, we have accurately interpreted the "wisdom of the body" as intending for the stress response to be consumated in some form of physical somatomotor expression, then a rationale quickly emerges for the consideration of physical exercise as a powerful therapeutic tool in prevention, treatment, and rehabilitation programs for stress-related disease and dysfunction.

HISTORY OF THERAPEUTIC EXERCISE

It can be assumed that our ancient ancestors suffered from few stress-related "hypokinetic" diseases, this owing to their physically demanding life styles. As our physically active culture evolved into a sedentary culture and the levels of physical exercise greatly diminished, at that point in human development did physical exercise gain the potential for therapeutic application.

Perhaps the earliest use of exercise in a therapeutic capacity, according to Ryan (1974), was in the fifth century B.C. It was during this time that the Greek physician Herodicus prescribed gymnastics for various diseases. In the second century B.C., Asclepiades prescribed walking and running in conjunction with diet and massage for disease as well as for the ills of an "opulent" society.

In sixteenth-century Europe, Joseph Duchesne is thought to be the first to use swimming as a therapeutic tool. He is said to have used such physical activity to strengthen the heart and lungs. From this time on in Europe, exercise gained great popularity in therapeutic and preventive applications.

Following World War I, therapeutic exercise and the study of exercise physiology gained momentum in the United States. Physical fitness came into vogue in the 1960s for the lay public with the urging of President Kennedy and with the advent of the President's Council on Physical Fitness in 1956.

As more and more individuals began exercising, more and more data became available regarding its nature and effects. Physical fitness found itself being promoted in the occupational world with the founding of organizations such as the American Association of Fitness Directors in Business and Industry, which vigorously promoted the "good health is good business" philosophy to millions at the jobsite.

Also in the 1960s, American culture saw the advent of the urban "health spa." These urban/suburban facilitates were centers for the promotion of a health-oriented culture. Yet the pursuit of physical fitness remained very much a segmented activity segregated by gender. The 1970s and the 1980s, however, witnessed two revolutions in the American pursuit of physical exercise that were to change this. The first revolution was centered around the invention of a type of exercise equipment that literally "revolutionized" the pursuit of physical health. Nautilus equipment was to make weightlifting easier, safer, and more efficient. And when practiced in the recommended protocol, it actually yielded the *potential* to facilitate skeletal muscular development while at the same time improving the efficiency of the cardiopulmonary system—thus achieving what exercise enthusiasts considered the "best of both worlds."

The second revolution involved the "image" of physical exercise. As noted earlier, there were two different psychologies of exercise, one for women and one for men. Under the influence of writes such as Kenneth Cooper (*Aerobics*) and Jim Fixx (*The Complete Book of Running*), as well as the marketing and development of sophisticated exercise facilities that foster social support, the social barriers to physical exercise fell. For the first time in American history exercise became a social, as well as physical, activity that both men and women could pursue and enjoy together. These two revolutions cannot be underestimated in terms of their importance to the proliferation of the American physical fitness culture. Today, exercise is enjoying its greatest popularity in the United States, and it has been "rediscovered" by health-care professionals.

The present discussion looks at exercise as a modern therapeutic tool for the treatment of excessive stress.

MECHANISMS OF ACTION

Exercise itself represents an intense form of stress response, yet it differs greatly from stress response implicated in the onset of psychosomatic disease. Why then is the stress of exercise health promoting, in most instances, and the emotionally related stress of living in a competitive urban environment, for example, health eroding? Let us examine the mechanisms that may answer this question.

There exist three therapeutic mechanisms of action that serve to explain the clinical effectiveness of exercise in the treatment of excessive stress. They entail:

1. Mechanisms active during exercise
2. Mechanisms active shortly after exercise
3. Long-term mechanisms

The therapeutic mechanisms at work during the acute process of exercising are manifest in the tendency for such physical activity to healthfully utilize the potentially harmful constituents of the stress response. During the stress response, the stress-responsive gluconeogenic hormones (primarily cortisol) begin to break down adipose tissue for energy. In this process, a form of fat, called free fatty acid (FFA), is released into the bloodstream (Mount Castle, 1980). During the stress of physical exercise, FFA levels actually decline because the FFA are utilized for energy by the active muscles. In contrast, however, during emotionally related stress, the FFA are not utilized as rapidly because of the sedentary nature of such stress. The FFA persist in the bloodstream and are converted to triglycerides and ultimately to low-density lipoproteins (LDL). LDL have shown to be the major source of atherosclerotic plaque (Haskell & Fox, 1974; Miller, 1980) associated with coronary artery disease.

A second point to consider during the stress response is that a significant demand is placed on the cardiovascular system. Cardiac output (heart rate times stroke volume), blood pressure, and resistance to peripheral blood flow all increase. By the use of moderate physical activity, however, these factors are manifest in a more healthful form. Although cardiac output must increase, the rhythmic use of the striate muscles actually assists the return of blood to the heart (increase in venous return). Blood pressure must increase during exercise as well, but not so dramatically as is seen when one remains inactive (as in a traffic jam, for example).

Third, during the stress response, it has been shown that the hormones epinephrine and norepinphrine are released. Research (Dimsdale & Moss, 1980) has shown that during the stress of exercise, norepinephrine is preferentially released, whereas during emotionally related stress, epinephrine is preferentially released. McCabe and Schneiderman (1984) conclude that circulating epinephrine represents the greatest risk to the integrity of the heart muscle because the ventricles are maximally responsive to epinephrine, not norepinephrine. In a heart that suffers from ischemia, or other problems, they conclude that high levels of epinephrine could induce a lethal arrhythmia. Finally, we see that during the stress response, the resistance to blood flow to the skin and other peripheral aspects increases. During the stress of exercise, resistance to blood flow in the skin actually decreases—this has implications for cooling of the body and declines in blood pressure (see Bar-Or & Buskirk, 1974; Mountcastle, 1980, for discussions of these cardiovascular dynamics).

The examples just described are indicative of the drastically different ways the body responds to the stress of exercise in contrast with the stress response that we undergo if we remain static, or inactive. Other examples in pulmonary functions and hemodynamics are similarly available. Clearly, the acute strain on the body is quite different if one undergoes a stress response while one is active, compared with remaining inactive. Although physical activity has the capability of using the constituents of the stress response in a constructive manner, the following passages discuss the therapeutic reactions that last beyond the acute exercise period itself.

The short-term therapeutic mechanisms associated with exercise entail the initiation of a state of relaxation following the physical activity. Clearly, exercise itself represents a powerful ergotropic response mediated by the sympathetic nervous system; however, according to Balog (1978), on completion of exercise, the organism may undergo psychophysiological recovery by the initiation of a trophotropic response mediated by the parasympathetic nervous system. According to de Vries (1966), gamma motor neural discharge may also be inhibited during recovery from physical activity. The gamma motor system is a complementary connection from the cerebral cortex to the striate musculature. The result of such inhibition is said to be a striate muscle relaxation.

The muscle-relaxant qualities of exercise have important implications for short-term declines in diffuse anxiety and ergotropic tone in autonomic as well as striate muscles. It has been demonstrated that striate muscle tension contributes to diffuse anxiety and arousal in striate and autonomic musculature through a complex feedback system (Gellhorn, 1964, 1967; Jacobson, 1978). This system involves afferent (incoming) proprioceptive stimulation from striate muscles to the limbic emotional centers, the hypothalamus and cerebral cortex. Therefore, reduction in striate tension should lead to a generalized decrease in ergotropic tone throughout the body, as well as a decrease in diffuse anxiety levels; and this has been demonstrated empirically by Gellhorn (1958b) and reviewed in greater detail by Everly (1985b). The research of de Vries (1981, 1968) has now clearly demonstrated the fact that exercise leads to decreased skeletal muscle tension following exercise.

Most recently, there has been speculation regarding the short-term psychological benefits of physical exercise. These have been observed to be related to antianxiety and analgesic outcome (Sime, 1984). Searching for the physiological basis for such effects has led researchers to (1) the ob-

served reduction in muscle tension and subsequent diminished proprioceptive bombardment of the emotional centers in the limbic system as
described above and (2) the release of endogenous opioids such as beta
lipotropin and beta endorphin. As indicated in Chapter 2, beta lipotropin is
released from the anterior pituitary during stress. Sime (1984) concludes
that even in light of conflicting data regarding opioid-blocking naloxone,
there still seems to be substantial evidence linking the postexercise antianxiety and analgesic states with the release of morphine-like endogenous
opiods. This phenomenon may also explain the so-called "runner's high"
that often accompanies vigorous exercise.

The most significant long-term mechanisms of health promotion inherent in exercise appear to emerge when exercise is aerobic or endurance
oriented and practiced for a minimum of about one month. These mechanisms appear to affect both physiological and psychological outcome.
Haskell (1984) concludes:

> Men who select a physically active lifestyle on their own generally demonstrate
> fewer clinical manifestations of coronary heart disease (CHD) than their seden-
> tary counterparts; when events do occur, they tend to be less severe and to
> appear at an older age. . . . A recent report from Finland provides evidence of a
> similar relationship for women . . . . (p. 413)

Biological mechanisms by which exercise may contribute to improved cardiovascular health are summarized from Haskell (1984) in Table 16.1.

Psychologically, reviews by Layman (1977) and Martin and Dubbert
(1982) suggest that regular aerobic exercise promotes improved psychological functioning as manifest by elevation of depressed mood, improved self-
esteem, enhanced sense of control, and reductions in felt anxiety. Sime
(1984) points out that such conclusions may need to be tempered with an
appreciation for the difficulties encountered in the design and measure-

Table 16.1. Biological Foundations of
Exercise and Cardiovascular Health

Maintained or increased myocardial oxygen
  supply
Increased cerebral blood flow
Diminished myocardial work demands
Increased blood supply to skeletal muscles
Increased myocardial efficiency
More rapid elimination of metabolic waste pro-
  ducts
Decreased adiposity
Improved lipoprotein profile (HDL:LDL ratio)
Increased electrical stability of myocardium
Diminished resting heart rate
Normalization of carbohydrate metabolism

---

ment of studies that investigate the relationship between exercise and mental health, however. Nevertheless, after reviewing a substantial amount of literature, he concludes there is a body of empirical and clinical evidence supporting the relationship between exercise and an improved state of mind.

Collectively, it may well be that the long-term physiological and psychological mechanisms of action that support the use of exercise in the treatment and prevention of stress-related disease represent a higher level of physical and psychological fitness and therefore a "higher level of stress resistance." This higher level of fitness may then aid the individual, both psychologically and physically, in withstanding the potentially injurious effects of excessive stress. One might consider such a level of fitness as a "buffer" again excessive stress. Indeed, based upon the reviews of Layman (1974), Wilmore (1982), Martin and Dubbert (1982), Haskell (1984), Sime (1984), Sachs and Buffone (1984), and Weller and Everly (1985), it may be argued the stress-resisting aspects of sustained, chronic exercise include:

1. Increased cardiovascular efficiency
2. Improved pulmonary function
3. Improved glucose utilization
4. Reduced body fat
5. Reduced resting blood pressure
6. Diminished autonomic nervous system reactivity
7. Reduced muscle tension
8. Reduced trait anxiety
9. Elevated self-concept
10. Improved sense of self-control and self-efficacy

To reiterate, these potential alterations are important to the present discussion of stress-reduction mechanisms because they all contribute to the patient's ability to tolerate high levels of stress, thus resisting pathologic outcome.

RESEARCH SUPPORTING THERAPEUTIC EXERCISE FOR STRESS

A review of relevant literature on the clinical use of exercise in the treatment of excessive stress and stress-related disease yields ample support and rationale for such an application:

1. A scholarly review by Donoghue (1977) supports the relationship between chronic exercise and improved work performance.

2. Fifteen minutes of walking (so as to maintain a sustained heart rate of 100 beats per minute) was found to be a more powerful muscle relaxant than 400 mg of meprobamate (deVries & Adams, 1972).

3. Comparing aerobically trained subjects with untrained subjects, research has shown that persons trained through exercise to improve aerobic capacity recovered more quickly from exposures to psychosocial stressors (Sinyor, Schwartz, Peronnet, Brisson, & Seraganian, 1983).

4. Ledwidge (1980) argues that exercise can be used to reduce chronic fatigue associated with depression. A well-controlled clinical trial conducted by Grist et al. (1978) found that exercise was equally as effective in reducing depression as time-limited psychotherapy (Grist et al., 1978).

5. In a ten-week study, programmed exercise was found to be associated with an increase in self-concept (Jasnoski, Holmes, Solomon, & Agular, 1981).

6. Research has shown that very light exercise, for as little as 12 minutes, as well as more vigorous exercise, can be useful in reducing muscle tension (Sime, 1977; de Vries, 1981), a major contributor to emotional instability and stress arousal (Everly, 1985b).

7. Epidemiological evidence has clearly shown that regular physical activity is capable of modifying cardiovascular disease risk profiles (Kannel & Sorlie, 1979).

Finally, let us summarize this section on research with a conclusion from Sime's (1984) review: "If stress is defined in the traditional fight-or-flight terminology, then exercise is a classic method of stress management through its active, dynamic release of physiological preparedness" (p. 502). Further, varied psychological propensities for excessive stress (e.g., poor self-esteem, hostility, poor body image), as well as varied characteristics that seem to prolong excessive stress (e.g., anxiety, physiological reactivity, depression, muscle tension) collectively, seem to be moved in a more healthful direction through the regular use of physical exercise (Kraus & Raab, 1961; Layman, 1977; Sime, 1984).

EXERCISE FOR STRESS MANAGEMENT

It is generally accepted that exercise for stress management is best if it meets three criteria:

1. Exercise should be aerobic, that is, any exercise that involves a sustained increase in oxygen demand (compared with basal metabolic levels). Such exercises are usually thought of as "endurance" exercises. Table 16.2 contains a list of exercises that can be useful in aerobic training for stress management.

2. Exercise should contain rhythmic movements that are coordinated, rather than random and uncoordinated. Further, such exercises should not put excessive strain on joints or connective tissue.

3. Exercise, from a psychological perspective, should be "egoless," that is, it should either avoid competitive paradigms or allow one to "win"

Table 16.2. Potentially Aerobic
Exercises

Walking
Aerobic weight lifting
Swimming
Running/jogging
Rope skipping
Racquetball
Cycling
Aerobic dance/movement

on every occasion, whatever winning means to the individual. Even the more vigorous aerobic exercise is for naught if after its completion one ruminates about having lost and how one can "get even." Ideally, exercise for stress management is exercise for the sake of exercise. Its goals are typically intrinsic—self-improvement, ventilation, long-range improvement in somatomotor coordination or motoric skill, and the like. Egoless exercise has been discussed by Gallwey (1976) as being void of an evaluative component. Whenever exercise and self-evaluation or self-esteem become intertwined, the healthful characteristics of exercise come into question.

EXERCISE GUIDELINES

Once an exercise has been chosen, the next issue that arises is "How much exercise is enough to promote health and better cope with stress?" The answer resides in the interaction of three variables: (1) exercise intensity, (2) exercise duration, and (3) the frequency of the exercise.

In determining the guidelines for health-promoting exercise it is first necessary to consider the physical status of the individual prior to programmed exercise. The first step in evaluating physical status is the implementation of a complete physical examination. The second step in the determination of physical status is the use of a standardized exercise tolerance test. There are four basic tests widely used for this purpose: (1) the Harvard Step Test, (2) Cooper's 12 minute run–walk, (3) the Astrand Ergometer Test, and (4) the Treadmill Electrocardiogram. Such evaluations, especially the latter two, are useful in determining fitness levels and target heart rate training ranges and screening for latent abnormalities that are only evident under physical exertion (Weller & Everly, 1985). Other variables that may be used to pretest/screen exercise participants include (Weller & Everly, 1985):

1. Body composition (% body fat)

2. Lung capacity
3. Body flexibility
4. General body strength
5. Resting heart rates and blood pressure

Returning to the issue of how much exercise is enough, the American College of Sports Medicine (1980) has provided minimum guides for enhancing the cardiopulmonary efficiency of otherwise healthy adults for whom physical exams were unremarkable. According to these guidelines, physical exercise generally needs to meet the following criteria:

1. Minimum intensity: 60% of maximum heart rate regardless of the specific exercise chosen (see Table 16.3)
2. Minimum duration: 15 minutes of continuous exercise so that the attained prescribed heart rate does not drop below 60% of maximum (see Table 16.4)
3. Minimum frequency: 3 times per week

Once the screening and planning stages for exercise have been completed and an exercise program has been selected, exercise sessions should be structured. According to Ribisl (1984), daily exercise sessions should contain a warm-up phase, an exercise phase, and a cool-down phase. An exercise session, which lasts 60 minutes, is typically structured with 10–20 minutes warm-up, 20–40 minutes actual aerobic exercise, and 10–20 minutes cool-down.

The warm-up, according to Ribisl (1984) accomplishes several important goals:

Table 16.3. Maximum Heart Rates Listed by Age[a,b]

Age	Maximum	85% maximum	80% maximum	70% maximum
25	200	170	160	140
30	194	165	155	136
35	188	160	150	132
40	182	155	145	128
45	176	150	141	124
50	171	145	136	119
55	165	140	132	115
60	159	135	127	111
65	153	130	122	107

[a]Values are listed in beats per minute (bpm).
[b]Beginning exercisers may need to begin at around a 40% to 50% maximum level (Ribisl, 1984).

Table 16.4. Minimum Activity for
Cardiovascular Fitness[a,b]

Swimming	900 yd
Running	9 mi
Walking	12 mi
Racquetball	4 hr
Cycling	24 mi

[a]Source: *American Health*, August, 1987, p. 23.
[b]Divided into 4 sessions per week.

1. Facilitation of enzymatic activity
2. Increased metabolic activity
3. Decreased total peripheral resistance
4. Increased perfusion of blood to the skeletal muscles
5. Increased speed of nerve conduction
6. Improved oxygen delivery

As for actual aerobic exercise activities, Table 16.2 contains a list of exercises that if practiced according to appropriately prescribed duration, intensity, and frequency guidelines can lead to improved cardiopulmonary efficiency and increased resistance to stress.

The cool-down period is extremely important, especially for adults, as it facilitates venous return thereby reducing cardiovascular strain. Similarly, the cool-down period facilitates the removal of lactic acid and other metabolic waste products. This third and final phase of daily exercise is perhaps the most often forgotten yet it is just as important as the preceding two phases for healthful, safe exercise.

A final consideration in developing exercise guidelines concerns compliance issues. Just providing a fitness program is obviously not enough. The mere availability of even the most modern of exercise facilities does not significantly improve exercise compliance. "The newest, most advanced exercise facilities available will simply rust from lack of use unless [individuals] can see exercise as personally rewarding" (Weller & Everly, 1985). Although most people recognize the need to exercise and the benefits of improving physical fitness, first year "dropout" rates exceed 50% (Stone, 1980). Dishman (1982) and Martin and Dubbert (1982) summarize major factors affecting exercise compliance:

1. Convenience of exercise facilities
2. Moderate exercise intensity
3. Social support

4. Perceived reinforcement
5. Perceived availability of time to exercise

It may well be that aspects of all five factors must be present if exercise is to be sustained.

CAVEATS ABOUT THE USE OF PHYSICAL EXERCISE

In this chapter, physical exercise has been discussed as a tool in stress management. The guidelines are offered *not* as an exercise prescription, but only as a model to show the clinician what considerations are active in the use of exercise for therapeutic purposes. Those readers interested in exercise prescriptions should refer to Ribisl (1984), Weller and Everly (1985), and the American College of Sports Medicine (1980). Yet, in continuing this overview of physical exercise, it is important to consider that there are precautions that should be taken.

The most critical point to be made in this section is that physical exercise represents a powerful stressor. Intense exercise not only stresses the cardiopulmonary system, but can greatly affect the musculoskeletal system as well.

Physical exercise has the potential to evoke a greater stress response than any psychosocial stressor we can imagine. Although the employment of physical exertion does appear to avoid most of the potential pathogenic qualities in psychophysiological stress arousal, the sheer quantity of the arousal during physical exercise can be overwhelming to the cardiopulmonary system. Cases are clearly on record of individuals who died from cardiac failure while exercising for their health.

The musculoskeletal system is vulnerable to the strain of physical exercise as well. Numerous joint and connective-tissue problems are related to excessive physical exercise. It is highly recommended that the person use only the proper equipment for exercise, in order to circumvent many of these potential problems.

Exercise is clearly individualistic; what is right for some may not be for others. It is always a good idea to have the family physician assess an individual's physiological readiness to participate in an exercise program and then to suggest reasonable guidelines, as noted earlier.

The success of an exercise program depends on its consistent utilization. Therefore, the question of motivation arises. It is important to find an exercise program that is not aversive for the patient. The mistake that most people make is to "overdo" an exercise program. The results are usually soreness, injuries, or the realization that it simply takes too much time. Therefore, people should engage in programs that will be continued. Emphasis should be placed on the need for patience and the need to integrate the exercise program into one's life style. It helps to find an exercise partner, one whom the person can exercise with—not compete with.

The cardiovascular, pulmonary, and weight-reducing aspects of the exercise program will manifest themselves within several weeks. The therapeutic psychological effects may take longer to realize, however, so once again the need for patience is required.

Finally, care must be taken in finding the best amount of exercise for the client. Dodson and Mullens (1969) found that "light exercise" actually made some psychiatric patients more anxious, whereas longer and more intense exercise, in this case jogging, reduced their anxiety.

SUMMARY

In this chapter, the use of physical exercise has been considered for its utility as an instrument in the treatment of excessive stress and its pathologic corollaries. Let us review the main points:

1. There is ample evidence to suggest that the stress response is nature's way of preparing the human animal for muscular exertion. Physical exercise may then represent nature's own prescription for how to healthfully ventilate and utilize the stress response once it has been initiated.

2. There is evidence that suppression of the intrinsic need for somatomotor expression that accompanies the stress response may well be pathogenic itself, hence the concept of "hypokinetic diseases" and related notions.

3. The idea that exercise can be therapeutic has persisted for literally thousands of years, dating back to the fifth century B.C. and the Greek physician Herodicus.

4. Within American society, regular physical exercise is becoming an accepted way of life fueled by the advent of more efficient exercise systems (e.g., Nautilus) and coeducational exercise facilities that foster socialization and interpersonal support across historic gender barriers. The efforts of well-known exercise advocates have done much to promote the widespread adoption of exercise practices.

5. Regular exercise appears to be therapeutic by virtue of three distinct mechanisms:

• During exercise, constituents of the stress response such as lactic acid, free fatty acid, and epinephrine are utilized in a healthful manner.

• Exercise induces a rebound relaxation effect, upon short-term cessation, leading to feelings of tranquility and reduced muscle tension.

• Exercise promotes the development of physical and psychological characteristics that appear to facilitate a certain degree of stress resistance, for example, reduced adipose tissue, electrical stabilization of the myocardium, improved lipoprotein profile, improved myocardial strength, and improved self-esteem and self-efficacy.

6. A key to exercise and stress reduction appears to be the use of consistent aerobic exercise, performed in a coordinated rhythmic manner, and with an "egoless" attitude.

7. The major criteria in designing exercise protocols involve appropriate intensity, duration, and frequency. Generally accepted minimum exercise guidelines for normal healthy adults include performing an exercise at 60% of the maximum heart rate for at least 15 minutes, at least three times a week.

8. Actual exercise sessions should contain warm-up, exercise, and cool-down periods. If exercise is not convenient, supported, and perceived as reinforcing, it will not be sustained regardless of attitudes.

9. In sum, research has provided ample evidence that physical exercise can promote psychological and physical alterations that are antithetical to the pathogenic processes of excessive stress. It may well be that physical exercise activates a form of coping mechanism that no other stress management intervention can—ventilation/utilization of the stress response before it leads to disease, as depicted in the introduction to Part II.

Part III

Special Topics in the Treatment of the Human Stress Response

This is the third and final section of this volume. Its purpose is to address specific issues that are of unique relevance to the treatment of the human stress response.

Chapter 17, entitled "Stress and the Contemporary Woman," provides a discussion of stress-related issues as they are uniquely applicable to woman. It reviews stressors unique to women as well as the female stress response. The goal of the chapter is sensitize the clinician to the uniqueness of the female patient who suffers from stress arousal or its pathological effects.

Stress at work has been an issue for three decades. Occupational stress and stress management have become topical issues in the 1980s. Though the matter is a problem by consensual validation, the behavioral sciences have only recently taken a serious look at it and how its manifestations can best be treated. The purpose of Chapter 18, entitled "Occupational Stress and Its Management," is to review those efforts and to offer one perspective on the nature and treatment of occupational stress.

Chapter 19 addresses posttraumatic stress syndrome. This psychiatric disorder may be the most florid stress-related disorder directed toward the mind as the target organ. Its importance to clinicians arises from the suggestion that it remains significantly underdiagnosed, while at the same time becoming the focus of some of the most hotly disputed litigation in the insurance industry.

Chapter 20 employs, for a final time, the system's phenemenological model as a graphic tool to summarize the treatment of the human stress response. A general treatment model is reviewed within this summary chapter as a means of integrating and summarizing the main thrust of this volume: the treatment of the human stress response.

Having provided a summation in the form of Chapter 20, there is an appendix that addresses itself to microdiscussions of selected topics of interest in the treatment of excessive stress arousal. Although far more lengthy and comprehensive discussions of the topics are available elsewhere, the goal of this appendix section is to provide a brief, practical introduction to these "special clinical considerations."

Stress and the Contemporary Woman

Eileen C. Newman

> She is a perfect mother
> the model wife
> the best housekeeper
> the greatest cook
> the most available daughter
> the most effective worker
> the most helpful friend . . .
> She is everything
> to everyone.
> But who is she?
> —Natasha Josefowitz

In the past few decades, social scientists have observed marked changes in the behavioral options for men and women in this society. The gender differences that were once predictable and taken for granted have been questioned as men and women are varying more in their roles, attitudes, and behaviors than ever before. Let us briefly review the social events that have resulted in these changes.

Most of us credit the Women's Movement of the 1960s and the 1970s for these changes. However, the Industrial Revolution precipitated the

Eileen C. Newman • University of Miami, Coral Gables, Florida 33134.

current changes in traditional sex-role stereotypes. Thus, the rise of feminism was not solely the result of the sexual revolution of the 60s and 70s but actually the product of a series of changes over the past two centuries, each wave of feminism being eventually more successful than the one preceding it. Briefly, the history of feminism over the past 150 years stars such early feminists as Elizabeth Cady Smith, Susan B. Anthony, and Lucy Stone. Unfortunately, their drive for equality included an attack on the institution of marriage that threatened the entire culture and ultimately failed. Subsequently, feminists became more socially acceptable, limiting their activities to supporting Prohibition, devoting themselves to social welfare causes, and securing the right to vote (Moulton, 1980). It took 72 years to secure this right. Despite this victory in 1920, women were still basically uneducated, lacking in social awareness, and dependent upon their husbands.

Some 60 years later, we see that more women than ever before are receiving postgraduate and professional education, are becoming more conscious of their ability to enter and succeed in occupational domains once exclusively male, and that there is a general sociological thrust for equality between the sexes (although such equality has yet to be realized). Socioeconomic conditions have wrought a situation where over half the female population is working outside the home. In 1950, for instance, two out of every three middle-income families had one wage earner, primarily because the husband was the sole breadwinner (Smith, 1979). Gurtin (1980) adds, "Since 1947, the number of working women has increased 205% and the number of women enrolled in previously male-dominated professional programs has tripled" (p. 29). Further, it is predicted that by 1990, "two thirds of all mothers with children under six will be working" (McCroskey, 1982, p. 32). This remarkable increase in the number of working mothers has, unfortunately, not been met by a coincidental increase in a commitment by business institutions and young men in general to help relieve women of some of their childcare responsibilities.

Thus, over the years we have seen a change in the status of women, but for all the "consciousness raising" of recent times and the vast research done in this area, the relationships between the sexes remain unchanged in many ways (see Table 17.1).

In light of this brief history of the societal changes relevant to North American women and the potential stress these changes pose, this chapter will focus on the nature and treatment of stress as it pertains to women from the perspective of the health practitioner. What is different about the ways women respond to stress? How do health practitioners' attitudes toward their female patients have an impact on the therapeutic process? What stressors are unique to women? The answers to these and other questions will be examined, as will the implications of this information for the treatment of the contemporary female patient experiencing stress.

Table 17.1. Gains and Losses in Women's Status in the Last Decade[a]

Gains	Losses
1. More women "firsts" and in traditionally male jobs . . .	but the great majority still clustered in "women's work."
2. Women entering law, medicine, and business in greater numbers . . .	and still earning less than men in the same fields.
3. Many more women are now running for public office . . .	but there are only two women in the Senate and twenty-one in the House (98th Congress).
4. Men no longer regard wives' working as a threat to their masculinity . . .	unless their wives earn more than they do.
5. The vast majority of young high-school and college women assume they will work for a large percentage of their lives, and that they will combine work and family . . .	but neither business institutions nor young men plan to make professional accommodations or compromises for child care.

[a]Adapted from Tavris & Wade, 1984, p. 32.

STRESSORS UNIQUE TO WOMEN

As contemporary women are finding themselves juggling more and more demands, they are particularly vulnerable to *burnout*. Freudenberger and North (1985) define burnout as:

> . . . a wearing down and wearing out of energy. It is an exhaustion born of excessive demands which may be self-imposed or externally imposed by families, jobs, friends, lovers, value systems, or society, which deplete one's energy, coping mechanisms, and internal resources. It is a feeling state which is accompanied by an overload of stress, and which eventually impacts on one's motivation, attitudes and behavior. (pp. 9–10)

They add:

> In light of women's unique position in our society, the definition takes on some unexpected coloration. Many women have become so inured to the stress and pressure endemic in their lives and roles, the feeling state of exhaustion is construed as normal living. Complaints of fatigue, lost motivation, and waning enthusiasm are tossed off as though they come with the female territory—not to be taken too seriously. And yet those complaints can act as crucial indicators of a burnout condition. (p. 10)

Thus, health care providers must be attuned to their own vulnerability to dismiss women's symptom reports as merely "neurotic" complaints. The following factors are common precipitators of the stress response and, potentially, burnout. The various stressors can be subsumed under two general groups, psychosocial stressors and physical stressors.

Psychosocial Stressors

Role Strain

Role strain is defined as the conflict produced by having to choose among multiple demands placed on the woman who works—the demands of her employer, the demands of her profession, and her obligations as a mother, wife, and person in her own right.

Traditionally, the wife has been viewed as a satellite of her husband with little knowledge of, or interest in, affairs outside the domestic sphere. The husband was the breadwinner and the wife provided him and the children with homemaking and emotional support. But the world of women has changed markedly in the last 20 to 30 years, and although women have always worked, the type of work and professional alternatives now open to them has broadened considerably. By 1975, women held 42% of the jobs in our country and, at this rate, will likely hold the majority of jobs by the end of the country (Bird, 1979). This has changed the traditional marriage described above, producing three alternative types of marriages: the dual-career marriage, the two-paycheck marriage, and the two-person career marriage.

Rapaport and Rapaport (1976) first coined the term "dual career families" in the late 1960s. They defined such a family as a "type of family structure in which both heads of household—the husband and wife—pursue active careers and family lives" (p. 9). Although the word "career" is defined as any sequence of jobs, in the true sense it means a sequence of jobs demanding commitment and is characterized by continuous development. Thus, the dual-career marriage may be thought of as a situation in which both husband and wife pursue not just employment but careers designed to provide personal and professional development.

The two-paycheck marriage differs from the dual-career marriage in that the former lacks the long-term commitment to professional development that is present in the dual-career marriage. Usually, in this second type of marriage, the husband is the primary provider and the wife works to supplement his income.

Finally, Hendrick and Hendrick (1983) describe the third family type, the "two-person career," and distinguish it from the former two families. Here one person, typically the husband, has a job that demands an enormous commitment on the part of the other spouse, typically the wife. For example, "a man may be hired to administer a community hospital: this involves management of hospital systems, hiring and firing of personnel, and frequent contact with governing board members and perhaps the community at large. This man's wife may be expected to support the hospital through volunteer work, participation in a number of related community activities, and entertainment of administrative staff, medical staff, board members, and community leaders. Thus, if both persons perform their designated roles, we have a two-person career or two for the price of one!" (p. 254)

Although these family models have similarities, it is the dual-career marriage that holds the greatest implications for both realizing and threatening personal and familial health.

What appears to be the most pressing problem for working women is the provision of childcare. Women have been conditioned to believe that motherhood is their most valuable and unique capability and this belief has resulted in keeping women safely at home, under the control of the husband. With the increasing sophistication of contraceptive techniques and the ability to regulate the number of children one has or to postpone having children, women may experience increasing anxiety about choosing between adopting the traditional role of wife and mother or the career options now available to her. Choosing to do both—to manage both motherhood and career—requires self-confidence, energy and drive, and the ability to not be as perfectionistic as she might be if managing only family or career. In a study of employed women's anxiety, depression, and hostility levels according to their perceived career and family role commitments, Light (1984) found that "women who step outside the socially ascribed roles of wife and mother by placing careers before families will experience emotional turmoil and stress" (p. 290).

Johnson and Johnson (1977) found that the greatest guilt and anxiety that occurs in mothers in dual-career families is over the time work takes from her role as mother. Yet Bernard (1974) points out that professional mothers are anything but rejecting of their children:

> They find as much pleasure as other women in motherhood. They have read the books and are now cowed by them. They believe they are better mothers when they have relief from full-time attention to their children and they think it is better for their children as well. Without their work, they could become resentful, sullen, angry, depressed. (p. 169)

Even when children aren't a consideration, women's interpersonal relationships are more likely to be impacted by stress than males'. In a study comparing the effects of stress between male and female public accountants, Pearson, Wescott, and Seiler (1985) found women perceive interpersonal relations as more stressful during the busy tax season. They also found that these women found it more difficult to leave work problems at work and relax at home and suspect that because women assume more home responsibilities than men, they have little time for leisure activities or relaxation.

Poloma (1972) found that those women who successfully managed the role strain inherent in juggling family and job, employed four types of stress management techniques: (1) they focused on the benefits of combining career and family rather than on the drawbacks; (2) they decided in advance which role would take precedence in a crisis, and usually the family is more important; (3) they compartmentalized the two roles, leaving job pressures at work and family problems at home; and (4) when any of the circumstances in their family lives changed, they compromised to adjust to their family's demands.

So we see that changes in work patterns for the sexes have produced an alternative to the traditional complementary marriage (where the husband works and the wife is responsible for the household and children). The dual-career couple is a growing phenomenon resulting from both the influx of women into the workplace and changing attitudes about appropriate behavior for the sexes. Unfortunately, most employees and employers are currently inadequately prepared to deal effectively with the problems created by the dual-career marriage, lacking comprehensive guidelines or precedents for such problems. Left to work out these problems for themselves, and often chastised by traditional families, these couples suffer extreme stress. Without existing role models, these couples must learn to deal not only with the conflicts inherent in balancing career and family responsibilities, but also with powerful societal norms working against adopting and maintaining role flexibility. The key to success in these marriages is compromise. Problems of geographic mobility, childcare, and equal division of household tasks must be negotiated, and the solutions agreed upon must be constantly reevaluated to ensure against regression to behavior stereotypic of one's sex role.

One final strategy worth mentioning is adopting and maintaining an androgynous, as opposed to a sex-role stereotyped, approach to living. Let us now turn to the problem of sex-role stereotyping and the opportunity for adopting this alternative androgynous philosophy.

Sex-Role Stereotyping

Rigid prescriptions by society for appropriate behaviors for the sexes begin at birth. The aforementioned problems encountered by the women in a dual-career or two-paycheck marriage are largely a result of the stress produced by not conforming to their prescribed sex role. Generally, men have been described as possessing traits that reflect competence, rationality, and assertiveness. They have been viewed as independent, active, competitive, self-confident, and ambitious, whereas women have been viewed as dependent, less competitive, lacking in self-confidence, and not ambitious.

As an alternative to this characterization of people as masculine or feminine, based on such stereotyped roles, Sandra Bem proposed the concept of psychological androgyny. Androgyny measures the extent to which a person believes he or she possess the desirable attributes of both sexes as opposed to being traditionally masculine or feminine in personality. Bem (1974) was particularly interested in how sex-typed masculine males and feminine females were restricted by rigid sex roles. In American society, the traits considered appropriate for a woman have put her at a disadvantage in terms of achieving what is seen as successful and important. Women have been viewed as sex objects, nurturant mothers, or domestic helpmates. Likewise, the male role restricts behavior, especially in areas such as sensuality, tenderness, and childcare. Bem's standard of psychological health for sexes—androgyny—allowed for the personal expression of the best traits of men and women. For example, traits typically associated with femininity are yielding, gentle, tender, sensitive to the needs of others, and childlike. Traits typically associated with masculinity are independent, willing to take risks, competitive, analytical, and forceful. Androgynous people would, theoretically, be able to express any of these traits no matter what their sex.

The extent to which men and women define themselves through their stereotyped sex roles is largely unconscious (Bem, 1975). Feminism and increasing awareness of male–female sex-role stereotyping is causing people to be more self-conscious about openly expressing a low opinion of women. However, a subtle, covert sex-role stereotyping still exists. Since her original conception of androgyny, Bem (1983) has discovered a flaw in her theory, namely that androgyny assumes the dichotomization by sex type (into masculine and feminine) in its construction, the very thing it attempts to eradicate. What she now calls for is a gender-free socialization process whereby the way we organize information via cognitive structures no longer results in gender schema (our perceptions are organized in terms of a male–female dichotomy—pink is for girls and blue is for boys, etc.). This perceptual organization takes place without our awareness as it has developed since birth and has become "second nature."

Despite this problem with the concept of androgyny, there is merit in its application to the dual-career dilemma. A behavior pattern that can grow out of an underlying androgynous attitude is that of "situation-dependent" behavior. Situation-dependent behavior involves having partners behave in a flexible, situation-specific manner in order to preserve the well-being of the family unit. Each partner must consider three aspects of the situation: (1) the objective demands of the situation, (2) the relative ability of each partner to perform the task at hand, and (3) the preferences of each partner, given the present task. If, on the other hand, a couple exhibits "role-dependent" behavior, it means that the couple's behavior, both interpersonally and socially, is dictated by social convention and existing socially approved sex roles, thereby often disregarding what may be more situationally effective behavior.

If you operationalize this idea, the principle of situation-dependent behavior dictates that the woman may handle the family finances, mow the lawn, or change the oil in the car if she can perform those activities better than her spouse, and/or she prefers to do such work, and she has the necessary time available. Likewise, the man may cook the meals, clean much of the house, or do the laundry if he can perform those activities better than his spouse and/or he prefers to do such work, and he has the necessary time available. The principle of role-dependent behavior, on the other hand, would dictate that the woman perform the duties that are are traditionally performed by the woman and the man perform the duties that are traditionally performed by the man.

Marital Stressors

As noted above, women are especially vulnerable in the area of inter-personal relations. Nowhere is this more evident than in a marital rela-tionship. For those women in a traditional marriage, it is typical that they gain a sense of security from the marriage and may be affected to a greater degree than those in less traditional marriages by the stressful events that adversely affect their husbands' lives. This has been noted by Makowsky (1980) in her review of stressful life-event inventories where she found there exists a "contagion of stress" from husband to wife that has been underestimated so that the stress in married women's lives is, in all like-lihood, greater than indicated by these inventories.

Moulton (1980) notes that changes have occurred in each sex's view of what marriage represents. Whereas marriage was once viewed as a trap by men only in the past, since the 1960s, it has become increasingly viewed as a trap by women as well. Housework and childcare began to feel restricting and unsatisfying, and outside work, where some pay and recognition were awarded, became more desirable. Thus, the primary outlets for women who felt trapped in a marriage were a return to work outside the home, an extramarital affair, or divorce.

Men seem to fare better as a result of being married than women. Carmen, Russo, and Miller (1981) compared psychiatric illness rates of married and never-married adults and found that marriage resulted in a 63% reduction in illness rates in white men and only a 28% reduction in white women. For minorities, the reduction in illness rates were 71% and 8% for men and women respectively. Russo and Sobel (1981) found the following hospital admission rates per 100,000 people in all marital status categories: 1,212 white men, 1,396 white women, 1,865 minority race men, and 1,773 minority race women. In contrast, for *married* people, the rates were 675 white men, 1,051 white women, 832 minority race men, and 1,631 minority race women. Thus, marriage significantly reduces hospital admis-sion rates for men but does not for women.

In his study of suicide statistics for women and men, Gove (1972) found that the loss of a spouse had a more debilitating effect on men than on women. Gove and his colleagues (see Gove, 1972, 1979; Gove & Geerlen, 1977; Gove & Tudor, 1973) have found women's overall higher rates of mental illness were largely accounted for by the higher rates of illness for married women. In all other marital status categories (single, divorced, or widowed), women had lower rates of mental illness than men. These authors conclude that women's higher rates are a function of their limited roles, noting that women have typically been restricted to the role of housewife—a role of frustration and low status, defined not in terms of their needs, but in the needs of *others*. We will return to this issue of the effects of sex-role limitation on physical health in a following subsection entitled "Doing It All."

Economic Stressors

Tavris and Wade (1984) found that half of all households headed by a woman with children live in poverty and that two-thirds of poor adults are female. They attribute this to the rising divorce rate, lower pay for women, lack of affordable childcare, and a preponderance of women in lower-paid jobs.

In his review of the literature, Phillips (1982) also found that women are paid less for equal work, and after equal preparation, than men. Although women are entering law, medicine, and business in greater numbers today, they are still earning less than the men in these same fields.

Gherman (1981) points out that there is a "ceiling to success" for women, in that they are now afforded the chance to achieve more than ever, but are still "frozen out" of the long-term management positions that pay over $50,000. In 1978, for example, women's median earnings were just slightly more than half that of men's, with women holding 35% of clerical jobs, 18% service positions, and only 5% in managerial and administrative positions.

Although the influx of women into better paying positions has improved the economic welfare of women to some extent, until economic differences are resolved, many other injustices and inequalities between men and women will not diminish.

Doing It All

If the pressures and responsibilities are juggled well, and the working mother successfully handles role strain, marital problems, sex-role stereotyping, economic strain, and other psychosocial stressors, she will actually be at an advantage. Bluestone (1965) found that women physicians between the ages of 35 and 55 who combined work, marriage, and motherhood were observed to have a general psychological well-being. They perceive more control over their lives, have satisfied their need for achievement, and fail to show as much depression at midlife as traditional women. A study by Verbrugge and Madans (1985) of government health statistics suggests that multiple roles improve health. Work outside the home was the strongest predictor of good health for women of all ages, with marriage second and parenthood third. Compared with nonemployed women, employed women had fewer days of illness, spent less time bedridden, had less chronic illness, and, in general, felt better.

Maracek (1978) points out that nonworking married women generally have one role that involves family life, whereas the working married man generally has two roles, one involving his occupation, the other his family. If he experiences a failure in one role he can still look to the other role to muster some sense of achievement and self-respect. Furthermore, the woman with only one role may feel much more anxious about failing because she has no other responsibilities that excuse her, nor does she have the alternative role that compensates for her failure in the other role. Much of the marital stress discussed in the earlier subsection may be explained by this phenomenon.

One way in which corporations or other employers may help working mothers is by offering Flextime. Flextime means giving employees a say in how they execute their prescribed work hours. Usually there are "core" times when all employees must be present and "flexbands" or flexible hours around starting time, lunch time, and closing time. Flextime seems very helpful to married women and mothers who's family demands often result in high absenteeism. In a study of single-parent and dual career women, it was found that they had a higher absenteeism than men on a fixed schedule, but approximately equal absenteeism rates when on a Flextime schedule (Johns, 1987). Flextime seems to help women meet family responsibilities without taking time off (e.g., children's doctor appointments, school functions, and the like).

Physical Stressors

Reproductive Functioning

Pregnancy and Childbirth The physical and psychological stress of childbirth is an experience unique to women. During pregnancy, hormonal changes occur, with estrogen and progesterone levels increasing significantly. Emotional reactions vary, and studies conflict as to whether pregnancy is always a period of radiant contentment, marked by urges for unusual food combinations. Hyde (1985) cites Sherman who concludes:

> So far as emotional state in pregnancy is concerned, the weight of the evidence suggests that it is not a period of unusual well-being. However, such feelings occur in some women during middle pregnancy, and there may be a decrease in psychotic reactions during pregnancy. Milder emotional disturbances, however, apparently increase, especially during the last six weeks. (p. 262)

Thus, the stage of pregnancy seems to affect emotional state, with the first trimester marked possibly by fatigue and depression, the second trimester by more positive emotions, and the third trimester by increasing anxiety as the mother-to-be anticipates the delivery and health of the newborn child.

For working women, pregnancy may still precipitate subtle discrimination in the form of employer justification in overlooking her for selection or advancement or giving her increasing responsibility. But Gomberg (1974) notes that whereas a women may lose a few months work postpartum for giving birth to a total of two children, because men are at a greater risk for alcoholism and coronary infarction, they may lose up to ten years of productivity. Despite this concern, employers may unwittingly discriminate against women by not looking at the broader picture.

Childbirth results in a drastic reduction in estrogen and progesterone levels and it may take several months before they reach homeostasis and for menstruation to resume. It seems that much of the childbirth experience can be modified, for example, through the use of the Lamaze method of natural childbirth and other pain control techniques and the support of the father or some significant other in the birthing or delivery room. Also, much of the variance in the experiences of childbirth may result from social influence or cultural expectations. In primitive tribal societies, for example, a childbirth ritual called *couvade* has been observed. In a couvade, it is typical for the man to exhibit the behaviors of a woman in labor (e.g., groaning, taking to bed, eating only certain foods, receiving guests) while the woman gives birth to the child and returns to work shortly thereafter.

Following delivery, a "postpartum depression" has been documented and occurs anywhere from 25% to 67% of the time (Hyde, 1985). During this brief period, generally a week or so, there are more suicide attempts than usual. The depression could be due to a combination of social and psychological factors (such as separation from the baby if he or she is ill, fear of responsibility, not wanting the child, or sudden change) and diminished estrogen and progesterone levels. Notman and Nadelson (1980) state that presently there is no definitive resolution as to whether postpartum reaction is a specific syndrome or a stress response to the psychological and physical changes of childbirth. Nonetheless, they note that less severe postpartum symptoms, like mild depression occur in 50% of parturient women and severe symptoms (e.g., psychotic-like reactions, severe depression) occur in one to two per thousand births.

Menstruation. The primary problems relating to menstruation are dysmennorhea (menstrual cramps) and premenstrual syndrome (PMS). Stress may induce amenorrhea (or loss of menstruation). Stress may also induce the onset of menstruation prematurely or interrupt the regularity of the menstrual cycle. Dysmenorrhea and PMS can act both as stressors themselves and to exacerbate existing stress. They can also be induced by stress.

Dysmenorrhea is thought to be a result of hormone-like agents called prostaglandins. Prostaglandins have been found at high levels in women with severe menstrual pain, and antiprostaglandin agents (e.g., Motrin, Ponstel), have been used to successfully treat cramps.

PMS generally occurs during the 7 to 14 days preceding menstruation (the luteal phase) and its symptoms can (but do not necessarily) include (see Wyngaarden & Smith, 1988):

Headaches/migraines
Anxiety and irritability
Fatigue
Negative feelings and/or
   depression
Moodiness
Backache and/or pelvic pain
Fluid retention and bloating
Food cravings (often for sweets)
Perspiration
Distention of the stomach with or
   without stomach upset

Breast engorgement and
   tenderness
Temperature changes
Lowered sex drive
An increase in mistakes or acci-
   dents
Swelling in the legs
Acne or blemishing
Flaring of allergic reactions
Outbursts of aggression

The mechanism by which stress influences menstrual problems is via the hypothalamus, which stimulates the anterior pituitary, which then effects the production of estrogen and progesterone in the ovaries. Thus, because PMS can contribute to stress in women and stress can affect PMS, any stress-management technique may make a difference in the experience of this monthly physical change.

Two excellent resources for females in this area of reproductive functioning are *Our Bodies, Ourselves* (1976), by the Boston Women's Health Book Collective, and *No More Menstrual Cramps and Other Good News* (1981) by Penny Budoff, M.D.

Menopause. Generally, at midlife, women experience the cessation of menstruation, a condition called menopause or, less frequently, "climacteric" changes. Menopause is marked by (1) a decrease in ovarian functioning, (2) a decrease in estrogen and progesterone, (3) eventual cessation of the menstrual cycle, (4) cessation of ovulation, and (5) eventual infertility. At this time, depression, anxiety, and irritability increase, as they usually do just before menstruation and just after childbirth when estrogen and progesterone levels drop. Physical symptoms include headaches, dizziness, pounding of the heart, hot flashes, and breast pains. Research suggests that cultural attitudes and a woman's emotional investment in the maternal role play an important part in the psychological response to menopause. Employed women, who were also mothers, tend to be less affected than unemployed mothers by menopause (Bart, 1971). Further-more, Bart found that in cultures where the woman's status rises at mid-life, these symptoms tend not to occur.

Estrogen replacement therapy has been successful in relieving many menopausal symptoms such as hot flashes, sweating, and irritability, sug-gesting a biological basis for menopausal symptoms as well as a cultural basis.

THE STRESS RESPONSE IN FEMALES

As seen in Chapter 2, the stress response is a complex process com-posed of a sequence of events involving the neural axes, the neuroen-docrine axes, and the endocrine axes. Generally, this process is identical for males and females. However, some differences exist.

The most notable difference between men and women in their physio-logical response to stress is in their adrenal-medullary reactivity. In her review of the literature, Collins (1985) notes that females are less prone than males to react with an increase of circulating epinephrine (or adrena-lin) when experiencing mental stressors (e.g., an achievement-demanding situation). However, females' *perceptions* of this stressful experience tend to be quite different than this lower level of adrenalin would indicate. Self-reports of subjective discomfort and lack of confidence tend to be greater in females than males. Similarly, Everly and Humphrey (1980) found that women had a significantly greater negative affective interpretation of the stress response than men.

Differences have also been noted in the behavioral inhibition systems of males and females. Men show a decrease in behavioral inhibition, be-coming proactive when faced with a stressor. Women, however, tend to show an increase in behavioral inhibition when faced with a stressor. There is some evidence that women's propensity to phobias, reactive de-pression, introversion, and susceptibility to anxiety, timidity, and fear, may be linked to a more highly reactive behavioral inhibition system in-volving the integrated activity of the frontal cortex, medial septal area, and the hippocampus (Martinson & Anderson, 1979). The question is still de-bated as to whether behavioral inhibition in females is learned or hormon-ally mediated.

In her attempt to compare the relationship between sex-related psy-chological characteristics (masculine and feminine interests) and measures of sympathetic-adrenal medullary hormones, Collins (1985) found, among her results, the following relationship. Comparing male and female en-gineering students, she found that not only had the females developed more masculine interests as they matured, but that adrenaline excretion during stress was higher in females with higher masculine interest scores.

Collins compares this to other research where career-oriented females excreted more adrenaline during stress than more traditional females and concluded, "It seems that sex-role orientation may have different implications for males and females, and this may be reflected in their psychophysiological responses in a stress situation" (Collins, 1985, p. 1229).

In an update on the current evidence on gender differences and health, Verbrugge (1985) states that although females have a life expectancy seven years longer than males and that *mortality rates*, at all ages and for all leading causes of death, are higher for males, *health statistics* show interesting differences (see Table 17.2).

Overall, she found that women show (1) higher morbidity from all acute conditions and nonfatal chronic conditions, (2) more short-term disability, (3) more medical services use, and (4) more medical drug use. She states:

> Over the adult life course, the size and components of sex differentials change. Gaps tend to be largest in young adulthood and smallest for elderly people. For adults 17–44, reproduction events are a prominent (but not sole) factor in women's excess morbidity and health care. At older ages, women's excess in such conditions persists and women have more short term disability and minor limitations. But older men catch up to them in health services use because their problems are more severe and pose immediate threats to life . . . the leading problems that spur limitation, ambulatory care and hospital episodes for men and women are very similar. What differs most is the rates, not the ranks. (Verbrugge, 1985, p. 163)

This author also points out two important things for physicians to keep in mind upon the initial evaluation of female clients: (1) health-reporting differences between men and women and (2) the potential for physician sex bias against female clients. Women are more likely to seek health care than are males and tend to give more complete, detailed health reports. There also seems to be a greater willingness among women to disclose their symptoms, perhaps because women tend to be more conforming or compliant and it is more socially acceptable for women to be sick. More frequent health-reporting behavior in women serves to buffer the debilitating effects of stress. Men are thought to withhold their symptoms and turn to alcohol, smoking, or recreational drugs to combat stress.

The second point to keep in mind is the potential to perceive male and female clients presenting with the same symptom differently. Although there is limited data supporting the existence of physician sex bias, no definitive evidence to date shows that different diagnoses and treatments of male and female clients with the same complaint result from the physician's sex bias. Many scientists and writers have purported, however, that women seem to obtain more psychologically related diagnoses, and seem to be the recipients of excessive diagnostic services and drug prescriptions.

The statistics in Table 17.2 shows that men die of heart attacks and that

Table 17.2. Health Statistics for American Men and Women by Age Based on National Health Surveys (in F/M)[a,b]

	No. of conditions per 100 persons per yr			
	Age 17–44			Age +45
Incidence of acute conditions (1981 and 1977–78)				
All acute conditions (1981)	1.27			1.22
Respiratory conditions	1.26			1.16
Digestive system conditions	1.18			1.24
Injuries	0.62			1.09
Prevalence of chronic conditions (1979)	Age 17–44		Age 45–64	Age 65+
Coronary heart disease	0.25		1.45	0.66
Hypertensive disease	0.95		1.11	1.38
Cerebrovascular disease	2.00		1.21	1.00
Atherosclerosis	1.00		0.54	1.02
Chronic bronchitis	1.94		1.09	1.44
Ulcer of stomach and duodenum	0.95		0.76	1.86
Frequent constipation	9.50		3.08	1.90
Gallbladder conditions	12.00		1.89	1.69
Chronic enteritis and colitis	3.25		2.50	2.30
Eczema, dermatitis, and urticaria	1.85		1.38	0.80
Thyroid conditions	7.00		5.38	3.08
Anemias	13.50		5.67	3.60
Migraine	3.00		3.71	2.50
Diseases of the urinary system	4.20		2.65	1.97
Drug Prescription (1977)	Age 19–34	Age 35–49	Age 50–64	Age 65+
No. of prescriptions per person for all people	2.56	1.70	1.58	1.36
No. of psychotropic prescriptions for all people (per 1,000 people)	2.16	1.98	1.99	1.64
Drug Use (1979)	Age 18–34	Age 35–49	Age 50–64	Age 65–79
Persons who used any psychotherapeutic drug in past yr (percentage)	2.18	2.21	1.45	1.70

[a]F/M = Female/Male sex ratio.
[b]Adapted from Verbrugge, 1985, pp. 159–162.

men are more likely to develop stress ulcers. What protects women from the higher incidence of vascular and hypertensive diseases and ulcerative colitis found in men? Estrogen appears to lower the incidence of vascular and hypertensive disease in women by facilitating lipid removal and by decreasing elastin, collagen, and mucopolysaccharides found in atherosclerotic lesions. Women also have been shown to have higher levels of high-density lipoproteins (HDL), which aid in the removal of cholesterol from the bloodstream, whereas men have been shown to have higher levels of low-density lipoproteins (LDL) which carry cholesterol to the arterial wall and promote plaque formation.

As for the formation of stress ulcers, the previously cited tendency for men to react to stress with higher levels of circulating catecholamines (particularly epinephrine) seems to have implications for the higher incidence of ulcers in men. Research indicates that not only does the activation of sympathetic (catecholamine) input into the digestive system decrease gastric blood flow, but these catacholamines also stimulate histamine release and histamines promote acid secretion in the gut (Martinson & Anderson, 1979). Again, the question as to whether the tendency to release greater amounts of catecholamines during stress in males is a biological difference between the sexes, a result of environmental conditioning, or some combination of the two, is still debated.

SUMMARY

This chapter focused on the nature and treatment of stress as it pertains to women, from the perspective of the health practitioner. Those stressors unique to women fall into two general groups: psychosocial and physical.

1. The primary psychosocial stressors are: (1) role strain, (2) marital stressors, (3) sex-role stereotyping, and (4) economic stressors. Role strain results from the demand to juggle a number of responsibilities, that is, professional and employee responsibilities, duties as wife and mother, and taking care of oneself. Nowhere has this strain been more evident than in the dual-career marriage, where both husband and wife pursue not just employment but careers designed to provide personal and professional development. Johnson and Johnson (1977) found that the greatest guilt and anxiety that occurs in mothers in dual-career families is over the time work takes from their role as mother. Choosing to manage both motherhood and career requires that the mother not berate herself for being less efficient than she might be if she was managing only the household or the career.

Without existing role models, dual-career couples must learn to deal both with the conflicts inherent in balancing family and career and the powerful societal norms working against adopting and maintaining role flexibility. Sex-role stereotyping plays the biggest part in making it difficult to maintain role flexibility. Rigid prescriptions for appropriate behavior for the sexes exist and violation of these norms often engenders subtle, adverse reactions in others. The alternative to sex-role stereotyped behavior is androgynous behavior, or the expression of the best traits of men *and* women, by either sex, to meet the demands of any situation. Although some objections have been voiced to this principle of psychological androgyny (see Bem, 1983), the notion of "situation-dependent" behavior, as opposed to "role-dependent" behavior, can serve as a model of behavior for dual-career couples.

2. Marital stressors for women of more traditional marriages include stressful events that adversely affect their husbands' lives and the often restricting, unrewarding, and unsatisfying nature of housework and childcare. Gove and his colleagues (Gove, 1972, 1979; Gove & Geerlin, 1977; Gove & Tudor, 1973) conclude that much of women's higher rate of mental illness can be attributed to their being primarily restricted to the role of housewife. This role is one of low status and frustration, which is defined not in terms of the housewife's needs, but the needs of others.

Finally, economic stressors include the lower pay women earn for equal work (Phillips, 1982) and the "ceiling to success" described by Gherman (1981) where women are still "frozen out" of the higher paying jobs.

3. The primary physical stressors are those related to reproductive functioning, namely pregnancy and childbirth, menstruation, and menopause. Hyde (1985) notes that the stage of pregnancy seems to have an effect on the emotional well-being of the mother. Hormonal changes, she says, both during pregnancy and following childbirth seem to play a great part in the emotional "ups and downs" and the postpartum depression. However, psychosocial factors such as cultural expectations and social support also seem to affect the woman's experience of pregnancy and childbirth. The most common problems due to menstruation are dysmenorrhea (menstrual cramps) and premenstrual syndrome (PMS). Prostaglandins have been found to be the major culprits responsible for dysmenorrhea, whereas fluctuations in estrogen and progesterone levels seem to play a major part in the PMS syndrome. Finally, menopause, or the cessation of menstruation, involves both the drop in estrogen and progesterone levels and the resultant symptoms associated with this change, as well as the psychological significance of losing the highly valued maternal role.

4. The stress response, as reviewed in Chapter 2, is virtually identical for males and females. The most notable difference is a greater tendency for males than females to react to an achievement-demanding situation with an increase in epinephrine or adrenaline. Furthermore, females tend to evidence greater behavioral inhibition (avoidance, fear, timidity, introversion) than males when faced with a stressor (Martinson & Anderson, 1979). The debate as to whether these differences are due to hormonal factors or environmental conditioning is still unresolved. The consequences of stress for women's health are that they show (1) higher morbidity from all acute conditions and nonfatal conditions, (2) more short-term disability, (3) more medical services use, and (4) more medical drug use. Men, on the other hand, suffer more severe problems that pose immediate threats to life (e.g., heart attacks) (Verbrugge, 1985).

5. In summary, the strides women have made can be health enhancing if the demands of home and career are juggled well (Verbrugge & Madans, 1985). It is important for the clinician to support the woman trying to maintain multiple roles. More than likely, her difficulty is not having more than one role but the fact that she is not managing these roles effectively. Stress-management techniques (e.g., relaxation training, time-management training, exercise, assertiveness training, and nutrition) can be employed with female clients to help them deal realistically with the limits imposed by juggling multiple roles.

Occupational Stress and Its Management

Even the most cost-conscious society should recognize that money spent on human capital is the single most important investment it can make.

Newsweek, October 18, 1982

As a society, we have gone to great lengths to see that the citizens of our society receive at least a basic education in reading, communications, and mathematics. These efforts are an attempt to assist our citizens in becoming better adjusted and productive members of society. Yet we have spent considerably less time and effort in helping our citizens develop a far more basic skill, the ability to cope with everyday life, especially the pressure associated with earning a living. The National Conference on Health Promotion Programs in Occupational Settings sponsored by the U.S. Public Health Service in 1979 recommended that occupational stress-management programs should be an integral part of any occupational health-promotion endeavor. The purpose of this discussion is to review the concept of occupational stress and to offer a basic framework for the development of occupational stress-management programs.

OCCUPATIONAL STRESS

Psychological Factors

"Can Companies Kill?" was the title of an article that appeared in *Psychology Today* (Rice, 1981). This article explored the question of "whether an employer can, in effect, by its own action or inaction, kill with stress" (p. 78). For example, there was the case of the secretary who was awarded $7,000 for what was determined to be "emotional distress" caused by her boss's "continual criticism and prying questions about her family life" (p. 81). Similarly, there was the case of a 20-year employee who successfully sued for damages incurred as a direct result of work-related stress. Just where does occupational stress come from and what are its consequences?

There can no longer be any reasonable doubt that excessive stress can lead to disease. In a comprehensive meta-analysis of 60 studies investigating the relationship between stress and illness, Towers (1984) provides a cogent argument for the pathogenic properties of excessive stress. Similarly, there is a growing body of evidence that the workplace may be injurious to the health of those who inhabit it and costly for those who control it.

This conclusion is supported by a series of investigations that culminate in what may be the single most eloquent analysis of work-related stress and illness yet conducted. Dotson, Manny, and Davis (1986) conducted intrigate multivariate path analyses in order to isolate both main effect and interactive effects attesting to ability of work-related stress to lead to illness and disfunction. Let us review some the earlier contributions to this line of investigation.

Historically, one of the earliest investigations into the relationship between excessive occupationally related stress and coronary heart disease (CHD) was that of Sales (1969). He notes: "It seems, from both the literature reviewed and the laboratory investigations, that organizational factors . . . can contribute to the etiology of coronary disease" (p. 334). Stanislav Kasl (1978) has comprehensively reviewed the area of occupational stress and concludes, "There is . . . a fair amount of suggestive evidence that job dissatisfaction and various complaints about work may be associated with CHD or CHD risk factors. . . . There is even some evidence that work satisfaction may make a modest contribution to overall longevity" (pp. 18–19).

Extending this influence to the corporation, Cooper and Marshall (1978) write:

> The mental and physical health effects of job stresses are not only disruptive influences on the individual . . . , but also a "real" cost to the organization, on whom many individuals depend: a cost which is rarely, if ever, seriously considered either in human or financial terms by the organizations, but one which they incur in their day-to-day operations. (p. 81)

More specifically, Greenwood and Greenwood (1979) found the "direct" costs of excessive executive stress in excess of $19 billion per year. Manuso (1983) suggests that the additional cost of employing a worker with stress-related symptoms may be an additional 25% of that employee's salary. Finally, Pelletier (1984) cites the following expenses related at least in part to excessive stress:

1. $44.2 billion for alcohol abuse
2. $3,394 for each employee/year with chronic headaches
3. $290 added to the cost of each car produced by Ford Motor Co. in 1980

If, indeed, this is the scope of the problem, what are the definable causes, or work-related stressors, in specific? This question is not easy to answer but some attempts of note have been made.

There have been many investigations into the nature of occupational stressors (see Everly, 1985a, for a review). Many of those studies have focused upon extremely narrow job-specific or occupation-specific factors. Such analyses yield little in terms of conceptual understanding or broad-spectrum programmatic intervention. Rather, those studies that define work-related stressors in far broader terms and that provide conceptual clarity to stress-at-work paradigms seem of greater value. There have been several noteworthy investigations of this genre.

In 1975, House published data that served as evidence that excessive job responsibilities were a precursor to ill health among employees. From this same study, there was also evidence that excessive or unwanted over-time assignments were a significant source of stress for employees. Upon closer examination, it may be argued that excessive job responsibilities and excessive overtime are actually forms of "overload," or excessive work demand (see Girdano & Everly, 1986) for a discussion of overload as a stressor).

In a later study of work-related stress, Weiman (1977) sought to dis-cover major generic stressors. In this study of over 1,500 management-level employees, he found four such generic factors: (1) job-role ambiguity, (2) job-role conflict, (3) too much, or too little, work, and (4) too much, or too little, responsibility. It may be of value to pause and make note of the fact that this study identified too little work and too little responsibility as potential stressors. These findings are consistent with Selye's notion of deprivational stressors (see Girdano & Everly, 1986). Deprivational stressors are stressors that cause stimulus "underload" as opposed to high demand stressors that cause a condition of stimulus overload, as mentioned earlier. There is evidence that both stimulus underload and stimulus overload can be powerful sources of stress (Selye, 1976). There is, however, no such thing as an absolute overload, or underload, threshold. Such thresholds will vary from worker to worker.

Another noteworthy effort toward the identification of major work-related stressors comes in the form of research by French and his col-leagues. In a review of a major investigative effort French and Caplan (1973) present data that isolate certain key concepts in occupational stress research. Their data suggest that the major source of occupationally related strain is poor "person–job fit." Role conflict was also a major direct cause of job strain, yet all other stressor factors could be defined within the context of a poor "person–job fit." Stated in a somewhat overly simplistic manner, the key to understanding occupational stress and illness depends largely upon an appreciation for the manner in which the needs, expectations, motives, personality, and so on of an individual is matched in a positive, health-promoting manner to the job description he or she is asked to assume.

In a summarizing report by Jaffee, Scott, and Orioli (1986), more specific job stressors were enumerated. They are offered here in concert with the previous findings of French and Caplan (1973) merely to provide some insight into some of the more generic and common factors that may serve to create undesirable person–job interactions:

—Work that does not allow the worker to participant in decisions about the work process;
—Jobs that place one in between two groups, such as supervisor and shop floor employees, or management and customers/clients;
—Jobs that demand more or less skill than one has;
—Receiving a job performance evaluation, or lack of clarity about expectations and standards about job performance;
—Changes in work demands, such as market shifts or restructuring;
—No clear career development path or opportunity for growth or advancement;
—Conflicts with co-workers or supervisors (Jaffe, Scott, & Orioli, 1986, p. 7)

The field of occupational stressor research owes perhaps its greatest debt to a group of Swedish researchers whose efforts have served to help clarify some of the broadest conceptual aspects of work-related stressors. Gardell (1977) was among the first to demonstrate that work environments that give rise to feelings of powerlessness and alienation are intrinsically stressful for most workers.

Frankenhaeuser (1986) extended this perspective from a psychophysiological point of view. Her research focused on the variables of "effort" and "distress." The factor of effort was defined as active coping procedures and a striving to gain and maintain control. The factor of distress, on the other hand, was defined as a feeling of dissatisfaction, boredom, and unpredictability. Figure 18.1 depicts Frankenhaeuser's model.

The interaction of effort and distress, according to Frankenhaeuser, represents the highest stress environment. Here, the daily quest to exert control over one's environment is met with a series of environmental factors that confront and antagonize that quest. Examples would include any environment that exerts a given demand on a worker within a context of boring, routinized, repetitive, or unpredictable constraints. Such environments give rise to extraordinary catecholamine *and* cortisol secretion and are highly associated with ill health, especially cardiovascular disease (Henry & Stephens, 1977).

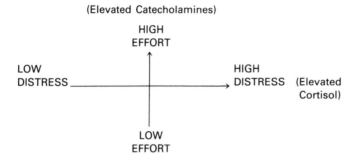

Figure 18.1. Frankenhaeuser's model.

The interaction of distress without effort represents any set of environmental conditions that cause the worker to experience the desire to give up and that engender feelings of a loss of control, helplessness, and hopelessness. Such conditions are associated primarily with cortisol elevations, depressive syndromes, and perhaps even neoplastic formation (Frankenhaeuser, 1986; Henry & Stephens, 1977).

The interaction of effort without distress represents a condition where the worker feels motivated to work within a given environment and sees a productive result to the efforts put forth. There is a high sense of personal control at work here, often combined with a sense of accomplishment and a sense of job commitment. Catecholamines moderately increase under such conditions, yet cortisol seems suppressed.

The interaction of a lack of effort without distress is virtually by definition not seen within the world of work for most of today's workers.

This brings us to the integrative efforts of Karasek *et al.* (1981). Karasek and his colleagues constructed a model of job stress that interfaced job demand with job control/flexibility. This model is portrayed in Figure 18.2 below.

Figure 18.2. Karasek's model.

According to Karasek's theory, the combination of excessive job demands and a lack of job flexibility and/or job control gives rise to a pathogenic work environment. In repeated empirical investigations encompassing several thousand employees, it was found that excessive demand without a perception of adequate control was associated with ill health, especially coronary heart disease. Such work situations carried the same risk of heart disease as the risk factors of smoking or elevated cholesterol levels.

In sum, the preceding has reviewed major sources of occupational stress. Three important themes can be extracted from what has been reviewed: overload (too much stimulation), underload (too little stimulation), and the issue of the perception of control. It may be that these three factors interact in such a way as to account for the vast majority of occupational stress. These factors are obviously psychological in origin. What of physical work-related factors that contribute to stress?

Physical Factors

There exist many physical (biogenic) work-related factors that are related to stress. These factors act by directly causing arousal within the organism. No higher cortical associations or meanings are required to induce a stress response.

Noise

The first factor to be examined will be that of noise. Noise is sound. Sound is an integration of mechanical waves. The strength, or volume, of sound is measured on the basis of pressure gradients called decibels (dB). Zero dB represents 20 micronewtons per square meter. The dB scale is a logarithmic scale (based upon powers of 10). Thus, sound intensity multiplies by 10 with every 10 dB. The frequency (tonal quality) of sound is measured in cycles per second, also known as Hertz (Hz).

Kryter (1970) showed that noise levels in excess of 90 dB can stimulate the sympathetic nervous system as well as the cardiovascular system. Reviews by Kryter (1970) and Glass and Singer (1972) have implicated excessive noise (in excess of 90 dB and 20,000 Hz) in decreased short-term memory, decreased learning ability, increased blood pressure, increased adrenal medullary function, increased adrenal cortical function, and increased accident rates.

Tables 18.1 and 18.2 provide additional information on noise levels.

Table 18.1. Effects of Noise Levels on Humans

dB Level	Effect
140+	Acute exposures may damage hearing
140	
130	Pain threshold
120	
110	
100	
90	
85	Hearing loss after repeated 8-hour exposures
80	
70	Potential for hearing loss begins
65	Evidence of a stress response begins
60	
55	Disruption of conversations
50	
40	Sleep disrupted
30	
20	
10	
0	Hearing begins

Table 18.2. Decibel Levels of Exposure to Common Sounds in Business and Industry

Common sounds	Average dB	Common sounds	Average dB
Rocket engine	180	Food disposal	85
Air raid siren	140	Inside a noisy restaurant	75
Police and fire siren at 100 feet	135	Inside a stenographic room	75
Jet takeoff at 200 feet	130	Loud conversation at 3 feet	75
Car horn at 3 feet	125	Electric shaver	75
Pneumatic (air) drill at 5 feet	125	Vacuum cleaner	75
Inside a discotheque	125	Noisy office	70
Rock concert	125	Dishwasher	70
Pile drivers at 25 feet	120	Washing machine	70
Inside a boiler room	110	Inside a classroom	68
Train passing at 10 feet	108	Clothes dryer	60
Inside a heavy manufacturing plant	100	Normal conversation at 3 feet	60
Chain saw at 3 feet	100	Average residential street	55
Riveting gun at 25 feet	100	Table fan	50
Garbage truck	100	Refrigerator	40
Gasoline mower	90	Quiet office	40
City traffic at 5 feet	90	Library	38
Outboard motor at 10 feet	85	Soft whisper at 15 feet	25
Home shop tools	85	Hearing begins	0

Lighting

Lighting within the occupational environment is another potential source of work-related stress. Either too much light or too little light can increase arousal levels. The luminance (brightness) of light can be measured in nits (candles per square meter). Tasks involving fine detail require greater than average light (around 800 to 1000 nits). General office work can be conducted around 100 nits. When lighting falls below minimum required values, muscular eye strain results. The most common characteristic of too much light is glare. Glare results in visual dysfunction because it makes it more difficult to focus upon objects. Once, again, glare contributes to muscular strain as well as excessive retinal stimulation.

Temperature

Temperature is another factor that can contribute to stress. The ideal range for sedentary work is 70 to 75 degrees Fahrenheit (at 50% humidity). Ambient temperatures in excess of 81 degrees Fahrenheit seem to erode productivity (Selye, 1976). Temperatures that drop below 68 degrees Fahrenheit may begin to erode productivity of some office workers. When discussing temperature, it is important to mention the concept of humidity. High humidity impedes the body's ability to cool itself via evaporation. Thus as humidity increases, so does the potential for becoming too hot. Fresh, circulating air aids in the natural cooling process.

OCCUPATIONAL STRESS MANAGEMENT

Having discussed the nature of human stress and its common occupationally related factors, it is now time to discuss the management of occupational stress. Let us briefly review several noteworthy stress-management efforts within the workplace.

In one early study, Peters, Benson, and Peters (1977) utilized a noncultic meditative intervention patterned after the writings of Herbert Benson (1975). Employees were taught this meditative technique along with some relevant health education over the course of a 12-week period. Results of the study indicated that employees benefited by improvements in psychological well-being, work performance, blood pressure, and general health.

A somewhat similar intervention was implemented by Carrington et al. (1980). In this study, 154 employees of the New York Telephone Company were taught to use a meditative technique including an audiotape and asked to practice twice a day. After five months, it was found that meditating employees experienced significant reductions in hostility, depression, anxiety, and somatization as measured by self-report inventories. In another study utilizing an audiotape delivery format, Bhalla (1980) tested a multidimensional intervention that allowed subjects to express personal preferences for intervention techniques. Assessment of cardiovascular and neuroendocrine-dependent measures found that giving subjects the opportunity to choose their own stress-management techniques in a multicomponent format led to superior health-related outcome.

Leclerc (1980) utilized biofeedback training for executives as a stress-management intervention. Results of this study found that participating executives reported lower levels of stress and more internal loci of control as a result of the biofeedback training.

Research by Everly (1980) tested a "nonclinical" educational intervention for working adults. The program was designed along guidelines described at the end of Chapter 1, in Table 20.2, and elsewhere (Girdano & Everly, 1986; Griffin, Everly, & Fuhrmann, 1982). Results of the research found that basic stress-management techniques focused on person–environment interaction led to improvements in self-esteem, internal locus of control, and the ability to relax.

These findings are in concert with the recommendations of Neale et al. (1983). In a comprehensive survey of occupational stress-management programs, these authors concluded that such programs could focus on (1) the person, and (2) the environment (workplace). Greatest efficacy is likely to be derived from interventions, however, that improve the person–work environment "fit." This suggestion is in agreement with the work of French and Caplan (1973) described earlier.

Let us now turn to published reviews of stress-management programs at the worksite. An analysis of the relevant literature reveals four separate and useful reviews of worksite stress-management programs: (1) Newman and Beehr (1979), (2) Murphy (1984), (3) Jaffee et al. (1986), and (4) Everly and Smith (1987).

The review offered by Newman and Beehr (1979) focuses on so-called "personal" and "organizational" stress-management interventions for worksite utilization. The authors review 24 published papers advocating "personal" interventions such as meditation and philosophical changes for managing job-related stress. Of those 24 papers, only 10 were based on empirical research. Of those 10, only 3 were able to offer empirically credible conclusions. Newman and Beehr continue their review by analyzing 23 published papers that address "organizational" strategies (e.g., human factors and organizational development interventions) for managing job-related stress. Of those 23 papers, only 9 were in any way based on empirical investigations. Of the 9 that were empirically based, 7 appeared to warrant serious consideration. The conclusion of the authors was that

" . . . there appears to be no single recipe or point of intervention to be recommended for the management of stress in all persons, in all organizations in all circumstances" (p. 39). In other words, there seems to be no single *best* stress-management intervention. They continue to suggest that future researchers should adopt a multicause and multieffect model of stress.

Lawrence Murphy (1984) offers a review of 13 empirical investigations into the management of work-related stress. Nine of the 13 studies used asymptomatic control groups. The interventions tested included cognitive restructuring, biofeedback, meditation, muscle relaxation exercises, and breathing exercises. Outcome included psychological symptoms, systolic blood pressure, diastolic blood pressure, electromyographic indices, frequency of health clinic visits, work attitudes, and performance. The author concludes:

> The studies reviewed in this paper indicate that worksite stress management programs are feasible and that a variety of techniques can be effective in helping workers reduce physiological arousal levels and psychological manifestations of stress. Although too few studies have been conducted to determine the relative merits of select techniques and compute cost-benefit ratios, such programs appear to have potential for improving worker well-being and partially offsetting the costs of occupational stress arising from productivity losses and stress related disorders. (p. 11)

The monograph by Jaffee *et al.* (1986) provides a useful overview of the field and the major evaluative studies, but fails to critically comment on their credibility.

Finally, there is the review by Everly and Smith (1987). In this select review, the authors focus primarily on empirical investigations that were empirically "credible" from a research design perspective. After conducting these analyses, they conclude that there is substantial evidence that stress-management programs can reduce psychological and behavioral factors otherwise adversely affected by excessive stress. This effect, they note, has been demonstrated only at immediate posttestings (usually 10 to 12 weeks after program initiation). Long-term data on programmatic efficacy has not been forthcoming because of the absence of such controlled longitudinal investigations. The authors further note, however, that the lack of a common valid financial metric has prohibited comprehensive investigations into the cost benefits of worksite stress management.

GUIDELINES FOR PROGRAM DEVELOPMENT

Stress-management programs may come in many shapes and sizes— from one-to-one counseling interventions to group training programs. Rather than select one "ideal" stress-management program, within this section we have elected to present a generalized set of developmental guidelines that are flexible enough to fit virtually any organizational setting. To date, the most popular format used for occupational stress-management programs has been the group training seminar format. Here, groups of 10 to 50 participants are brought together for training in stress management. Such seminars may last for several hours or several days. Some in-house programs may even meet once a week for several months. The guidelines presented in this section are ideally suited for the training seminar format, but may be adapted for individual one-to-one counseling interventions as well.

Components of a Stress Management Program

Participants in stress-management programs appear to benefit the most when certain generic components are provided within the scope of the intervention (Everly & Rosenfeld, 1981; Levi, 1979). They include

1. An explanation of what stress is
2. An explanation of the personal health and performance implications for eustress and distress
3. A method for identifying personal symptoms of excessive stress
4. A method for identifying personal causes of stress
5. An explanation of and practice in various stress-management strategies, preferably organized around a cogent rationale and coherent structure

Before discussing each component in detail, it is important to note that preceding all intervention will be selection and measurement, if applicable of any outcome (dependent) variables that will be used to measure the success of the stress-management intervention. Following such determination, actual intervention begins.

1. The word "stress" means many things to many people. The first component of a stress-management intervention should entail discovering what stress means to the participants, noting connotations as well as denotations (both correct and incorrect) of the word. This represents a form of audience analysis. This discussion should conclude by reaching some generally acceptable and technically correct definition of stress. Thus, general agreement will be reached as to what stress really is and existing misconceptions will have been corrected by the end of this stage.

2. The second stage of the stress management model includes some form of explanation of the nature of the stress response itself. Included in this discussion should be an explanation of how stress can physiologically act to be a positive, motivating force as well as a debilitating, destructive force. Although it is important to keep this discussion simple, it is of

particular value in demystifying stress and removing it from the realm of a "mental illness" in the minds of the participants.

3. The third component in the program involves helping participants identify the symptoms of excessive stress. Because symptoms are idiosyncratic and are even dynamic within the same individual, this process requires personal practice on the part of each participant. It is helpful to begin with a stress symptom checklist and then instruct participants in how to recognize these symptoms in themselves. Even more important is the cognitive interpretation assigned to these symptoms. If the participants view these symptoms as wholly negative, a self-perpetuating feedback mechanism could be created. The result would be greater stress arousal and even panic states being initiated at the symptom's first appearance. On the other hand, recognition of some symptoms could be interpreted positively as the initiation of a eustress response that can be controlled and actually be helpful to the individual, in that it represents the mobilization of resources not previously available to the individual. Therefore, not only should recognition of symptoms be taught, but a positive interpretation of these symptoms should be encouraged when possible.

Of course, it is essential to note that certain stress symptoms could be early warning signs of a significant health problem. The participants should be instructed in the recognition of such symptoms and encouraged to seek medical consultation. Such symptoms might include prolonged dizziness, prolonged gastrointestinal pain, persistent visual disturbances, persistent heart conduction abnormalities, or any severe pain or dysfunction at all.

4. The next component in the stress management program involves the identification of sources of stress—called stressors. Effective stress management is often predicated upon stressor identification. To achieve that goal, it is advisable to have participants complete a "personal stressor profile." I use a series of self-assessment exercises (Girdano & Everly, 1986). These self-assessment exercises yield a profile of each participant's personal sources of stress, including psychosocial stressors such as overload, underload, deprivation, frustration, and the need for control. Other domains assessed include diet and personality factors. When participants know what their source of stress are, they can better begin to render those sources benign.

5. The most lengthy and most complex component in the stress-management program involves explanation of and practice in various stress-management strategies. The model that has been created represents a "multidimensional" or "holistic" model for intervention. By this we mean that stress management should attack the problem of excessive stress from multiple dimensions, or perspectives, in order to be comprehensive (Everly & Rosenfeld, 1981; Girdano & Everly, 1986; Levi, 1979) in the same way that the individual's total life is affected by multiple influences. Such per-

spectives should consider the roles of environment, personality, life style, and biology in the cause and management of excessive stress.

Based upon a review of the literature and practical application it may be concluded that there are basically three generic perspectives, or dimensions, from which individual stress management may be initiated. (Everly & Rosenfeld, 1981; Girdano & Everly, 1986) They are:

1. Helping the individual develop strategies by which to avoid/ minimize/ modify exposures to stressors, thus reducing the tendency to experience the stress response
2. Helping the individual develop skills in relaxation, thus reciprocally inhibiting the stress response
3. Helping the individual develop techniques for the healthful expression of the stress response
4. Organizational development and redesign to reduce/eliminate occupational stressors

The fourth dimension of stress management intervention may be only indirectly under the control of the individual and is only sometimes found in occupational stress-management programs. Effecting changes in the work environment itself involves organizational sanctions that may range from microcosmic changes in job descriptions or the office environment to macrocosmic changes that might include alteration of the organizational structure. This last option has been added with the understanding that some corporate climates and some jobs are inherently stressful and are unalterable; therefore, stress-management interventions must put an emphasis on the individual rather than the job.

Table 18.3 lists the multidimensional stress-management model described above, including some specific strategies. In reviewing Table 18.3, it is important for the stress-management trainer to be cognizant of the fact that there is no single best way to manage stress. Rather, effective stress management is based on identifying stress-management strategies that the participant finds personally useful at a given point in time. Because all human beings are unique, what may be right for one person may not be for another. Similarly, because people are dynamic, stress management cannot be static but must be dynamic and flexible as well. Table 18.3 simply lists options that may be considered under each of the major headings.

EVALUATION

Fundamentally speaking, there are two evaluation models that may be used to assess the effectiveness of worksite stress-management programs:

Table 18.3. A Multidimensional Model for Stress
Management

I. Helping the individual develop strategies by which to
avoid/minimize/modify exposures to stressors
  A. Time-management training
  B. Assertiveness training
  C. Communications training
  D. Hostility-management training
  E. Management-by-objectives
  F. Practice in rational thinking; cognitive restructuring
  G. Diet
II. Helping the individual develop skills in relaxation (see
Everly & Rosenfeld, 1981, for a review)
  A. Deep breathing techniques
  B. Meditation
  C. Biofeedback
  D. Progressive relaxation
  E. Coping with anxiety
  F. Mental imagery
III. Helping the individual develop techniques for healthful
expression of the stress response
  A. Physical exercise
  B. Emotional catharsis
IV. Organizational development

(1) the behavioral science model and (2) the financial model. The behavioral science model evaluates the effectiveness of stress-management programs by their ability to bring about some positive health-related or work-related change in one or more behavioral outcome variables. Does, for example, the worksite health promotion program lead to a reduction in alcohol use, sick days, self-reports of anxiety, blood pressure, production errors, and the like? The financial models, on the other hand, begin where the behavioral science models leaves off. Financial models would ask questions such as how much money was saved when the alcoholism, sick days, anxiety, blood pressure, production errors, and the like were converted to dollars and cents? Further, the financial models may ask these questions in light of the actual costs of implementing the stress-management programs. That is to say, the behavioral scientist is usually most concerned in an evaluation paradigm with the question "Did the program work or not?" The financial expert typically goes one step further and asks the question "What did the program cost in view of its behavioral outcome?"

In the most useful evaluation of stress-management programs, positive behavioral/medical outcome may be insufficient to completely answer the question of the effectiveness of such programs. Rather, cost-conscious managers are beginning to ask cost-related questions. More and more health-promotion programs may soon have to justify their existence on more than just humanitarian grounds; enter the financial model.

The evaluation of occupational health programs using financial criteria may be something that behavioral scientists are unfamiliar with. Reviews by Smith and Everly (1988), Spencer (1984), and Smith, Haight, and Everly (1986) will prove of value to those interested in such methods. A brief review at this point is in order.

One means of evaluating the financial value of any occupational health-promotion program is the cost-effectiveness model. Cost effectiveness typically assumes that the intervention is of value and then seeks to calculate the cost in relation to some other means of obtaining the same end. The cost-effectiveness model yields no data on absolute value provided by the intervention, but rather is used to compare interventions on units of outcome. Mathematically, cost-effectiveness can be expressed as:

$$\frac{\text{Program cost} + \text{No. employees served}}{\text{No. of behavioral change units achieved}}$$

A financial model that is superior to the cost-effectiveness in terms of its ability to answer the "How much?" question is the cost-benefit model. Cost-benefit models evaluate the efficiency of the investment. Mathematically, absolute cost-effectiveness is calculated as:

Sum of all program's income + cost savings − sum of all
program investments (costs)

Extending this model, the rate-of-return model can be used to calculate financial benefits of health-promotion investments. Mathematically,

$$\text{Rate of return} = \frac{\text{Sum of all benefits (income} + \text{savings) per year}}{\text{Yearly cost}}$$

In a recent evaluation of a large corporate health-promotion program, Smith (1986) evaluated the cost benefits of a corporate weight-loss program. In what was designed to be the most critical appraisal of corporate health promotion yet conducted, Smith utilized stringent internal auditing standards to calculate the financial impact of this health-promotion program. The study followed 33 employees who participated in the weight-loss program and compared them with 33 matched controls. Smith found that the weight-loss program yielded a 23% return on investment per annum. This was certainly a striking return and needs to be replicated.

SUMMARY

This chapter provided a basic discussion of the nature of occupational stress and its management aimed at better insight into the problems associated with the design, implementation, and evaluation of an occupational stress-management program.

A review of previous research yields the following conclusions:

1. The superordinate occupational stressor appears to be conditions where there is a high demand placed on the worker in combination with few opportunities to exert control over the high-demand environment.

2. There exists a paucity of well-controlled occupational stress-management studies.

3. Those that do exist often employ outcome variables of questionable clinical/behavioral significance.

4. Despite the aforementioned problems, there does appear to be some controlled, empirically generated evidence that stress management at the worksite can be useful in reducing certain psychological and behavioral factors with the potential to be meaningful.

5. Current evidence points to the conclusion that there is no such thing as one *best* stress-management intervention. Rather, evidence indicates the value of multimodel and personalized/flexible interventions.

6. At this time there exists no convincing replicated evidence that worksite stress management is clearly cost-beneficial when opportunity costs (the benefits derived from alternative investments) are factored in. This evidence is lacking not because of a failure of programs to show such evidence, but because of a failure to employ financial models that would argue effectively to such a conclusion.

7. There is a great need for worksite stress-management programs to be conducted and replicated showing both behavioral and financial efficacy when opportunity costs are considered.

Posttraumatic Stress Disorder

The posttraumatic stress syndrome has been recognized for decades (Freud, 1921). Even systematic empirical inquiry dates back to the 1940s (Kardiner, 1941). Yet it was not until 1980 that the now highly recognizable posttraumatic stress syndrome was officially catalogued within the official nosological compendium of the American Psychiatric Association, the *Diagnostic and Statistical Manual of Mental Disorders*—3rd edition (DSM–III) (APA, 1980). With this recognition of the syndrome as an official mental disorder came a surge of research efforts designed to lead to better diagnostic refinement as well as improved treatment.

Whereas once the syndrome was viewed almost exclusively as a result of armed combat, now posttraumatic stress disorder (PTSD) has been found to result not only from war-related situations but from a host of noncombat-related experiences as well. In 1987, the American Psychiatric Association revised its official nosology (APA, 1987). PTSD remained, albeit somewhat modified, reflecting the phenomenological opinion of the preceding years. Are we coming closer to a comprehensive understanding of PTSD, or are we just beginning to scratch the surface of what may be a uniquely complex interaction of pathophysiological and psychopathological constituents? The purpose of this chapter is to review current evidence on the nature of PTSD as well to as offer an integrating phenomenological hypothesis regarding this disorder, which appears to be playing more and more a role in Western society.

DIAGNOSTIC SYMPTOMATOLOGY

In 1941, Kardiner (1941) described five consistent clinical features of the syndrome now referred to as PTSD:

Table 19.1. Diagnostic Criteria for Posttraumatic Stress Disorder—DSM—III (1980)

A. Existence of a recognizable stressor that would evoke significant symptoms of distress in almost everyone
B. Re-experiencing of the trauma as evidenced by at least one of the following:
   (1) recurrent and instrusive recollections of the event
   (2) recurrent dreams of the event
   (3) sudden acting or feeling as if the traumatic event were reoccurring, because of an assoication with an environmental or ideational stimulus
C. Numbing of responsiveness to or reduced involvement with the external world, beginning some time after the trauma, as shown by at least one of the following:
   (1) markedly diminished interest in one or more significant activities
   (2) feeling of detachment or estrangement from others
   (3) constricted affect
D. At least two of the following symptoms that were not present before the trauma:
   (1) hyperalertness or exaggerated startle response
   (2) sleep disturbance
   (3) guilt about surviving when others have not or about behavior required for survival
   (4) memory impairment or trouble concentrating
   (5) avoidance of activities that arouse recollection of the traumatic event
   (6) intensification of symptoms by exposure to events that symbolize or resemble the traumatic event

1. Constriction of personality functioning
2. Exaggerated startle reflex and irritability
3. Psychic fixation upon the trauma
4. Atypical dream experiences
5. A propensity for explosive and aggressive reactions

In 1942, Gillespie (1942) described an acute "war neurosis" as having as an important clinical feature an increased startle reaction characterized by increased and generalized muscular tension, palpitations, and a "sinking feeling," thus emphasizing a distinct autonomic nervous system component to this posttrauma syndrome.

In 1980, the American Psychiatric Association described PTSD as a form of anxiety disorder.

> The essential feature is the development of characteristic symptoms following a psychologically traumatic event that is generally outside the range of usual human experience. . . . The characteristic symptoms involve re-experiencing the traumatic event; numbing of responsiveness to, or reduced involvement with, the external world; and a variety of autonomic, dysphoric, or cognitive symptoms. (p. 236)

The specific criteria are listed in Table 19.1.

PTSD was described in subvariations, as well:

1. "Acute," where the onset of symptoms occurred within 6 months of the trauma and lasted less than 6 months; and
2. "chronic or delayed," where either or both of the following applied—duration of the symptoms for 6 months or more (chronic) and/or the onset of symptoms at least 6 months after the trauma (delayed).

In 1987, the American Psychiatric Association revised its criteria for PTSD (APA, 1987). In doing so, the traumata giving rise to PTSD were somewhat better defined. Once again, the notion of a psychologically distressing event outside the normal range of human experience was emphasized. Yet specific instances were cited:

a serious threat to one's life or physical integrity; a serious threat or harm to one's children, spouse, or other close relatives and friends; sudden destruction of one's home or community; or seeing another person who has recently been, or is being, seriously injured or killed as a result of an accident or physical violence. In some cases the trauma may be learning about a serious threat or harm to a close friend or relative. . . . (pp. 247–248)

Table 19.2 describes the specific criteria requisite for the PTSD diagnosis.

In reviewing Tables 19.1 and 19.2, one sees a fundamental convergence on four equally weighted phenomenological factors that are believed to constitute PTSD:

1. Exposure to an extraordinary stressor outside the usual realm of human experience
2. Intrusive psychological reexperiencing of the traumatic event
3. Psychological numbing to, or reduced involvement with, the external environment
4. Autonomic nervous system hyperreactivity and/or hyperfunction

Let us move to a review of recent research and clinical findings with an appreciation for a reformulation of the PTSD concept.

PSYCHOLOGICAL PHENOMENOLOGY

As the preceding section described, in addition to exposure to an extraordinary stressor, PTSD represents three major symptom clusters: (1) psychological reexperiencing of the traumatic event, (2) a psychological numbing, or avoidance, of the external environment, and (3) autonomic nervous system hyperfunction. In diagnostic formulation, these three symptom clusters are equally weighted. Although, when revising the DSM–III, the updated description of PTSD that appeared in the DSM-III-R seemed to reflect a new emphasis being placed upon the numbing/ avoidance cluster. In the DSM–III, only one of three criteria was needed to satisfy this symptom requirement. In the DSM–III-R, three of seven criteria are now

Table 19.2. The Diagnostic Criteria for Posttraumatic Stress Disorder, DSM-III-R (1987)

A. The person has experienced an event that is outside the range of usual human experience and that would be markedly distressing to almost anyone, e.g., serious threat to one's life or physical integrity; serious threat or harm to one's children, spouse, or other close relatives and friends; sudden destruction of one's home or community; or seeing another person who has recently been, or is being, seriously injured or killed as the result of an accident or physical violence.

B. The traumatic event is persistently re-experienced in at least one of the following ways:
  (1) recurrent and intrusive distressing recollections of the event (in young children, repetitive play in which themes or aspects of the trauma are expressed)
  (2) recurrent distressing dreams of the event
  (3) sudden acting or feeling as if the traumatic event were recurring (includes a sense of reliving the experience, illusions, hallucinations, and dissociative (flashback) episodes, even those that occur upon awakening or when intoxicated)
  (4) intense psychological distress at exposure to events that symbolize or resemble an aspect of the traumatic event, including anniversaries of the trauma

C. Persistent avoidance of stimuli associated with the trauma or numbing of general responsiveness (not present before the trauma), as indicated by at least three of the following:
  (1) efforts to avoid thoughts or feelings associated with the trauma
  (2) efforts to avoid activities or situations that arouse recollections of the traumas
  (3) inability to recall an important aspect of the trauma (psychogenic amnesia)
  (4) markedly diminished interest in significant activities (in young children, loss of recently acquired development skills such as toilet training or language skills)
  (5) feeling of detachment or estrangement from others
  (6) restricted range of affect, e.g., unable to have loving feelings
  (7) sense of a foreshortened future, e.g., does not expect to have a career, marriage, or children, or a long life

D. Persistent symptoms of increased arousal (not present before the trauma), as indicated by at least two of the following:
  (1) difficulty falling or staying asleep
  (2) irritability or outbursts of anger
  (3) difficulty concentrating
  (4) hypervigilance
  (5) exaggerated startle response
  (6) Physiologic reactivity upon exposure to events that symbolize or resemble an aspect of the traumatic event (e.g., a women who was raped in an elevator breaks out in a sweat when entering any elevator)

E. Duration of the disturbance (symptoms in B, C, and D) of at least one month.

needed to satisfy this symptom domain. Yet evidence does not necessarily support such a revised emphasis, or even equal consideration for the three major symptom clusters themselves.

Kolb (1987) has suggested that the symptoms of PTSD fall within four categories: (1) impaired perceptual, cognitive, and affective functions; (2) symptoms of released activation; (3) reactive affect and avoidance; and (4) restitutive symptoms and behaviors.

Yet Kolb argues that the symptoms of released activation are the "constant" symptoms of the condition. These symptoms are the exaggerated startle reaction, irritability, hyperalertness, nightmares, and related psychophysiological expressions of autonomic nervous system hyperfunction.

Similarly, Foy *et al.* (1984) in a comparison of methods for the concurrent discrimination of PTSD found that self-report indices of anxiety and autonomic nervous system arousal alone were capable of correctly identifying more than 90% of the study's subjects. The investigation employed 21 Vietnam veteran PTSD patients and 22 Vietnam veterans with other psychiatric complaints.

In a review of three psychophysiological investigations into PTSD, Kolb (1984, 1987) concluded that indices of sympathetic nervous system arousal were capable of differentiating PTSD from non-PTSD subjects.

PTSD subjects showed more autonomic arousal in response to trauma-related stimuli than did non-PTSD subjects. Thus, Kolb (1987) concluded that "psychophysiological assessment offers strong potential not only for diagnostic identification . . . but also for assessment of severity of the disorder" (p. 991).

Finally, Horowitz *et al.* (1980) investigated the signs and symptoms of PTSD. Using a multi-inventory battery of self-report indices, Horowitz investigated the three major PTSD clusters: (1) intrusive reexperiencing of the trauma, (2) numbing/avoidance reactions, and (3) anxiety/stress reactions. The authors concluded that intrusive thinking and general symptoms of distress were of primary clinical prevalence and importance in the PTSD phenomenon. They add that the numbing and avoidance signs and symptoms are best understood as efforts of the PTSD patient to control the primary PTSD symptomatology.

In sum, within this section a review of current evidence addresses a reformulation of the PTSD syndrome so as to support a primary phenomenological role for (1) intrusive trauma-related ideation and (2) autonomic nervous system hyperfunction and/or hyperactivity. The DSM–III and DSM–III-R formulations of equally weighted symptom clusters may well be called into question.

ANATOMY AND PHYSIOLOGY OF PTSD

Without question the work of van der Kolk and his colleagues (van der Kolk, Greenberg, Boyd, & Krystal, 1985) and Kolb (1984, 1987) stand at the forefront with respect to the anatomical and physiological formulations of PTSD. Prior emphasis has been placed upon adrenergic hypersensitivity within the hindbrain locus ceruleus and its projections to the limbic and neocortical regions as the physiological and anatomical foundations of PTSD. This formulation will be reconstructed in view of the "limbic hypersensitivity phenomenon" hypothesis of Everly and Benson (Everly, 1985b;

Everly & Benson, in press) and recent phenomenological research within the limbic system.

From an anatomical perspective, in concert with the formulation of MacLean (1949), Gray (1982) has identified the septal hippocampal complex as the neuroanatomical epicenter for the intergration of exteroceptive as well as interoceptive, proprioceptive, and cognitive stimuli (Van Hoesen, 1982; Seifert, 1983). More specifically, Gray argues, as do Reiman *et al.* (1986), that the noradrenergic system within the septal hippocampal nuclei bears primary responsibility for integrating and responding, via hypothalamic efferent mechanisms, to novel and unpleasant stimuli, and further, that stimulation of these projections results in a heightened sensitivity and reactivity within all innervated regions, including neuroendocrine effector mechanisms, to environmental cues seen in any way as novel, threatening, or otherwise aversive. Similarly, Madison and Nicoll (1982) found that noradrenergic neurons from the locus ceruleus to the hippocampus serve to impair the ability of the septal hippocampal region to accommodate to excitatory stimuli.

Reiman *et al.* (1986) have demonstrated through position emission tomography that the septal hippocampal complex plays a major role in panic attacks. They further conclude that via the septal amygdalar complex, the septal hippocampal nuclei can initiate a hypothalamically mediated stress response.

Gloor (1986) has reported that the hippocampus plays a major role in memory and fear reactions. Electrophysiological investigations of awake patients having surgery for epilepsy found that activation of the hippocampus was capable of engendering "flashbacks," affective lability, perceptual distortions, fear, worry, and even guilt reactions (see also Post, 1986, and Seifert, 1983).

In sum, to this point, there is a wide range of evidence indicating that residing with the confines of the septal-hippocampal-amygdalar complex are nuclei responsible for engendering all of the major symptoms of PTSD, including intrusive recollections and flashbacks (Gloor, 1986), neurologic hypersensitivity, hyperstartle reactions, and inhibited stimulus accommodation (Gray, 1982; Madison & Nicoll, 1982), panic-like responses (Reiman *et al.*, 1986), fear, rumination, worry, guilt-like reactions (Gloor, 1986), and affective lability (Post, 1986). Cooper, Bloom, and Roth (1982) have suggested that the role of the locus ceruleus is to act as a general orienting system, rather than as a specific organizing epicenter for panic and related dysfunction.

If, indeed, the anatomical basis for PTSD is in the septal-hippocampal-amygdalar noradrenergic system, what extraordinary physiology serves to sustain the phenomenon? The noradrenergic hypersensitivity formulations of van der Kolk *et al.* (1985) and Kolb (1987) as generically extended within this text and elsewhere (Everly, 1985b; Everly & Benson, in press) seem reasonable. Using the disorders of arousal model described earlier it may be argued that PTSD represents a limbic-system-based condition of neurological hypersensitivity where a pathognomic propensity for limbic hyperreactivity is related to intraneuronal alterations that result from, and lead to, neuronal hyperexcitability. The intraneuronal alterations within the noradrenergic projections may include an extraordinary synthesis of tyrosine hydroxylase (Black *et al.*, 1987), an extraordinary availability of excitatory postsynaptic receptors, and/or an extraordinary diminution of inhibitory presynaptic receptors (Frank, 1987; Hoehn-Saric, 1982; Post & Ballenger, 1981).

Thus, PTSD may well represent a classic "physioneurosis," as Kardiner (1941) had originally suggested, consisting of anatomical and physiological neuronal transformations that serve as the basis for a hypersensitivity and subsequent extraordinary condition of neural excitability residing within the locus-ceruleus-born noradrenergic projections of the septal-hippocampal-amgydalar regions of the limbic system.

THE PSYCHOLOGICAL PROFILE OF PTSD

The work of Keane and his colleagues is preeminent in the search for the psychological PTSD prototype. Using Minnesota Multiphasic Personality Inventory (MMPI) patients and 100 patients with other psychiatric diagnoses, Keane, Malloy, and Fairbank (1984) were able to identify an MMPI profile that was capable of correctly classifying 74% of all patients. The MMPI decision rule was F ≥ 66, Depression (2) ≥ 78, Schizophrenia (8) ≥ 79 (using T scores). Item analysis led to the creation of a 49-item MMPI PTSD subscale that was able to correctly identify 82% of the patients studied. On this MMPI subscale, patients who score 35 out of 49 have an 87% chance of possessing a valid PTSD diagnosis, whereas patients who score above 40 have a 90% chance of a true positive PTSD diagnosis.

In a cross-validation of the aforementioned MMPI PTSD subscale, Fairbank, McCaffrey, and Keane (1985) found that patients with a T score above 88 on the F scale were most likely to possess a factitious disorder. Thus, the F decision rule became 66 ≤ F ≤ 88 and correctly identified 93% of the sample studied when combined with the previous (2) ≥ 78 and (8) ≥ 79.

The work of McDermott (1987) sought to extend the psychometric diagnosis of PTSD beyond the MMPI. Using the Millon Clinical Multiaxial Inventory (MCMI), McDermott evaluated 22 Vietnam combat veterans, 11 of whom had been diagnosed with PTSD. The results of his study indicate that PTSD patients may present elevations on the MCMI schizoid and avoidant scales (x > 80) with a concommitant depression on the histrionic scale. These data are in concert with the report of Everly and Humpston (unpublished) who found that similar profiles successfully identified 17 out of 21 women (80%) who had been sexually abused.

Based on Kolb's (1987) hypothesis that PTSD represents a partial cognitive deficit, in combination with the belief that PTSD resides within the hippocampal complex, Everly and Horton (unpublished report) hypothesized that there would be a short-term memory deficit among PTSD patients. Using 15- and 30-second trials of the Peterson Memory Paradigm, these authors found that 9 out of 12 (75%) noncombat-related PTSD patients failed to meet the 55% correct cutting-line criterion for the 15-second trials, and 10 out of 12 (83%) of the patients failed to meet the 45% correct cutting-line criterion for the 30-second trials. These data served to support the hypothesis that PTSD patients are likely to possess a cognitive deficit manifest as an impairment to immediate and short-term memory function. Long-term memory was unimpaired in these subjects.

Finally, it should be noted that despite the growing interest in PTSD, as Brett and Ostroff (1985) have suggested, PTSD remains underrated and underdiagnosed. They conclude that PTSD patients are likely to be misdiagnosed as substance abusers, alcohol abusers, antisocial personalities, and malingerers (Silverman, 1986). It is clear that although our data base is growing, there remains much to learn about PTSD. Special care should be taken to expand our PTSD subject pools. Currently, most of what we know about PTSD is based on Vietnam veteran studies. We may significantly increase our risk of false negative diagnoses unless we gather additional data on noncombat-related PTSD.

THE STRESSOR CRITERION IN PTSD

Using current diagnostic guidelines for PTSD, the *sine qua non* of the diagnosis is a stressor beyond the scope of usual human experience. Yet there exists theoretical and empirical evidence that PTSD can be engendered by toxins, stimulants, and chronic stressor exposure.

Silverman (1986) reported on the development of PTSD in response to pentaborane, a highly volatile liquid boron hydride. Such exposure caused significant CNS lesions, which resembled PTSD upon behavioral manifestation.

Schottenfeld and Cullen (1985) and Dager *et al.* (1987) found that PTSD and panic disorder, respectively, could be engendered on the basis of exposure to toxic chemicals.

Finally, Davidson and Baum (1986), investigating the incident at Three Mile Island and Breslau and Davis (1987) report evidence that cumulative exposure to both noncombat and combat experiences, respectively, is capable of engendering PTSD.

TREATMENT OF PTSD

PTSD may well represent an intimately interwoven fabric consisting of psychological and physiological dysfunction. Constructing a linear, causal algorithm for each and every symptom and sign of PTSD currently would be a labyrinthine undertaking, but one can get a sense that PTSD represents a psychophysiological phenomenon that may well benefit from an applied combination of psychological and physiological therapies (Everly, 1985c). Indeed, Hogben and Cornfeld (1981) report on the treatment of five PTSD patients for whom neuroleptics, tricyclic antidepressants, and psychotherapy had proven ineffectual. Yet when phenelzine (a monoamine oxidase inhibitor) was tried, improved treatment outcome was reported. These authors suggested that the phenelzine provided its own therapeutic "main effect" while enhancing the effects of psychotherapy so as to provide a therapeutic "interaction effect." It may well be that the successful treatment of PTSD is that which provides an interaction of psychotherapeutic and physiotherapeutic effects. Everly (1985c) has elsewhere described and emphasized the need to combine psychotherapeutic and physiotherapeutic actions in just such a treatment model for PTSD.

Let us review several therapeutic interventions that have thus far been employed.

Psychotherapy

Group therapy has been used on a large scale for the treatment of PTSD. Lifton (1973) recommended the use of self-help groups for Vietnam veterans. More formal group therapy exercises have been used extensively and are nicely summarized in van der Kolk (1987). Rationales for the use of formal group therapy have included the reduction of resistance, an avoidance of regression, the provision of peer support, avoidance of transference problems, the provision of a safe format for abreaction, and the provision of a place for reality orienting and consensual validation. Horowitz (1974) has supported the use of individual psychotherapy when directed toward the goals of: (1) cognitive control, (2) improving self-image, (3) improving interpersonal relationships, (4) decreasing stress, and (5) working though the "meaning" of the trauma.

Pharmacotherapy

A wide variety of psychopharmacologic agents have been used in the treatment of PTSD. As van der Kolk (1987) has stated, "Psychotherapy is rarely helpful as long as the patient continues to respond to contemporary events and situations with a continuation of physiological emergency reactions . . ." (p. 75).

The benzodiazepines are agents that serve to mobilize the existing inhibitory neurotransmitter gamma amino butyric acid (GABA) within the brain. The successful use of benzodiazepine anxiolytics in the treatment of PTSD has been reported by van der Kolk (1983). Sheehan (1983) has reported on the successful use of a specific benzodiazepine, alprazolam, in the treatment of panic disorder and what he has called "endogenous anxiety."

Perhaps somewhat counterintuitively, antidepressants have been reported to be of value in treating PTSD. Both tricyclic (Burstein, 1984) and monoamine oxidase inhibiting (Hogben & Cornfeld, 1981) antidepressants have been shown to diminish the autonomic hyperactivity of PTSD. Recent evidence has emerged that the monamine oxidase inhibitors (MAOI) may be of superordinate value in treating PTSD when compared with tricyclics (Frank, 1987).

This conclusion is similar to those of a study that found phenelzine, an MAOI, slightly superior to imipramine for treating panic attacks (Sheehan, Ballenger, & Jacobson, 1980). The mechanism by which antidepressants serve to inhibit PTSD symptomatology is currently unclear; implicated are either a decreased beta (excitatory) adrenergic sensitivity or an increased alpha-2 (inhibitory) adrenergic sensitivity (Hoehn-Saric, 1982).

Finally, the newest major pharmacologic initiative in the treatment of PTSD involves the use of anticonvulsant and other CNS-stabilizing medications. Lipper *et al.* (1986) reported the successful use of carbamazepine in the treatment of PTSD in 7 out of 10 combat veterans. They indicated that the success of carbamazepine in PTSD argued for the presence of a pathophysiological phenomenon of CNS instability such as "kindling" as being at the foundation of PTSD. This conclusion is consistent with the speculation of Everly (Everly, 1985b; Everly & Benson, in press) who sees PTSD as a condition whose pathophysiology is first and foremost that of limbic-system hypersensitivity and instability, especially within the noradrenergic projections.

Thus, it may well be that anticonvulsants and other CNS stabilizers such as clonazempam, dilantin, and lithium may be of some value in the treatment of PTSD and related symptomatology by eliminating or reducing the hyperexcitability of limbic mechanisms and the subsequent repeated arousal of emergency neuroendocrine phenomena.

It seems clear that PTSD represents an exquisitely woven phenomenon consisting of complexly intertwined psychological and physiological pathognomonic constituents (not just symptoms). If this conclusion is correct, as current evidence suggests, then the effective treatment of PTSD may require a combination of psychotherapeutic and physiotherapeutic technologies, as suggested and delineated by Everly (1985c). Such a therapeutic paradigm would most likely include psychotherapy targeted toward amelioration of dysfunctional cognitive themes and patterns in combination with physiotherapeutic technologies aimed at diminishing pathological arousal (e.g., the behavioral elicitation of the relaxation response and/or the use of various psychopharmacotherapeutics as described above.

SUMMARY

This chapter has addressed the subject of PTSD, one of the most underrated and underdiagnosed of the psychiatric disorders. Historically, in its more severe forms, PTSD has led to permanent partial disabilities. In some cases, permanent total disabilities have resulted. Because of the prevalence and propensity to remain undiagnosed for protracted periods of time, this stress-related disorder has been included in the present volume. Let us review the main points:

1. PTSD is generally thought to possess four key phenomenological constituents: (1) the presence of stressful experience generally accepted to be outside the usual realm of human experience; (2) intrusive, recollective experiences; (3) autonomic nervous system hyperactivity; and (4) avoidance and numbing-like symptoms.

2. Within this chapter, it has been argued that the "essence" of PTSD is the intrusive, recollective experience in combination with the autonomic nervous system hyperfunction. The avoidant and numbing symptoms have been reformulated as attempts by the patient to control the pathological syndrome. Exposure to a stressor remains a necessary but insufficient diagnostic criterion.

3. Once viewed in the context of a combat-related syndrome, PTSD is now recognized as having the potential to arise out of virtually any life-threatening experience. Recent evidence has even suggested that PTSD can arise out of an accumulation of stressor experiences, exposure to certain solvents, toxins, and stimulants, and the experience or observation of traumatic, but not necessarily life-threatening, event such as the loss of personal property and/or physical injury.

4. Once suggested as residing within the hindbrain, PTSD has been reformulated from a physiological perspective as residing primarily as a condition of neurological hypersensitivity within the noradrenergic projections of the septal-amygdalar-hippocampal complexes. Potential causes of the neuronal hypersensitivity include an augmentation of tyrosine hydroxalase, an increase in beta-1 postsynaptic excitatory receptors, a decrease in alpha-2 presynaptic inhibitory receptors, and an increase in postsynaptic dendritic spines.

5. Attempts to identify the psychological profile of the PTSD patient have focused upon the use of the MMPI. The $66 \leq F \leq 88$, $(2) \geq 78$, and $(8) \geq 79$ decision rule for the MMPI seems a useful starting point. Other

research has utilized the MCMI and found elevations on the schizoid and avoidant subscales coupled with a diminution of the histrionic subscale to be useful in identifying PTSD patients. Research has also found an impairment of short-term memory among PTSD patients. Finally, it was noted that PTSD patients may be frequently misdiagnosed as being sociopathic, hypochondriacal, and/or substance abusers.

6. From a treatment perspective, PTSD, especially in its chronic forms, may require a combination of psychotherapeutic and pharmacologic efforts to be truly effective. Antidepressants and anticonvulsants appear to be promising agents for the cases that do not respond to benzodiazepines.

Chapter 20

Summation and Conclusions

With all its sham, drudgery and broken dreams, it is still a beautiful world. Be cheerful. Strive to be happy.

—Max Ehrmann

"First study the science. Then practice the art which is born of that science." These words of Leonardo da Vinci have served as the guiding spirit of this volume. Perhaps more than any other pathological process, stress arousal represents the epitome of mind/body interaction. I have suggested earlier in this volume that proper clinical understanding and treatment of such conditions that so intimately intertwine psychology and physiology demand that the clinician's attention be directed toward the "science" of physiology (and pathophysiology) as well as the art/science of behavior change. Thus, to be consistent with this stated bias, this volume has first introduced the reader to a rather detailed exploration of the physiological nature and foundations of the human stress response. This, as a preface to the subsequent chapters that directly addressed the treatment of excessive stress arousal and its pathological consequences.

A TREATMENT MODEL

In order to assist the reader in seeing the phenomenology of pathogenic stress arousal in its larger context, this volume has introduced an epiphenomenological model of the human stress response, from stressor to target-organ effect. This model was first introduced in Chapter 2 as Figure 2.6. It represents the larger "overview" of not just stress arousal but its antecedent and consequent constituents. This basic figure was employed again in Chapter 5 (Figure 5.1) but this time with measurement technologies superimposed. The same basic model was again employed in the introduction to Part II, this time to demonstrate how treatment interventions might be conceptualized in a coherent and cogent manner via a unifying model. Finally, that same figure will be replicated once again to assist in the summary of the text (see Figure 20.1).

The stress response is predicated upon an event called a *stressor*. The stressor can be real or imagined. The stressor is typically then perceived and some *cognitive interpretation* is rendered by the individual. The obvious exception would be sympathomimetic and vasoactive stressors, which bypass interpretation (see Appendixes C and D). On the basis of the interpretation, the individual will experience some *affect* emerging from the limbic circuitry. Intimately intertwined with the creation of this affect is the activation of a *neurological triggering mechanism* that transduces psychological events into somatic realities. The most important of these somatic realities is the initiation of the stress response itself: a psychophysiological mechanism of mediation characterized by arousal and possessing three basic efferent limbs: the neural, the neuroendocrine, and the endocrine. These stress arousal mechanisms then exert some *target-organ effect*, that is, signs and symptoms. If *coping* mechanisms employed by the person are not successful, continued arousal and a *psychosomatic disease* is the likely consequence (refer to Figure 20.1).

Given an understanding of this oversimplified process, treatment interventions can be more appropriately selected and implemented.

Listed in Table 20.1 are the major treatment interventions discussed within this volume and summarized in Figure 20.1.

Having used a treatment model to summarize this volume, let us turn to a clinical protocol to see how it all fits together.

A TREATMENT PROTOCOL

In Chapter 1, the reader may recall that on the basis of a review by Girdano and Everly (1986), it was suggested that the treatment of excessive stress arousal may be categorized into three therapeutic genres, or "dimensions":

1. Strategies to avoid/minimize/modify stressors
2. Strategies to reduce excessive arousal and target-organ reactivity/ dysfunction
3. Strategies to ventilate, or express, the stress response

The use of such a summarial schema facilitates the creation of a gener-

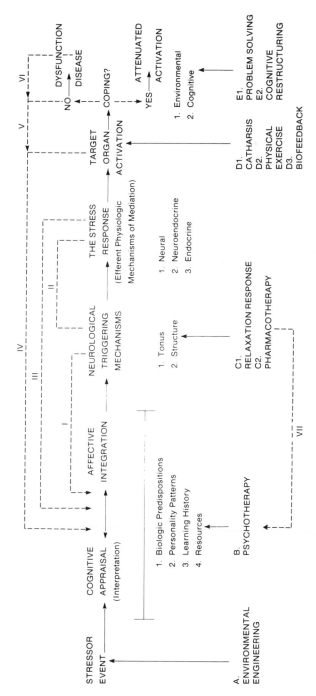

Figure 20.1. A multidimensional treatment model for the human stress response.

Table 20.1. Treatment Interventions

Treatment options	Chapter discussions	Purpose
Environmental engineering	Chapter 8; Appendixes C and D	To allow the patient to avoid or minimize exposure to stressors
Psychotherapy	Chapters 6, 7, and 8 See also Chapters 10–14	To avoid stressors; to reinterpret stressors; to increase perception of self-efficacy
Relaxation response	Chapters 10–14, 16	To reduce pathogenic arousal; to increase perception of self-efficacy
Psychopharmacotherapy	Chapter 15	To reduce arousal
Reduction of target-organ activation	Chapters 8, 13, 14, 16	To ventilate the stress response in a health promoting manner; to reduce target-organ arousal or dysfunction
Problem-solving and cognitive restructuring	Chapter 8	To attentuate excessive arousal

ic, multidimensional treatment protocol. This protocol, compared with Figure 20.1 and Table 20.1, more readily translates into a step-by-step guide for clinical practice and is summarized below in Table 20.2.

Having the patient undergo a physical examination is desirable, especially if target-organ disease or dysfunction are manifest. The stress response is the epitome of mind/body interaction. For this reason, it is sometimes difficult to distinguish psychologically induced problems from those problems that possess little or no psychogenic etiology. In some cases, what appears to be stress-related signs and symptoms may in reality be indicative of some neurological pathology or neoplastic phenomenon.

As previous pages have indicated, psychological assessment, especially personologic assessment, can play an important role in treatment planning. The concept of personologic diathesis, when operationalized, provides insight not only into diagnosis but treatment as well (see Chapter 6). A broad-spectrum psychological assessment tool such as the Minnesota Multiphasic Personality Inventory or the Millon Clinical Multiaxial Inventory are useful and efficient assessment tools, especially the latter, which integrates personality assessment (refer also to Chapter 5).

The general protocol described in Table 20.2 is not designed to be "blindly" adhered to by the practicing clinician; rather it is provided as a general guide to allow the clinician to formulate a multidimensional, individualized treatment protocol. A multidimensional treatment protocol is far superior to a unidimensional one. Further, aided by the psychological

Table 20.2. A General Treatment Protocol

Physical examination
Psychological assessment (especially personality assessment, see Chapters 5 and 6)
Interventions (3 dimensions):
1. Helping the patient develop and implement strategies for the avoidance/minimization/modification of stressors.
   A. Patient education (see Chapter 7 for a rationale)
   B. Environmental engineering—Chapter 8; Appendices C and D
   C. Psychotherapy—Chapter 8
2. Helping the patient develop and implement skills which reduce excessive stress arousal and target organ reactivity/dysfunction.
   A. Meditation—Chapter 10
   B. Neuromuscular relaxation—Chapter 11; Appendix B
   C. Respiratory control—Chapter 12
   D. Hypnosis—Chapter 13
   E. Biofeedback—14
   F. Psychopharmacotherapy—Chapter 15
3. Helping the patient develop and implement techniques for the healthful ventilation/expression of the stress response.
   A. Catharsis—Chapter 8
   B. Physical exercise—Chapter 16

---

assessment, the treatment plan can be tailored to the specific needs of the patient. Bhalla (1980) found that multidimensional, individualized treatment protocols were generally superior to those that were unidimensional or otherwise "boiler-plate" protocols (see also Meichenbaum & Turk, 1987).

To reiterate the approach of this book, effective treatment emerges from accurate and specific diagnosis. To assess the notion of a personologic diathesis, to actively involve the patient in his or her own therapy, and to recognize the therapeutic value of patient education (see Chapter 7) seems a useful and humanistic approach to the treatment of the human stress response and its target-organ consequences.

A WORD ABOUT TREATMENT ADHERENCE

It would be naive to believe or expect that if all of the guidelines in this text are followed treatment adherence would approach 100%. This is simply not the case. Patient adherence to life-style management programs designed to reduce health-related risk factors (e.g., stress-management programs) reportedly range from a high of 80% to a low of 20%. It has been suggested that adherence to daily home relaxation sessions is as low as 40%. Even adherence to antihypertensive drug regimens may be as low as

60%. See Meichenbaum and Turk (1987) for a review of these and other treatment adherence issues.

Nevertheless, it is hoped by reviewing the phenomenology of stress arousal and its measurement and treatment that treatment adherence and clinical success will be superior to those treatment conditions where such has not been the case. It is also highly recommended that before designing any treatment protocols the reader review a manual on facilitating treatment adherence (e.g., Meichenbaum & Turk, 1987).

SUMMARY

In conclusion, within this summary chapter, we have seen two forms of summary: the first, a treatment model, provided more of a conceptual summary; the second, a treatment protocol, provided more of a clinically practical summary. It is hoped that by providing both not only will a sense of clinical practicality be conveyed but also a conceptual understanding that will allow the reader to move beyond the constraints of this volume.

Special Considerations in Clinical Practice

Self-Report Relaxation Training Form

When teaching patients to engender the relaxation response, the typical protocol requires the patient to visit the office between one and three times per week. This limited frequency would make it difficult to realize the desired therapeutic effect of a cultivated lower arousal status. Therefore, patients commonly receive relaxation training "homework." This usually consists of asking the patient to employ the relaxation response once or twice a day. In order to provide a useful forum for communications, and to improve compliance, it is highly desirable to have the patient complete a relaxation training report form each time the relaxation response is practiced. The patient is then asked to return the completed forms to the therapist at the beginning of each office session. The therapist then uses these forms as a means of reviewing the patient's progress.

Following this introduction is an example relaxation report form that may be used for reporting on the progress made in home relaxation training.

Relaxation Report Form

Name: _____   Time Started _____
Date: _____   Time Finished _____

Beginning SURS* _____   (before the relaxation exercise begins)
Ending SURS   _____   (after the relaxation exercise has ended)

Were you able to relax?   YES   NO   (Circle one)
   If "No", why not? _____
_____

Did your mind wander?   YES   NO
   If "Yes", what were you distracted by? _____
_____

Did you experience anything unusual?   YES   NO
   If "Yes", what? _____
_____

Is there anything else you would like to report? _____
_____
_____
_____
_____
_____

*The SURS (Subjective Units of Relaxation) indication is a method by which you may indicate your subjective levels of relaxation. A SURS of 10 will be indicative of a dream-like state of profound relaxation; a SURS of 5 is indicative of how you believe the "average" person feels on an "average" day; and a SURS of 1 is indicative of a panic attack. Choose any number between 1 and 10, inclusive, to indicate your beginning and ending SURS levels.

Physically Passive
Neuromuscular Relaxation

Earlier in this text, it was stated that "neuromuscular relaxation" was the term usually reserved for isotonic and isometric contractions of the striate musculature designed to teach the client to relax. The entire preceding discussion on neuromuscular relaxation has addressed that type of physically active procedure. By far the greater part of the literature has been generated on this active form of neuromuscular relaxation—hence our emphasis on reviewing that form. There does exist, however, what may be considered a physically passive form of neuromuscular relaxation. In this appendix we shall address that form of relaxation.

Physically passive neuromuscular relaxation fundamentally consists of having the patient focus sensory awareness on a series of individual striate muscular groups and then relax those muscles through a process of direct concentration. In the passive neuromuscular relaxation procedure described here, there is no actual muscular contraction initiated as part of the relaxation cycle—hence "passive" neuromuscular relaxation.

The procedure of physically passive neuromuscular relaxation may be considered a form of mental imagery and directed sensory awareness. Mental imagery as a therapeutic intervention has a long and effective history for a wide range of clinical problems (see Leuner, 1969; Sheehan, 1972). When applied to the reduction of muscle tension, the basic mechanism involved in passive neuromuscular relaxation appears to be useful in tension reduction. In a review of investigations into the role of neuromuscular relaxation in general tension reduction, Borkovec, Grayson, and Cooper (1978) conclude: "Apparently, frequent attempts to relax while focusing on internal sensations are sufficient to promote tension reduction" (p. 527). In our own clinical experience, we have found passive neuromuscular relaxation to be quite effective in reducing subjective as well as electromyographically measured muscle tension.

There do appear to be several distinct advantages and disadvantages when comparing passive neuromuscular relaxation with a physically active form of neuromuscular relaxation. Passive neuromuscular relaxation has the advantage of having no potential limitations based on physical handicaps, as compared with neuromuscular relaxation that involves actual muscle tensing. Another advantage is entailed in the fact that the patient can execute a passive protocol without distracting others or drawing attention to himself or herself. Such is obviously not the case with a protocol that involves actual muscle contraction. A final advantage is that a passive protocol generally takes much less time to complete (usually half the time). The major disadvantage in using a passive form of neuromuscular relaxation resides in the fact that, like meditation or other forms of mental images, it leaves the patient more vulnerable to distracting thoughts. This may be a significant drawback when using a passive protocol with obsessive-type patients or patients who have a tendency to get bored easily.

Let us now examine one sample passive protocol (written as if being spoken directly to the patient). The "preparation for implementation" phase will be fundamentally the same as for the physically active form of neuromuscular relaxation, except with a few alterations (refer to Chapter 11). In Step 1 of the preparation for implementation (precautions), the precautions will be the same as described for general relaxation. However, the special precautions for meditation will prevail here, as opposed to those for the physically active neuromuscular relaxation. The physically passive component here is what dictates this alteration. Steps 2 through 4 may remain the same. Steps 5 through 8 may be omitted because of their reference to the actual tensing of muscles. The patient should be instructed to breathe normally, in a relaxed manner.

BACKGROUND INFORMATION

It has long been known that muscle tension can lead to stress and anxiety—thus, if you can learn to reduce excessive muscle tension, you will reduce excessive stress and anxiety.

What you are about to do is relax the major muscle groups in your body. You can do this by simply focusing your attention on each set of muscles that I describe. Research has shown that with *patience* and *practice*, you can learn to achieve a deeply relaxed state by simply concentrating on relaxing any of the various muscle groups in your body.

First, you should find a quiet place without interruptions or glaring lights. Find a comfortable chair or bed to support your weight. Feel free to loosen restrictive clothing and remove glasses and contact lens if you desire.

ACTUAL INSTRUCTIONS

OK, let's begin. I'd like you to close your eyes and get as comfortable as you can. Let the chair or bed support all your weight. Remember, your job is to concentrate on allowing the muscles that I describe to relax completely.

CHEST AND STOMACH

I'd like you to begin by taking a deep breath. Ready? Begin . . . (*pause three seconds*) and now exhale as you feel the tension leave your chest and stomach. Let's do that one more time. Ready? Begin . . . (*pause three seconds*) and now relax and exhale as the tension continues to leave and your chest and stomach are relaxed.

HEAD

I'd like you to focus your attention on the muscles in your head. Now begin to feel those muscles relax as a warm wave of relaxation begins to descend from the top of your head. Concentrate on the muscles in your forehead. Now begin to allow those muscles to become heavy and relaxed. Concentrate as your forehead becomes heavy and relaxed (*pause 10 seconds*). Now switch your focus to the muscles in your eyes and cheeks and begin to allow them to become heavy and relaxed. Concentrate as your eyes and cheeks become heavy and relaxed (*pause 10 seconds*). Now switch your focus to the muscles in your mouth and jaw. Allow those muscles to become heavy and relaxed. Concentrate as your mouth and jaw become heavy and relaxed (*pause 10 seconds*).

NECK

Now you can begin to feel that wave of relaxation descend into the muscles of your neck. Your head will remain relaxed as you now shift your attention to your neck muscles. Allow your neck muscles to become heavy and relaxed. Concentrate as your neck becomes heavy and relaxed (*pause 10 seconds*).

SHOULDERS

Now you can begin to feel that wave of relaxation descend into your shoulder muscles. Your head and neck muscles will remain relaxed as you now shift your attention to your shoulder muscles. Allow your shoulder muscles to become heavy and relaxed. Concentrate as your shoulders become heavy and relaxed (*pause 10 seconds*).

ARMS

Now you can begin to feel that wave of relaxation descend into your arms. Your head, your neck, and your shoulders will remain relaxed as you now shift your attention to the muscles in both your arms. Allow both your arms to become heavy and relaxed. Concentrate as your arms become heavy and relaxed (*pause 10 seconds*).

HANDS

Now you can begin to feel that wave of relaxation descend into your hands. Your head, your neck, your shoulders, and your arms will remain relaxed as you now shift your attention to the muscles in both your hands. Allow both your hands to become heavy and relaxed. Concentrate as your hands become heavy and relaxed (*pause 10 seconds*).

THIGHS

Now you can begin to feel that wave of relaxation descend into your thighs. Your head, your neck, your shoulders, your arms, and your hands will remain relaxed as you now shift your attention to the muscles in both your thighs. Allow both your thighs to become heavy and relaxed. Concentrate as your thighs become heavy and relaxed (*pause 10 seconds*).

CALVES

Now you can begin to feel that wave of relaxation descend into your calves. Your head, your neck, your shoulders, your arms, your hands, and your thighs will remain relaxed as you now shift your attention to the muscles in both your calves. Allow both your calves to become heavy and relaxed. Concentrate as your calves become heavy and relaxed (*pause 10 seconds*).

FEET

Now you can begin to feel that wave of relaxation finally descend into your feet. The entire rest of your body will remain relaxed as you now shift your attention to the muscles in both your feet. Allow both your feet to become heavy and relaxed. Concentrate as your feet become heavy and relaxed (*pause 10 seconds*).

CLOSURE

All the major muscles in your body are now relaxed. To help you remain relaxed, simply repeat to yourself each time you exhale, "I am relaxed." Take the next few minutes and continue to relax as you repeat to yourself, "I am relaxed" . . . "I am relaxed" (*pause about five minutes*).

REAWAKEN

Now I want to bring your attention back to yourself and the world around you. I shall count from 1 to 10. With each count, you will feel your mind become more and more awake, and your body become more and more responsive and refreshed. When I reach 10, open your eyes, and you will feel the *best* you've felt all day—you will feel alert, refreshed, full of energy, and eager to resume your activities. Let's begin: 1–2 You are beginning to feel more alert, 3–4–5 you are more and more awake, 6–7 now begin to stretch your hands and feet, 8– now begin to stretch your arms and legs, 9–10 open your eyes, *now!* You feel alert, awake, your mind is clear and your body refreshed.

On concluding the initial passive neuromuscular procedure, inform the patient that he or she can use this procedure to relax once or preferably twice a day—before lunch and before dinner. Other times can also be useful as well, particularly when used as an aid for sleeping.

In summary, Appendix B has presented the clinician with a physically passive alternative form of neuromuscular relaxation, not as prescription, but as an example of how such a protocol could be created. This option is designed simply to expand the clinician's arsenal of stress-reduction interventions with which to meet the idiosyncratic needs of individual patients. The ultimate assessment of clinical suitability remains with the clinician, and should be made on an individual case-by-case basis.

Stress-Inducing Sympathomimetic Chemicals

Sympathomimetics are chemical substances that initiate a stress response by the biochemical stimulation of the sympathetic branch of the autonomic nervous system. Sympathomimetics are also known to stimulate noradrenergic central nervous system tracts as well. In the psychological domain, sympathomimetics are known to act as psychotropic stimulants causing a sense of stimulation and well-being. The primary mechanism of action for sympathomimetics is the augmentation of norepinephrine and epinephrine release.

Some of the more common sources for sympathomimetics are listed below:

1. Coffee (*Coffee arabica*) contains the sympathomimetic substance caffeine. The standard clinical adult dosage of caffeine is 200 milligrams (mg). The lethal dose is thought to range between 2,000 and 10,000 mg. A 5-ounce cup of drip brewed coffee contains about 150 mg, the same quantity percolated would contain about 100 mg, and the same quantity if it were instant and freeze-dried would contain about 65 mg.

2. Tea (*Camelia theca*) contains caffeine as well. Five ounces of tea if allowed to brew for 5 minutes contains about 50 mg; if allowed to brew for only one minute it would contain about 25 mg.

3. Cocoa contains about 15 mg of caffeine (5 ounces).

4. "Soft drinks" range from 30 to 65 mg (12 ounces).

5. A 1-ounce chocolate bar contains about 40 mg of caffeine or similar substances.

6. Caffeine will also be found in many over-the-counter and prescription medications. For example:

Cafergot—100 mg	Fiorinal—40 mg
Ergocaf–100 mg	Norgesic—30 mg
Fioricet—40 mg	Wigraine—100 mg
Anacin—32 mg	No Doz—100 mg
Acqua Ban—100 mg	Prolamine—140 mg
Acqua Ban Plus—200 mg	Stay-Alert—250 mg
Dietac—200 mg	Stay Awake—200 mg
Enerjets—65 mg	Slim Plan Plus—200 mg
Excedrin Extra—65 mg	Triaminicin—30 mg
Midol—32 mg	Vivarin—200 mg

The "half-life" of caffeine is about 3 hours. Thus this chemical can accumulate quite easily over the course of an entire day.

It is generally believed that quantities greater than 350 mg/day can lead to a physical dependence upon caffeine.

7. Other sympathomimetic chemicals include theobromine, theophylline, and amphetamine. Cocaine and nicotine exert sympathomimetic effects as well, yet appear to be far more addicting for some individuals.

The pharmacologic information contained within this Appendix C was derived from Schwartz (1987), the 1987 volume of the *Physician's Desk Reference*, and Stephenson (1977); while believed to be accurate at the time of writing, the information cannot be guaranteed.

Vascular Headaches and Vasoactive Substances

Many vascular headaches, including the classical migraine, can be induced by vasoactive stimuli. These stimuli interact with what may be a biogenic predisposition for vascular spasticity so as to set the stage for a vascular headache. More specifically, vasoactive stimuli are factors that have the ability to stimulate the sympathetic neural constituency of thusly innervated blood vessels. Through what may be either a vasospastic phenomenon or a singular vascular rebound phenomenon, these stimuli are believed to have the capability of inducing a vascular headache syndrome, including the classical migraine syndrome.

The primary vasoactive substances include:

1. Tyramine (a pressor amine)
2. Monosodium glutamate
3. Sodium nitrate
4. Histamine
5. Bright light that creates glare
6. Changes in barometric pressure, especially rapid declines
7. Strenuous physical exercise
8. Loud noise
9. Some sympathomimetics (Despite the fact that sympathomimetic pharmaceuticals are prescribed to treat vascular headaches, the initial ingestion of some "hidden" or naturally occurring sympathomimetics may be sufficient to induce a vasospasm.)

Foods that are relatively high in vasopressor action include:

1. Liver
2. Most cheeses
3. Caviar
4. Sausages
5. Coffee (depending upon quantity)
6. Tea (depending upon quantity)
7. Chocolate (depending upon quantity)
8. Marinated herring
9. Hot dogs (if containing nitrates)
10. Chianti wine
11. Red wines
12. Many foods that contain brewer's yeast
13. Fava beans
14. Many fermented or overripened foods.

These lists within Appendix D are provided as general information for the practicing clinician. They should not be used to prescribe medication or to alter the dietary regimen of patients. Rather the information contained herein is designed to serve as a general guide to assist in formulating diagnostic and/or treatment impressions with the intent of appropriate medical and nutritional consultation.

The Etiology of Panic
Nonpsychological Factors

Panic attacks represent a very specific form of pathological stress response. Shader (1984) has suggested its prevalence in the United States to be 2% to 4.7%. Any clinician who treats stress and anxiety-related disorders will invariably be confronted with patients presenting some form of panic disorder and its predictable pattern of subsequent behavioral avoidance.

Panic attacks are characterized by paroxymal episodes of autonomic nervous system hyperfunction usually combined with cognitive/affective symptoms that include dissociation, depersonalization, a generalized morbid fear, fear of dying, fear of losing control, and/or intense emotional manifestation. Proprioception is often interrupted, thus leaving the patient neuromuscularly unstable. Panic attacks typically may last but several minutes, although some attacks could last more than an hour, depending upon etiology.

Although it is widely known that panic attacks can be initiated by psychological factors, it is less widely known that panic attacks are sometimes secondary to variant medical/physiological conditions. Before treating a patient with panic-like symptomatology via psychotherapeutic or psychopharmacological interventions, the clinician should first attempt to determine to what degree medical or physiological factors serve as the etiological basis for the attacks.

Listed below are the most common primary medical/physiological factors that may give rise to secondary panic attacks. Clinicians should be sensitive to these factors when constructing a medical history for the patient with some form of panic syndrome:

1. Acute hypoglycemia may serve as a panicogenic. It is well-established that the arcuate and ventromedial hypothalamic nuclei contain receptors responsible for the neurological monitoring of glucose. Buckley (1985) has argued that acute hypoglycemic inhibition of the hypothalamic glucoreceptor mechanisms prevent the release of the neurotransmitter beta endorphin and its inhibitory effect upon the panic-related neural networks of the locus ceruleus. When this inhibitory effect is removed, the locus ceruleus becomes far more likely to be massively depolarized. If such depolarization were to occur, a noradrenergically mediated panic attack would most likely result.

2. It has been suggested that some women will suffer panic-like symptoms at the point in their menstrual cycle where progesterone reaches its zenith. This point is usually within seven days of the onset of menses. This conclusion is based upon the hypothesis that, for some, high levels of progesterone can act as a panicogenic (see Carr & Sheehan, 1984).

3. Vigorous anaerobic exercise is believed to be able to induce a panic in those patients biologically inclined to suffer from panic disorders. One of the by-products of anaerobic exercise is lactic acid. Pitts and McClure (1967) found that some individuals manifest a biogenic hypersensitivity to lactate (a relative to lactic acid) and this hypersensitivity was manifest in the form of panic attacks. Thus, factors that lead to a rise in lactic acid may be associated with panic.

4. According to Gorman, Liebowitz, and Klein (1984), there exist several medical disorders that either mimic or induce panic attacks. They include:

- Hyperthyroidism
- Hypothyroidism
- Mitral valve prolapse
- Cardiac arrhythmias
- Pheochromocytoma
- Drug or alcohol withdrawal
- Coronary insufficiency
- Amphetamine overdose
- Caffeine overdose

In sum, the assessment of any medical or physiological factors known to serve in the primary etiology of the panic syndrome seems a reasonable course of action for the clinician to assume prior to treating a patient with a history of panic-like symptoms.

Biochemical Bases of Arousal

Throughout this volume, it has been emphasized that pathogenic stress represents a disorder of "arousal." Arousal within the human body is mediated through a series of complex neurological networks. Nevertheless, the basis for the activation of these neurological networks resides in the biochemistry of their respective neurotransmitters (refer to Chapter 2). In this appendix, a brief summary of the major neurotransmitters that mediate arousal will be provided. Also provided will be a description of the drugs that affect these neurotransmitters.

There are three major arousal mediating neurotransmitters: dopamine, norepinephrine, and serotonin.

DOPAMINE

Dopamine is one of the monoaminergic catecholamines. Its synthesis, which is primarily in the neuronal terminals, is described below:

Phenylalnine
 ↓ Phenylalnine hydroxylase
Tyrosine
 ↓ Tyrosine hydroxylase
Dopa
 ↓ Dopa carboxylase
Dopamine (DA)

Dopamine is inactivated by monoamine oxidase (MAO) and catechol-O-methyl-transferase (COMT).

Drugs that affect dopamine are:

Synthesis inhibitor—alpha Methyl-p-tyrosine
Depletor—Reserpine
Reuptake inhibitor—Cocaine
Releaser—Amphetamine
Receptor blockers—Chlorpromazine, Haloperidol
Catabolic inhibitor—Pargyline
Receptor agonist—Apomorphine

NOREPINEPHRINE

Norepinephrine (noradrenalin) is the primary excitatory neurotransmitter. Its synthesis, which occurs primarily in the synaptic vesicles, is described below:

Phenylalanine
↓ Phenylalanine hydroxylase
Tyrosine
↓ Tyrosine hydroxylase
Dopa
↓ Dopa decarboxylase
Dopamine
↓ Dopamine-beta-hydroxylase
Norepinephrine (NE)

Norepinephrine is inactivated by MAO and COMT.
Drugs that affect norepinephrine are

Synthesis inhibitor—Disulfiram
Depletor—Reserpine
Reuptake Inhibitor—Cocaine
Releaser—Amphetamine
Receptor blocker—Phentolamine
Catabolism inhibitor—Iproniazid
Receptor agonists—Ephedrine, Clonidine (alpha-2 agonist)

SEROTONIN

The synthesis of Serotonin (5-Hydroxytryptamine)(5-HT) is described below:

Tryptophan
↓ Tryptophan hydroxylase
5-Hydroxytryptophan
↓ 5-HTP decarboxylase
5-Hydroxytryptamine

Serotonin is inactivated primarily by MAO. Drugs that affect serotonin are

Synthesis inhibitor—alpha Methyl 5-HTP
Depletor—Reserpine
Reuptake inhibitor—Nortryptaline
Releaser—p-Chloramphetamine
Receptor blocker—Methysergide
Catabolic inhibitor—Iproniazid
Receptor agonist—LSD, psilocin

Professional Journals for Stress Research

American Journal of Health Promotion
Annals of Behavioral Medicine
Archives of General Psychiatry
Behavioral Medicine (formerly *Journal of Human Stress)*
Biofeedback and Self-Regulation
Health Education
Health Psychology
Journal of Clinical and Consulting Psychology
Journal of Psychosomatic Research
Journal of Traumatic Stress
Psychology and Health
Psychophysiology
Psychosomatic Medicine
Psychosomatics

How Do You Cope With Stress?

A Self-Report Checklist Designed for Health Education Purposes

DIRECTIONS: There are many ways to cope with the stress in your life. Some coping techniques are more effective than others. The purpose of this checklist is to help you, the reader, assess how effectively you cope with the stress in your life. Upon completing this checklist, you will have identified many of the ways you choose to cope with stress, while at the same time, through a point system, ascertaining the relative desirability of the coping techniques that you now employ. This is a health education survey, not a clinical assessment instrument. Its sole purpose is to inform you of how you cope with the stress in your life.

In order to complete the checklist, simply follow the instructions given for each of the 14 items listed below. When you have completed all of the 14 items, place your total score in the space provided.

_____   1. Give yourself 10 points if you feel that you have a supportive family.
_____   2. Give yourself 10 points if you actively pursue a hobby.
_____   3. Give yourself 10 points if you belong to some social or activity group that meets at least once a month (other than your family).

_____ 4. Give yourself 15 points if you are within five pounds of your "ideal" bodyweight, considering your height and bone structure.

_____ 5. Give yourself 15 points if you practice some form of "deep relaxation" at least three times a week. Deep relaxation exercises include meditation, imagery, yoga, etc.

_____ 6. Give yourself 5 points for each time you exercise 30 minutes or longer during the course of an average week.

_____ 7. Give yourself 5 points for each nutritionally balanced and wholesome meal you consume during the course of an average day.

_____ 8. Give yourself 5 points for each time you do something that you really enjoy, "just for yourself," during the course of an average week.

_____ 9. Give yourself 10 points if you have some place in your home that you can go to in order to relax and/or be by yourself.

_____ 10. Give yourself 10 points if you practice time-management techniques in your daily life.

_____ 11. Subtract 10 points for each pack of cigarettes you smoke during the course of an average day.

_____ 12. Subtract 5 points for each evening during the course of an average week that you take any form of medication or chemical substance (including alcohol) to help you sleep.

_____ 13. Subtract 10 points for each day during the course of an average week that you consume any form of medication or chemical substance (including alcohol) to reduce your anxiety or just calm you down.

_____ 14. Subtract 5 points for each evening during the course of an average week that you bring work home; work that was meant to be done at your place of employment.

_____   Total Score

Now that you've calculated your score, consider that the higher your score, the greater your health-promoting coping practices. A "perfect" score would be around 115. Scores in the 50–60 range are probably adequate to cope with most common sources of stress.

Also keep in mind that items 1–10 represent adaptive health-promoting coping strategies, and items 11–14 represent maladaptive, health-eroding coping strategies. These maladaptive strategies are self-sustaining because they do provide at least some temporary relief from stress. In the long run, however, their utilization serves to erode one's health. Ideally, health-promoting coping strategies (items 1–10) are the best to integrate into your life style and will ultimately prove to be an effective preventive program against excessive stress.

References

AMA Drug Evaluations. Acton, MA: Publishing Services Group, Latest edition.

Abboud, F. M. (1976). Relaxation, autonomic control and hypertension. *New England Journal of Medicine, 294*, 107–109.

Abramson, L. Y., Seligman, M. E. P., & Teasdale, J. D. (1978). Learned helplessness in humans: Critique and reformulation. *Journal of Abnormal Psychology, 87*(1), 49–74.

Adler, C., & Morrissey-Adler, S. (1983). Strategies in general psychiatry. In J. Basmajian (Ed.), *Biofeedback* (pp. 239–254). Baltimore: Williams & Wilkins.

Agras, W. S. (1983). Relaxation therapy in hypertension. *Hospital Practice, 25*, 129–137.

Alexander, A. B. (1975). An experimental test of the assumptions relating to the use of EMG. Biofeedback as a general relaxation training technique. *Psychophysiology, 12*, 656–662.

Alexander, F. (1950). *Psychosomatic medium*. New York: Norton.

Allen, R. (1981). Controlling stress and tension. *Journal of School Health, 17*, 360–364.

Almy, T. P., Kern, F., & Tulin, M. (1949). Alterations in colonic function in man under stress. *Gastroenterology, 12*, 425–436.

Amenta, P. S. (1983). *Histology*. New Hyde Park, NY: Excerpta Medica.

American College of Sports Medicine (1980). *Guidelines for graded exercise testing and exercise prescription*. Philadelphia: Lea & Febiger.

American Psychiatric Association (1968). *Diagnostic and statistical manual of mental disorders* (2nd ed.). Washington, DC: Author.

American Psychiatric Association. (1980). *Diagnostic and statistical manual of mental disorders* (3rd ed.) Washington, DC: Author.

American Psychiatric Association. (1987). *Diagnostic and statistical manual of mental disorders* (3rd ed., revised). Washington, DC: Author.

Ametz, B., Fjellner, B., Eneroth, P., & Kallner, A. (1986). Neuroendocrine response selectivity to standardized psychological stressors. *International Journal of Psychosomatics, 33*, 19–27.

Amkraut, A., & Solomon, G. (1974). From symbolic stimulus to the pathophysiologic response: Immune mechanisms. *International Journal of Psychiatry in Medicine, 5*, 541–563.

Andersson, B., Hovmoller, S., Karlsson, C., & Svensson, S. (1974). Analysis of urinary catecholamines. *Clinica Chimica Acta, 51*, 13–28.

Andreassi, J. (1980). *Psychophysiology*. New York: Oxford University Press.

Araoz, D. L. (1983). Use of hypnotic techniques with oncology patients. *Journal of Psychosocial Oncology*, Winter, *1*(4), 47–54.

Ardell, D. (1977). *High level wellness*. Emmaus, PA: Rodale.

Arnarson, E., & Sheffield, B. (1980, March). *The generalization of the effects of EMG and temperature biofeedback*. Paper presented at the Annual Meeting of the Biofeedback Society of America, Colorado Springs, CO.

Arnold, M. (1970). *Feelings and emotions*. New York: Academic Press.

Arnold, M. (1984). *Memory and the brain*. Hillsdale, NJ: Erlbaum.

Averill, J. (1973). Personal control over aversive stimuli and its relationship to stress. *Psychological Bulletin, 80,* 286–307.

Avorn, J., & Langer, E. J. (1982). Induced disability in nursing home patients. *Journal of the American Geriatrics Society, 30*(6), 379–400.

Axelrod, J., & Reisine, T. (1984). Stress hormones. *Science 224,* 452–459.

Backus, F., & Dudley, D. (1977). Observations of psychosocial factors and their relationship to organic disease. In Z. J. Lipowski, D. Lipsitt, & P. Whybrow (Eds.), *Psychosomatic medicine* (pp. 187–205). New York: Oxford University Press.

Bainton, C., Richter, D., Ballantyne, D., and Klein, J. (1985). Respiratory modulation of sympathetic activity. *Journal of the Autonomic Nervous System, 12,* 77–90.

Baldessarini, R. (1985). *Chemotherapy in Psychiatry*. Cambridge, MA: Harvard University Press.

Ballentine, R. (1976). *Science of breath*. Glenview, IL: Himalayan International Institute.

Balog, L. F. (1978). *The effects of exercise on muscle tension and subsequent muscle relaxation.* Unpublished doctoral dissertation, University of Maryland.

Bandura, A. (1977). Self-efficacy. *Psychological Review, 84,* 191–215.

Bandura, A. (1982a). Self-efficacy mechanism in human agency. *American Psychologist, 37*(2), 122–147.

Bandura, A. (1982b). The self and mechanisms of agency. In J. Suls (Ed.), *Psychological perspectives on the self* (pp. 3–39). Hillsdale, NJ: Erlbaum.

Bandura, A., Taylor, C. B., Williams, S. L., Mefford, I. N., & Barchas, J. D. (1985). Catecholamine secretion as a function of perceived coping self-efficacy. *Journal of Consulting and Clinical Psychology, 53*(3), 406–414.

Bar-Or, O., & Buskirk, E. (1974). The cardiovascular system and exercise. In W. Johnson & E. Buskirk (Eds.), *Science and medicine of exercise and sport*. New York: Harper & Row.

Barlow, D., & Beck, J. (1984). The psychosocial treatment of anxiety disorders. In J. B. Williams & R. Spitzer (Eds.), *Psychotherapy research* (pp. 29–69). New York: Guilford Press.

Barnett, E. A. (1984). Hypnosis in the treatment of anxiety and chronic stress. In W. B. Wester II & A. H. Smith, Jr. (Eds.), *Clinical hypnosis: A multidisciplinary approach* (pp. 458–462). Philadelphia: Lippincott.

Bart, P. B. (1971). Depression in middle-aged women. In V. G. Gornick & B. K. Moran (Eds.), *Women in sexist society* (pp. 163–186). New York: Basic Books.

Bartlett, E. E. (1971). The use of hypnotic techniques without hypnosis per se for temporary stress. *American Journal of Clinical Hypnosis, 13*(4), 273–278.

Basmajian, J. (1963). Control and training of individual motor units. *Science, 141,* 440–441.

Basmajian, J. V. (Ed.). (1983). *Biofeedback*. Baltimore: Williams & Wilkins.

Basmajian, J., & Hatch, J. (1979). Biofeedback and the modification of skeletal muscular dysfunctions. In R. Gatchel & K. Price (Eds.), *Clinical applications of biofeedback* (pp. 97–111). Oxford: Pergamon.

Baum, A., Fleming, R., & Davidson, L. M. (1983). Natural disaster and technological catastrophe. *Environment and Behaviour, 15*(3), 333–354.

Beck, A. (1984). Cognitive approaches to stress. In R. Woolfolk & P. Lehrer (Eds.), *Principles and practice of stress management* (pp. 255–305). New York: Guilford Press.

Beck, A., & Emery, G. (1985). *Anxiety disorders and phobias: A cognitive perspective*. New York: Basic Books.

Beck, A., Rush, A., Shaw, B., & Emory, G. (1979). *Cognitive therapy of depression*. New York: Guilford Press.

Belicki, K., & Bowers, P. (1982). The role of demand characteristics and hypnotic ability in dream change following a presleep instruction. *Journal of Abnormal Psychology, 91*, 426–432.

Bem, S. (1974). The measurement of psychological androgyny. *Journal of Personality and Social Psychology, 42*, 155–162.

Bem, S. (1975). Androgyny vs. tight little lives of fluffy women and chesty men. *Psychology Today, 9*, 58–59.

Bem, S. (1983). Gender schema theory and its implications for child development: Raising gender-aschematic children in a gender-schematic society. *Signs, 8*(4), 598–616.

Benjamin, L. (1963). Statistical treatment of the Law of the Initial Values in autonomic research. *Psychosomatic Medicine, 25*, 556–566.

Benson, H. (1969). Yoga for drug abuse. *New England Journal of Medicine, 281*, 1133.

Benson, H. (1974). Decreased blood pressure in borderline hypertensive subjects who practice meditation. *Journal of Chronic Diseases, 17*, 163–169.

Benson, H. (1975). *The relaxation response.* New York: Morrow.

Benson, H. (1983). The relaxation response: Its subjective and objective historical precedents and physiology. *Trends in Neuroscience, 6*, 281–284.

Benson, H. (1987). *Your maximum mind.* New York: Times Books.

Benson, H., Alexander, S., & Feldman, C. (1975). Decreased premature ventricular contractions through the use of the relaxation response. *Lancet, 2*, 380–382.

Benson, H., Beary, J., & Carol, M. (1974). The relaxation response. *Psychiatry, 37*, 37–46.

Benson, H., & Friedman, R. (1985). A rebuttal to the conclusions of David S. Holme's article: Meditation and somatic arousal reduction. *American Psychologist, 40*, 725–728.

Benson, H., Marzetta, B., & Rosner, B. (1974a). Decreased blood pressure in borderline hypertensive subjects who practiced meditation. *Journal of Chronic Diseases, 27*, 163–169.

Benson, H., Marzetta, B., and Rosner, B. (1974b). Decreased blood pressure in pharmacologically treated hypertensive patients who regularly elicited the relaxation response. *Lancet, 1*, 289–291.

Berkun, M. (1962). Experimental studies of psychological stress in man. *Psychological Monographs, 76* (Whole no. 534).

Bernard, J. (1974). *The future of motherhood.* New York: Penguin Books.

Berstein, D., & Borkovec, T. (1973). *Progressive relaxation training.* Champaign, IL: Research Press.

Bhalla, V. (1980). *Neuroendocrine, cardiovascular, and musculoskeletal analyses of a holistic approach to stress reduction.* Unpublished doctoral dissertation, University of Maryland.

Bielski, R., & Friedel, R. (1976). Prediction of tricyclic antidepressant response. *Archives of General Psychiatry, 33*, 1479–1489.

Bio-Science, Inc. (1982). *The bio-science handbook.* Van Nuys, CA: Author.

Bird, C. (1979). *The two-paycheck marriage.* New York: Rawson-Wade.

Black, I., Adler, J., Dreyfus, C., Friedman, W., Lagamma, E., & Roach, A. (1987). Biochemistry of information storage in the nervous system. *Science, 236*, 1263–1268.

Bluestone, N. (1965). Marriage and medicine. *Journal of the American Medical Womens Association, 20*, 1048–1053.

Borkovec, T., Grayson, J., & Cooper, K. (1978). Treatment of general tension: Subjective and physiological effects of progressive relaxation. *Journal of Consulting and Clinical Psychology, 46*, 518–528.

Borysenko, J. (1984). Stress, coping, and the immune system. In J. Matarazzo, et al. (Eds.), *Behavioral Health* (pp. 248–274). New York: Wiley.

Borysenko, M. (1987). The immune system. *Annals of Behavioral Medicine, 9*, 3–10.

Boston Women's Health Book Collective (1976). *Our bodies, ourselves.* New York: Simon & Schuster.

Bowers, K. S., & Kelly, P. (1979). Stress, disease, psychotherapy, and hypnosis. *Journal of Abnormal Psychology, 88*(5), 4909–505.

Brende, J. O., & Benedict, B. D. (1980). The Vietnam combat delayed stress response syndrome: Hypnotherapy of "dissociative symptoms." *American Journal of Clinical Hypnosis*, 23, 34–40.

Breslau, L., & Baum, A. (1986). Chronic stress and PTSD. *Journal of Consulting and Clinical Psychology*, 54, 303–308.

Breslau, N., & Davis, G. (1987). PTSD: The stressor criterion. *Journal of Nervous and Mental Disease*, 175, 255–276.

Brett, E., & Ostroff, R. (1985). Imagery and PTSD. *American Journal of Psychiatry*, 142, 417–424.

Brod, J. (1959). Circulatory changes underlying blood pressure elevation during acute emotional stress in normotensive and hypertensive subjects. *Clinical Science*, 18, 169–270.

Brod, J. (1971). The influence of higher nervous processes induced by psychosocial environment on the development of essential hypertension. In L. Levi (Ed.), *Society, stress, and diseases* (Vol. 1: pp. 312–323). New York: Oxford University Press.

Brown, B. (1977). *Stress and the art of biofeedback*. New York: Harper & Row.

Brown, B. (1980). Perspectives on social stress. In H. Selye (Ed.), *Selye's guide to stress research* (pp. 21–45). New York: Van Nostrand Reinhold.

Brown, C. C. (1967). *Methods in psychophysiology*. Baltimore: Williams & Wilkins.

Brown, D. P., & Fromm, E. (1987). *Hypnosis and behavioral medicine*. Hillsdale, NJ: Erlbaum.

Brown, G. W. (1972). Life events and psychiatric illness. *Journal of Psychosomatic Research*, 16, 311–320.

Buckley, R. (1985, November). *Post-prandial hypoglycemic anxiety*. Paper presented to the thirty-second annual meeting of Psychosomatic Medicine, San Francisco, CA.

Budoff, P. (1981). *No more menstrual cramps and other good news*. New York: Penguin Books.

Budzynski, T. (1978). Biofeedback in the treatment of muscle contraction (tension) headache. *Biofeedback and Self-Regulation*, 3, 409–434.

Budzynski, T. (1979, November). *Biofeedback and stress management*. Paper presented at the Johns Hopkins Conference on Clinical Biofeedback, Baltimore, MD.

Budzynski, T., & Stoyva, J. (1969). An instrument for producing deep muscle relaxation by means of analog information feedback. *Journal of Applied Behavioral Analysis*, 2, 231–237.

Burstein, A. (1984). Treatment of post traumatic stress disorder with imipramine. *Psychosomatics*, 25, 681–686.

Byrne, S. (1973). Hypnosis and the irritable bowel: Case histories, methods and speculation. *American Journal of Clinical Hypnosis*, 15(4), 263–265.

Calabrese, J., Kling, M., & Gold, P. (1987). Alterations in immunocompetence during stress, bereavement, and depression. *American Journal of Psychiatry*, 144, 1123–1134.

Campernolle, T., Kees, H., & Leen, J. (1979). Diagnosis and treatment of the hyperventilation syndrome. *Psychosomatics*, 20, 612–625.

Cannistraci, A. (1975–1976). *A voluntary stress release and behavior therapy in the treatment of clenching and bruxism* (Vol. 1) [Cassette tape]. New York: Biomonitoring Applications.

Cannon, W. B. (1914). The emergency function of the adrenal medula in pain and in the major emotions. *American Journal of Physiology*, 33, 356–372.

Cannon, W. B. (1929). *Bodily changes in pain, fear, hunger, and rage*. New York: Appleton.

Cannon, W. B., & Paz, D. (1911). Emotional stimulation of adrenal secretion. *American Journal of Physiology*, 28, 64–70.

Capra, F. (1975). *The tao of physics*. Boulder: Shambala.

Carmen, E. H., Russo, N. F., & Miller, J.B. (1981). Inequality and mental health. *American Journal of Psychiatry*, 10, 1319–1330.

Carr, D., & Sheehan, D. (1984). Panic anxiety: A new biological model. *Journal of Clinical Psychiatry*, 45, 323–330.

Carrington, P. (1977). *Freedom in meditation*. New York: Anchor Press.

Carrington, P., *et al.* (1980). The use of meditation relaxation techniques for the management of stress in a working population. *Journal of Occupational Medicine*, 22, 221–231.

Carruthers, M., & Taggart, P. (1973). Vagotonicity of violence. *British Medical Journal, 3,* 384–389.

Cassel, J. (1974). *Psychosocial processes and "stress." The Behavioral Sciences and Preventive Medicine.* Washington, DC: Public Health Service.

Cattell, R. B. (1972). *The Sixteen Personality Factor.* Champaign, IL: Institute for Personality and Ability Testing, IPAT.

Cattell, R. B., & Sheier, I. (1961). *The meaning and measurement of neuroticism and anxiety.* New York: Ronald Press.

Chavat, J., Dell, P., & Folkow, B. (1964). Mental factors and cardiovascular disorders. *Cardiologia, 44,* 124–141.

Chiasson, S. W. (1986). Hypnosis in other related medical conditions. In W. C. Wester II & A. H. Smith, Jr. (Eds.), *Clinical hypnosis: A multidisciplinary approach* (pp. 288–304). Philadelphia: Lippincott.

Cicchetti, D., & Hesse, P. (1983). Affect and intellect. In R. Plutchik and H. Kelleman (Eds.), *Emotion* (pp. 115–169). New York: Academic Press.

Cohen, F., & Lazarus, R. S. (1973). Active coping processes, coping dispositions, and recovery from surgery. *Psychosomatic Medicine, 35*(5), 375–387.

Cohen, F., & Lazarus, R. S. (1979). Coping with the stresses of illness. In G. Stone, F. Cohen, & N. Adler (Eds.), *Health psychology* (pp. 217–254). San Francisco: Jossey-Bass.

Cohen, J. (1984). The benefits of meta-analysis. In J. Williams and R. Spitzer (Eds.), *Psychotherapy research* (pp. 332–339). New York: Guilford Press.

Collins, A. (1985). Interaction of sex-related psychological characteristics and psychoneuroendocrine stress responses. *Sex Roles, 12,* 1219–1230.

Collison, D. R. (1968). Hypnotherapy in the treatment of asthma. *American Journal of Clinical Hypnosis, 11*(1), 6–11.

Collison, D. R. (1970). Cardiological applications of the control of the autonomic nervous system by hypnosis. *American Journal of Clinical Hypnosis, 12,* 150–156.

Collison, D. R. (1975). Which asthmatic patients should be treated by hypnotherapy? *Medical journal of Australia, 1,* 776–781.

Collison, D. R. (1978). Hypnotherapy in asthmatic patients and the importance of trance depth. In F. H. Frankel & H. S. Zamansky (Eds.), *Hypnosis at its bicentennial: Selected papers.* New York: Plenum Press.

Cooper, C., & Marshall, J. (1978). Sources of managerial and white collar stress. In C. Cooper & R. Payne (Eds.), *Stress* (pp. 81–105). New York: Wiley.

Cooper, J. R., Bloom, F., & Roth, R. (1982). *The biochemical basis of neuropharmacology.* New York: Oxford University Press.

Corley, K. (1985). Psychopathology of stress. In S. Burchfield (Ed.), *Stress* (pp. 185–206). New York: Hemisphere.

Corson, S., & Corson, E. (1971). Psychosocial influences on renal function: Implications for human pathophysiology. In L. Levi (Ed.), *Society, stress, and disease* (Vol. 1: pp. 338–351). New York: Oxford University Press.

Cox, D., Freundlick, A., & Meyer, R. (1975). Differential effectiveness of EMG feedback, verbal relaxation instructions, and medication placebo with tension headaches. *Journal of Consulting and Clinical Psychology, 43,* 892–898.

Coyne, J. C., & Holroyd, K. (1982). Stress, coping, and illness. In T. Millon, C. Green, & R. Meagher (Eds.), *Handbook of clinical health psychology* (pp. 103–128). New York: Plenum.

Crasilneck, H. B., & Hall, J. A. (1985). *Clinical hypothesis: Principles and applications.* New York: Grune & Stratton.

Cromwell, R. L., Butterfield, E. C., Brayfield, F. M., & Curry, J. J. (1977). *Acute myocardial infarction: Reaction and recovery.* St. Louis, MO: Mosby.

Daebler, H. (1973). The use of relaxation and hypnosis in lowering high blood pressure. *American Journal of Clinical Hypnosis, 16,* 75–83.

Dager, S., Holland, J., Cowley, D., & Dunner, D. (1987). Panic disorder precipitated by exposure to organic solvents in the workplace. *American Journal of Psychiatry, 144,* 1056–1058.

Dahlstrom, W., Welsh, G., & Dahlstrom, L. (1975). *An MMPI handbook* (Vol. 2): *Research developments and applications.* Minneapolis: University of Minnesota Press.

Damon Corporation. (1981). *Evaluation of adrenocortical function.* Needham Heights, MA: Author.

Daniels, L. K. (1977). Treatment of migraine headache by hypnosis and behavior therapy: A case study. *American Journal of Clinical Hypnosis, 19*(4), 241–244.

Datey, K. (1969). A yogic exercise in the management of hypertension. *Angiology, 20,* 325–333.

Davidson, J. (1976). The physiology of meditation and mystical states of consciousness. *Perspectives in Biology and Medicine, 19,* 345–379.

Davidson, L., & Baum, A. (1986). Chronic stress and PTSD. *Journal of Consulting and Clinical Psychology, 54,* 303–308.

Davidson, L. M., Baum, A., & Collins, D. L. (1982). Stress and control-related problems at Three Mile Island. *Journal of Applied Social Psychology, 12*(5), 349–359.

Deabler, H. L., Fidel, E., Dillenkoffer, R. L., & Elder, S. T. (1973). The use of relaxation and hypnosis in lowering high blood pressure. *American Journal of Clinical Hypnosis, 16,* 75–83.

Deadwyler, S., Gribkoff, V., Cotman, D., & Lynch, G. (1976). Long-lasting chances in the spontaneous activity of hippocampal neurons following stimulation of the entorhinal cortex. *Brain Research Bulletin,* 1–7.

Delanoy, R., Tucci, D., & Gold, P. (1983). Amphetamine effects on LTP in dendate granule cells. *Pharmacology, Biochemistry, and Behavior, 18,* 137–139.

Delmonte, M. (1984). Physiological concomitants of meditation practice. *International Journal of Psychosomatics, 31,* 23–36.

Dembroski, T. & Costa, P. (1988). Assessment of coronary-prone behavior. *Annals of Behavioral Medicine, 10,* 60–63.

Derogatis, L. (1977). *The SCL-90-R: Administration, scoring and procedures manual 1.* Baltimore: Clinical Psychometric Research.

Derogatis, L. (1980). *The Derogatis stress profile.* Baltimore: Clinical Psychometric Research.

deVries, H. (1963, May). *The effects of exercise upon residual neuromuscular tension.* Paper presented to the American Association of Health, Physical Education and Recreation National Convention, Minneapolis.

deVries, H. (1966). *Physiology of exercise.* Dubuque, IA: Brown.

deVries, H. (1968). Immediate and long-term effects of exercise upon resting muscle action potential level. *Journal of Sports Medicine and Physical Fitness, 8,* 1–11.

deVries, H. (1970). Physiological effects of exercise training regimen upon men aged 52 to 88. *Journal of Gerontology, 25,* 325–336.

deVries, H. (1981). Tranquilizer effect of exercise. *America's Journal of Physical Medicine, 60,* 57–66.

deVries, H., & Adams, G. (1972). Electromyographic comparison of single doses of exercise and meprobamate as to effects or muscular relaxation. *American Journal of Physical Medicine, 52,* 130–141.

Dimsdale, J. E., & Moss, J. (1980). Plasma catecholamines in stress and exercise. *Journal of the American Medical Association, 243,* 340–342.

Dishman, R. (1982). Compliance/adherence in health-related exercise. *Health Psychologist, 1,* 237–267.

Doane, B. (1986). Clinical psychiatry and the physiodynamics of the limbic system. In B. Doane & K. Livingston (Eds.), *The limbic system* (pp. 285–315). New York: Raven Press.

Doane, B., & Livingston, K. (Eds.). (1986). *The limbic system.* New York: Raven Press.

Dodson, L., & Mullens, W. (1969). Some effects of jogging on psychiatric patients. *American Corrective Therapy Journal, 10,* 130–134.

Donoghue, S. (1977). The correlation between physical fitness, absenteeism, and work performance. *Canadian Journal of Public Health, 68,* 201–203.

Dorpat, T. L., & Holmes, T. H. (1955). Mechanisms of skeletal muscle pain and fatigue. *Archives of Neurology and Psychiatry, 74,* 628–640.

Dotevall, G. (1985). *Stress and the common gastrointestinal disorders.* New York: Praeger.

Dotson, C., Manny, P., & Davis, P. (1986). *A study of occupational stress among poultry and red meat inspectors.* Langley Park, MD: Institute of Human Performance.

Duffy, E. (1962). *Activation and behavior.* New York: Wiley.

Dunbar, H. F. (1935). *Emotions and bodily changes.* New York: Columbia University Press.

Dunn, F., & Howell, R. (1982). Relaxation training and its relationship to hyperactivity in boys. *Journal of Clinical Psychology, 38,* 92–100.

Edelberg, R. (1972). Electrical activity of the skin. In N. Greenfield & R. Sternbach (Eds.), *Handbook of psychophysiology.* New York: Holt, Rinehart & Winston.

Edinger, J. (1982). Incidence and significance of relaxation treatment side effects. *Behavior Therapist, 5,* 137–138.

Eichelman, B. (1985). Hypnotic change in combat dreams of two veterans with post-traumatic stress disorder. *American Journal of Psychiatry, 142*(1), 112–114.

Eisler, R., & Polak, P. (1971). Social stress and psychiatric disorder. *Journal of Nervous and Mental Disease, 153,* 227–233.

Eliot, R. (1979). *Stress and the major cardiovascular diseases.* Mt. Kisco, NY: Futura.

Ellis, A. (1971). Emotional disturbance and its treatment in a nutshell. *Canadian Counselor, 5,* 168–171.

Ellis, A. (1973). *Humanistic psychology: The rational-emotive approach.* New York: Julian.

Emery, G. (1987). *Stress free program: Therapist manual.* Los Angeles: Association for Advanced Training in the Behavioral Sciences.

Emery, G., & Lesher, E. (1982). Treatment of depression in older adults: Personality consideration. *Psychotherapy Theory, Research and Practice, 19,* 500–505.

Emmons, M. (1978). *The inner source: A guide to meditative therapy.* San Luis Obispo, CA: Impact.

Engel, B. T. (1972). Operant conditioning of cardiac function: A status report. *Psychophysiology, 9,* 161–177.

Engel, G. L. (1968). A life setting conducive to illness. *Annals of Internal Medicine, 69,* 293–300.

Engel, G. L. (1971). Sudden and rapid death during psychological stress. *Annals of Internal Medicine, 74,* 771–782.

Engels, W. (1985). Dermatological disorders. In W. Dorfman & L. Cristofar (Eds.), *Psychosomatic illness review* (pp. 146–161). New York: Macmillan.

English, E., & Baker, T. (1983). Relaxation training and cardiovascular response to experimental stressors. *Health Psychology, 2,* 239–259.

Epstein, S., & Coleman, M. (1970). Drive theories of schizophrenia. *Psychosomatic Medicine, 32,* 114–141.

Euler, U. S. V., & Lishajko, F. (1961). Improved techniques for the fluorimetric estimation of catecholamines. *Acta Physiologica Scandinavia, 51,* 348–355.

Evans, F. J. (1967). Suggestibility in the normal waking state. *Psychological Bulletin, 67,* 114–129.

Evans, F. J. (1968). Recent trends in experimental hypnosis. *Behavioral Science, 13,* 477–487.

Everly, G. S. (1978). *The Organ Specificity Score as a measure of psychophysiological stress reactivity.* Unpublished doctoral dissertation, University of Maryland.

Everly, G. S. (1979a). *Strategies for coping with stress: An assessment scale.* Washington, DC: Office of Health Promotion, Department of Health and Human Services.

Everly, G. S. (1979b). A technique for the immediate reduction of psychophysiologic stress reactivity. *Health Education, 10,* 44.

Everly, G. S. (1979c). A psychophysiologic technique for the rapid onset of a trophotropic state. *IRCS Journal of Medical Science, 7,* 423.

Everly, G. S. (1980). The development of less stressful personality traits in adults through educational interventions. *Maryland Adult Educator, 2,* 63–66.

Everly, G. S. (1985a). Occupational stress. In G. S. Everly & R. Feldman (Eds.), *Occupational health promotion* (pp. 49–73). New York: Wiley.

Everly, G. S. (1985c, April). *Neurocognitive therapy and rehabilitation of psychiatric syndromes in response to stress.* Paper presented to the International Conference on Stress and Behavioral Emergencies, University of Maryland, Baltimore County Campus.

Everly, G. S. (1985b, November). *Biological foundations of psychiatric sequelae in trauma and stress-related "Disorders of Arousal."* Paper presented to the 8th National Trauma Symposium, Baltimore, MD.

Everly, G. S. (1986). A "Biopsychosocial Analysis" of psychosomatic disease. In T. Millon & G. Klerman (Eds.), *Contemporary Directions in Psychopathology* (pp. 535–551). New York: Guilford Press.

Everly, G. S. (1987). The principle of personologic primacy. In C. Green (Ed.), *Prodeedings of the conference on the Millon Clinical Inventories* (pp. 3–7). Minneapolis: National Computer Systems.

Everly, G. S., & Benson, H. (1988, September), *Disorders of arousal and the relaxation response: A reformulation of the nature and treatment of stress-related disease.* Paper presented to the IV International Conference on Psychophysiology, Prague, Czechoslovokia.

Everly, G. S., & Benson, H. (1989). Disorders of Arousal and the Relaxation Response. *International Journal of Psychosomatics, 36,* 15–21.

Everly, G. S., Harnett, C., Henderson, R., Plasay, M., Sherman, M., Allen, R., and Newman, E. (1986). The development of an instrument to measure stress in adults. In J. Humphrey (Ed.), *Human stress* (pp. 43–57). New York: AMS Press.

Everly, G. S., & Horton, A. M. Cognitive Impairment and PTSD. Unpublished report.

Everly, G. S., & Humphrey, J. (1980, November–December). Perceived dimensions of stress responsiveness in male and female students. *Health Education, 11,* 38–39.

Everly, G. S., & Humpston, P. The MCMI and sexually abused females. Unpublished report.

Everly, G. S., & Rosenfeld, R. (1981). *The nature and treatment of the stress response.* New York: Plenum Press.

Everly, G. S., Shapiro, S., Levine, S., Newman, E., & Sherman, M. (1987). An investigation into the relationships between personality and clinical syndromes. In C. Green (Ed.), *Proceedings of the conference on the Millon Clinical Inventories* (pp. 295–307). Minneapolis: National Computer Systems.

Everly, G. S., & Smith, K. (1987). Occupational stress and its management. In J. Humphrey (Ed.) *Human stress: Current selected research, Vol. 2.* (pp. 235–246) New York: AMS Press.

Everly, G. S., & Sobelman, S. H. (1987). *The assessment of the human stress response: Neurological, biochemical, and psychological foundations.* New York: AMS Press.

Everly, G. S., & Spollen, M., Hackman, A., & Kobran, E. (1987). Undesirable side-effects and self-regulatory therapies. *Proceedings of the Eighteenth Annual Meeting of the Biofeedback Society of America* (pp. 166–167).

Everly, G., Welzant, V., Machado, P. and Miller, K. (1989). The correlation between frontalis muscle tension and sympathetic nervous system activity. Unpublished research report.

Fabian, J. J., & Manus, G. I. (1986). Using hypnosis in groups. In B. Zilbergeld, M. G. Edelstien, & D. L. Araoz (Eds.), *Hypnosis: Questions and answers* (pp. 350–354. New York: Norton.

Fair, P. (1983). Biofeedback assisted relaxation strategies in psychotherapy. In J. Basmajian (Ed.), *Biofeedback* (pp. 170–191). Baltimore: Williams and Wilkins.

Fairbank, J., McCaffery, R., & Keane, T. (1985). Psychometric detection of fabrication symptoms of PTSD. *American Journal of Psychiatry, 142,* 501–503.

Feldman, R., & Quenzer, L. (1984). *Neuropsychopharmacology*. Sunderland, MA: Sinauer Association.

Fifkova, E., & Van Harreveld, A. (1977). Long lasting morphological changes in dendritic spines and dentate granule cells following stimulation of the entorhinal area. *Journal of Neurocytology, 6*, 211–230.

Fiske, D. W. (1983). The meta-analysis revolution in outcome research. *Journal of Consulting and Clinical Psychology, 51*, 65–70.

Folkow, B., & Neil, E. (1971). *Circulation*. London: Oxford University Press.

Foon, A. E. (1985). Similarity between therapists and client's locus of control: Implications for therapeutic expectations and outcome. *Psychotherapy, 22*(4), 711–717.

Foy, D., Sipprelle, R., Rueger, D., & Carroll, E. (1984). Etiology of PTSD in Vietnam veterans. *Journal of Consulting and Clinical Psychology, 52*, 79–87.

Frances, A. (1982). Categorical and dimensional systems of personality diagnosis. *Comprehensive Psychiatry, 23*, 516–527.

Frances, A., & Hale, R. (1984). Determining how a depressed woman's personality affects the choice of treatment. *Hospital and Community Psychiatry, 35*, 883–884, 954.

Frank, J. D. (1974). The restoration of morale. *American Journal of Psychiatry, 131*, 271–274.

Frank, J. (1987, October). *Antidepressant treatments for PTSD*. Paper presented to the Third Annual Meeting of the Society for Traumatic Stress Studies, Baltimore, MD.

Frankel, F. H. (1976). *Hypnosis: Trance as a coping mechanism*. New York: Plenum Press.

Frankenhaeuser, M. (1980). Psychoneuroendocrine approaches to the study of stressful person-environment transactions. In H. Selye (Ed.), *Selye's guide to stress research* (pp. 46–70). New York: Van Nostrand Reinhold.

Frankenhaeuser, M. (1986). A psychological framework for research on human stress and coping. In Mortimer H. Appley & R. Trumbell (Eds.), *Dynamics of stress: Physiological, psychological, and social perspectives* (pp. 101–116). New York & London: Plenum Press.

Frankenthal, K. (1969). Autohypnosis and other aids for survival in situations of extreme stress. *International Journal of Clinical and Experimental Hypnosis. 17*(3), 153–159.

Frazier, T. (1966). Avoidance conditioning of heart rate in humans. *Psychophysiology, 3*, 188–202.

Freeman, G. L. (1939). Toward a psychiatric Plimsoll Mark. *Journal of Psychology, 8*, 247–252.

French, J., Caplan, R., & Harrison, R. (1982). *The mechanisms of job stress and strain*. New York: Wiley.

French, J., & Caplan, R. (1973). Organizational stress and individual strain. In A. Marrow (Ed.), The failure of success (pp. 30–66). New York: AMACOM.

Freud, S. (1921). *Forward in psychoanalysis and the war neurosis*. New York: International Psychoanalytic Press.

Friedman, H., & Booth-Kewley, S. (1987). The "disease-prone personality." *American Psychologist, 42*, 539–555.

Friedman, M., & Rosenman, R. (1974). *Type A behavior and your heart*. New York: Knopf.

Friedman, H., & Taub, H. A. (1977). The use of hypnosis and biofeedback procedures for essential hypertension. *International Journal of Clinical and Experimental Hypnosis, 20*(3), 184–188.

Friedman, M. (1969). *Pathogenesis of coronary artery disease*. New York: McGraw-Hill.

Froberg, J., Karlsson, C., Levi, L., & Lidberg, L. (1971). Physiological and biochemical stress reactions induced by psychosocial stimuli. In L. Levi (Ed.), *Society, stress, and disease* (Vol. 1: pp. 280–295). New York: Oxford University Press.

Fromm, E. (1980). Values in psychotherapy. *Psychotherapy: Theory, research and practice, 17*, 4.

Fuller, G. (1972). *Biofeedback: Methods and procedures in clinical practice*. San Francisco: Biofeedback Institute of San Francisco.

Gaarder, K., & Montgomery, P. (1977). *Clinical biofeedback: A procedural manual.* Baltimore: Williams & Wilkins.

Galwey, T. (1976). *Inner tennis.* New York: Random House.

Gardell, B. (1977). Autonomy and participation at work. *Human Relations, 30,* 515–533.

Gatchel, R., & Price, K. (1979). Biofeedback: An introduction and historical overview. In R. Gatchel & K. Price (Eds.), *Clinical applications of biofeedback: Appraisal and status.* New York: Pergamon.

Gellhorn, E. (1957). *Autonomic imbalance and the hypothalamus.* Minneapolis: University of Minnesota Press.

Gellhorn, E. (1958a). The physiological basis of neuromuscular relaxation. *Archives of Internal Medicine, 102,* 392–399.

Gellhorn, E. (1958b). The influence of curare on hypothalamic excitability and the electroencephalogram. *Electroencephalography and Clinical Neurophysiology, 10,* 697–703.

Gellhorn, E. (1964a). Sympathetic reactivity in hypertension. *Acta Neurovegetative, 26,* 35–44.

Gellhorn, E. (1964b). Motion and emotion. *Psychological Review, 71,* 457–472.

Gellhorn, E. (1965). The neurophysiological basis of anxiety. *Perspectives in Biology and Medicine, 8,* 488–515.

Gellhorn, E. (1967). *Principles of autonomic-somatic integrations.* Minneapolis: University of Minnesota Press.

Gellhorn, E. (1968). Central nervous system tuning and its implications for neuropsychiatry. *Journal of Nervous and Mental Disease, 147,* 148–162.

Gellhorn, E. (1969). Further studies on the physiology and pathophysiology of the tuning of the central nervous system. *Psychosomatics, 10,* 94–104.

Gellhorn, E., & Kiely, W. (1972). Mystical states of consciousness. *Journal of Nervous and Mental Disease, 154,* 399–405.

Gellhorn, E., & Loofbourrow, G. (1963). *Emotions and emotional disorders.* New York: Harper & Row.

Gevarter, W. (1978). *Psychotherapy and the brain.* Unpublished paper. Washington, DC: NASA.

Gherman, E. M. 91982). *Stress and the bottom line.* New York: AMACOM.

Gifford, S., & Gunderson, J. G. (1970). Cushing's disease as a psychosomatic disorder: A selective review. *Perspectives in Biology and Medicine, 13,* 169–221.

Gillespie, R. D. (1942). *Psychological effects of war on citizen and soldier.* New York: Norton.

Girdano, D. A. (1977). Performanced based evaluation. *Health Education, 8,* 13–15.

Girdano, D., & Everly, G. (1986). *Controlling stress and tension* (2nd ed.). Englewood Cliffs, NJ: Prentice-Hall.

Girodo, M. (1974). Yoga meditation and flooding in the treatment of anxiety neurosis. *Journal of Behavior Therapy and Experimental Psychiatry, 5,* 157–160.

Gittelman-Klein, R., & Klein, D. (1969). Premorbid asocial adjustment and prognosis in schizophrenia. *Journal of Psychiatric Research, 7,* 35–53.

Glass, D. C., & Singer, J. E. (1972). *Urban stress: Experiments on noise and social stressors.* New York & London: Academic Press.

Glick, B. S. (1970). Some limiting factors in reciprocal inhibition therapy. *Psychiatric Quarterly, 44,* 223–230.

Gloor, P. (1986). Role of the human limbic system in perception, memory, and affect. In B. Doane & K. Livingston (Eds.), *The limbic system* (pp. 159–169). New York: Raven Press.

Glueck, G., & Stroebel, C. (1975). Biofeedback and meditation in the treatment of psychiatric illness. *Comprehensive Psychiatry, 16,* 309.

Glueck, B., & Stroebel, C. (1978). Psychophysiological correlates of relaxation. In A. Sugarman & R. Tarter (Eds.), *Expanding dimensions of consciousness.* New York: Springer.

Goddard, G., & Douglas, R. (1976). Does the engram of kindling model the engram of normal long-term memory? In J. Wads (Ed.), *Kindling* (pp. 1–18). New York: Raven Press.

Goddard, G., McIntyre, D., & Leech, C. (1969). A permanent change in brain function resulting from daily electrical stimulation. *Experimental Neurology, 25,* 295–330.

Goleman, D., & Schwartz, G. (1975). Meditation as an intervention in stress reactivity. *Journal of Consulting and Clinical Psychology, 15,* 110–111.

Gromberg, E. S. (1974). Women and alcoholism. In V. Franks & V. Burtle (Eds.), *Women in therapy: New psychotherapies for a changing society* (pp. 169–190). New York: Brunner-Mazel.

Gorman, J., Dillon, D., Fyer, A., Liebowitz, M., & Klein, D. (1985). The lactate infusion model. *Psychopharmacology Bulletin, 21,* 428–433.

Gorman, J., Liebowitz, M., Klein, D. (1984). *Panic disorder and agoraphobia.* Kalamazoo, MI: Upjohn.

Gove, W. R. (1972). Marital status and suicide. *Journal of Health and Social Behavior, 13,* 204–213.

Gove, W. R. (1979). Sex differences in epidemiology of mental illness: Evidence and explanations. In F. Gomberg & V. Franks (Eds.), *Gender and disordered behavior.* New York: Brunner/Mazel.

Gove, W. R., & Geerlen, R. (1977). The effects of children and employment on the mental health of married men and women. *Social Forces, 56,* 66–76.

Gove, W. R., & Tudor, J. F. (1973). Adult sex roles and mental illness. *American Journal of Sociology, 78,* 812–835.

Grace, W., Seton, P., Wolf, S., & Wolff, H. G. (1949). Studies of the human colon:I. *American Journal of Medical Science, 217,* 241–251.

Graham, D. T. 1972). Psychosomatic medicine. In N. Greenfield & R. Sternbach (Eds.), *Handbook of psychophysiology.* New York: Holt, Rinehart & Winston.

Gray, J. (1985). Issues in the neuropsychology of anxiety. In A. Tuma and J. Maser (Eds.) *Anxiety and Anxiety Disorders* (pp. 5–26). Hillsdale, N.J.: Lawrence Erlbaum.

Gray, J. (1982). *The neuropsychology of anxiety.* New York: Oxford University Press.

Greden, J. F. (1974). Anxiety or caffeinsim: A diagnostic dilemma. *American Journal of Psychiatry, 131,* 1089–1092.

Green, E., & Green, A. (1977). *Beyond biofeedback.* San Francisco: Delta.

Green, E., & Green, A. (1983). General and specific applications of thermal biofeedback. In J. Basmajian (Ed.), *Biofeedback* (pp. 211–227). Baltimore: Williams & Wilkins.

Greenfield, N., & Sternbach, R. (1972). *Handbook of psychophysiology.* New York: Holt, Rinehart & Winston.

Greengard, P. (1978). Phosphorylated proteins and physiological affectors. *Science, 199,* 146–152.

Greenleaf, E. (1974). Defining hypnosis during hypnotherapy. *International Journal of Clinical and Experimental Hypnosis, 22*(2), 120–130.

Greenspan, K. (1979). Biological feedback: Some conceptual bridges with analytically oriented psychotherapy. *Psychiatric Opinion,* pp. 17–20.

Greenwood, J., & Greenwood, J. (1979). *Managing executive stress.* New York: Wiley.

Griffin, D., Everly, G. S., & Fuhrmann, C. (1982, September). Designing an effective stress management training program. *Training,* 20–31.

Grossman, P., deSwart, J., & DeFares, P. (1985). A controlled study of breathing therapy for treatment of hyperventilation syndrome. *Journal of Psychosomatic Research, 29,* 49–58.

Gurtin, L. (1980). The dual career family. *Journal of College Placement, 40,* 28–31.

Guyton, A. C. (1982). *Textbook of medical physiology.* Philadelphia: Saunders.

Hamberger, L., & Lohr, I. (1984). *Stress and stress management.* New York: Springer.

Harlem, O. (1977). *Communication in medicine.* New York: Karger.

Harper, H. A. (1975). *Review of physiological chemistry.* Los Altos, CA: Lange.

Harvey, J. (1978). Diaphragmatic breathing: A practical technique for breath control. *The Behavior Therapist, 1,* 13–14.

Haskell, W. (1984). Overview: Health benefits of exercise. In J. Matarazzo, S. Weiss, J. Heid, N. Miller, & S. Weiss (Eds.), *Behavioral Health* (pp. 409–423). New York: Wiley.

Haskell, W., & Fox, S. (1974). Physical activity in the prevention and therapy of cardiovascular disease. In W. Johnson & E. Burskirk (Eds.), *Science and medicine of exercise and sport.* New York: Harper & Row.

Hassett, J. (1978). *A primer of psychophysiology.* San Francisco: Freeman.

Hathaway, S., & McKinley, J. (1967). *Manual for the MMPI.* New York: The Psychological Corporation.

Hegstrand, L. R., & Eichelman, B. (1981). Determination of rat brain tissue catecholamines using liquid chromatography with electrochemical detection. *Journal of Chromatography, 22,* 107–111.

Heide, F., & Borkovec, T. (1983). Relaxation induced anxiety. *Journal of Consulting and Clinical Psychology, 51,* 171–182.

Heisel, J. S. (1972). Life changes as etiologic factors in juvenile rheumatoid arthritis. *Journal of Psychosomatic Research, 17,* 411–420.

Hendrick, C., & Hendrick, S. (1983). *Liking, loving and relating.* Monterey, CA: Brooks/Cole.

Henry, J. P., & Ely, D. (1976). Biologic correlates of psychosomatic illness. In R. Grenell & S. Galay (Eds.), *Biological foundations of psychiatry* (pp. 945–986). New York: Raven Press.

Henry, J. P., & Stephens, P. (1977). *Stress, health, and the social environment.* New York: Springer-Verlag.

Herbert, C. P., & Gutman, G. M. (1980). Practical group autogenic training for management of stress-related disorders in family practice. In H. J. Wain (Ed.), *Clinical hypnosis in medicine* (pp. 109–117). Miami: Symposia Specialists.

Hess, W. (1957). *The functional organization of the diencephalon.* New York: Grune & Stratton.

Hewitt, J. (1977). *The complete yoga book.* New York: Schocken.

Hilgard, E., & Hilgard, J. (1975). *Hypnosis in the relief of pain.* Los Altos, CA: Kaufman.

Hillenberg, J., & Collins, F. (1982). A procedural analysis and review of relaxation training research. *Behavior Research and Therapy, 20,* 251–260.

Hoehn-Saric, R. (1982). Neurotransmitters in anxiety. *Archive of General Psychiatry, 39,* 735–742.

Hoffman, J., Benson, H., Arns, P., Stainbrook, G., Landsberg, L., Young, J., & Gill, A. (1982). Reduced sympathetic relaxation response. *Science, 215,* 190–192.

Hogben, G., & Cornfeld, R. (1981). Treatment of traumatic neurosis with phenelzine. *Archives of General Psychiatry, 38,* 40–45.

Holmes, T. H., and Rahe, R. (1967). The social readjustment rating scale. *Journal of Psychosomatic Research, 11,* 213–218.

Holmes, T. H., Trenting, T., & Wolff, H. (1951). Lift situations, emotions, and nasal disease. *Psychosomatic Medicine, 13,* 71–82.

Holmes, T. H., & Wolff, H. G. (1952). Lift situations, emotions and backache. *Psychosomatic Medicine, 14,* 18–33.

Horowitz, M. (1974). Stress response syndrome. *Archives of General Psychiatry, 31,* 768–781.

Horowitz, M., Wilner, N., Kaltreider, N., & Alvarez, W. (1980). Signs and symptoms to post-traumatic stress disorder. *Archives of General Psychiatry, 37,* 85–92.

House, J. (1975). Occupational stress as a precursor to coronary disease. In W. D. Gentry & R. B. Williams (Eds.), *Psychological aspects of myocardial infarction and coronary care.* St. Louis: Mosby.

Humphrey, J., & Everly, G. (1980). Factor dimensions of stress responsiveness in male and female students. *Health Education, 11,* 38–39.

Hunter, M. E. (1986). Hypnosis in medical practice. In W. C. Webster II & A. H. Smith, Jr. (Eds.), *Clinical hypnosis: A multidisciplinary approach* (pp. 288–304). Philadelphia: Lippincott.

Hyde, J. S. (1985). *Half the human experience.* Lexington, MA: Heath.

Hymes, A. (1980). Diaphragmatic breath control and post surgical care. *Research Bulletin of the Himalayan International Institute, 1,* 9–10.

Issacson, R. L. (1982). *The limbic system.* New York: Plenum Press.

Jacobson, E. (1929). *Progressive relaxation.* Chicago: University of Chicago Press.

Jacobson, E. (1938). *Progressive relaxation.* Chicago: University of Chicago Press.

Jacobson, E. (1970). *Modern treatment of tense patients.* Springfield, IL: Charles C Thomas.

Jacobson, E. (1978). *You must relax.* New York: McGraw-Hill.

Jaffee, D., Scott, C., Orioli, E. (1986). *Stress management in the workplace.* Washington, DC: Washington Business Group on Health.

Jana, H. (1967). Effect of hypnosis on circulation and respiration. *Indiana Journal of Medical Research, 55,* 591–598.

Jasnoski, M., Holmes, D., Solomon, S., & Agular, C. (1981). Exercise, changes in aerobic capacity and changes in self-perceptions. *Journal of Research in Personality, 15,* 460–466.

Jasper, H. (1949). Diffuse projection systems. *Electroencephalography and Clinical Neuropsychology, 1,* 405–420.

Jemmott, J., & Locke, S. (1984). Psychosocial factors, immunologic mediation, and susceptibility to infectious disease. *Psychological Bulletin, 95,* 78–108.

Jencks, B. (1977). *Your body: Biofeedback at its best.* Chicago: Nelson-Hall.

Johns, G. (1987). *Organizational behavior: Understanding life at work.* Glenview, IL: Scott-Foresman.

Johnson, C., & Johnson, F. (1977). Attitudes toward parenting in dual career families. *American Journal of Psychiatry, 134,* 4.

Johnson, R., & Spalding, J. (1974). *Disorders of the autonomic nervous system.* Philadelphia: Davis.

Jones, R. (1977). *Self-fulfilling prophecies.* Hillsdale, NJ: Erlbaum.

Joy, R. (1985). The effects of neurotoxicants on kindling and kindled seizures. *Fundamental and Applied Toxicology, 5,* 41–65.

Kamiya, J. (1969). Operant control of the EEG alpha rhythm and some of its reported effects on consciousness. In C. Tart (Ed.), *Altered states of consciousness.* New York: Wiley.

Kannel, W., & Sorlie, P. (1979). Some health benefits of physical activity: The Framingham study. *Archives of Internal Medicine, 139,* 857–861.

Kanner, A. D., Coyne, J. C., Schaefer, C., & Lazarus, R. S. (1981). Comparison of two modes of stress measurement: Daily hassles and uplifts versus major life events. *Journal of Behavioral Medicine, 4,* 1–39.

Karasek, R., *et al.* (1981). Job decision latitude, job demands, and cardiovascular disease. *American Journal of Public Health, 71,* 694–705.

Kardiner, A. (1941). The traumatic neuroses of war. *Psychosomatic Medicine Monographs, 11.*

Kasl, S. (1978). Epidemiological contributions to the study of work stress. In C. Cooper & R. Payne (Eds.), *Stress at work* (pp. 4–48). New York: Wiley.

Katz, N. W. (1979). Comparative efficacy of behavioral training, training plus relaxation, & a sleep-trance hypnotic induction in increasing hypnotic susceptibility. *Journal of Consulting and Clinical Psychology, 47,* 119–127.

Kayser, A., Robinson, D., Nies, A., & Howard, D. (1985). Response to phenelzine among depressed patients with features of hysteroid dysphoria. *American Journal of Psychiatry, 142,* 486–488.

Keane, T., Malloy, P., & Fairbank, J. (1984). Empirical development of an MMPI scale for combat related PTSD. *Journal of Consulting and Clinical Psychology, 52,* 888–891.

Kendal, B. (1967). Clinical relaxation for neurosis and psychoneuroses. In E. Jacobson (Ed.), *Tension in medicine.* Springfield, IL: Charles C Thomas.

Kerr, T., Schapira, K., Roth, M., & Garside, R. (1970). Relationship between the Maudsley Personality Inventory and the course of affective disorders. *British Journal of Psychiatry, 116,* 11–19.

Kihlstrom, J. F. (1979). Hypnosis and psychopathology: Retrospect and prospect. *Journal of Abnormal Psychology, 88*(5), 459–473.

Kirtz, S., & Moos, R. H. (1974). Physiological effects of social environments. *Psychosomatic Medicine, 36,* 96–114.

Klajner, F., Hartman, L., & Sobell, M. (1984). Treatment of substance abuse by relaxation training. *Addictive Behaviors, 9,* 41–55.

Knapp, P. (1982). Pulmonary disorders and psychosocial stress. In W. Fann, I. Karacan, A. Pakorny, & R. Williams (Eds.), *Phenomenology and treatment of psychophysiological disorders* (pp. 15–34). New York: Spectrum.

Kobasa, S., & Puccetti, M. (1983). Personality and social resources in stress resistance. *Journal of Personality and Social Psychology, 45,* 839–850.

Kobasa, S. (1979). Stressful life events, personality, and health. *Journal of Personality and Social Psychology, 37,* 1–11.

Kolb, L. C. (1984). The post traumatic stress disorders of combat. *Military Medicine, 149,* 237–243.

Kolb, L. C. (1987). A neuropsychological hypothesis explaining post traumatic stress disorders. *American Journal of Psychiatry, 144,* 989–995.

Kopin, I. (1976). Catecholamines, adrenal hormones, and stress. *Hospital Practice, 11,* 49–55.

Krantz, D. S. (1980, September). Cognitive processes and recovery from heart attack: A review and theoretical analysis. *Journal of Human Stress,* 27–38.

Kraus, H., & Raab, W. (1961). *Hypokinetic disease.* Springfield, IL: Charles C Thomas.

Kroger, W. S., & Fezler, W. D. (1976). *Hypnosis and behavior modification: Imagery conditioning.* Philadelphia: Lippincott.

Kryter, K. (1970). *The effects of noise on man.* New York: Academic.

Kupfer, D., Pickar, D., Himmelhoch, J., & Detre, T. (1975). Are there two types of unipolar depression? *Archives of General Psychiatry, 32,* 866–871.

Kutz, I., Borysenko, J., & Benson, H. (1985). Meditation and psychotherapy. *American Journal of Psychiatry, 142,* 1–8.

Lacey, J., & Lacey, B. (1958). Verification and extension of the principle of autonomic response-stereotype. *American Journal of Psychology, 71,* 50–73.

Lacey, J., & Lacey, B. (1962). The Law of Initial Value in the longitudinal study of autonomic constitution. *Annals of the New York Academy of Sciences, 98,* 1257–1290, 1322–1326.

Lachman, S. (1972). *Psychosomatic disorders: A behavioristic interpretation.* New York: Wiley.

Lader, M. H. (1969). Psychophysiological aspects of anxiety. In M. H. Lader (Ed.), *Studies of anxiety* (pp. 53–61). Ashford, Kent, England: Headly Brothers.

Lake, C. R., Ziegler, M., & Kopin, I. (1976). Use of plasma norepinephrine for evaluation of sympathetic neuronal function in man. *Life Sciences, 18,* 1315–1326.

Lang, I. M. (1975). *Limbic involvement in the vagosympathetic arterial pressor response of the rat.* Unpublished master's thesis, Temple University.

Lang, P. J., Lazovick, A. D., & Reynolds, D. (1985). Desensitization, suggestibility, and pseudotherapy. *Journal of Abnormal Psychology, 70,* 395–402.

Lang, R., Dehof, K., Meurer, K., & Kaufmann, W. (1979). Sympathetic activity and Transcendental Meditation. *Journal of Neural Transmission, 44,* 117–135.

Langer, E. J. (1983). *The psychology of control.* Beverly Hills, CA: Sage.

Langer, E. J., & Benevento, A. (1978). Self-induced dependence. *Journal of Personality and Social Psychology, 36*(8), 886–893.

Langer, E. J., Janis, I. L., & Wolfer, J. A. (1975). Reduction of psychological stress in surgical patients. *Journal of Experimental Social Psychology, 11,* 155–165.

Langer, E. J., & Rodin, J. (1976). The effects of choice and enhanced personal responsibility for the aged: A field experiment in an institutional setting. *Journal of Personality and Social Psychology, 34*(2), 191–198.

Latimier, P. (1985). Irritable bowel syndrome. In W. Dorfman & L. Cristofar (Eds.), *Psychosomatic Illness Review* (pp. 61–75). New York: Macmillan.

Laudenslager, M., Ryan, S., Drugan, R., Hyson, R., & Maier, S. (1983). Coping and immunosuppression. *Science, 221,* 568–570.

Lavey, R., & Taylor, C. (1985). The nature of relaxation therapy. In S. Burchfield (Ed.), *Stress* (pp. 329–358). New York: Hemisphere.

Layman, E. (1977). Psychological effects of physical activity. In J. H. Wilmore (Ed.), *Exercise and sports sciences reviews* (pp. 107–135). New York: Academic.

Lazar, A. (1975). Effects of the TM program on anxiety, drug abuse, cigarette smoking and alcohol consumption. In D. Orne-Johnson, L. Domash, and J. Farrow (Eds.), *Scientific research on the TM program* (pp. 243–250). Geneva: MIV Press.

Lazarus, A. A. (1971). *Behavior therapy and beyond.* New York: McGraw-Hill.

Lazarus, A. A. (1973). "Hypnosis" as a facilitator in behavior therapy. *International Journal of Clinical and Experimental Hypnosis, 31,* 25–31.

Lazarus, A. A. (1977). *In the mind's eye: The power of imagery for personal enrichment.* New York: Rawson.

Lazarus, R. S. (1966). *Psychological stress and the coping process.* New York: McGraw-Hill.

Lazarus, R. S. (1975). A cognitively oriented psychologist looks at biofeedback. *American Psychologist, 30,* 553–561.

Lazarus, R. S. (1982). Thoughts on the relations between emotions and cognition. *American Psychologist, 37,* 1019–1024.

Lazarus, R. S. (1984). On the primacy of cognition. *American Psychologist, 39,* 124–129.

Lazarus, R. S., & Alfert, E. (1964). The short-circuiting of threat. *Journal of Abnormal and Social Psychology, 69,* 195–205.

Lazarus, R. S., & Folkman, S. (1984). *Stress, appraisal, and coping.* New York: Springer.

Le Blanc, J. (1976, July). *The role of catecholamines in adaptation to chronic and acute stress.* Paper presented at the proceedings of the International Symposium on Catecholamines and Stress, Bratislava, Czechoslovakia.

Lebaron, S., & Zeltzer, L. K. (1984). The role of psychotherapy in the treatment of children with cancer. *Psychotherapy in Private Practice, 2*(3), 45–49.

Leclerc, G. (1980). *Effects of biofeedback and relaxation training on stress management in business executives.* Unpublished doctoral dissertation, University of Rochester.

Ledwidge, B. (1980). Run for your mind. *Canadian Journal of Behavioral Science, 12,* 126–140.

Lee, K., Schottler, F., Oliver, M., & Lynch, G. (1980). Brief bursts of high-frequency stimulation produce two types of structural change in rat hippocampus. *Journal of Neurophysiology, 44,* 247–258.

Lehmann, J., Goodale, I., & Benson, H. (1986). Reduced pupillary sensitivity to topical phenylephrine associated with the relaxation response. *Journal of Human Stress, 12,* 101–104.

Lehrer, P., & Woolfolk, R. (1984). Are stress reduction techniques interchangeable, or do they have specific effects? In R. Woolfolk & P. Lehrer (Eds.), *Principles and practice of stress management* (pp. 404–477). New York: Guilford Press.

Leuner, H. (1969). Guided affective imagery. *American Journal of Psychotherapy, 23,* 4–21.

Levi, L. (1972). Psychosocial stimuli, psychophysiological reactions and disease. *Acta Medica Scandinavica* (entire Supplement 528).

Levi, L. (1975). *Emotions: Their parameters and measurement.* New York: Raven Press.

Levi, L. (1979). *Psychosocial factors in preventive medicine. The Surgeon General's report on health promotion and disease prevention: Background papers.* Washington, DC: U.S. Government Printing Office.

Levi, L., & Anderson, L. (1975). *Psychosocial stress.* New York: Wiley.

Liebowitz, M., et al. (1985). Psychopharmacologic validation of atypical depression. *Journal of Clinical Psychiatry, 45,* 22–25.

Liebowitz, M., & Klein, D. (1981). Interrelationship of hysteroid dysphoma and borderline personality disorder. *Psychiatric Clinics of North America, 4,* 67–87.

Lifton, R. J. (1973). *Home from the war.* New York: Simon & Schuster.

Light, H. 91984). Differences in employed women's anxiety, depression, and hostility levels according to their career and family role commitment. *Psychological Reports, 55,* 290.

Lindsley, D. B. (1951). Emotion. In S. S. Stevens (Ed.), *Handbook of experimental psychology.* New York: Wiley.

Lindsley, D. B., & Sassaman, W. (1938). Autonomic activity and brain potentials associated with "voluntary" control of pilomotors. *Journal of Neurophysiology, 1,* 342–349.

Lipowski, Z. J. (1984). What does the word "psychosomatic" really mean? *Psychosomatic Medicine, 46,* 153–171.

Lipper, S., et al. (1986). Preliminary study of Carbamazepine in PTSD. *Psychosomatics, 27,* 849–854.

Lown, B., *et al.* (1976). Basis for recurring ventricular fibrillation in the absence of coronary heart disease and its management. *New England Journal of Medicine, 294,* 623–629.

Lubar, J. (1983). Electroencephalographic biofeedback and neurological applications. In J. Basmajian (Ed.), *Biofeedback* (pp. 37–61). Baltimore: Williams & Wilkins.

Lum, L. C. (1975). Hyperventilation: The tip of the iceberg. *Journal of Psychosomatic Research, 19,* 375–383.

Lundberg, U., & Forsman, L. (1978). *Adrenal medullary and adrenal cortical responses to understimulation and overstimulation.* Stockholm: Department of Psychology, University of Stockholm, Report No. 541.

Luria, A. R. (1958). *The mind of a mnemonist* (L. Solotaroff, trans.). New York: Basic Books.

Luthe, W. (Ed.). (1969). *Autogenic therapy* (Vols. I–VI). New York: Grune & Stratton. *Psychosomatic medicine.* New York: Harper & Row.

MacHovec, F. J. (1985). Treatment variables and the use of hypnosis in the brief therapy of post-traumatic stress disorder. *International Journal of Clinical and Experimental Hypnosis, 33* (1), 6–14.

MacLean, P. D. (1949). Psychosomatic disease and the "visceral brain." *Psychosomatic Medicine, 11,* 338–353.

MacLean, P. D. (1975). On the evolution of three mentalities. *Man-Environment System, 5,* 213–224.

Madison, D., and Nicoll, R. (1982). Noradrenaline blocks accommodation of pyramidal cell discharge in the hippocampus. *Nature, 299,* 636–638.

Maher-Loughnan, G. P. (1975). Intensive auto-hypnosis in resistant psychosomatic disorders. *Journal of Psychosomatic Research, 1*(5–6), 361–365.

Mahl, G. F., & Brody, E. (1954). Chronic anxiety symptomatology, experimental stress and HCI secretion. *Archives of Neurological Psychiatry, 71,* 314–325.

Makara, G., Palkovits, M., & Szentagothal, J. (1980). The endocrine hypothalamus and the hormonal response to stress. In H. Selye (Ed.), *Selye's guide to stress research* (pp. 280–337). New York: Van Nostrand Reinhold.

Makowsky, V. (1980). Stress and the mental health of women: A discussion of research and issues. In M. Guttentag, S. Salasin, & D. Belle (Eds.), *The mental health of woman* (pp. 111–127). London, England: Academic Press.

Malmo, R. B. (1966). Studies of anxiety. In C. Spielberger (Ed.), *Anxiety and behavior.* New York: Academic Press.

Malmo, R. B. (1975). *On emotions, needs, and our archaic brain.* New York: Holt, Rinehart, & Winston.

Malmo, R. B., & Shagass, C. (1949). Physiologic study of symptom mechanisms in psychiatric patients under stress. *Psychosomatic Medicine, 11,* 25–29.

Malmo, R. B., Shagass, C., & Davis, J. (1950). A method for the investigation of somatic response mechanisms in psychoneurosis. *Science, 112,* 325–328.

Mandler, G. (1984). *Mind and body.* New York: Norton.

Manuck, S., & Krantz, D. (1984). Psychophysiologic reactivity in coronary artery disease. *Behavioral Medicine Update, 6,* 11–15.

Manuso, J. (1978). Testimony to the President's Commission on Mental Health. *Report of the President's Commission on Mental Health* (Vol. 2, Appendix). Washington, DC: U.S. Government Printing Office.

Manuso, J. (1983). The equitable life assurance society program. *Preventive Medicine, 12,* 658–662.

Maracek, J. (1978). Psychological disorders in women: Indices of role strain. In I. Frieze, J. Parsons, P. Johnson, D. Ruble, & G. Zellman (Eds.), *Women and sex roles: A social psychological perspective* (pp. 255–276). New York: Norton.

Maranon, G. (1924). Contribution a l'etude de l'action emotive de l'ademaline. *Revue Francais d'Endrocrinologie, 2,* 301–325.

Martin, J., & Dubbert, P. (1982). Exercise application and promotion in behavioral medicine. *Journal of Consulting and Clinical Psychology, 50,* 1004–1017.

Martinson, I., & Anderson, S. (1979). Male and female response to stress. In D. Kjervik & I. Martinson (Eds.), *Women in stress: A nursing perspective* (pp. 89–95). New York: Appleton-Century-Crofts.

Mason, J. B. (1971). A re-evaluation of the concept of non-specificity in stress theory. *Journal of Psychiatric Research, 8,* 323–333.

Mason, J. B. (1972). Organization of psychoendocrine mechanisms: A review and reconsideration of research. In N. Greenfield & R. Sternbach (Eds.), *Handbook of psychophysiology* (pp. 3–76). New York: Holt, Rinehart & Winston.

Mason, J. W. (1968a). A review of psychendocrine research on the sympathetic-adrenal medullary system. *Psychosomatic Medicine, 30,* 631–653.

Mason, J. W. (1968b). Organization of psychoendocrine mechanisms. *Psychosomatic Medicine, 30* (Entire Part 2).

Mason, J. W. (1968c). A review of psychoendocrine research on the pituitary-adrenal cortical system. *Psychosomatic Medicine, 30,* 576–607.

Mason, J. W., Maher, J., Hartley, L., Mougey, E., Perlow, M., & Jones, L. (1976). Selectivity of corticosteroid and catecholamine responses to various natural stimuli. In G. Servan (Ed.), *Psychopathology of human adaptation* (pp. 147–171). New York: Plenum Press.

Matussek, P., & Wiegand, M. (1985). Partnership problems as causes of endogenous and neurotic depressions. *Acta Psychiatrica Scandinavia, 71,* 95–104.

McCabe, P., & Schneiderman, N. (1984). Psychophysiologic reactions to stress. In N. Schneiderman & J. Tapp (Eds.), *Behavioral medicine* (pp. 3–32). Hillsdale, NJ: Erlbaum.

McCaul, K., Solomon, S., & Holmes, D. (1979). The effects of paced respiration and expectations on physiological responses to threat. *Journal of Personality and Social Psychology, 37,* 564–571.

McClelland, D. C., Ross, G., & Patel, V. (1985). The effect of an academic examination on salivary norepinephrine and immunoglobulin levels. *Journal of Human Stress, 11,* 52–59.

McClure, C. (1959). Cardiac arrest through volition. *California Medicine, 90,* 440–448.

McCroskey, J. (1982). Work and families: What is the employer's responsibility? *Personnel Journal, 61,* 30–38.

McDermott, W. (1987). The diagnosis of PTSD using the MCMI. In C. Green (Ed.), *Proceedings of the conference on the Millon inventories.* Minneapolis: National Computer Systems.

McGuigan, F. J. (1984). Progressive relaxation. In R. Woolfolk & P. Lehrer (Eds.), *Stress management* (pp. 12–42). New York: Guilford Press.

McGuigan, F. J., Sime, W., & Wallace, J. (1984). *Stress and tension control* (Vol. 2). New York: Plenum Press.

McKerns, K., & Pantic, V. (1985). *Neuroendocrine correlates of stress.* New York: Plenum Press.

McNair, D., Lorr, M., & Droppleman, L. (1971). *Profile of mood states manual.* San Diego: Educational and Industrial Testing Service.

Medansky, R. S. (1971). Emotion and the skin. *Psychosomatics, 12,* 326–329.

Meehl, P. (1973). *Psychodiagnosis.* New York: Norton.

Mefferd, R. (1979). The developing biological concept of anxiety. In W. Fann *et al.* (Eds.), *Phenomenology and treatment of anxiety.* (pp. 111–124). New York: Spectrum.

Mei-tal, V., Meyerowitz, S., & Engel, G. L. (1970). The role of psychological processes in a somatic disorder—Multiple sclerosis. *Psychosomatic Medicine, 32,* 67–86.

Meichenbaum, D. (1977). *Cognitive-behavior modification.* New York: Plenum Press.

Meichenbaum, D. (1985). *Stress innoculation training.* New York: Plenum Press.

Meichenbaum, D., & Jaremko, M. (1983). *Stress reduction and prevention.* New York: Plenum Press.

Meichenbaum, D., & Turk, D. (1987). *Facilitating Treatment Adherence.* New York: Plenum Press.

Michaels, R., Haber, M., & McCann, D. (1976). Evaluation of Transcendental Meditation as a method of reducing stress. *Science, 192,* 1242–1244.

Michaels, R., Parra, J., McCann, D., & Vander, A. (1979). Renin, cortisol, and aldosterone during Transcendental Meditation. *Psychosomatic Medicine, 41,* 49–54.

Miehlke, A. (1973). *Surgery of the facial nerve.* Philadelphia: Saunders.

Miller, G. J. (1980). High density lipoproteins and atherosclerosis. *Review of Medicine, 31,* 97–108.

Miller, L., & Smith, A. (1982). *The Stress Audit Questionnaire.* Boston: Neuromedical Consultants.

Miller, N. E. (1978). Biofeedback and visceral learning. *Annual Review of Psychology, 29,* 373–404.

Miller, N. E. (1979). General discussion and a review of recent results with paralyzed patients. In R. Gatchel & K. Price (Eds.), *Clinical applications of biofeedback* (pp. 215–225). Oxford: Pergamon.

Miller, N. E., & Dworkin, B. (1977). Critical issues in therapeutic applications of biofeedback. In G. Schwartz & J. Beatty (Eds.), *Biofeedback: Theory and research* (pp. 129–162). Chicago: Aldine.

Millon, T. (1981). *Disorders of personality: DSM-III, Axis II.* New York: Wiley.

Millon, T. (1983). *Millon clinical multiaxial inventory manual.* (3rd ed.). Minneapolis: National Computer Systems.

Millon, T., (1988). Personologic Psychotherapy. *Psychotherapy, 25,* 209–219.

Millon, T., & Everly, G. (1985). *Personality and its disorders.* New York: Wiley.

Millon, T., Green, C. J., & Meagher, R. B. (1982). *Millon behavioral health inventory manual* (3rd ed.). Minneapolis: National Computer Systems.

Mitchell, C. M., & Drossman, D. (1987). The irritable bowel syndrome. *Annals of Behavioral Medicine, 9,* 13–18.

Mittelman, B., & Wolff, H. G. (1942). Emotions and gastroduodenal function. *Psychosomatic Medicine, 4,* 5–19.

Monroe, R. (1970). *Episodic Behavioral Disorders.* Cambridge, MA: Harvard University Press.

Monroe, R. (1982). Limbic ictus and atypical psychosis. *Journal of Nervous and Mental Disease, 170,* 711–716.

Monroe, S. (1983). Major and minor life events as predictors of psychological distress. *Journal of Behavioral Medicine, 6,* 189–206.

Moorefield, C. W. (1971). The use of hypnosis and behavior therapy in asthma. *American Journal of Clinical Hypnosis, 13*(3), 162–168.

Moos, R., & Engel, B. (1962). Psychophysiological reactions in hypertensive and arthritic patients. *Journal of Psychosomatic Research, 6,* 227–241.

Morse, D., Cohen, L., Furst, M., & Martin, J. (1984). A physiological evaluation of the Yoga concept of respiratory control of the autonomic nervous system. *International Journal of Psychosomatics, 31,* 3–19.

Moulton, R. (1980). Anxiety and the new feminism. In I. Kutash (Ed.), *Handbook of stress and anxiety* (pp. 267–284). San Francisco: Jossey-Bass.

Mountcastle, V. B. (1980). *Medical physiology.* St. Louis: Mosby.

Murphy, M., & Donovan, S. (1984). *Contemporary meditation research.* San Francisco: Esalen Institute.

Murphy, L. (1984). Occupational stress management: A review and appraisal. *Journal of Occupational Psychology, 57,* 1–15.

Musaph, H. (1977). Itching and other dermatoses. In E. Wittower & H. Warnes (Eds.), *Psychosomatic medicine* (pp. 307–316). New York: Harper & Row.

Myer, E., & Brady, J. (1979). *Research in the psychobiology of human behavior.* Baltimore: Johns Hopkins Press.

Naranjo, C., & Ornstein, R. (1971). *On the psychology of meditation.* New York: Viking.

Nauta, W. (1979). Expanding borders of the limbic system concept. In T. Rasmussen & R. Marino (Eds.), *Functional neurosurgery.* New York: Raven Press.

Nauta, W., & Domesick, V. (1982). Neural associations of the limbic system. In A. Beckman (Ed.), *Neural substrates of behavior* (pp. 3–29). New York: Spectrum.

Neale, M., Singer, J., Schwartz, J., & Schwartz, G. (1983, March). *Yale-NIOSH occupational stress project.* Paper presented to the Society of Behavioral Medicine Meeting, Baltimore, MD.

Newman, J., & Beehr, T. (1979). Personal and organizational strategies for handling job stress. *Personnel Psychology, 32*, 1–43.

Nicassio, P., & Bootzin, R. (1974). A comparison of progressive relaxation and autogenic training as a treatment for insomnia. *Journal of Abnormal Psychology, 83*, 253–260.

Nidich, S. (1973). Influence of TM on a measure of self-actualization: A replication. *Journal of Counseling Psychology, 20*, 565–566.

Notman, M., & Nadelson, C. (1980). Reproductive crises. In A. Brodsky & R. Hare-Mustin (Eds.), *Women and psychotherapy* (pp. 307–338). New York: Guilford Press.

Ogden, E., & Shock, N. (1939). Voluntary hypercirculation. *American Journal of Medical Sciences, 98*, 329–342.

Omer, H., & Everly, G. (in press). Psychological influences on pre-term labor. *American Journal of Psychiatry.*

Orme-Johnson, D., & Farrow, J. (1978). *Scientific research on the Transcendental Meditation program.* Collected paper, New York: Maharishi International University Press.

Orne, M. T. (1965). Psychological factors maximizing resistance to stress: With special reference to hypnosis. In S. Z. Klausner (Ed.), *The quest for self-control* (pp. 286–328). New York: Free Press.

Ornstein, R. (1972). *The psychology of consciousness.* San Francisco: Freeman.

Ornstein, R., & Sobel, D. (1987). *The healing brain: Breakthrough discoveries about how the brain keeps us healthy* (pp. 99). New York: Simon & Schuster.

Overmier, J. B., & Seligman, M. E. P. (1967). Effects of inescapable shock upon subsequent escape and avoidance learning. *Journal of Comparative and Physiological Psychology, 63*, 28–33.

Pagano, R., & Frumkin, L. (1977). The effect of Transcendental Meditation on right hemisphere functioning. *Biofeedback and Self-Regulation, 2*, 407–415.

Papez, J. (1937). A proposed mechanism of emotion. *Archives of Neurology and Psychiatry, 38*, 725–743.

Patel, C. (1975). Twelve month follow-up of Yoga and biofeedback in the management of hypertension. *Lancet, 2*, 62–64.

Patel, C., Marmot, M., & Terry, D. (1981). Controlled trial of biofeedback and behavioral methods in reducing mild hypertension. *British Medical Journal, 282*, 2005–2008.

Paul, G. (1967). Strategy of outcome research in psychotherapy. *Journal of Consulting and Clinical Psychology, 31*, 109–118.

Paul, G. (1969a). Physiological effects of relaxation training and hypnotic suggestion. *Journal of Abnormal Psychology, 74*, 425–437.

Paul, G. (1969b). Inhibition of physiological response to stressful imagery by relaxation training and hypnotically suggested relaxation. *Behavior Research and Therapy, 7*, 249–256.

Paull, A., & Hislop, I. G. (1974). Etiologic factors in ulcerative colitis: Birth, death and symbolic equivalents. *International Journal of Psychiatry in Medicine, 5*, 57–63.

Paykel, E., Myers, J., Dienelt, M., Klerman, G., Lindenthal, J., & Pepper, J. (1969). Life events and depression: A controlled study. *Archives of General Psychiatry, 21*, 753–760.

Pearson, D., Wescott, S., & Seiler, R. (1985). A comparative study of stress in public accounting. *The Woman CPA*, 16–18.

Pelletier, K. (1984). *Healthy people in unhealthy places.* New York: Dell.

Penfield, W. (1975). *The mystery of the mind.* Princeton, NJ: Princeton University Press.

Peper, E. (1976). Problems in biofeedback training. *Perspectives in Biology and Medicine, 19*, 404–412.

Peters, R. K., Benson, H., & Peters, J. (1977). Daily relaxation response breaks in a working population: II. effects on blood pressure. *American Journal of Public Health, 67,* 954–959.

Peterson, C., & Seligman, M. E. P. (1984). Causal explanations as a risk factor for depression: Theory and evidence. *Psychological Review, 91*(3), 347–374.

Phillips, E. L. (1982). *Stress, health and psychological problems in the major professions.* Washington, DC: University Press of America.

Pitts, F., & McClure, J. (1967). Lactate metabolism in anxiety neurosis. *New England Journal of Medicine, 277,* 1329–1336.

Poloma, M. (1972). Role conflict and the married professional woman. In C. Safilios-Rothschild (Ed.), *Toward a sociology of women* (pp. 187–199). Lexington, MA: Xerox College Publishing.

Post, R. (1985). Stress sensitization, kindling, and conditioning. *Behavioral and Brain Sciences, 8,* 372–373.

Post, R. (1986). Does limbic system dysfunction play a role in affective illness? In B. Doane & K. Livingston (Eds.), *The limbic system* (pp. 229–249). New York: Raven Press.

Post, R., & Ballenger, J. (1981). Kindling models for the progressive development of psychopathology. In H. van Pragg (Ed.), *Handbook of biological psychiatry* (pp. 609–651). New York: Marcel Dekker.

Post, R., Rubinow, D., & Ballenger, J. (1986). Conditioning and sensitisation in the longitudinal course of affective illness. *British Journal of Psychiatry, 149,* 191–201.

Post, R., Uhde, T., Putnam, F., Ballenger, J., & Berrettini, W. (1982). Kindling and Carbamazepien in affective illness. *Journal of Nervous and Mental Disease, 170,* 717–731.

Powell, L. (Ed.). (1984). Stress, type A behavior, and cardiovascular disease. *Behavioral Medicine Update, 6.*

Praeger-Decker, I., & Decker, W. (1980). Efficacy of muscle relaxation in combating stress. *Health Education, 11,* 39–42.

Pratap, V., Berrettini, W., & Smith, C. (1978). Arterial blood gases in pranayama practice. *Perceptual and Motor Skills, 46,* 171–174.

Pratt, G. J. (1986). Hypnosis and stress management. In B. Zilbergeld, M. G. Edelstien, & D. L. Araoz (Eds.), *Hypnosis questions and answers* (320–324). New York: Norton.

Pratt, G. J., Wood, D. P., & Alman, B. M. (1984). *A clinical hypnosis primer.* La Jolla, CA: Psychology and Consulting Associates Press.

Public Health Service (1979). *Healthy people.* Washington, DC: U.S. Government Printing Office.

Pitts, F., & McClure, J. (1967). Lactate metabolism in anxiety neurosis. *New England Journal of Medicine, 277,* 1329–1336.

Rabkin, J. G. (1982). Stress and psychiatric disorders. In L. Goldberger & S. Brenitz (Eds.), *Handbook of stress* (pp. 566–584). New York: Free Press.

Rachman, S. (1968). The effect of muscular relaxation or desensitization therapy. *Behavior Therapy and Research, 6,* 159–166.

Racine, R., Tuff, L., & Zaide, J. (1976). Kindling unit discharge patterns and neural plasticity. In J. Wada & R. Ross (Eds.), *Kindling* (pp. 19–39). New York: Raven Press.

Rapaport, R., & Rapaport, R. N. (1976). *Dual-career families re-examined.* New York: Harper-Colophon Books.

Raskin, N. (1985). Migraine. In W. Dorfman & L. Cristofar (Eds.), *Psychosomatic illness review* (pp. 11–22). New York: Macmillan.

Ray, C., Lindop, J., & Gibson, S. (1982). The concept of coping. *Psychological Medicine, 12,* 385–395.

Redmond, D. E. (1979). New and old evidence for the involvement of a brain norepinephrine system in anxiety. In W. Fann, I. Karacan, A. Pikorney, & R. Williams (Eds.), *Phenomenology and treatment of anxiety* (pp. 153–204). New York: Spectrum.

Redmond, D. E., & Huang, Y. (1979). New evidence for a locus ceruleus-norepinephrine connection with anxiety. *Life Sciences, 25,* 2149–2162.

Reiman, E., *et al.* (1986). The application of positron emission tomography to the study of panic disorder. *American Journal of Psychiatry, 143,* 469–477.

Reisenzein, R. (1983). The Schachter theory of emotion. *Psychological Bulletin, 94,* 239–264.

Ribisl, P. (1984). Developing an exercise prescription for health. In J. Matarazzo *et al.* (Eds.), *Behavioral health* (pp. 448–466). New York: Wiley.

Rice, B. (1981, June). Can companies kill? *Psychology Today,* pp. 78–85.

Roberts, A. (1985). Biofeedback. *American Psychologist, 40,* 938–941.

Roberts, A., Kewman, D. G., & MacDonald, H. (1973). Voluntary control of skin temperature: Unilateral changes using hypnosis and feedback. *Journal of Abnormal Psychology, 82,* 163–168.

Rochefort, G. J., *et al.* (1959). Depletion of pituitary corticotropin by various stresses and by neurohypophyseal preparations. *Journal of Physiology, 146,* 105–116.

Rodin, J. (1986). Aging and health: Effects of the sense of control. *Science, 233,* 1271–1276.

Rodin, J., & Langer, E. J. (1977). Long-term effects of a control-relevant intervention with the institutionalized aged. *Journal of Personality and Social Psychology, 35*(12), 897–902.

Rodolpha, A., Kraft, W., & Reilly, R. (1985). Current trends in hypnosis and hypnotherapy. *American Journal of Clinical Hypnosis, 28,* 20–26.

Roessler, R., & Greenfield, M. (Eds.) (1962). *Physiological correlates of psychological disorders.* Madison: University of Wisconsin Press.

Roldan, E., Alvarez-Pelaez, P., & deMolina, F. (1974). Electrographic study of the amygdaloid defense response. *Physiology and Behavior, 13,* 779–787.

Romano, J. (1982). Biofeedback training and therapeutic gains. *Personnel and Guidance Journal, 60,* 473–475.

Rosch, P. (1986). Forward. In J. Humphrey (Ed.), *Human stress* (pp. ix–xi). New York: AMS Press.

Roseman, I. (1984). Cognitive determinants of emotion. In P. Shaver (Ed.), *Review of personality and social psychology* (pp. 11–36). Beverly Hills: Sage.

Rosenbaum, J. (1984). *Psychobiological model of panic and phobic avoidance.* Unpublished manuscript, Massachusetts General Hospital, Boston.

Rosenbaum, M. (1985). Ulcerative colitis. In W. Dorfman & L. Cristofar (Eds.), *Psychosomatic illness review* (pp. 61–75). New York: Macmillan.

Rosenberg, S., Hayes, J., & Peterson, R. (1987). Revising the Seriousness of Illness Rating Scale. *International Journal of Psychiatry in Medicine, 17,* 85–92.

Rosenweig, M., & Leiman, A. (1982). *Physiological psychology.* Lexington, MA: Heath.

Rossier, J., Bloom, F., & Guillemin, R. (1980). In H. Selye (Ed.), *Selye's guide to stress research* (pp. 187–207). New York: Van Nostrand Reinhold.

Rubin, L. R. (1977). *Reanimation of the paralyzed face.* St. Louis: Mosby.

Russo, N. F., & Sobel, S. B. (1981). Sex differences in the utilization of mental health facilities. *Professional Psychology, 12,* 7–19.

Ryan, A. (1974). A history of sports medicine. In A. Ryan and F. Allman (Eds.), *Sports medicine.* (pp. 1–3). New York: Academic.

Sacher, E. J., Fishman, J. R., & Mason, J. W. (1965). Influence of the hypnotic trance on plasma 17-hydroxy-corticosteroid concentration. *Psychosomatic Medicine, 27,* 33–34.

Sachs, M. C., & Buffone, G. (1984). *Running as therapy.* Lincoln: University of Nebraska Press.

Sales, S. (1969). Organizational role as a risk factor in coronary disease. *Administrative Science Quarterly, 14,* 325–336.

Salk, J. (1973). *Survival of the Wisest.* New York: Harper and Row.

Sarason, I., Johnson, J., & Siegel, J. (1978). Assessing the impact of life changes. *Journal of Consulting and Clinical Psychology, 46,* 932–946.

Sarnoff, D. (1982). Biofeedback: New uses in counseling. *Personnel and Guidance Journal, 60,* 357–360.

Schachter, S., & Singer, J. (1962). Cognitive, social, and physiological determinants of emotional states. *Psychological Review, 65,* 379–399.

Schnore, M. M. (1959). Individual patterns of physiological activity as a function of task differences and degree of arousal. *Journal of Experimental Psychology, 58,* 117–128.

Schottenfeld, R., & Cullen, M. (1985). Occupation-induced PTSD. *American Journal of Psychiatry, 142,* 198–202.

Schuster, M. (1983). Biofeedback and the control of gastrointestinal motility. In J. Basmajian (Ed.), *Biofeedback* (pp. 275–281). Baltimore: Williams & Wilkins.

Schwartz, G. (1977). Psychosomatic disorders and biofeedback. In J. Maser & M. Seligman (Eds.), *Psychopathology.* San Francisco: Freeman.

Schwartz, G. (1979). The brain as a health care system. In G. Stone, F. Cohen, & N. Adler (Eds.), *Health psychology* (pp. 549–573). San Francisco: Jossey-Bass.

Schwartz, G., Fair, P., Mandel, M., Salt, P., Mieske, M., & Klerman, G. (1978). Facial electromyography in the assessment of improvement in depression. *Psychosomatic Medicine, 40,* 355–360.

Schwartz, M. (1987). *Biofeedback.* New York: Guilford Press.

Seifert, W. (Ed.) (1983). *Neurobiology of the hippocampus.* New York: Academic Press.

Seligman, M. E. P. (1975). *Helplessness: On depression, development and death.* San Francisco: Freeman.

Seligman, M. E. P., & Maier, S. F. (1967). Failure to escape traumatic shock. *Journal of Experimental Psychology, 74,* 1–9.

Selye, H. (1951). The General Adaptation Syndrome and the gastrointestinal diseases of adaptation. *American Journal of Proctology, 2,* 167–184.

Selye, H. (1956). *The stress of life.* New York: McGraw-Hill.

Selye, H. (1974). *Stress without distress.* Philadelphia: Lippincott.

Selye, H. (1976). *Stress in health and disease.* Boston: Butterworth.

Selye, H. (1980). Preface. In H. Selye (Ed.), *Selye's guide to stress research* (pp. v–xiii). New York: Van Nostrand Reinhold.

Serban, G. (1975). Stress in schizophrenics and normals. *British Journal of Psychiatry, 126,* 397–407.

Shader, R. (1984). Epidemiologic and family studies. *Psychosomatics, 25* supplement, 10–15.

Shaevitz, M. H. (1984). *The superwoman syndrome.* New York: Warner Books.

Shagass, C., & Malmo, R. (1954). Psychodynamic themes and localized muscular tension during psychotherapy. *Psychosomatic Medicine, 16,* 295–313.

Shapiro, D. (1978). *Precision nirvana.* Englewood Cliffs, NJ: Prentice-Hall.

Shapiro, D. (1985). Clinical use of meditation as a self-regulation strategy. *American Psychologist, 40,* 719–722.

Shapiro, D., & Giber, D. (1978). Meditation and psychotherapeutic effects. *Archives of General Psychiatry, 35,* 294–302.

Sharpley, C. F. and Rogers, H. (1984). A meta-analysis of frontal EMG levels with biofeedback and alternative procedures. *Biofeedback and Self-Regulation, 9,* 385–393.

Shearn, D. (1962). Operant conditioning of heart rate. *Science, 137,* 530–531.

Sheehan, D. (1983). *The anxiety disease.* New York: Scribner.

Sheehan, P. (1972). *The function and nature of imagery.* New York: Academic Press.

Sheehan, D., Ballenger, J., & Jacobson, G. (1980). Treatment of endogenous anxiety with phobic, hysterical, and hypochondriacal symptoms. *Archive of General Psychiatry, 37,* 51–59.

Shellenberger, R., & Green, J. (1986). *From the ghost in the box to successful biofeedback training.* Greeley, CO: Health Psychology Publications.

Shepherd, J., & Weiss, S. (Eds.). (1987). Behavioral Medicine and Cardiovascular Disease. *Circulation, 76,* Entire Monograph #6.

Shoemaker, J., & Tasto, D. (1975). Effects of muscle relaxation on blood pressure of essential hypertensives. *Behavior Research and Therapy, 13,* 29–43.

Silverman, J. (1986). PTSD. *Advances in Psychosomatic Medicine, 16,* 115–140.

Sime, W. (1977). A comparison of exercise and meditation in reducing physiological response to stress. *Medicine and Science in Sport, 9,* 55 (Abstract).

Sime, W. (1984). Psychological benefits of exercise training in the healthy individual. In J. Matarazzo, S. Weiss, J. Heid, N. Miller, & S. Weiss (Eds.), *Behavioral Health* (pp. 488–508). New York: Wiley.

Simons, D. J., Day, E., Goodell, H., & Wolff, H. (1943). Experimental studies on headache. *Research Publication of the Association of Nervous and Mental Disorders, 23,* 228–244.

Sinyor, D. S., Schwartz, S., Peronnet, F., Brisson, G., & Seraganian, P. (1983). Aerobic fitness level and reactivity to psychosocial stress. *Psychosomatic Medicine, 45,* 205–217.

Smith, K. (1986). *Development of an internal auditing methodology for evaluating corporate wellness investments.* Unpublished doctoral dissertation, George Washington University.

Smith, K., & Everly, G. S. (1988). Problems in the evaluation of occupational health promotion programs. *American Journal of Health Promotion, 3,* 43–51.

Smith, K., Haight, T., & Everly, G. S. (1986). Evaluating corporate wellness investments. *The Internal Auditor, 43,* 28–34.

Smith, M., Glass, G., & Miller, T. (1980). *The benefits of psychotherapy.* Baltimore: Johns Hopkins University Press.

Smith, R. E. (1979). *The subtle revolution: women at work.* Washington, DC: The Urban Institute.

Sowers, J., Raj, R., Hershman, J., Carlson, H., & McCallum, R. (1977). The effect of stressful diagnostic studies and surgery on anterior pituitary hormone release in man. *Acta Endocrinologica, 86,* 25.

Spencer, L. (1984). How to calculate the costs and benefits of an HRD program. *Training, July,* 40–50.

Spiegel, D. (1981). Vietnam grief work using hypnosis. *American Journal of Clinical Hypnosis, 24* (1), 33–40.

Spiegel, D., & Bloom, J. R. (1983). Group therapy and hypnosis reduce metastic breast carcinoma pain. *Psychosomatic Medicine, 45*(4), 333–339.

Spiegel, H., & Spiegel, D. (1978). *Trance and treatment: clinical uses of hypnosis.* New York: Basic Books.

Spielberger, C., Gorsuch, R., & Lushene, R. (1970). *The STAI Manual.* Palo Alto, CA: Consulting Psychologists Press.

Stavraky, K. M. (1968). Psychological factors in the outcome of cancer. *Journal of Psychosomatic Research, 12,* 251–259.

Stein, L., Wise, C., & Berger, B. (1973). An antianxiety action of benzodiazepines. In S. Garattini, E. Mussini, & L. Randall (Eds.), *The benzodiazepines.* New York: Raven Press.

Steinmark, S., & Borkovec, T. (1973). *Assessment of active and placebo treatment of moderate insomnia.* Paper presented at the Midwestern Psychological Association, Chicago.

Stephenson, P. (1977). Physiologic and psychotropic effects of caffeine on man. *Journal of the American Dietetic Association, 71,* 240–247.

Steptoe, A. (1981). *Psychological factors in cardiovascular disorders.* New York: Academic Press.

Sterman, M. B. (1973). Neurophysiological and clinical studies of sensorimotor EEG biofeedback training: Some effects on epilepsy. In L. Birk (Ed.), *Biofeedback: Behavioral medicine.* New York: Grune & Stratton.

Sterman, M. B., & Friar, L. (1972). Suppression of seizures in an epileptic following sensorimotor EEG feedback training. *Electroencephalography and Clinical Neurophysiology, 33,* 89–95.

Stern, R., Ray, W., & Davis, C. (1980). *Psychophysiological recording.* New York: Oxford University Press.

Sternbach, R. (1966). *Principles of psychophysiology.* New York: Academic Press.

Stone, J. (1986). Presentations of doctor and office to facilitate hypnosis. In B. Zilbergard, M. G. Edelstein, & D. Araoz (Eds.), *Hypnosis questions and answers* (pp. 69–75). New York: Norton.

Stone, W. (1980). Motivation for fitness. *Arizona Journal of HPRR, 24,* 5–7.

Stoyva, J. M. (1965). Posthypnotically suggested dreams at the sleep cycle. *Archives of General Psychiatry, 12,* 287–294.

Stoyva, J. M. (1976). Self-regulation and stress-related disorders: A perspective on biofeedback. In D. I. Mostofsky (Ed.), *Behavior control and modification of physiological activity*. Englewood Cliffs, NJ: Prentice-Hall.

Stoyva, J. M. (1977). Guidelines in the training of general relaxation. In J. Basmajian (Ed.), *Biofeedback: Principles and practices for clinicians*. Baltimore: Williams & Wilkins.

Stoyva, J. M. (1979). Musculoskeletal and stress-related disorders. In O. Pomerleau & J. Brady (Eds.), *Behavioral medicine* (pp. 155–176). Baltimore: Williams & Wilkins.

Stoyva, J. M., & Anderson, C. (1982). A coping-rest model of relaxation and stress management. In L. Goldberger & S. Breznitz (Eds.), *Handbook of Stress* (pp. 745–763). New York: Free Press.

Stoyva, J. M., & Budzynski, T. (1974). Cultivated low-arousal: An anti-stress response? In L. DiCara (Ed.), *Recent advances in limbic and autonomic nervous systems research* (pp. 369–394). New York: Plenum Press.

Strelau, J., Farley, F., & Gale, A. (1985). *The biological basis of personality and behavior*. New York: McGraw-Hill.

Stroebel, C. F. (1979, November). *Non-specific effects and psychodynamic issues in self-regulatory techniques*. Paper presented at the Johns Hopkins Conference on Clinical Biofeedback, Baltimore, MD.

Strupp, H. H. (1970). Specific vs. nonspecific factors in psychotherapy and the problem of control. *Archive of General Psychiatry, 23*, 393–401.

Strupp, H. H. (1980). Success and failure in time-limited psychotherapy. *Archives of General Psychiatry, 37*, 947–954.

Stutman, R. K., & Bliss, E. L. (1985). Posttraumatic stress disorder, hypnotizability and imagery. *American Journal of Psychiatry, 142*(6), 741–743.

Suler, J. R. (1985). Meditation and somatic arousal reduction: A comment on Holme's review. *American Psychologist, 40*, 717.

Suls, J., & Mullen, B. (1981). Life events, perceived control and illness: The role of uncertainty. *Journal of Human Stress*, 30–34.

Suter, S. (1986). *Health psychophysiology*. Hillsdale, NJ: Erlbaum.

Swonger, A., & Constantine, L. (1976). *Drugs and therapy: A psychotherapist's handbook of psychotropic drugs*. Boston: Little, Brown.

Tart, C. (1964). A comparison of suggested dreams occuring in hypnosis and sleep. *International Journal of Clinical and Experimental Hypnosis, 12*, 263–289.

Tart, C. (1975). *States of consciousness*. New York: Dutton.

Taub, E., & Stroebel, C. (1978). Biofeedback in the treatment of vasonconstrictive syndromes. *Biofeedback and Self-Regulation, 3*, 363–374.

Tavris, C., & Wade, C. (1984). *The longest war: Sex differences in perspective* (2nd ed.). San Diego, CA: Harcourt Brace Jovanovich.

Taylor, C. B. (1978). Relaxation training and related techniques. In W. S. Agras (Ed.), *Behavioral modification* (pp. 30–52). Boston: Little, Brown.

Taylor, J. (1953). A scale for manifest anxiety. *Journal of Abnormal and Social Psychology, 48*, 285–290.

Taylor, M., & Abrams, R. (1975). Acute mania. *Archives of General Psychiatry, 32*, 863–865.

Theorell, T., & Rahe, R. H. (1971). Psychosocial factors and myocardial infarction: An inpatient study in Sweden. *Journal of Psychosomatic Research, 15*, 25–31.

Thomas, C., & McCabe, L. (1980). Precursors of premature disease and death: Habits of nervous tension. *Johns Hopkins Medical Journal, 147*, 137–145.

Thompson, S. C. (1981). Will it hurt less if I can control it? A complex answer to a simple question. *Psychological Bulletin, 90*(1), 89–101.

Todd, F. J., & Kelly, R. J. (1970, December). The use of hypnosis to facilitate conditioned relaxation responses: A report of three cases. *Journal of Behavior Therapy and Experimental Psychiatry, 1*(4), 295–298.

Tomasi, T. B. (1984). The secretory immune system. In D. P. Stites, J. D. Stobo, H. H.

Fudenberg, & J. V. Wells (Eds.), *Basic and clinical immunology* (pp. 187–196). Los Altos, CA: Lange.

Tomita, T. (1975). Action of catecholamines on skeletal muscles. In S. Geigor (Ed.), *Handbook of physiology*, Vol. 6 (pp. 537–552). Washington, DC: American Physiological Society.

Torem, M. (1987). Hypnosis in the treatment of depression. In W. C. Wester (Eds.), *Clinical hypnosis* (pp. 288–301). Cincinnati, OH: Behavioral Science Center.

Towers, J. F. (1984). *A meta-analysis of the relationships among stress, social supports, and illness and their implications for health professions education.* Unpublished doctoral dissertation, University of Pennsylvania.

Trimble, M. (1981). *Post-traumatic Neurosis.* New York: Wiley.

Tucker, D. M. (1981). Lateral grain function, emotion, and conceptualization. *Psychological Bulletin, 89,* 19–46.

Tyrer, P., Casey, P., & Gall, J. (1983). Relationship between neurosis and personality disorder. *British Journal of Psychiatry, 142,* 404–408.

Usdin, E., Kretnansky, R., & Kopin, I. (1976). *Catecholamines and stress.* Oxford, Pergamon.

Vahia, N. (1972). Psychophysiologic therapy based on the concepts of Pantanjali. *American Journal of Psychotherapy, 27,* 557–565.

van der Kolk, B. A. (1983). Psychopharmacological issues in post traumatic stress disorder. *Hospital and Community Psychiatry, 34,* 683–691.

van der Kolk, B. A. (1987). *Psychological trauma.* Washington, DC: American Psychiatric Press.

van der Kolk, B., Greenberg, M., Boyd, H., & Krystal, J. (1985). Inescapable shock, neurotransmitters, and addition to trauma. *Biological Psychiatry, 20,* 314–325.

Van Hoesen, G. W. (1982). The para-hippocampal gyrus. *Trends in Neuroscience, 5,* 345–350.

Vanderhoof, L. (1980). *The effects of a simple relaxation technique on stress during pelvic examinations.* Unpublished Master's Thesis, University of Maryland School of Nursing.

Verbrugge, L. (1985). Gender and health: An update on hypotheses and evidence. *Journal of Health and Social Behavior, 26,* 156–182.

Verbrugge, L., & Madans, J. (1985). Social role and health trends of American women. *Melbank Memorial Fund Quarterly/Health and Society, 63,* Fall.

Verrier, R., & Lown, B. (1984). Behavioral stress and cardiac arrhythmias. *Annual Review of Physiology, 46,* 155–176.

Visintainer, M. A., Volpicelli, J. R., & Seligman, M. E. P. (1982). Tumor rejection in rats after inescapable or escapable shock. *Science, 216,* 437–439.

von Bertalanffy, L. (1968). *General systems theory.* New York: Braziller.

Wadden, T. A., & Anderton, C. H. (1982). The clinical use of hypnosis. *Psychological Bulletin, 91*(2), 215–243.

Weil, J. (1974). *A neurophysiological model of emotional and intentional behavior.* Springfield, IL: Charles C Thomas.

Weiman, C. (1977). A study of occupational stressors and the incidence of disease/risk. *Journal of Occupational Medicine, 19,* 119–122.

Weiner, H. (1977). *Psychobiology and human disease.* New York: Elsevier.

Weiner, H., Thaler, M., Reiser, M., & Mirsky, I. (1957). Etiology of duodenal ulcer. *Psychosomatic Medicine, 19,* 1–10.

Weinstock, L., & Clouse, R. (1987). A focused overview of gastrointestinal physiology. *Annals of Behavioral Medicine, 9,* 3–6.

Weissman, M., Prusoff, B., & Klerman, G. (1978). Personality and the prediction of long-term outcome of depression. *American Journal of Psychiatry, 135,* 797–800.

Weitz, R. D. (1983). Psychological factors in the prevention and treatment of cancer. *Psychotherapy in Private Practice, 1*(4), 69–76.

Weller, D., & Everly, G. (1985). Occupational health through physical fitness programming. In G. Everly and R. Feldmen (Eds.), *Occupational health promotion* (pp. 127–146). New York: Macmillan.

Wenger, M. A., Clemens, T., Coleman, D., Cullen, T., & Engel, B. (1960). Autonomic response patterns during intravenous infusion of epinephrine and norepinephrine. *Psychosomatic Medicine, 22,* 294–307.

Wester, W. C., II. (Ed.) (1987). *Clinical hypnosis: A case management approach.* Cincinnati, OH: Behavioral Science Center.

Wester, W. C., II., & Smith, A. H., Jr. (Eds.) (1980). *Clinical hypnosis: A multidisciplinary approach.* Philadelphia: Lippincott.

White, J. (1974). *What is meditation?* New York: Doubleday Anchor.

Whitehead, W. (1978). Biofeedback in the treatment of gastrointestinal disorders. *Biofeedback and Self-Regulation, 3,* 375–384.

Wickramasekera, I. (1976). Biofeedback, behavior therapy and hypnosis: Convergences and the placebo response. In I. Wickramasekera (Ed.), *Biofeedback, behavior therapy and hypnosis: Potentiating the verbal control of behavior for clinicians.* Chicago: Nelson-Hall.

Wickramasekera, I. (1986). A model of people at high risk to develop chronic stress-related somatic symptoms: Some predictions. *Experimental Psychology: Research and Practice, 17(5),* 437–447.

Widiger, T., & Frances, A. (1985). Axis II personality disorders. *Hospital and Community Psychiatry, 36,* 619–627.

Wilder, J. (1950). The Law of Initial Values. *Psychosomatic Medicine, 12,* 392–401.

Williams, R. B. (1984). Type A behavior and coronary artery disease. *Behavioral Medicine Update, 6,* 29–33.

Williams, R. B. (1986). Patterns of reactivity and stress. In K. Matthews *et al.* (Eds.), *Handbook of stress, reactivity, and cardiovascular disease* (pp. 109–125). New York: Wiley.

Williams, R. B., Haney, T., Lee, K., Kong, Y., Blumenthal, J., & Whalen, R. (1980). Type A behavior, hostility, and artherosclerosis. *Psychosomatic Medicine, 42,* 539–549.

Wilmore, J. (1982). *Training for sport and activity.* Boston: Allyn and Bacon.

Witkin-Lanoil, G. (1984). *The female stress syndrome.* New York: Newmarket Press.

Wolf, S. (1985). Peptic ulcer. In W. Dorfman & L. Cristofar (Eds.), *Psychosomatic illness review* (pp. 52–60). Ne York: Macmillan.

Wolf, S., & Glass, G. B. (1950). Correlation of conscious and unconscious conflicts with changes in gastric function and structure. In H. G. Wolff, S. Wolf *et al.* (Eds.), *Life stress and bodily disease* (pp. 17–35). Baltimore: Williams & Wilkins.

Wolff, H. G. (1963). *Headache and other head pain.* New York: Oxford University Pres.

Wolpe, J.(1958). *Psychotherapy by reciprocal inhibition.* Stanford: Stanford University Press.

Wyler, R. A., Masuda, M., & Holmes, T. H. (1968). Seriousness of illness rating scale. *Journal of Psychosomatic Research, 11,* 363–374.

Wyler, R. A., Masuda, M., & Holmes, T. H. (1971). Magnitude of life events and seriousness of illness. *Psychosomatic Medicine, 33,* 115–122.

Wyngaarden, J., & Smith, L. (1988). *Cecil textbook of medicine.* Philadelphia: Saunders.

Yates, F., & Maran, J. (1972). Stimulation and inhibition of ACTH release. In W. Sawyer & E. Knobil (Eds.), *Handbook of Physiology* (pp. 37–62). Washington, DC: American Physiological Society.

Young, L., Richter, J., Bradley, L., & Anderson, K. (1987). Disorders of the upper gastrointestinal system. *Annals of Behavioral Medicine, 9,* 7–12.

Yuwiler, A. (1976). Stress, anxiety and endocrine function. In R. Grenell and S. Galay (Eds.), *Biological foundations of psychiatry.* New York: Raven Press.

Zajonc, R. B. (1984). On the primacy of affect. *American Psychologist, 39,* 117–123.

Zuckerman, M. (1960). The development of an affect adjective checklist for the measurement of anxiety. *Journal of Consulting Psychology, 24,* 457–462.

Zuckerman, M., & Lubin, B. (1965). *Manual for the Multiple Affect Adjective Checklist.* San Diego: Educational and Industrial Testing Service.

About the Author

George S. Everly, Jr., Ph.D. is currently Director of the Division of Psychological Services at the Homewood Hospital Center of the Johns Hopkins Health System. In addition, Dr. Everly is Professor of Psychology and Director of the Health Psychology Research Laboratory at Loyola College in Maryland. He is also on the adjunct faculty of the Johns Hopkins University.

Dr. Everly is a Fellow of the American Institute of Stress and a Fellow of the Academy of Psychosomatic Medicine. He is the author or co-author of several other textbooks on stress, including *Controlling Stress and Tension* (with Daniel Girdano), *The Assessment of the Human Stress Response* (with Steven Sobelman), and *Occupational Health Promotion* (with Robert Feldman). He is also a Contributing Editor to the *American Journal of Health Promotion*.

This volume was written while Dr. Everly was a Visiting Scholar in Psychology at Harvard University, and later a member of the Section on Behavioral Medicine at New England Deaconess Hospital, and a Visiting Lecturer on Medicine at Harvard Medical School.

Index